D0060456

THE RIGHT
TO LITERACY

Edited by

*Andrea A. Lunsford, Helene Moglen,
and James Slevin*

THE MODERN LANGUAGE ASSOCIATION OF AMERICA
NEW YORK   1990

Copyright © 1990 by The Modern Language Association of America

Library of Congress Cataloging-in-Publication Data
The Right to literacy / edited by Andrea A. Lunsford, Helene Moglen, and James Slevin.
  p.   cm.
  Papers originally presented at the Right to Literacy Conference sponsored by the Modern Language Association in 1988.
  Includes bibliographical references.
  ISBN 0-87352-197-8   ISBN 0-87352-198-6 (pbk.)
  1. Literacy—United States—Congresses. 2. English language—Study and teaching—United States—Congresses.   3. Censorship—United States—Congresses.   I. Lunsford, Andrea A., 1942–   . II. Moglen, Helene, 1936–   . III. Slevin, James F., 1945–   . IV. Modern Language Association. V. Right to Literacy Conference (1988 : Ohio State University)
LC151.R54 1990
302.2'244—dc20   90-33855

Cover design by Laurie Smollett

Published by The Modern Language Association of America
10 Astor Place, New York, New York 10003-6981

CONTENTS

INTRODUCTION
Andrea A. Lunsford, Helene Moglen, and James Slevin   1

PART ONE CONTEXTS

National Contexts

Public Literacy: Puzzlements of a High School Watcher
Theodore R. Sizer   9

Producing Adult Readers: 1930–50
David Bartholomae   13

Particular Contexts

Becoming Literate: A Lesson from the Amish
Andrea R. Fishman   29

Time to Write: Resistance to Literacy in a Maine Fishing Community
John S. Lofty   39

Collaboration, Collaborative Communities, and Black Folk Culture
Keith D. Miller and Elizabeth A. Vander Lei   50

Rural Poverty and Literacy in the Mississippi Delta: Dilemmas,
    Paradoxes, and Conundrums
Anthony Petrosky   61

Professional Contexts

Literacy and the Politics of Education
C. H. Knoblauch   74

The English Department and Social Class: Resisting Writing
James Thomas Zebroski   81

PART TWO SPEAKING OUT OF THE SILENCES

"Knowledge Is Power": The Black Struggle for Literacy
Thomas Holt   91

Perspectives on the Intellectual Tradition of Black
    Women Writers
Jacqueline Jones Royster   103

Censorship and Spiritual Education
James Moffett   113

Caliban in the Composition Classroom
Donald Rothman   120

Censorship, Identification, and the Poetics of Need
Deanne Bogdan   128

On Teaching Convicts
Maurice Laurence, Jr.   148

The Rhetoric of Empowerment in Writing Programs
  Harriet Malinowitz   152
Literacy and Citizenship: Resisting Social Issues
  David Bleich   163

PART THREE   LITERACY AND ITS ENEMIES, ILLITERACY AND ITS FRIENDS

Language, Logic, and Literacy
  Keith Walters   173
Literacy and Knowledge
  Deborah Brandt   189
The Situation of Literacy and Cognition: What We Can Learn
    from the Uzbek Experiment
  Beth Daniell   197
In Praise of the Local and Transitory
  Kathryn Thoms Flannery   208
Bloomsday: Doomsday Book for Literacy?
  C. Jan Swearingen   215
The Ideology of Literacy: A Bakhtinian Perspective
  Charles Schuster   225

PART FOUR   CREATING AND SUSTAINING LITERACY

Toward a Social-Cognitive Understanding of Problematic
    Reading and Writing
  Glynda Hull and Mike Rose   235
Cross-Age Tutoring: The Right to Literacy
  J. Elspeth Stuckey and Kenneth Alston   245
Enacting Critical Literacy
  John Clifford   255
Adolescent Vernacular Writing: Literacy Reconsidered
  Miriam P. Camitta   262
The World, the Text, and the Reader
  Paula M. Salvio   269
Collaboration, Resistance, and the Teaching of Writing
  Suzanne Clark and Lisa Ede   276

PART FIVE   TOWARD THE RESPONSIBILITIES OF LITERACY

The Fourth Vision: Literate Language at Work
  Shirley Brice Heath   288

INTRODUCTION

The essays gathered together in this volume grew out of presentations featured at the 1988 Right to Literacy Conference, an event sponsored by the Modern Language Association with support from the Ohio State University, the Ohio Humanities Council, and the Federation of State Humanities Councils. The conference represented a bold new venture for the Modern Language Association in that it sought, for the first time, to address an audience far beyond the bounds of Modern Language Association membership. The impetus for the conference can be traced back at least as far as the Modern Language Association's 1982 "Report of the Commission on the Future of the Profession," which urged that the definition of the discipline we call literature be broadened and that a new commission be established to examine and make recommendations to improve existing relations between literature and writing. In forming that commission, the Executive Council charged it with (1) improving communication between members who teach writing and literature; (2) developing programs, publications, and projects that would improve the teaching and study of both fields and our understanding of the relation between them; (3) encouraging departments to develop policies adequate to the range of programs within a department; and (4) identifying ways in which the Modern Language Association and the Association of Departments of English can support the teaching of writing and literature in the secondary schools. In pursuing its charge, the Commission on Writing and Literature held open hearings at major professional meetings, interviewed various scholars and researchers, sponsored a Modern Language Association forum, organized a Conference on the Future of Doctoral Studies in English, and worked toward issuing a final report.

For members of the commission, all university professors, the most difficult charge to address effectively was the last one. How could we best reach out to schools and communities to affect the teaching of reading and writing? Time and time again, commission members circled around this question, producing voluminous notes on the need for university-school-community collaboration but settling on few concrete ways to allow for such collaboration. Heated discussions of this issue eventually led to the realization that our questions could best be addressed in the context of literacy education, that teachers of reading and writing in classes from first grade through graduate school, as well as teachers without institutional affiliations in rural communities and in urban centers, could all appropriately be described as literacy workers. We also came to understand that few of us who teach reading and writing appreciate the extent to which we have common concerns and similar uncertainties because we rarely have the opportunity to share with one another—across the bureaucratic structures that divide us—our perceptions, frustrations, hopes, and sometimes despair. It was to initiate just such discussions—in order to discover how we might support one another and how the Modern Language Association might support us all—that The Right to Literacy Conference was planned. The conference call for papers invited participants to consider differing definitions and historical understandings of literacy and the political, pedagogical, and theoretical implications of the many approaches to literacy education that have been taken both in this country and abroad.

Our conference title, The Right to Literacy, established a context for the presentations. It posits that literacy is a right and not a privilege: a right that has been denied to an extraordinary number of our citizens. It implies, therefore, that illiterate persons are not themselves dysfunctional but are, rather, the signs of a dysfunctional society. Such an assertion, while obvious, may also be misleading, for it may be interpreted as suggesting that, once all citizens have learned to read and write, justice will have been done and we will have achieved a more nearly perfect democratic society. This is, of course, not true. Literacy is not in itself a panacea for social inequity; it does, in fact, guarantee little. It will not effect the redistribution of this nation's wealth. It will not grant more influence or power to those who have been disempowered by their race, their class, their gender, their sexual orientation, or their nationality. Nor will it ensure freedom or democracy. Indeed, totalitarian governments have never underestimated the effectiveness of language and the importance, therefore, of a literate citizenry. We know that many adults and children have been subjugated through language and that some have learned, in turn, how they can use language against others. We know that our schools often function as machines to mangle children—to destroy their curiosity, their independence, their vitality, their cultural identity—rendering them silent, obedient, and passive and keeping them in their places by mystifying the oppressive circumstances of their lives.

Paolo Freire has written:

> Illiteracy is one of the concrete expressions of an unjust social reality. Illiteracy is not a strictly linguistic or exclusively pedagogical or methodological problem. It is political, as is the very literacy through which we try to overcome illiteracy. (10)

Because, as Freire says, both illiteracy and literacy education are inevitably political, literacy workers in all contexts do well to refrain from jumping on the literacy bandwagon without first questioning the motives of both those who are driving it and those who are funding its operations. It is necessary to ask what kind of literacy we want to support: literacy to serve which purposes and on behalf of whose interests. Since the teaching of reading and writing can never be innocent, literacy workers must choose pedagogical methods with care, mindful of the theoretical assumptions with which those methods are informed.

One of the major goals of the conference was to question a series of assumptions about literacy that continue to go unrecognized and unquestioned only at our peril: that literacy takes both its characteristics and its significance solely from its contributions to the economic and political well-being of the state; that literacy can be mandated; that literacy is simply and neutrally defined as the ability to read and write, unaffected by issues of, for instance, gender, race, and class; and that literacy will be acquired outside the contexts of compelling personal and social purposes. Probing such assumptions leads to the sobering realization of how inextricably embedded literacy is in culture, how context-dependent is its realization. Thus, to be only functionally literate in a hyper-literate society is to live as an oppressed stranger in an overwhelming world. On the other hand, to achieve cultural literacy, as it has been defined by E. D. Hirsch and others, is to live in passive comfort as a tourist in an alien world. In both roles the literate agent is constructed by an external agency that has as a primary goal its own reproduction. Such a situation has led Andrew Sledd and others to call for "dysfunctional" literacy, a subversive form of knowing and being that interrogates social meanings, instead of accommodating to them.

As the assumptions that underlie notions of literacy are problematically disguised, so are its definitions. Thus, the conference sought to anatomize the term itself, rejecting narrow conceptions of literacy as a set of discrete rudimentary skills. Unfortunately, school, community, and scholarly groups have traditionally approached literacy in that way, as a phenomenon to be analyzed into discrete segments or categories to carry out largely instrumental and unexamined purposes. Of course, such dysfunctional practices reflect in many ways the isolation, fragmentation, and dissociation in American society at large, a tendency nowhere more detrimental than in those places where literacy—as literate practice—has traditionally been nurtured and sustained. The family, itself now fragmented and reduced, exists separate from community and community organizations. These community organizations are, in turn, unconnected to the workplace (another site of literacy development), and the schools are often the most radically separate of all—separated from families, communities, and workplaces. The work of Shirley Brice Heath in particular demonstrates how altered social contexts have changed patterns of behavior in ways that hinder literate practices by both children and adults.

A second major goal of the Right to Literacy Conference, therefore, was to challenge this tendency to fragment and dichotomize literacy by inviting participants to situate literacy in epistemological, ideological, pedagogical, and political contexts. Recognizing that to see literacy whole demands a loosening of borders, a willingness to listen hard to many voices, the conference mixed teachers and scholars from all institutional levels, as well as school superintendents, principals, literacy tutors, adult learners, lawyers, community volunteers, researchers, librarians, and representatives from state humanities councils, labor unions, and prison literacy projects in forty-two states, Canada, the United Kingdom, and South Africa. What evolved from this unique moment of collaboration was not a clear agenda of the sort urged by those who have rushed to claim a quick national fix for illiteracy. Conference participants eschewed closure and refused solutions. Joining in what they recognized to be an important national conversation, they attempted, rather, to explore and understand literacy's many faces. Many present at the conference had believed themselves to be functioning in isolation; instead, they found themselves to be part of a large and engaged community. The perception developed that an active, diverse, and extraordinarily committed literacy movement does exist in this country and that, while its members have not communicated very much with one another in the past, they will have a great deal to say to one another in the future.

This volume aims to re-create a sense of the conference's complexity, to provide an opportunity for members of the Modern Language Association to join the rich and fruitful conversation initiated in Ohio. The essays are divided into five parts, reflecting the range of questions engaged at the conference. Our groupings are intended to suggest similar emphases, but individual essays are as likely as not to belong in several sections; we trust that our arrangement of them does not obscure the interrelations among the volume's several parts. The first part explores the national, local, and professional contexts of literacy; it raises critical questions both about the large social and political perspectives that inform our understanding of literacy and about the social and political conditions that restrain or enable the realization of literacy. Part 2, "Speaking out of the Silences," explores how literacy is denied not only by overt censorship but also by the subtler and more insidious forces of racism, sexism, homophobia, and elitism; these essays offer ways of helping others to envision and attain the power to speak out. Part 3, "Literacy and Its Enemies, Illiteracy and Its Friends," offers critical perspectives on those conceptions of literacy and methods of literacy education that ultimately subvert its attainment as a right of citizens. Part 4, "Creating and Sustaining Literacy," offers curricular and pedagogical models for successful literacy efforts at different educational levels and in diverse cultural situations. The volume concludes, as the conference itself concluded, with Shirley Brice Heath's provocative synthesis of the conference's themes and her articulation of concerns that require our continued critical scrutiny.

This volume helps ensure that continued scrutiny. The essays open up a range of questions that the follow-up Modern Language Association conference, "The Responsibilities of Literacy" (September 1990), was designed to address. This 1990 conference, held in Pittsburgh, was conceived as a way of carrying on the conversation begun in Ohio—in particular, by exploring the following issues:

> What interests are represented in the literacy practices of communities, schools, and workplaces? What assumptions lie behind the terms and metaphors that govern current discussions of literacy?
>
> What current practices promote or inhibit collaborations among communities, schools, and workplaces? What are the benefits and dangers of such collaborations?
>
> What tensions are there between a focus on the individual learner or worker and an emphasis on cooperative learning, union-management collaboration, and work teams?

What are examples of teachers working effectively with institutional, corporate, community, or state mandates? What are the tensions between institutional or government policy and individual practice?

What approaches to measurement, assessment, and evaluation promote or inhibit literacy?

Are there literacies we do not see? What alternative varieties exist in communities, schools, and workplaces, and how are these being supported or discouraged?

What are the implications of arguments that literacy should foster either social assimilation or resistance to mainstream culture?

What are the relations between our desires for mass literacy and the realities of contemporary mass culture?

What institutional structures and conditions of national life are necessary for a literate America?

The polylogue in these pages is intended to inform forthcoming conferences on literacy and to influence the national debate. As many essays in this volume suggest, there is no one enemy of full literacy—not the schools, not poverty, not the government. Indeed, perhaps the most threatening enemy of all is what James Moffett calls "agnosis": not wanting to know, the fear of knowing. Agnosis functions on all levels on behalf of hegemonic interests—in government, in the media, on school boards, and, not least of all, in our own minds. It is not wanting to know that sustains our sense of who we are by protecting us from the knowledge both of who we are not—of who the other is—and of what we may, with more courage, become. It is the fear of knowing that leads us to embrace simplistic solutions to complex literacy problems. It is with the fear of knowing that we struggle not only as teachers and students of literacy but as human beings committed to self-transcendence and social change.

The essays presented in this volume resist agnosis. Key words that emerge through repetition in their titles and arguments—*perspective, contexts, interpretive, struggle, resisting, reinventing, restructuring, reconceptualizing, censorship, value, community, empowerment*—suggest that the authors are not as a group drawn to easy answers or reductive definitions, that they are actively trying to identify creative pedagogical methods from positions at the intersection of the personal and the social. These essays offer national and international perspectives—the perspectives of teachers, adolescents, and children; of immigrants, blacks, native Americans, Hispanics, and latinos; of women and men, heterosexual and gay; of those who teach in prisons, in public schools, in community colleges and universities, in rural areas, and in inner cities. A review of the table of contents reveals a volume concerned not with a monolithic literacy or pedagogy but with the many dimensions of literacy in contemporary life, with the many ways of understanding and debating it, and ultimately with the many ways that teachers and students have come together to achieve it.

WORKS CITED

Freire, Paolo. *The Politics of Education: Culture, Power, and Liberation.* Trans. Donaldo Macedo. South Hadley: Bergen, 1985.

Heath, Shirley Brice. *Ways with Words: Language, Life, and Work in Communities and Classrooms.* Cambridge: Cambridge, 1983.

Hirsch, E. D., Jr. *Cultural Literacy: What Every American Needs to Know.* Boston: Houghton, 1987.

Modern Language Association. "Report of the Commission on the Future of the Profession." *PMLA* 97 (1982): 940–58.

———. "Report of the Commission on Writing and Literature." *Profession* 88 (1988): 70–76.

Sledd, Andrew. "Readin' not Riotin': The Politics of Literacy." *College English* 50 (1988): 495–508.

Part One
CONTEXTS

NATIONAL CONTEXTS

Public Literacy:
Puzzlements of a High School Watcher

Theodore R. Sizer

To visit among American high schools is to be struck by how similar these venerable social institutions are. Certainly, there is variety, best explained by differences in social class and, to a smaller extent, the race and the ethnicity of the students. The feel of a school serving the poor is profoundly different from the feel of its cousin in a Gold Coast suburb. However, it is the similarities that impress—the ubiquitous routines, the seven-period day, the bells, home-coming, school defined as English-math-science-social studies-language, each purveyed to students in isolation from every other. There are the texts, the sequence of topics, the testing, and, most important, the assumptions about learning and teaching and schooling that undergird these practices and the wry, usually genial cynicism of the teachers. In a nation priding itself on its local schooling, the consistencies are surprising. And the consistencies are exhibited by the students themselves—their clothing, lingo, enthusiasms, symbols. Again, class counts here, as does geography. But the wonder is why the differences are not far greater. Americans are mesmerized by their differences. Perhaps they should reflect a bit more on their similarities.

There is a wealth of shared knowledge reflected in high school regimens. Kids can move from Bangor to Butte and lose few steps. Not only are the language and the school routines relatively the same, but the nuances and the gestures of getting along remarkably transcend geography. The starker differences among Americans portrayed in basic training barrack scenes from World War II movies seem quaint today to most of us. The fact is that we clearly have a pervasive and powerful public literacy, a set of widely accepted symbols and ideas that give meaning to being American.

At a recent seminar my Brown University colleague Robert Scholes neatly demonstrated this public literacy by asking us to examine carefully what we must already know if we are to understand a twenty-eight-second Budweiser beer television commercial. The spot portrayed a fledgling black baseball umpire. In the half minute he moves from a scruffy minor-league ballpark to a major-league stadium to a close play at third and the resultant tirade from an offended, beefy white manager to the predictable smoke-filled bar where, with a glamorous black woman dutifully at his side, he accepts the tip of a bottle across the room from that same manager. It's all about making it, with Bud. The segment is redolent with assumed meanings. Most foreigners would miss most of it, as Scholes found. We Americans share a culture so completely that we are barely aware of it.

During the week of 19 June 1988, a typical early-summer span, the television sets that reside in more than 95% of America's 89 million homes were on some seven hours a day; 14.5 million households tuned in to *Night Court* and *Cheers*; *The Cosby Show* and *Sixty Minutes* drew barely fewer. Earlier that year, 37 million households watched the football Super Bowl. Shared experience, necessarily articulated in widely shared language and symbols, is a stunning reality. This shared experience shapes our expectations and discourse. It is no wonder that our adolescents are so much more alike than we, considering the expanse and the heterogeneous ethnicity of this country, might otherwise expect.

One might easily mock the results of this shared experience, this American public literacy. It is better to test it undefensively and perhaps try to harness it. Our public literacy is characterized by at least four properties. First, it is centrally driven, usually for purposes of merchandising. Whether with jeans or biology textbooks, the name of the commercial game is national saturation. Only large companies survive in this big league, even if they appear to be little companies. For example, in the textbook field, Silver Burdett, Ginn, Allyn and Bacon, Simon and Schuster, and Prentice Hall are all Gulf and Western satraps. National symbols are expertly crafted. We have a substantial national curriculum, one with few professional educators' or elected school boards' fingerprints on it.

Second, our public literacy is commercial. The vehicle for our shared culture emerges from the selling of things, usually products or services of some sort but also people, in electoral campaigns, and even ideas, as Jim and Tammy Bakker and their kin would have us believe. Much of the message is about demands in the making, provoking us to want things we previously didn't even know about. Thus, it's expansive, broadening. If you've never tried oat bran, you haven't lived. Move up to a Buick.

Third, our public literacy simplifies, synthesizes, unifies, focuses. *USA Today*. The McDonald's arches. Stylized logos. The *Harpers* short-essay format. The point is to be made simply, easily, quickly, and, above all, effectively. The sound bite. The powerful metaphor: an iron curtain. The utterly memorable modern version of Confucian analects. The reduction of a full life-style to the snapshot of a celebrity: *People* magazine.

Finally, our public literacy is pedagogically sophisticated, using understandings about human learning and a range of technologies far beyond the schoolteacher's ken. There are tie-ins—film to video to books to T-shirts. Clustered media characterize this pedagogy, the carefully coordinated use of sight and sound and print in artful, powerful combination. It is tough for your average French teacher to compete with MTV. As teachers, we school and college folk limp far behind our cousins in the communications industry.

The questions all this provokes are as demanding as they are obvious. Is this shared experience, this public literacy, a good thing? Is it tasteless? Is some of it, in fact, a vicious form of "acceptable" lying? Or is it modestly more benign, merely purveying corrupting fictions? Does it, with an artfulness that provokes acceptance and passivity, undermine habits of thoughtfulness? Is it undemocratic?

Why do we have it? Or, put more cogently, who wants it? (Public acceptance to date seems to be almost universal.) Should it be changed? That is, should there be rules of public discourse, as well as rules of the road, or is the First Amendment the inevitable protector of tawdriness and dishonesty, as well as free expression? Can, in fact, a public literacy be changed? What are the costs in trying to change it? Who should change it? Government? If so, by direct regulation, a national assessment of all the educating media? Or by indirection, through the tax code, with great business advantages given to alternative or public (not-for-profit) enterprises? Or do we leave change to the market, hoping that an aroused public will clean up mindlessness and worse in the common domain, somewhat as it appears to be doing to rid publicly shared air of cigarette-smoke pollution?

There must be answers to these questions. My concern here, however, is not to pursue these but to express some puzzlements. Why aren't we talking much about this ubiquitous public literacy? The intense and visible concern for illiteracy, for the inability of many to read and to find meaning in that reading—as reflected in this conference—is as sincere and important as it is conventional; folks have to be able to read, understand, and articulate to survive in this society. But what of the shared symbol systems, the public literacy, that we already have? It is shaping, in an unprecedented way, a national culture. Its power seems greater in some important respects than the formal teaching in schools and colleges.

The academy itself accepts the megaculture, the machine for public literacy, in a revealing way: it barely studies the matter. Higher education has been largely mute, for example, about the threat to academic freedom implicit in national testing or a de facto nationalized and virtually monopolistic textbook industry. The effects of television on American thought are remarkably little studied. We accept cultural gigantism, little reflecting on its meaning. By contrast, our savage little debates about critical theory rarely focus on the texts that saturate our cultural life but turn around intense little obscurities that, while perhaps of intellectual merit, have no cultural significance.

I am puzzled by how easily we rely on quick fixes in these matters—acceptance of a single score on a forty-minute machine-graded test to rate a school or to rank a student against hundreds of thousands of others; a glib dismissal of the mass media, one resting on precious little empirical data; an avoidance of that army of people in the communications industry who are, in fact, teaching our people their shared values; concession to the encroachments on individual freedom implicit in the increasingly centralized character of our institutions. We aren't paying enough attention, and a charge of myopia against the academy is not too strong. However, there is not just inattention; there is in all too many quarters active hostility to studying the popular culture in general, much less its aspect as a form of literacy. Such concerns are considered soft, unworthy activity for the bright person seeking tenure. It is both strange and sad.

The academy must recognize the reality of a public literacy, see it in perspective, and study it carefully. We must adopt a rich definition of this public literacy. As E. D. Hirsch has reminded us, it has a content, and we must see it as a content in context—gregarious, changeable, reflected and used in a rich variety of media. But content is only a part; no functioning literacy is merely facts; it is the ways of using those facts, of using style, of exhibiting habits. This use or exhibition arises from incentives, and the incentives that a culture presents its citizens shape their willingness to use and to be in the habit of using the values, content, and symbols that tie that culture together. Incentives arise from politics, both formal and informal, and the social system in which those politics proceed. Americans need to know more about the real content of our literacy, about its exhibition, and about the incentives and the politics that produce such incentives, that provoke that exhibition. It is the duty of the academy to pursue these complex issues.

In sum, we have an unprecedented wide public literacy in this country. All those adolescents roiling through their schools' standardized routines and responding collectively to mass media's messages are evidence enough of that. Let us pay close attention to this new phenomenon, this product of affluence and technology. And if we find it wanting, let us be about changing it.

Producing Adult Readers: 1930–50

David Bartholomae

> The selection of the right material for the right reader, then, is a
> problem of no small consequence. Recreation for leisure hours,
> intellectual progress, even literacy itself, depends in a large measure
> on how well the problem is solved by the reader himself or by
> someone from whom he seeks advice and counsel.
>
> William S. Gray and Bernice E. Leary,
> What Makes a Book Readable: With Special
> Reference to Adults of Limited Reading Ability:
> An Initial Study (1935)

I

The right material for the right reader. This essay explores the large-scale organization of reading in the United States before, during, and after World War II but particularly during the depression, when unemployment or "enforced leisure" created a new and, to some, dangerous population of adults with time on their hands—time, it was felt, that might best be spent with a book. There were adult readers, of course, before the *adult reader* became a key term in a diverse program of research and instruction. For my purposes in this essay, the "adult reader" is a figure of speech, a character in the professional literature whose name is invoked to justify a research agenda, the expense of public funds, or the organization of a curriculum.

This adult reader is not the common reader, since the adult reader had to be conceived of as abnormal, needing special direction or assistance. The adult reader, however, was still a reader, able to read words or sentences, able to make some sense out of letters on a page. I will not, then, be reviewing programs for nonreading adults. I will be looking at those programs designed for adults who were said to read poorly or randomly or not enough—to be the wrong readers reading the wrong books. In the words of one document,

> These include the adults who acquired laborious, inefficient reading habits in
> youth, who symbolize all books and reading matter by dull textbooks of a passing
> era, those who are deterred by the formal aspects and the literary traditions of
> libraries, those 40 (or 50)? millions living in regions unserved by any library, those
> too busy and limited in time to tolerate the academic style and verbosity of a large

portion of our books on serious topics, and especially that very large group of persons who simply do not know that there is matter in print that is of interest to them. (National Commission 3)

The negative references to "literary traditions" and "academic style and verbosity," a fairly common gesture in the professional literature of the 1930s and 1940s, represent the rhetorical front of a new consituency's efforts to claim reading as its subject—to take it, that is, from the institutionally established representatives of English. The field is thus divided, with an idealized educated reader on one side (a reader who goes to the library to select literary texts) and the adult reader on the other side (a reader who does not know what to read or how to read properly).[1] Both readers are figures that enable a certain conception of reading and instruction, of books and readers. The rejection of "literary traditions" by reading specialists was a rhetorical move whose effect was to clear a space for newly conceived programs of research and instruction: the "scientific" study of reading, a pedagogy based on efficiency and utility, the application of readability measures; the development of adult education programs, readers' advisory services, the Great Books series. All, in a sense, fill a space made possible by the definition of a different class of reader.

It was possible, of course, to name this difference in terms of a reader's position in relation to the usual channels for distributing books. There were readers who either literally couldn't get hold of books (they couldn't afford them or, as in the reference above, they lived outside regions served by libraries), or they were readers who couldn't imagine themselves being served by the existing channels of distribution. These would be readers who could get their hands on books but who couldn't imagine that books "belonged" to them or that they could manage them. Or the difference could be named in terms of class. In the 1930s particularly, the Affiliated Schools for Workers (later the American Labor Education Service) defined the adult reader as a person who, in most cases because of unemployment, had not only the time to read but also the motive—for retraining, for leisure, for understanding. And the workers' education movement produced materials—that is, teaching materials, reading lists, collections of workers' autobiographies—that are strikingly different from those produced through the universities and funded research programs directed at the adult reader. (See, for example, Hourwich and Palmer; *Annotated List*; Carter.)

In general, the representation of the adult reader as a worker or as a person needing newly conceived access to books was displaced by a more powerful representation of the adult reader as a reader lower on a developmental scale —a figure more powerful, that is, for the way it commanded and organized the field. The problem of reading was thus conceived of as a problem residing primarily in books (they were too hard) and in readers (they were poorly prepared) and not in a system of production and distribution. The argument I want to make is that during this period publishers, librarians, educators, and reading specialists constructed an abstraction called the adult reader. This figure functioned as a way of organizing a way of speaking, but it was also a way of organizing the market, since the adult reader was a potential consumer of those products controlled by publishers, librarians, educators, and reading specialists; the adult reader was a consumer, that is, of both books and education.

Let me set the scene for this brief history by referring to those challenges to the figure of the adult and the adult reader that preoccupied contemporary commentators. It was, the literature says over and over again, a period when education had produced a reading public unimaginable by earlier terms and standards—unimaginable in both its size and its heterogeneity. It was a time when publishing practices, schools, and libraries could bring more books to more people than ever before—a time, that is, of what was thought to be a great opportunity for the spread of culture (the culture of books and writing) and a time of great danger, since the reading public (suddenly imagined as a mass audience) could be shaped and moved by the production of reading material under no one's direct control. The wartime concern for propaganda as a technology for the control of hearts and minds was both a reflection of and a comment on the general awareness of the mass media and the masses. And it was, it was said, a time when the scientific approach to education would erase cultural stereotypes and force a new look at students and readers. It was no longer quite so easy to imagine what the other person was thinking or reading.

For my purposes I will divide the literature into three camps. There were those, like William Gray, who played a major role in the development of the scientific study of reading and reading pedagogy; those like I. A. Richards and Mortimer Adler, who were imagining the "proper" education of the educated public (worried about college graduates and undergraduates who lacked the proper understanding of "great books"); and those like Douglas Waples, researchers affiliated with library schools, receiving funding from the American Library Association and other organizations, and concerned with the use of libraries to direct adult reading (through reading lists and readers' advisory services). Waples, like Gray, was a member of the faculty at the University of Chicago, and, like Gray, he drew on the new techniques of the social sciences for studying individual and group behavior.

I will illustrate my argument by drawing primarily from Gray and his students and from Waples and the work funded by the American Library Association. Let me note in passing, however, a parallel set of texts, texts written out of a different tradition and from different institutional sites and yet with pragmatic how-to titles and an underlying concern for social order that make them quite similar to the work of the social scientists. I am referring to books like *How to Read* (Ezra Pound, 1931), *How to Teach Reading* (F. R. Leavis, 1932), *How to Read a Book* (Mortimer Adler, 1940), and *How to Read a Page* (I. A. Richards, 1942).[2]

In some ways the Leavis-Adler axis is the least interesting to those who have been reading recent critiques of English, English as the practice of university English departments. The figure of the reader here is a familiar one. The reader is a convenient abstraction constructed in terms of absence (what the reader didn't or couldn't do), and what the reader didn't or couldn't do is just what the scholar would have easily done, what the teacher would be happy or, at least, prepared to teach. The reader was a person who did not (or could not) read like Leavis, but Leavis would be happy to show him the way. It was the classic gesture of imperialism: to define the others in terms of what they lack, something we have, and to plan a program to provide for the needs of the impoverished.

When I turned to an alternative literature on reading—librarians' reports, reports of federal commissions, research by reading specialists—I found a similar pattern, authorized not by the powerful presence of a great reader (like Leavis) who could stand single-handedly for the culture but by the powerful rhetoric of social science research, which could speak for truths that were objectively there in the traces of human choice and behavior, which could tell a story that did not seem to be written by a single person or set of interests.

The project of constructing this figure brought together opposing schools, both progressive and conservative educators. The motive to construct the adult reader, in other words, was greater than the differing motives represented by differences in educational philosophy. It would be wrong, however, to assume that the governing motive here was simply economic, narrowly conceived as a desire to sell books or course credits. The project was driven also by the desire to imagine a unified culture, which could be read generously as a desire to extend education across divisions of race and class but which could also be read symptomatically as the dominant (literate) culture's desire to reproduce itself.

To tell this story as a story, I need to identify actors and agents. These are not the actors and agents identified by the researchers I have taken as my primary sources. The key agent in my account is something I loosely call English—not narrowly conceived as the practice of professional critics and university English departments but the more general field—including librarians, educators, publishers, and public policy makers who are concerned with the organization of reading and writing in American culture. When I refer to *English*, I am referring to a way of speaking about reading, writing, language, and culture and also to something more historically specific and present, scholarly disciplines made up of practitioners and their texts, and, in the mid-1930s, a variety of institutions: the United States Office of Education, the Modern Language Association, the National Council of Teachers of English, the University of Chicago and its graduate programs, the American Library Association, the Affiliated Schools for Workers, the Progressive Education Association, the American Council on Education, local teachers' groups, academic departments, the publishing industry—all concerned to organize reading and writing. In what I take as a complex and difficult reference, *English* stands for an organized attempt to produce readers and writers. It is, among other things, an expression of the literate culture's desire to reproduce itself, to match the right books with the right readers.

II

Perhaps the best way to begin a story about the construction of the adult reader is to begin with adolescence. I do not want to suggest that the development of the "adolescent reader" led to the construction of the adult reader, but the issues in adolescent literature are more clear-cut, both as they are represented in schooling and in the wider distribution circuits of the library and the marketplace; therefore, it is not difficult to show how the construction of the adolescent reader served interests and purposes other than those of actual adolescents who needed or wanted to read.

The adolescent reader is a familiar figure; today there are book lists at libraries, publication programs in the major publishing houses, book clubs, and sections of bookstores all labeled in the name of the adolescent or young adult reader. These do not contain all the books that adolescents can or do read, nor do they contain all the books by or about adolescents. Another principle of selection is at work here. Those books that are excluded are said to be too long or too difficult; some contain "inappropriate" content; some are determined to lie outside the interests of adolescents; some authors and publishers are seeking a wider audience. All these decisions are made through reference to the adolescent reader, a figure that could be said to be a product of developmental psychology or statistical measure but one that is also the product of a more generalized desire to reproduce a predictable image of adolescence. In other words, the programs designed to produce adolescent readers do not assist a "natural" fit of reader and text. Those prescriptions for matching the adolescent with the right books propose as normal a stereotype of the adolescent; they reorganize the distribution system so that certain choices become predictable and others unlikely.[3]

The figure of the adolescent reader is partly a product of the same progressive movement that produced the current concept of adult education. This was the movement to formalize a general education, one separate from vocational education or college preparation and designed to prepare the general population for full lives. In a particularly apt phrase from a resolution offered at the close of the 1944 United States Office of Education Conference on General Education, general education was referred to as "life adjustment training":

> If the vocational schools served 20% of the population and college prep another 20%, we do not believe that the remaining 60% of our youth of secondary school age will receive the life adjustment training they need and to which they are entitled as American citizens. (Applebee 144)

To provide teenagers with the experiences that would prepare them for life, English needed to define the common field of adolescent experience. The problems unique to adolescence would be represented in a literature designed to explicate and solve these problems—books to illustrate "normal" or "mature" responses to the difficult experiences of adolescence. A Baltimore librarian described her job this way: When students came into the library, she was to prescribe books "very much as physicians prescribe sulfa drugs, . . . by prescribing as best she can, and by keeping a sharp lookout for reactions" (Applebee 147).

The creation of an adolescent literature required the creation of a typical adolescent, one version of the right reader for these books. Here is a recent account of that adolescent:

> The "image" of the American Boy that emerges is of a clean-cut, socially poised extrovert, an incurious observer of life rather than a participant, a willing conformer, more eager to get than to give, a bit of a hypocrite but a rather dull companion—a well-adjusted youth not much above a moron. And the "image" of the American Girl? She is the one who likes the American boy.   (Lynch and Evans 413)

The point I want to argue is that the new terms changed not only the production and the distribution of images but the production and the distribution of books. One set of books was substituted for another. Here, for example, is a 1937 report from the Tulsa school board to Tulsa parents:

> As you read the list of seventy four book titles which follow, you will not find therein the titles of outstanding works of literature excepting "A Message to Garcia," "The Gettysburg Address," and "The Declaration of Independence."
>
> The reason for this is explained in consideration of the criterion on which they were chosen: namely, what contribution does this book make toward:
>
> 1. Building and maintaining physical and mental health;
> 2. An understanding of the fundamental principles and institutions of a democratic society;
> 3. Knowledge of the interaction between man and the natural environment;
> 4. Individual guidance and counseling?
>
> The application of this criterion brought into our list practically none of the works of literature which are in themselves great works of art; and it did bring into our list many books that reflect the common problems of health, understanding, knowledge, and guidance. They are all well written (the poorest of them from a literary point of view is probably "Work of Art" by Sinclair Lewis); and when read by young people of the secondary-school age under the competent direction and clear understanding of an intelligent teacher, they should be of great educational value in the various areas to which they are recommended.   (LaBrant 210)

It is interesting to consider why these criteria should rule out the earlier material in the high school curriculum ("outstanding works of literature"),

material that at several points in the history of American education were said
to provide health, understanding, knowledge, guidance, and counseling. In part,
this was simply the result of the application of social science measurement to
the canon. Surveys had shown that the kids hated great books and that neither
their teachers nor their parents read them when they didn't have to. On those
grounds it made sense to require students to read books that would work, that
would produce the expected social or psychological effects. Great books were
an inefficient way to produce the goals of general education. It is also possible
to find arguments against "outstanding works of literature" based on democratic
principles (great books had little to do with the experience of the majority of
those in school). The wider the circle of readers, the more difficult it became
to assume that reading would be valued generally or without question. As Lou
L. LaBrant put it, "What is regarded by the teacher as a normal, desirable, and
even necessary activity, is in the mind of the students' parents a luxury or
perhaps sheer idleness" (190). In general, the work of both the reading specialists
and the librarians is based on a rejection of those values represented by literature
and by reading as the reading of literature. Partly, the specialists and librarians
are staking a claim to reading as a subject by conceiving of it as separate from
the study of literature, particularly as practiced in colleges and universities. It
is against this representation of reading, in fact, that we should read the work
of Leavis and others to preserve the canon as a means for propagating taste and
sensibility.

The program to produce a new class of reader, whether adolescent or adult,
was accompanied by a program to produce a new class of book—the adolescent
novel or, for the adult market, the "readable book," a kind of no-nonsense
democratic text, without the "academic style and verbosity of a large portion
of our books on serious subjects." According to the American Library Association Commission on Adult Education (1924), "The dearth of books that are
at once simple, informal, interesting, adult in tone, and reliable in content
greatly limit the effectiveness of the adult education services of libraries" (National Commission 1).

For young adults in school full-time, as well as for adults in school at night,
the new reading programs represented a desire to reject traditional conceptions
of literary value while retaining reading as a value—valued, in particular, as a
way to organize, guide, and inform a heterogeneous public, not the common
reader but the masses, reading. This was the program: to fill leisure time and
to produce a common sensibility—not a common culture in an Arnoldian sense
but a set of shared goals and understandings. In place of outstanding works of
literature, the curriculum and the libraries and the publishing industry were
prepared to offer useful books, books of information, guidance, and self-help
organized by "level."

When the figure of the reader was reconceived, the market was reorganized
according to categories of age and mental development, and books were redis-
tributed (and in some cases newly produced) to serve specialized audiences. This

is a crude formula, but the general supply of reading material, certainly not undistinguished but divided along class lines (high and low), became redivided, with the reader's stage of development introduced as a factor. Older readers, readers who no longer needed primers or packaged material, were conceived of as a special audience requiring the right books to be the right readers. English, that is, both preserved and reproduced its construction of the adolescent by creating a genre called "adolescent literature" and by removing adolescents from a more general market. And the shift for adolescents was reproduced with adults. Readers or potential readers characterized primarily by their economic situation (unemployed workers, immigrants, adults with the time or the motive to seek out additional education) were reconceived in terms that erased their economic status. For educators, researchers, and publishers—all of whom had an interest in this newly conceived consumer—these readers' distinguishing differences were defined in terms of ability level, rather than their positions as members of a class, culture, or work force.

III

Adults are not captive consumers like adolescents; adults are not necessarily in school, and, if they are in school, it is under different terms and with different expectations. They get their books from bookstores, friends, and libraries. And, significantly, much of the early research on reading was sponsored by library associations and library schools. Researchers argued that with the new methods of the social sciences, they would find and describe the real "adult reader," by survey, by case study, by interview, by tracking down all those readers who checked out a preselected sample of books in a given year. The search was on to find out what adults wanted to read and what they could read—to find the right books and the right readers.

The general assumption was that the increased number of readers and the increasing availability of books had made it increasingly difficult to imagine the reader as the relatively stable figure he once was.

> To prepare for all types of students—those from the prairies, towns, and industrial cities; from wealthy suburban homes, slums, and tenant farms; from religious and irreligious homes; from Catholic, Protestant, and Jewish environments; from black, white and yellow races; from families supporting and opposing trade unions; from provincial and sophisticated groups—and to attempt to inculcate in all an appreciation of literature, requires an almost infinitely wide and flexible program. (LaBrant 190)

To prepare for and to inculcate all types of students requires an almost infinitely wide and flexible program. The remainder of this essay considers how this program—infinitely wide and flexible—is translated, at least through adult education, into a program of the right books for the right readers. These terms mark the culture's desire and anxiety to both contain and control the various readers of a diverse society.

One response to the rigidity of prior programs was the creation of what, characteristically, was called "free reading." If the reading conventionally assigned to readers was neither free nor flexible and if, as studies had shown, neither students nor their teachers would read outside of class the sorts of books the curriculum assumed they should read, then perhaps the answer was to add on a reading program that was open—one in which students could read what they wanted to read. This, after all, is one way of reproducing the circumstances of adult reading. Readers, it was argued, read what they want to read. That, then, is what they should do in a program of instruction.

There is, of course, no such thing as free reading—not only because books are commodities and controlled by a variety of market forces but also because readers do not have clear, single motives. What was perhaps most surprising to the researchers who studied these new readers was the recognition that free reading did not produce the expected results: readers didn't know what they wanted to read, or they didn't want to read anything, or they chose books that scandalized those who oversaw their reading. The researchers learned that free choice and an open field did not produce the desired results—that is, the right people reading the right books. Here is Douglas Waples, one of the leading reading researchers of the 1930s and 1940s, working through the problematics of a reader's will:

> Most of us actually read what lies within easiest reach, what demands the least mental effort, and what concerns our special interests. Our reading is thus determined by accessibility, readability, and subject interests—in this order. Accessibility best explains why we seldom read on subjects we are most curious about. Mass reading is much more accessible. The records show that we seldom do read what we really like, except when, by some miracle, our favorite subjects are discussed in a congenial style in some publication we hold in our hands. . . .
>
> Why people read what they read, we will never know exactly. About all we can say is that whenever anybody reads anything at all, certain incentives have triumphed over various inhibitions. Whenever we decide not to read and so decide to do something else, our inhibitions have prevailed. . . . On a desert island, we would read the phone book if we happened to have one. . . . But since a wide variety of reading matter is easily accessible to most of us, it is readability that largely explains our selections.   (Anderson 217–18)

What is most interesting here is how the question of accessibility, the first in importance, is translated into a question of readability; the key question becomes not how books are produced and distributed but how they are written.

In the face of what seemed to be random or uncontrolled reading, English set to work to organize a field that seemed to defy organization—by creating book lists, by surveying readers to see what they wanted (and needed), by standardizing response (or "comprehension"), by shaping adult taste (prohibiting or discouraging the reading of "cheap" novels, to use one of Waples's phrases), and by trying to stimulate the production of a new type of book, the readable book.[4] This, in some ways, tells the story of the development of the figure of the adult reader—from a person with limited access to books to a person with a limited ability to process text. And the story of adult education became the story of reading drills and comprehension exercises (to ensure that all readers agree), reading tests (to sort out levels of readers), readability formulas (to create levels of texts), and a newly created genre of readable writing (The *Reader's Digest* is perhaps the most lasting example of this).

One of the achievements of reading researchers in the 1940s was the development of formulas to measure readability, the most notable of which was developed by William Gray at the University of Chicago. Gray's formula is significantly different in its intent from Rudolf Flesch's better known formula for "plain" English. Flesch's index is part of an argument for a universally efficient language—clear prose for all people. Gray's formula was, initially, a diagnostic tool for teachers and librarians and, secondarily, a guide for would-be writers of adult books. He is not idealizing clear prose but arguing for a specific kind of simplified prose for the adult reader of limited ability. A librarian would use the formula (based on the number of clauses, the number of words in a clause, and so on) to guide readers toward a graded series of readers. Similarly, writers and publishers could use the formula to develop graded materials for adult readers. Here, for example, is an expression of the expectations created by Gray's work:

> The need for readable books is not yet met but is at least recognized. Publishers and educators are now convinced and experimentation in the production of the needed simple books on topic of current interest, addressed to adult minds, is under way in the "Readability Laboratory" recently established at Teachers College, Columbia University, under the direction of Professor Lyman Bryson, a member of the American Library Association Board on the Library and Adult Education.   (National Commission 2)

As a device for organizing research and curriculum and as a device for thinking about the problems of reading, the concept of the readable book takes the available supply of books—books that are being read by adults, including those who are working class or with limited formal education or limited English—and defines many of them as "unreadable," inappropriate. This shift is the most surprising and has had the most lasting and negative effect on adult education, where readers are often directed away from the books that other adults read. There are enough examples of readers of all ages and classes taking inspiration from books that are difficult, books they cannot completely understand, to suggest that a move to easy or efficient books is neither inevitable nor necessarily preferable in assisting adult readers (or any reader, for that matter).

The abstraction, "adult reader," came to represent those who did not or could not read what they were supposed to read. There remained something monstrous (or mysterious) about these subjectivities that were not the recognizable products of the "standard" culture. In the 1930s and 1940s, largely through the influence of Gray and Waples, the survey became the standard instrument to probe these mysteries. As was the case with the construction of the typical adolescent, the process organized adult types according to fixed stereotypes of race, class, and gender. Here, for example, is a 1936 report:

> Whereas the women's list is dotted with such "cream-puff" items as *The Magnificent Obsession, Forgive Us Our Trespasses*, and *Imitation of Life*, the men's list impresses by its general virility. The women select heavily from fiction; the men compose their reading diet with more substantial stuff. Even the fiction they read is of a decidedly more vigorous sort.   (Anderson 228)

To determine subject interests among prospective adult readers, Douglas Waples asked people to rate their interest in a variety of subjects, like public morality, and he surveyed the following groups: prisoners, post office employees, machinists, farmers, medical students, and high school teachers. He found that interest in public morals ranged from the prisoners (with the highest interest rate) to Vermont farmers (with the lowest). Waples concluded, "The prisoners' interest is self-explanatory. [!] The farmers' indifference suggests aloofness from urban frivolity" (Waples and Tyler 27). In *Who Reads What?* (1935), Charles H. Compton reports on a survey of seven hundred recent readers of Thomas Hardy, their names taken from the circulation records at the St. Louis Public Library. The list includes ninety-six salesmen and saleswomen.

> They are mostly department store clerks and Piggly Wiggly or neighborhood grocery clerks. The women generally call themselves sales ladies. There are a number of traveling salesmen and others who hit the front doors in disposing of their wares. It is incredible that these salesfolks who sell us sox and ties and BVD's, bread and butter, sugar and tea, can really understand Hardy—at least not in the way our wives do, who write papers on him for women's club programs. It must be a mere coincidence that those of Hardy's works which critics generally consider his greatest are also the most popular with these salespeople.   (36)

Across the literature, one finds researchers fitting readers into prior types or predictable categories.

This process is seen perhaps most dramatically in the case studies of the period, in which individual cases are read in terms of English's powerful agenda. Here, for example, are excerpts from a case study reported by Ruth Strang, one of Gray's students. It is the case study of a "Negro" busboy living in Chicago, called by his initials, N. T., whose age is between forty-one and fifty and whose last grade of public education was grade 9:

> Reading is one of his three leisure time activities, the other two being attending the movies and playing an instrument. To these he devoted, on the average,

fourteen hours a week. When interviewed he was reading *Mein Kampf*, which he had bought. During the last month he had read Wells's *Outline of History*, Coon's *Measuring Ethiopia*, and Voltaire's *Candide*. (51)

The researcher administered a test, written responses to set passages. The responses, she said, showed N. T.'s tendency to "include his own personal opinion and additional ideas which he attributes to the author but which were not included in the article." She says, "He makes no attempt to separate his summary of what the author said from his own comments." Her conclusion was that N. T. "need[s] help in getting a more adequate idea of what he reads and especially in selecting reading material which is within his range of ability to comprehend. For what does it profit N. T. to read if he gains from his reading only erroneous ideas?" (53)

This investigation into the practice of a reader became a measure of whether, to English, he was a reader or not. As a consequence, N. T.—who read Wells, Hitler, Coon, and Voltaire, all in a three-month period—is defined as a nonreader, someone who can best be served by the introduction of books he would find more "readable." He was the wrong reader reading the wrong books.

The measure of his failure as a reader, at least beyond the numerical measure of the comprehension test (or, perhaps, the researcher's inability to see an order in his reading—after all, what conventional program would bring together *Mein Kampf, Measuring Ethiopia, Candide*, and Wells's *Outline of History*?) was the degree to which N. T. failed to separate his beliefs from an author's. He did not, or could not, call attention to the difference between what he knew and what a book said. He identified with what he read; he let an author speak for him, saw himself as an equal partner in the conversation, or took as his own that which was said by another. What might be identified as the source of N. T.'s pleasure as a reader is, for English, a source of anxiety. He failed to achieve the kind of distance from the text that is, under various names, still one of the goals of literacy education, in which students are asked to talk about an author's devices or to read "critically," to resist becoming taken by or lost in what they read.

One can detect a similar anxiety in many of the examples Waples, Berelson, and Bradshaw offer in *What Reading Does to People: A Summary of Evidence on the Social Effects of Reading and a Statement of Problems for Research* (1940). For example:

A still more satisfactory account, for our purposes, of what the *New Masses* does to its readers might be given in terms of the motives responsible for the reading —motives which the reading generally satisfies. It is safe to suggest that readers of the *New Masses* are most numerous among the "deprived" groups. They generally lack the security which larger incomes would provide. They lack the prestige enjoyed by other classes with higher social status, more respectable occupations, wider social contacts, and a generally larger share of the things that everyone wants. Hence, to say that an effect of reading the *New Masses* is an increase in the readers' sense of security and prestige through their identifications with the social platform of the Communist party is more explanatory than to say that they read the *New Masses* because they are communists or that the reading increases their loyalty to the Communist party.   (20)

The concern expressed here is a concern for uncontrolled reading, heightened by the newly realized sense of the power of mass media, including print, to move a large and relatively unknown readership. Waples, Berelson, and Bradshaw, who believe they are opening up the possibilities for the study of the "social effects" of reading, are blunt about the social and political backdrop to their research. The opening pages of their book refer to necessary changes in social policy in a time of crisis, to "the international events of 1940" and the "domestic social experiments of the New Deal":

> Whether such changes occur with or without the violence and distress of international or civil wars depends in large part upon how the several agencies of mass communication—print, radio, and cinema combined—are used to clarify and to interrelate the interests of contending factions. Mass communications can be used to show where common interests lie, to encourage rational and deliberate changes; or they may be used by each faction to antagonize rival factions and to precipitate violence.   (1)

And, they conclude, "Conditions beyond our control define the problems of adjustment to social forces which can be met by intelligent changes in the conditions within our control" (2).

IV

The selection of the right material for the right reader. These terms have served as the key terms in my account of reading research and instruction in the twenty-year period, 1930–50. Their force can be felt in current practice. Let me turn to a brief example, one that came to me through the Modern Language Association Literacy Conference in September 1988.

A handsome series of materials for adult new readers, called Writers' Voices, was recently developed by the Literacy Volunteers of New York City with an impressive advisory committee and funding and assistance from a long list of companies and foundations. In a sense, the series represents the cooperative efforts of concerned persons from business, education, and the community— the best we have to offer. Let me turn to one book in the series, an anthology containing selections from two books by Maya Angelou, *I Know Why the Caged Bird Sings* and *The Heart of a Woman* (Literacy Volunteers).

There are fifty-five pages of text in this book; only twenty-one of them contain selections from Angelou's two books. The rest of the pages are preface, preparation, questions, and apparatus. The first seventeen pages are made up of the following sections: "About *Writers' Voices*," "Note to the Reader," "About Maya Angelou," "Maya Angelou's Family Tree," "About Joe Louis," and "About the Selection from *I Know Why the Caged Bird Sings*." A reader is given seventeen pages of preparation for seven pages of *Caged Bird*.

The headnote for each of the books in Writers' Voices is a statement by a literacy student, Mamie Moore, from Brooklyn: "I want to read what others do—what I see people reading in libraries, on the subway, and at home." One could argue that Writers' Voices is one example of how the culture prevents Mamie Moore from doing what other readers do. She is not, after all, reading the paperback copy of *Caged Bird*, something people read in libraries, on the subway, and at home; she is reading a substitute version, one that is significantly different from the original and, in a sense, harder to read, since its opening seventeen pages argue that the reader cannot read the book, that the reader is not prepared.

If one steps outside the standard texts of reading pedagogy and adult education, outside their conception of the right book and the right reader, it is possible to see Writers' Voices as a carefully organized attempt to keep *I Know Why the Caged Bird Sings* out of the hands of new readers by giving them an alternative text and by making Angelou's words seem difficult, unapproachable (or unapproachable without the assistance of a specialist and special preparation). As an example of practice, Writers' Voices effectively reproduces the very problems it is designed to address and, in doing so, maintains the tradition I've charted in the 1930s and 1940s. This is not the result of bad faith or crass commercialism. Literacy workers are, after all, often volunteers.[5] It is, rather, the product of a way of thinking and speaking about reading, books, and the adult reader that deserves critical reappraisal. The habits of past practice are limiting the options available to literacy volunteers today.

The purpose of this brief history is to provide a context for current practice, a way of seeing certain terms and assumptions as situated in particular historical moments or specific academic projects. It is possible, I have argued, to see the problems of adult reading as problems of access, and it is possible to see the dominant programs for adult readers as limiting access to books, by taking readers out of the open market and by presenting reading as something to be done only through a program of assistance. To do this, however, we have to read against the figure of the adult reader as it is part of the legacy of adult education. When we read the tradition this way, it suggests that we (*we* as representatives of English) should be cautious of certain instincts, certain predictable gestures or conclusions, certain unconscious practices, like the practice of determining for others the right books—good books, readable books. We need to resist what seems to be an inevitable move—to define the sensibilities of others in terms of their differences from our own, to imagine that teaching inevitably involves giving others what we have and they lack—our books, our habits, our version of critical consciousness. Perhaps the money and the energy spent guiding readers might be better spent changing the ways we, as a society, produce and distribute texts, the material goods of a literate culture.[6]

NOTES

[1]Here, as an additional example, is Douglas Waples and his colleagues. Waples was Professor of Researches in Reading at the University of Chicago Graduate Library School and one of the original figures in the "scientific" study of reading:

> Certain values have been imputed to reading by the scholars and writers who have made their reputations by reading and criticizing the writings of others. It is not remarkable that those for whom reading is thus a vested interest should declare that reading is a good thing, that readers are wiser people than nonreaders, that those who read and approve what the contemporary critics approve are persons of superior taste, nor that those who read the more abstruse and more scholarly works are persons of superior wisdom. (*What Reading Does to People* 23).

[2]To this list I would add the volumes by Thompson and Rosenblatt. There is almost no reference back and forth between the Adler-Leavis list and the Gray or Waples groups. At best, there are a few references to Adler, whose book was on the best-seller list for more than a year.

[3]I recently felt the force of this economy in my own family. When we set out on summer vacation, we brought books—some for ourselves and some for our children, including my adolescent son. For my son, we took books from the adolescent list at the library (a list also provided by his school): *Lord of the Flies, The Call of the Wild*. He said he wanted to read war books and, through my selection, took *Battle Cry* and *For Whom the Bell Tolls*. My wife and I took what we were calling three Pittsburgh novels: *The Car Thief, Second Brother*, and *An American Childhood*. These are all either set in our town or have an author who lives in Pittsburgh. The adult books could also be said to have been adolescent literature, however, since all have an adolescent as the central character, although with a presentation of crime or sexuality that could be deemed inappropriate for adolescents. My son read all the books except *The Call of the Wild, For Whom the Bell Tolls*, and *An American Childhood*.

[4]It is interesting to consider how a positive term in a discussion of the distribution of books may become a term of moral disapprobation. One could argue that a wide range of cheap books widely distributed and skillfully presented is an appropriate and powerful way to deal with the problem of adult reading. The translation of the book as a commodity into the book as a cultural force (cheap books to "cheap" books) is one strategy in the construction of the adult reader.

[5]The Literacy Volunteers of New York, however, is also in the business of selling books. Each volume in the Writers' Voices series is priced at $2.95, making one of their books only a dollar less than an inexpensive paperback. If you pay the additional $2.00 required to order a copy, it is more. My point is that Writers' Voices is competing for the book buyer's money and attention.

[6]This project would not have been possible without the advice, consultation, and assistance of Chris Ross, who spent hours in the library reviewing material.

WORKS CITED

Adler, Mortimer Jerome. _How to Read a Book._ New York: Simon, 1940.

Anderson, Harold A. "Reading Interests and Tastes." _Reading in General Education: An Exploratory Study._ Ed. William S. Gray. Washington: American Council on Education, 1940. 217–70.

Annotated List of Materials for Workers' Classes. New York: Affiliated Schools for Workers, 1934.

Applebee, Arthur N. _Tradition and Reform in the Teaching of English._ Urbana: NCTE, 1974.

Carter, Jean. _Mastering the Tools of the Trade: Suggestive Material for Experimental Use in the Teaching of English in Workers' Classes._ New York: Affiliated Schools for Workers, 1932.

Compton, Charles H. _Who Reads What? Essays on the Readers of Mark Twain, Hardy, Sandburg, Shaw, William James, the Greek Classics._ New York: Wilson, 1935.

Flesch, Ruldolf. _The Art of Readable Writing._ New York: Harper, 1949.

Gray, William S., and Bernice E. Leary. _What Makes a Book Readable: With Special Reference to Adults of Limited Reading Ability: An Initial Study._ Chicago: U of Chicago P, 1935.

Hourwich, Andria Taylor, and Gladys L. Palmer. _I Am a Woman Worker._ New York: Arno, 1974.

LaBrant, Lou L. "American Culture and the Teaching of Literature." _Reading in General Education: An Exploratory Study: A Report of the Committee on Reading in General Education._ Ed. William S. Gray. Washington: American Council on Education, 1940. 186–216.

Leavis, F. R. _How to Teach Reading: A Primer for Ezra Pound._ Cambridge: Minority, 1932.

Literacy Volunteers of New York City. _Selected from_ I Know Why the Caged Bird Sings _and_ The Heart of a Woman. By Maya Angelou. Writers' Voices. New York: Literacy Volunteers of New York City, 1989.

Lynch, James Jeremiah, and Bertrand Evans. _High School English Textbooks._ Boston: Little, 1963.

National Commission on the Enrichment of Adult Life, National Education Association. "Committee Report on Adult Education in the Library," No. 33. Washington: 1936.

Pound, Ezra L. _How to Read._ London: D. Harmsworth, 1931.

Richards, I. A. _How to Read a Page: A Course in Efficient Reading with an Introduction to a Hundred Great Words._ New York: Norton, 1942.

Rosenblatt, Louise. _Literature as Exploration._ For the Commission of Human Relations of the Progressive Education Association. New York: Appleton, 1938.

Strang, Ruth. _Explorations in Reading Patterns._ Chicago: U of Chicago P, 1942.

Thompson, Denys. _Reading and Discrimination._ London: Chatto, 1934.

Waples, Douglas, Bernard Berelson, and Franklyn R. Bradshaw. _What Reading Does to People: A Summary of Evidence on the Social Effects of Reading and a Statement of Problems for Research._ Chicago: U of Chicago P, 1940.

Waples, Douglas, and Ralph W. Tyler. _What People Want to Read About: A Study of Group Interests and a Survey of Problems in Adult Reading._ Chicago: American Library Assn. and U of Chicago P, 1931.

PARTICULAR CONTEXTS

Becoming Literate:
A Lesson from the Amish

Andrea R. Fishman

One clear, frost-edged January Sunday night, two families gathered for supper and an evening's entertainment. One family—mine—consisted of a lawyer, a teacher, and their twelve-year-old son; the other family—the Fishers—consisted of Eli and Anna, a dairy farmer and his wife, and their five children, ranging in age from six to seventeen. After supper in the Fisher's large farm kitchen—warmed by a wood stove and redolent of the fragrances of chicken corn soup, homemade bread, and freshly baked apples—the table was cleared and an additional smaller one set up to accommodate games of Scrabble, double Dutch solitaire, and dominoes. As most of us began to play, adults and children randomly mixed, Eli Fisher, Sr., settled into his brown leather recliner with the newspaper, while six-year-old Eli, Jr., plopped on the corner of the couch nearest his father with a book.

Fifteen or twenty minutes later, I heard Eli, Sr., ask his son, "Where are your new books?" referring to a set of outgrown Walt Disney books we had brought for little Eli and his seven-year-old brother, Amos. Eli, Jr., pointed to a stack of brightly colored volumes on the floor, from which his father chose *Lambert, the Sheepish Lion*. As Eli, Jr., climbed onto the arm of the recliner and snuggled against his father, Eli, Sr., began reading the book out loud in a voice so commandingly dramatic that soon everyone was listening to the story, instead of playing their separate games. Broadly portraying the roles of both Lambert and his lioness mother and laughing heartily at the antics of the cub who preferred cavorting with the sheep to stalking with the lions, Eli held his enlarged audience throughout the rest of the story.

As most of us returned to our games when he finished reading, Eli, Sr., asked of anyone and everyone, "Where's the *Dairy?*" Daniel, the Fishers' teenage son, left his game and walked toward his father. "It's in here," he said, rummaging through the newspapers and magazines in the rack beside the couch until he found a thick newsletter called *Dairy World*, published by the Independent Buyers Association, to which Eli belonged.

Eli leafed through the publication, standing and walking toward the wood stove as he did. Leaning against the wall, he began reading aloud without preface. All conversation stopped as everyone once again attended to Eli's loudly expressive reading voice, which said:

> A farmer was driving his wagon down the road. On the back was a sign which read: "Experimental Vehicle. Runs on oats and hay. Do not step in exhaust."

Everyone laughed, including Eli, Sr., who then read the remaining jokes on the humor page to his attentive audience. All our games forgotten, we shared the best and the worst riddles and jokes we could remember until it was time for bed.

Occasions like this one occur in many homes and have recently attracted the interest of family literacy researchers (Heath; Taylor; Wells). The scene at the Fishers could have been the scene in any home where parents value reading and writing and want their children to value them as well. It would not be surprising if Eli and Anna, like other literacy-oriented parents, read bedtime stories to their children, helped with their homework, and encouraged them to attain high school diplomas, if not college degrees. But Eli and Anna do none of these things: they read no bedtime stories, they are annoyed if their children bring schoolwork home, and they expect their children to go only as far in school as they did themselves, as far as the eighth grade.

So, although Eli and Anna appeared on that Sunday night to be ideal pro-literacy parents, they may not be, according to commonly described standards, and one significant factor may account for their variations from the supposed ideal: Eli and Anna are not mainstream Americans but are Old Order Amish, raising their family according to Old Order tradition and belief. The Sunday night gathering I just described took place by the light of gas lamps in a house without radio, stereo, television, or any other electrical contrivance. Bedtime in that house is more often marked by singing or silence than by reading. Schoolwork rarely enters there because household, field, and barn chores matter more. And the Fisher children's studying is done in a one-room, eight-grade, Old Order school taught by an Old Order woman who attended the same kind of school herself. So while Eli, Jr., like his siblings, is learning the necessity and the value of literacy, what literacy means to him and the ways in which he learns it may differ in both obvious and subtle ways from what it means and how it's transmitted to many mainstream children, just as Eli's world differs from theirs, both obviously and subtly.

As suggested earlier, Eli, Jr., lives in a house replete with print, from the kitchen bulletin board to the built-in bookcases in the playroom to the tables and magazine rack in the living room. There are children's classics and children's magazines. There are local newspapers, shoppers' guides, and other adult periodicals. And there are books of children's Bible stories, copies of the King James Version of the Bible, and other inspirational volumes, none of which mark the Fishers' home as notably different from that of many other Christian Americans.

Yet there are differences, easily overlooked by a casual observer but central to the life of the family and to their definition of literacy. One almost invisible difference is the sources of these materials. Eli and Anna attempt to carefully control the reading material that enters their home. Anna buys books primarily from a local Christian bookstore and from an Amish-operated dry goods store, both of which she trusts not to stock objectionable material. When she sees potentially interesting books in other places—in the drugstore, in the book and card shop, or at a yard sale—she uses the publisher's name as a guide to acceptable content. Relatives and friends close to the family also supply appropriate titles both as gifts and as recommendations, which Anna trusts and often chooses to follow up.

Another, slightly more visible difference comes in the form of books and periodicals around the Fisher house that would not be found in many mainstream, farm, or Christian homes. Along with the local newspaper in the rack beside the couch are issues of *Die Botschaft*, which describes itself as "A Weekly Newspaper Serving Old Order Amish Communities Everywhere." On the desk is a copy of *The Amish Directory*, which alphabetically lists all the Amish living in Pennsylvania and Maryland by nuclear family groups, giving crucial address and other information, along with maps of the eighty-seven church districts included.

On top of the breakfront in the sitting area are copies of songbooks, all in German: some for children, some for adults, and one—the *Ausbund*—for everyone, for this is the church hymnal, a collection of hymns written by tortured and imprisoned sixteenth-century Anabaptists about their experiences and their faith. Kept with these songbooks is a German edition of the Bible and a copy of the *Martyrs Mirror*, an oversized, weighty tome full of graphic descriptions in English of the tortured deaths of early Anabaptists, each illustrated by a black-and-white woodcut print.

Despite what may seem to be the esoteric nature of these texts, none remain in their special places gathering dust, for all are used regularly, each reinforcing in a characteristic way the Amish definition of literacy and each facilitating the image Eli, Jr., has of himself as literate.

Because singing is central to Amish religious observance and expression, the songbooks are used frequently by all members of the family. Because singing requires knowing what is in the text and because Amish singing, which is unaccompanied and highly stylized, requires knowing how to interpret the text

exactly as everyone else does, the songbooks represent a kind of reading particularly important to the community, a kind that must be mastered to be
considered literate. Yet because singing may mean holding the text and following
the words as they appear or it may mean holding the text and following the
words from memory or from others' rendition, children of Eli's age and younger
all participate, appearing and feeling as literate as anyone else.

Functioning similarly are the German Bible and the *Martyrs Mirror*. Though
only the older Fishers read that Bible, they do so regularly and then share what
they've read with their children. It is the older Fishers, too, who read the
Martyrs Mirror, but that text Eli, Sr., usually reads aloud during family devotions,
so that Anna and all the children, regardless of age, participate similarly through
his oral presentations.

While it may seem easier to accept such variant definitions of reading in
shared communal situations like these, the participation of Eli, Jr., was equally
welcome and equally effective in shared individual reading. When individual
oral reading was clearly text-bound, as it is during family devotions, Eli was
always enabled to participate in ways similar to his brothers' and sisters', making
him a reader like them. When all the Fishers took turns reading the Bible aloud,
for example, someone would read Eli's verse aloud slowly, pausing every few
words, so that he could repeat what was said and thereby take his turn in the
rotation.

When the older children were assigned Bible verses or *Ausbund* hymn stanzas
to memorize, Eli was assigned the same one as Amos, the sibling closest in age.
Their assignment would be shorter and contain less complex vocabulary than
the one the older children got, yet Amos and Eli would also practice their verse
together, as the older children did, and would take their turns reciting, as the
older children did, making Eli again able to participate along with everyone
else.

Because oral reading as modeled by Eli, Sr., is often imitated by the others,
Eli, Jr., always shared his books by telling what he saw or knew about them.
No one ever told him that telling isn't the same as reading, even though they
may look alike, so Eli always seemed like a reader to others and felt like a reader
himself. When everyone else sat reading or playing reading-involved games in
the living room after supper or on Sunday afternoons, Eli did the same, to no
one's surprise, to everyone's delight, and with universal, though often tacit,
welcome and approval. When the other children received books as birthday
and Christmas presents, Eli received them too. And when he realized at age
six that both of his brothers had magazine subscriptions of their own, Eli asked
for and got one as well. Eli never saw his own reading as anything other than
real; he did not see it as make-believe or bogus, and neither did anyone else.
So, despite the fact that before he went to school Eli, Jr., could not read
according to some definitions, he always could according to his family's and his
own.

Just as all the Fishers read, so they all write, and just as Eli was enabled to define reading in a way that made him an Amish reader, so he could define writing in a way that made him an Amish writer. Letter writing has always been a primary family activity and one central to the Amish community. Anna writes weekly to *Die Botschaft*, acting as the scribe from her district. She, Eli, Sr., and sixteen-year-old Sarah all participate in circle letters, and the next three children all write with some regularity to cousins in other Amish settlements.

Yet, no matter who is writing to whom, their letters follow the same consistently modeled Amish format, beginning with "Greetings . . . ," moving to recent weather conditions, then to family and community news of note, and ending with a good-bye and often a philosophical or religious thought. I've never seen anyone in the community instructed to write this way, but in the Fisher family, letters received and even letters written are often read out loud, and though this oral sharing is done for informative rather than instructive purposes, it provides an implicit model for everyone to follow.

With all the other family members writing letters, reading them out loud, and orally sharing those they have received, Eli, Jr., wanted to write and receive letters, too, and no one said he couldn't. When he was very young, he dictated his messages to Sarah and drew pictures to accompany what she wrote down for him. Then, even before he started school, Eli began copying the dictated messages Sarah recorded, so that the letters would be in his own hand, as the drawings were.

Other forms of writing also occur in the Fisher household for everyone to see and use. Greeting cards, grocery lists, bulletin board reminders, and bedtime notes from children to absent parents were all part of Eli's life to some extent, and his preschool writing and drawing always adorned the refrigerator, along with the school papers of his brothers and sisters.

In addition, the Fishers played writing-involved games—including Scrabble and Boggle—in which everyone participated, as the family revised the rules to suit their cooperative social model and their definition of literacy. In any game at the Fishers, the oldest person or persons playing may assist the younger ones. No question of fairness arises unless only some players go unaided. Older players, too, may receive help from other players or from onlookers. Score is always kept, and, while some moves are ruled illegal, age or aid received neither bars nor assures a winner. Eli, Jr., therefore, has always played these games as well as anyone else.

Obviously, Eli, Jr., learned a great deal about literacy from all these preschool experiences, but what he learned went far beyond academic readiness lessons. More important, Eli learned that literacy is a force in the world—his world—and it is a force that imparts power to all who wield it. He could see for himself that reading and writing enable people as old as his parents and as young as his siblings to fully participate in the world in which they live. In fact, it might have seemed to him that, to be an Amish man, one must read and write, and to be a Fisher, one must read and write as well.

So, even before the age of six, Eli began to recognize and acquire the power of literacy, using it to affiliate himself with the larger Amish world and to identify himself as Amish, a Fisher, a boy, and Eli Fisher, Jr. However, what enabled Eli to recognize all these ways of defining and asserting himself through literacy was neither direct instruction nor insistence from someone else. Rather, it was the ability that all children have long before they can read and write print text, the ability, as Friere puts it, "to read the world." "It is possible," Friere asserts, "to view objects and experiences as texts, words, and letters, and to see the growing awareness of the world as a kind of reading, through which the self learns and changes" (6). Eli, Jr., clearly illustrates this understanding of how children perceive and comprehend the seemingly invisible text of their lives. What he came to understand and accept this way were the definition and the role of print literacy as his society and culture both consciously and tacitly transmit them.

When Eli, Jr., began school, therefore, he was both academically and socially ready to begin. To smooth the transition from home to school, Eli's teacher— like most in Old Order schools—held a "preschool day" in the spring preceding his entry to first grade. On that day, Eli and Mary, the two prospective first-graders in Meadow Brook School, came to be initiated as "scholars." Verna, their teacher, had moved the two current first-graders to other seats, clearing the two desks immediately in front of hers for the newcomers; all that day Mary and Eli sat in the first-grade seats, had "classes," and did seatwork like all the other children. They seemed to know they were expected to follow the rules, to do what they saw others doing, to practice being "scholars," and Verna reinforced that notion, treating those two almost as she would anyone else.

To begin one lesson, for example, "Let's talk about bunnies," she instructed, nodding her head toward the two littlest children, indicating that they should stand beside her desk. She then showed them pictures of rabbits, with the word *bunnies* and the number depicted indicated in word and numeral on each picture. After going through the pictures, saying, "three bunnies," "four bunnies," and having the children repeat after her, Verna asked three questions and got three choral answers.

> "Do bunnies like carrots?" she asked.
> "Yes," the two children answered together.
> "Do they like lettuce?"
> "Yes."
> "Do they sometimes get in Mother's garden?"
> "Yes."

Were it not for some enthusiastic head nodding, Eli, Jr., and Mary could have been fully matriculated students.

When she was ready to assign seatwork, Verna gave the preschoolers pictures of bunnies to color and asked, "What do we do first? Color or write our names?"

"Write our names," the pair chorused, having practiced that skill earlier in the day.

"Yes, we always write our names first. Go back to your desk, write your name, then color the picture. Do nothing on the back of the paper." And the children did exactly that, doing "what we do" precisely "the way we do it."

Verna also conducted what she called a reading class for the two preschoolers, during which they sat, and she held an open picture book facing them. Talking about the pictures, Verna made simple statements identifying different aspects of and actions in the illustrations. After each statement Verna paused, and the children repeated exactly what she had said. The oral text accompanying one picture said:

Sally is eating chips and watching TV.
Sally has a red fish.
Sally has spilled the chips.

After "reading" the text this way, the children answered questions about it.

"What does Sally have?" Verna asked.
"A fish," they replied.
"What color is her fish?"
"Red."
"Did Sally spill the chips?"
"Yes."
"Did the cat eat the chips?"
"Yes."

While the content of this lesson seems incongruous, I know, its form and conduct fit the Meadow Brook model perfectly. Precise recall and yeses are all that the questions demand. Even the last question, while not covered in the "reading," requires recognition of only what happens in the picture.

What happened in Meadow Brook School that day—and what would happen in the eight school years to follow—reinforced, extended, and rarely contradicted what Eli already knew about literacy. Reading and writing at school allowed him to further affiliate and identify himself with and within his social group. While his teacher occasionally gave direct instructions, those instructions tended to be for activities never before seen or experienced; otherwise, Eli and Mary knew to follow the behavioral and attitudinal lead of the older children and to look to them for assistance and support, just as they looked to the teacher. In other words, reading the school world came as naturally to these children as reading the world anywhere else, and the message in both texts was emphatically the same.

Most important here, however, may be the remarkable substantive coherence that Meadow Brook School provided, a coherence that precluded any conflict over what, how, or even whether to read and write. Eli's experience as a Fisher had taught him that reading comes in many forms—secular and religious, silent and oral, individual and communal—and they all count. Through his at-home experience, Eli had also learned which other, more specific, less obvious abilities count as reading in his world. He had learned to value at least four significant abilities: (1) the ability to select and manage texts, to be able to find his mother's letter in *Die Botschaft* or to find a particular verse in the Bible; (2) the ability to empathize with people in texts and to discern the implicit lessons their experiences teach: to empathize with Lambert the lion, who taught the possibility of peaceful coexistence, and to empathize with the Anabaptist martyrs, who taught the rightness of dying for one's faith; (3) the ability to accurately recall what was read, to remember stories, riddles, and jokes or to memorize Bible and hymn verses; and (4) the ability to synthesize what is read in a single text with what is already known or to synthesize information across texts in Amish-appropriate ways.

When Eli got to school, he found a similar definition of reading in operation. He and Mary were helped to select and manage text. Their attention was directed toward what mattered in the text and away from what did not. They were helped to discover the single right answer to every question. They had only to recall information without interpreting or extending it in any significant way. And they were expected to empathize with the people in Verna's lunchtime oral reading without questioning or hypothesizing about what had happened or what would happen next.

Similarly, before Eli went to school, he knew what counted as writing in his world, just as he knew what counted as reading. He learned at home that being able to write means being able to encode, to copy, to follow format, to choose content, and to list. And, when he arrived at school, this same definition, these same abilities, were all that mattered there, too.

While the dimensions of reading and writing that count at Meadow Brook and elsewhere in Eli's life seem little different from those that count in mainstream situations—a terrifying fact, I would suggest—it is important to recognize that several mainstream-valued skills are completely absent from the Amish world as I've experienced it. Critical reading—individual analysis and interpretation—of the sort considered particularly important by most people who are mainstream-educated or mainstream educators is not valued by the Amish because of its potentially divisive, counterproductive power.

Literary appreciation, too, is both irrelevant and absent because the study of text-as-object is moot. How a writer enables a reader to empathize with his characters doesn't matter; only the ability to empathize matters. Text, whether biblical or secular, is perceived not as an object but as a force acting in the world, and it is the impact of that force that counts.

When it comes to writing, the existing Amish definition also differs in what is absent, rather than what is present. While grammar, spelling, and punctuation do count for the Old Order, they do so only to the extent that word order, words, and punctuation must allow readers to read—that is, to recognize and make sense of their reading. If a reader readily understands the intention of an adjective used as an adverb, a singular verb following a plural noun, a sentence fragment, or a compound verb containing a misplaced comma, the Amish do not see these as errors warranting attention, despite the fact that an outside reader may.

Equally irrelevant in Old Order schools is the third-person formal essay—the ominous five-paragraph theme—so prevalent in mainstream classrooms. Amish children never learn to write this kind of composition, not because they are not college-bound but because the third-person-singular point of view assumed by an individual writer is foreign to this first-person-plural society; thesis statements, topic sentences, and concepts like coherence, unity, and emphasis are similarly alien.

One final distinction separates the Amish definition of literacy from that of many mainstream definitions: the absence of originality as a desirable feature. Not only do community constraints limit the number of appropriate topics and forms an Amish writer may use, but original approaches to or applications of those topics and forms is implicitly discouraged by the similarity of models and assignments and by the absence of fiction as an appropriate personal genre. All aspects of community life reward uniformity; while writing provides an outlet for individual expression and identification, singular creativity stays within community norms.

For Eli Fisher, Jr., then, the definition of literacy he learned at home was consistent with the one he found at school, though it differed in several important ways from those of most MLA members, for example. Yet for Eli, as for Friere, "deciphering the word flowed naturally from reading the immediate world" (7). From reading his world, this six-year-old derived a complete implicit definition that told him what literacy is and whether literacy matters. I can't help but wonder, however, what would have happened had Eli gone to school and been told, explicitly or through more powerful behaviors, that he really didn't know what counted as reading and writing, that his reading and writing were not real but other unknown or alien varieties were. What would have happened had his quiet imitative behavior made him invisible in the classroom or, worse yet, made his teacher assume that he was withdrawn, problematic, or less than bright? What if his work were devalued because it was obviously copied or just unoriginal? What if he had been called on to perform individually in front of the class, to stand up and stand out? Or what if he had been asked to discuss private issues in public? Or to evaluate what he read?

Had any of these things happened, I suspect that Eli would have had to make some difficult choices that would have amounted to choosing between what he had learned and learned to value at home and what he seemed expected to learn at school. To conform to his teacher's demands and values, he would have had to devalue or disavow those of his parents—a demand that public schools seem to make frequently of children from cultural or socioeconomic groups differing from those of their teachers or their schools, a demand that seems unfair, uncalled for, and unnecessary, not to mention counterproductive and destructive.

Eli Fisher's experience suggests, therefore, that those of us who deal with children unlike ourselves need to see our classrooms and our students differently from the way we may have seen them in the past. We need to realize that students, even first-graders, have been reading the world—if not the word—for at least five, six, or seven years; they come to school not devoid of knowledge and values but with a clear sense of what their world demands and requires, including what, whether, and how to read and write, though their understandings may differ significantly from our own. We need to realize that our role may not be to prepare our students to enter mainstream society but, rather, to help them see what mainstream society offers and what it takes away, what they may gain by assimilating and what they may lose in that process. Through understanding their worlds, their definitions of literacy, and their dilemmas, not only will we better help them make important literacy-related decisions, but we will better help ourselves to do the same.

WORKS CITED

Freire, Paulo. "The Importance of the Act of Reading." *Journal of Education* Winter 1983: 5–10.

Heath, Shirley Brice. *Ways with Words: Language, Life, and Work in Communities and Classrooms*. Cambridge: Cambridge UP, 1983.

Taylor, Denny. *Family Literacy*. Portsmouth: Heinemann, 1983.

Wells, Gordon. *The Meaning Makers*. Portsmouth: Heinemann, 1986.

Time to Write: Resistance to Literacy in a Maine Fishing Community

John S. Lofty

In 1978, on an island off the Maine coast, I began teaching a group of junior high school students who enjoyed class discussion but who resisted writing. My students wrote scant amounts in moody silence, responded indifferently to encouragement, and studiously refused to write more than a single draft. Their spare, thin prose was shorn of the rich descriptions characteristic of their talk. A small very vocal group successfully disrupted writing sessions by asking, "Why do we need to learn how to write?" Their question not only challenged the way in which writing was being taught by a process approach but also echoed their skepticism toward the value of writing itself.[1]

When my students described their lives at home, a set of cultural values emerged that contrasted significantly with the values taught in school. One of the most visible features of the difference was related to conceptions of time. Teachers now recognize that learning to write is influenced by students' sociolinguistic backgrounds, specifically by their oral language, but we often overlook the influence of cultural frameworks so fundamental as learners' modes of perceiving time and space.[2] Similarly, the ways in which the quality of time in school influences how students feel, think, and act remains largely unexamined (Leichter).

When Thoreau spoke of time as "the stream I go a-fishing in" (68), he appropriately pointed to time as the stream of human activities in which we create self, for it is in the context of our daily lives that we construct and shape the contours of time to serve our primary needs.[3] Thus, for many adults in the island community in which I taught, time is working at some fishing-related activity; for the students, time is both the experience of being at home and the experience of being in school. Here I speak of time, therefore, as a measure of the location, the duration, and the rhythm of events and as a means by which members of a community create their identity. I argue that a significant part of my students' resistance to writing was embedded in the tension that they experienced between how time was constructed and valued in the home and how it was constructed and valued in the school.

In island homes, life is attuned less to the uniform periods measured by a clock than to the fluid fluctuations of tide, season, and sun. The fishermen live according to "island time," and they define their personal rhythms of work and play in harmony with those of nature. Adults' time values reflect the ways in which work is done, and people seldom stop to consider the hour of day or the day of week when planning their daily round of activities. Islanders say, "We follow the sun until the job is finished." Men seldom watch the clock when they cut wood, haul lobster pots, or dig clams, nor do women as they work in the home and the garden, rake blueberries, and make Christmas wreaths. In contrast, the school day is part of the culture of clock and calendar. School time demands observance of the bell, celebrates punctuality, and organizes learning in units of time efficiently used for maximum productivity.

The island teachers applied practices based on assumptions about learning that had less currency in this community than they would have had in communities more directly influenced by bureaucratic, corporate, and industrial powers. The problems that I describe here are grounded in fundamental conflicts between the cultural values of home and of school and do not reflect on the professional skill, caring attitudes, and dedication of the teachers. During the three years that I taught on the island, I asked my students to hand in work on time, to allow sufficient time for reflection between drafts, and to work productively for a whole fifty-minute period. While these expectations appear reasonable to those of us habituated to the time order of the school day, they conflicted with the familiar temporal rhythms of life in many of the students' homes.

When these students wrote in school, they applied their knowledge of how they had seen adults in the community temporally organize their work. Their strategy was potentially rich because it drew on local knowledge, but, in applying that strategy, the students imported practices and values that conflicted with the ways in which the teachers asked them to prewrite, revise, and meet deadlines. My former students and those currently enrolled in the school gave their views on these topics when I returned, first in 1984 and again in 1986, to study resistance to writing.

Prewriting

A phrase that island people frequently use to describe their attitude toward work is, "Do it until it's done." Whenever possible, labor is not distributed consciously into stages to reflect and to prepare for the next step. The stages of designing and making a project usually evolve together, as Jeff explained in his comments about building a barn:

> If I'd done it before, I'd probably just do it. If it's somethin that I ain't never done before, I would talk about it. If it was somethin simple that didn't take much, just do it in your head. Some people would have to draw everythin out right to start with. Other people wouldn't have to draw nothin. An island person would be more likely to just go ahead and do it.

When I asked Andrea, a former student then in her senior year, how she and her mother made a quilt together, she told me: "I did it all at once. We stayed up real late one night. My mother and I finished it. We just started it and did it all day. That's the way I am. When I get started, I never stop."

My students wrote their papers in a similar fashion. I wanted to teach them different ways to start writing—such as making lists, free writing, and provisional outlining—but these preliminary activities conflicted with their preferred one-shot approach. Andrea preferred to write intensely for short periods until her writing was completed.

> I don't wanna stop when I get started writin a paper. I couldn't do it in any other way, 'cause if I kept stoppin, I'd like lose my train of thought, and I'd have all these sentences and paragraphs flowin in my mind, and then I'd just lose them, if I just don't do it all at once.

The students' practice of writing a paper at one sitting led them to resist any kind of prewriting, following Todd's advice: "Get it off, get it over with. Do it once and get it right." The students argued that they already knew what they wanted to write and, therefore, should produce one finished copy without preliminary drafting. It was an argument grounded in their culture-based experience of completing an activity in one session, whenever possible, instead of prolonging its duration by interrupting its progress.

Revision

Resistance to revision is by no means unique to students in this community. The reasons for their particular resistance, however, become more intelligible when we view that resistance in the light of local practices, rather than regard it as typical student laziness. To make and remake writing within a short time period is a fundamental feature of revision, but the islanders seldom revise their performance while telling stories, providing directions, or giving explanations. The islanders construct the material texts of their houses, boats, and fishing gear with clear conceptions of the final product that preclude revision. The islanders say: "If it works, leave it alone. This is good enough—finest kind."

Minor changes in cultural texts occur in successive versions of artifacts, but those variations evolve over a period of years. The maker and user of familiar objects locates a creation within a far longer span of time than does the teacher, whose temporal perspective anticipates a relatively brief process of making and remaking. The islanders tend to see events within a cycle of natural recurrence, in contrast to a linear stream of unretrievable opportunities. Their perspective suggests why my students were more willing to produce an altogether new paper than to go back and revise what they saw as completed writing.

When teachers asked the students in the lower elementary school to revise their writing, the children readily complied and did not see revision as repetitious busywork. However, by grade 6, the students were more acculturated to the community's time values, and many students were reluctant to write multiple drafts. In the upper high school, the students often resisted writing more than one draft for the reasons that Jeff described:

> The way the stories are written, you have to go through all kinds of study. You just can't write the story. You have to have a draft and all that stuff. Takes quite a bit of time. If we could write them our way, it would be all right.

Writing papers "our way" meant using the approach that Ann described: "If it's due Monday, I usually do it on the Sunday before it's due. . . . I think everybody writes about the same way, just wait until the last minute." When I asked Dave if he ever began his writing well in advance of the due date, he replied negatively:

> I've done things over a long time, and I lose all the information, 'cause I keep most of it in my head. When I do my book report, I have two things to do in two days. So one night I just do all the research, 'cause I speed read. I take three or four books home, and I read them all that night, take my notes, then any page numbers I want. Then the next night I'll make the finished copy.

The students believed that to revise what was adequate for their purposes was a poor use of time and did not produce better writing or a higher grade, the final issue for students like Lynn, who planned on college:

> Last year I had a teacher that we had to hand in our bibliography cards, hand in our note cards, and we got graded on every single thing. Rough drafts and every single thing we had to hand in. So we had to do it her way. I got an 86 on that, and the papers that I always do at the last minute, I usually get a 97 or a 98.

Because many parents needed their children's support by grade 9, the school's demands for homework took time away from the essential tasks of making money to pay for clothes, for transport, and in some homes to put food on the table. The students would say, "Time in school belongs to the teachers, but time at home should be ours." One major consequence of this attitude was that the students allocated only sufficient time to write one draft at the last minute and revised only if a paper received a failing grade. Moreover, the students often misinterpreted a teacher's encouragement to revise a paper as leniency toward failure, a second chance that the sea seldom offered to those who made mistakes.

The students' approaches to writing paralleled the "fisherman's style" of making, a poesis driven by the pragmatics of necessity, the aesthetics of improvisation, and limited time. For example, a quilt maker assembles different squares of material from those on hand, and the builder of a small rowing skiff recycles wood and fastenings from materials appropriated from previous projects. The maker pieces and patches a new project together from what fits and works with little concern for the intended purpose or the formal qualities of the old pieces. In a comparable way the students fashioned their writing from the language they heard at home, on the waterfront, and from their teachers. The students appropriated these prior texts into the language game of writing in school.[4] From personal experience, observation, and memories of tales told, they wove stories with scant regard for such conventions as a formally delineated beginning, middle, and end. In school the students expressed who they were and who they wanted to become as they attempted to manage both time and writing. (For a discussion of the interplay between time and narrative, see Ricoeur.)

In this six-sentence story by Cortinee from grade 6, her four-sentence orientation suggests that the time and familial setting of her narrative interest her as much as the single run-on sentence that narrates what actually happens.

Before my sister was born, when I was two years old, Dad, Mom and I lived downtown, upstairs over the liquor store. There was a small building on a rock where the bricks are near the new peer. Where there is "like" old gray boards on the top is where a little building used to be "at one time or another." I don't know anyone that knows where it is, but I do know somebody who knows what happened to it, my mother. It was a very stormy day, my father had gone out to haul lobster traps and Mom looked out to see if she could possibly see Dad but he had already come in so of course she couldn't see him but what she did see was the little building I was talking about that was once on the rock floating down the bay. That was almost nine years ago so I don't think it's floating down the bay or farther out to sea.

In fisherman's style, Cortinee weaves her story from remembering what her mother has told her about the event, from playing in this setting, and from knowing how island people tell stories. The presence of the old gray boards and logs provide an occasion for a written narrative in which Cortinee inscribes herself within local history. She assumes authority and creates a personal identity by narrating an event from the town's past and her family's place within it.[5] Part of her identity as a writer emerges from managing time in ways consonant with the islanders' practice of interweaving their past and present personal experiences.

Her teacher's well-intended suggestions for revision instruct Cortinee that acceptable stories should move linearly from past to present, should maintain a consistent temporal viewpoint, and should be separated into several sentences. Yet the teacher's suggestions potentially edit out modes of expression and techniques of invention that characterize her world and are fundamental to how these students use writing and time to shape their identity. The shape of her original story creates legitimate concerns for her writing teacher, who knows that his students will need a broad repertoire of language competences if they are to gain access to the cultural, educational, and professional opportunities available in other linguistic communities.

As teachers attempt to provide this repertoire, however, they encounter objections from students that are, from their perspective, equally legitimate. Students often view their teachers as taking away the ownership of a piece of writing by asking that it be done in the teacher's own way. At the same time, students begin to see the talk that they have learned at home, one resource for their writing, as somehow inferior in form to the writing that they have learned in school. In an effort to provide students with a range of written dialects, teachers are often regarded as imposing a standard English. The challenge for teachers, therefore, is to promote a more inclusive literacy, a literacy that will empower students to participate in larger linguistic communities without diminishing the power of regional forms and uses of language.

Time Frames and Due Dates

In school, the students learned quickly that their teachers expected writing to be submitted on time, rather than to arrive in the students' own time. While some students believed that they would not write without the pressure of a due date, most resented the deadline. The teachers frowned on students who tried to negotiate paper deadlines. When I asked my students for late papers, they would say: "Stop buggin us. It's comin." They promised to get their work to me when they could. The writing usually did arrive, often when least expected and not always during the same ranking period. If I protested that it was too late to count for that term, the reply was: "I thought you wanted this. Here, you better read it." When I became frustrated, the students sympathetically advised me that in time I would get over the frustration of not always getting work on time.

Andrea soon became irritated when I asked her how she used her time to write a paper: "I'll start my paper when I feel like it. If I feel like Monday, I wanna take the day off from school, that's how I work, whenever I feel like it." Andrea, who did not value her writing except for the grade she received, resented investing time in what she saw as a task only for the teacher. To assert her independence in school, Andrea invested minimal time in writing at her own convenience and accepted the consequences of late work.

In the community, calendar deadlines seldom determine when work or a payment is due. For example, local bankers know that, as soon as the ice leaves the bay and boats can begin fishing, winter loans will be paid, a flexibility essential to the islanders' survival. Fishermen deliver their goods and services according to a schedule controlled by the priorities of other work and ever-changing natural constraints. In contrast, rigid deadlines enforced by social authorities are the norm of schooltime.

My students' problems with meeting the time lines that were set by convention, rather than by the time needs of particular activities, surfaced in response to the master schedule that organized secondary-level education into a school day of seven fifty-minute periods. Sherrie, a seventh-grade student who enjoyed writing, described her experience of moving between classes:

Here, when it's English, do your English, math, do your math, science, do your science, social studies, do your social studies. Then just cut right off in the middle of it, finished or not. And then you do it again, and you cover it up, and then you go home, and then you do the other half of everything. . . . If you're sitting down in English and the bell rings, there's no choice, you have got to leave. But if you're sittin down at your house, and you are in the middle of your English, and supper is done, you could just say, "Well, could you please wait?" But you can't up here. It's just bang, the bell rings and you've gotta go, that minute, and you're all done.

The change was disorienting also for senior students like Greg, who related the confined time frames of learning to his difficulties in achieving a high quality of education in school:

Cramming all those classes into one little short day is too much. In the elementary school, I don't think they had that many classes in one day. I might have had three subjects, and we worked on those for a couple of hours, and I think that was more comfortable. You'd have a lot longer time to work on a specific thing, and you could get it really embedded in your head.

My interpretation of resistance to writing in school from the context of the community's time values may suggest that the patterned behaviors characteristic of this community caused the students to act in similar ways when in school. Procedures and values learned in the home could be observed in the students' behavior in school, but the influence was one of association, rather than one of direct causality. The students watched how the adults at home organized their activities, and they expected to find some continuity of that approach in schoolwork. Instead, the students discovered other ways of learning that often perplexed and frustrated them, partly because the new approaches made familiar ways of proceeding invisible. This discovery has much educational value if students and teachers discuss the differences between home learning and school learning and the logic for each.

To interpret differences in the temporal logics of home and school as markers of cultural values does not implicitly endorse resistance to writing. Students like Andrea and Jeff need a different kind of literacy than that of their parents and grandparents. Over the past decade, the fishing has failed more dramatically than in previous cycles of recession, and the island people are selling their property to highly literate professional people. If the local students are to manage their island and govern the schools, if they are to effect change and do more than survive a future different from the past, they need to achieve a full literacy.

Students vary in their political awareness of how literacy will affect their future lives and the development of their island. In 1988 many students continued to claim that talk would serve most of their communicative needs on the island. However, since 1978, when I first taught on the island, an increasing number of students and parents have come to believe that the students will need to graduate to attain the minimal level of literacy that their work will require. Many young people now choose to pursue nontraditional careers away from home, so a college education is becoming more essential. One graduating high school senior wrote:

> I can only see people returning to the island after they're retired. Otherwise their jobs will keep them away. If they couldn't handle the business world, then they might return rather quickly. The loss of local people is a problem, because it's a loss of culture. . . . I think students drop out before graduating because they don't realize the importance of school and an education, but I think that will decrease in the future, because it is becoming obvious that one needs at least a high school diploma to succeed.

I have argued that the island students are caught in a tension between values located at different positions on the spectrum of time: values conventionally ordered to serve an institution and values derived from the natural world. Although many of us do not teach in communities where time values are predicated on the activity patterns of rural life, this example strongly suggests the possibility that other communities may also experience time in ways that are unfamiliar to us. Consequently, I think our task is to examine the time values evident in our own communities and classrooms and then to assess how these values influence the teaching of writing and, more broadly, the promotion of literacy. This project has already been initiated in several critiques of the sociotemporal values that the educational system has inherited and transmitted to our English classes. In *Hidden Rhythms: Schedules and Calendars in Social Life* Eviatar Zerubavel shows that the principles apparent in the monastic table of hours continue to influence the time values of the school day (31–69). The bells of Saint Benedict coordinated the medieval activities of work, study, and prayer to ensure that all time was devoted to the service of God. In the context of penitentiary life, Michel Foucault in *Discipline and Punish: The Birth of the Prison* compares the philosophy of temporal control manifest in our contemporary schedule to the method for panoptically controlling inmates' movements in the nineteenth century (195–228). Can we expect the constructs of time derived from settings that feature uniform codes of behavior to serve adequately our mission of teaching pluralistic literacies in the late twentieth century?

In *Time Wars: The Primary Conflict in Human History*, Jeremy Rifkin argues that the ideologies of the business community reinforce the ethic of "time is money" (59). This identification reduces time to quantified units of production, a value that our educational system has substantially incorporated into its own practices.[6] Consequently, schools seldom recognize the problems that confront the English teacher who needs to provide time of a quality that helps students to hear the muse in their own writing and to listen for it in the writing of others.

As we continue to define the kinds of literacy that our society needs, an increasing number of teachers report the success of classes conceived as communities of writers and readers.[7] Students and teacher write together, interpret textual meanings collaboratively, and develop empathic relations, rather than autocratic relations. Teacher and students participate democratically in decisions not only about the forms and the topics of writing but also about each writer's time needs. When writers develop such communities within a context of time values that model hierarchical and economic power relations, their practice must run counter to many of the principles on which writing communities are based. If students are to own the writing by which they define who they are and who they want to become, both students and teachers need to negotiate the politics of time entailed in this process.

How do we conceptualize time in ways that are congruent with our philosophies of teaching students to become literate? Which ways of thinking about time enhance our students' experiences with language? What are we doing already that helps students attune their rhythms of writing to the temporal logics of composition? How can we establish connections between students' experiences of time at home and the attitudes toward time in the literacy class? Because we experience time within a wide spectrum of modes from diurnal rhythms to the nanoseconds of computer education—where, according to Rifkin, "time is information" (182)—our answers will be specific to and evolve within the varied contexts in which we teach. Our students can help us here by reflecting on the qualities of time that enable them to discover and to shape their identities in writing.

We value our schedules, time frames, and due dates because they allow us to coordinate our various activities so that we can predict with a fair degree of certainty the location, the duration, and the rhythm of the key events in our lives. In schools the management of time is one major strategy used to organize the contours of learning. However, as teachers, we often believe that we cannot change the institutionally determined structures of time that control our classrooms. If we cannot easily reconstruct the time values of our institutions, we can at least negotiate time with our students. To negotiate time is to observe how the particular time values of one group can be related to those of another. Both teachers and students can then plan work together with mutual respect for the time perspectives shaped by the institutional and cultural identities of each.

Teachers in grade school and in college have often argued that their students cannot yet handle the responsibilities of managing their own time. If this is true, we need to involve students more directly in making decisions about the temporal aspects of their education generally and about the area of composition specifically. Before we can involve students in such decisions, we need to know more about the temporal perspectives from which our students' rhythms of writing are derived. My students on the island taught me the importance of respecting their need to write without interruption, to work at their own pace, and to have time to be silent. Our students will assume greater responsibility for their writing and see more reasons to own it as we involve them in shaping their own timescapes of writing.[8]

NOTES

[1]Process approaches to teaching writing vary, but the method that has most influenced this school district since 1981, particularly in the elementary schools, owes much to a series of in-service workshops broadly following the pedagogy of Donald Graves. See, in particular, Graves.

[2]In the words of Shirley Brice Heath from the epilogue to *Ways with Words*, "Patterns of language use in any community are in accord with and mutually reinforce other cultural patterns, such as time and space ordering, [and] problem solving techniques . . ." (344).

[3]Central here is the idea that we perceive time as reified and seldom recognize the extent to which it is a social product grounded in part on biophysical rhythms and in part on social convention. See Zerubavel 42–43; Berger and Luckman 26.

[4]Many thanks to Alton L. Becker at the University of Michigan for his insights into how writers take the prior texts of their old language and make them new. Ludwig Wittgenstein describes this phenomenon as a language game. See Wittgenstein 7.5e.

[5]For those interested in pursuing further the relation between time and identity, see Martin Heidegger, the philosopher who established the major dimensions for how we think about this subject.

[6]For a discussion of the historical development of the influence of the business community on education, see Spring.

[7]See Atwell's discussion of the elements of a writing community at the junior high school level.

[8]My deepest thanks go to the students, teachers, and adults in the Maine fishing community where I taught and where I subsequently studied resistance to literacy. Their interest in my work and their patience in answering my questions deserve special recognition. For her editorial suggestions and for insights into the relations between narrative time and personal identity, many thanks go to Ellen Westbrook at the University of Southern Mississippi, Hattiesburg. To Helene Moglen at the University of California, Santa Cruz, my appreciation for her editorial assistance.

WORKS CITED

Atwell, Nancy. *In the Middle: Writing, Reading and Learning with Adolescents.* Upper Montclair: Boynton, 1987.

Berger, Peter L., and Thomas Luckman. *The Social Construction of Reality: A Treatise in the Sociology of Knowledge.* Garden City: Anchor, 1967.

Foucault, Michel. *Discipline and Punish: The Birth of the Prison.* Trans. Alan Sheridan. New York: Vintage, 1979.

Graves, Donald. *Writing: Teachers and Children at Work.* Portsmouth: Heinemann, 1983.

Heath, Shirley Brice. *Ways with Words: Language, Life, and Work in Communities and Classrooms.* Cambridge: Cambridge UP, 1983.

Heidegger, Martin. *Being and Time.* Trans. John Macquarrie and Edward Robinson. London: SCM, 1962.

Leichter, Hope Jensen. "A Note on Time and Education." *Teachers College Record* 81 (1980): 360–63.

Ricoeur, Paul. "Narrative Time." *Critical Enquiry* 7 (1980): 169–90.

Rifkin, Jeremy. *Time Wars: The Primary Conflict in Human History.* New York: Holt, 1987.

Spring, Joel H. *Education and the Rise of the Corporate State.* Boston: Beacon, 1972.

Thoreau, Henry David. *Walden.* Ed. Sherman Paul. Boston: Houghton, 1960.

Wittgenstein, Ludwig. *Philosophical Investigations.* Trans. G. E. M. Anscombe. Oxford: Blackwell, 1953.

Zerubavel, Eviatar. *Hidden Rhythms: Schedules and Calendars in Social Life.* Berkeley: U of California P, 1981.

Collaboration, Collaborative Communities, and Black Folk Culture

Keith D. Miller and Elizabeth A. Vander Lei

In recent years Kenneth Bruffee, Karen Burke LeFevre, Anne Gere, Peter Elbow, and other leading composition theorists have promoted the theory, history, and methods of collaborative learning and collaborative writing. Through their efforts, peer editing and other forms of collaboration have become important components of composition theory and instruction at all levels. In addition, John Trimbur and James Zebroski have schooled us to accept a more radically social, Vygotskyan conception of language development in place of Piaget's more solitary model. While these developments are all salutary, this view of collaboration is flawed because Bruffee (and the thinkers he cites), LeFevre, Gere, Elbow, and others have erected models of collaboration that virtually ignore minority cultures and much minority writing.[1]

For black America this omission is especially perilous because to ignore black folk culture is to bypass its effective, time-honored procedures for oral exchanges among collaborators. African-American folk culture offers an interactive system of oral collaboration that has ably served such rhetors as Martin Luther King, Jr., and Jesse Jackson and that can serve our composition students as well.

After offering a brief background on collaboration in black folk culture, we examine three of its major strategies of oral communication: communal collaboration, call-and-response collaboration, and historical collaboration. Each strategy originated and matured in black oral culture and operated in the integrated community of the civil rights movement; each can become a valuable component of composition classrooms.

Collaboration in Black Folk Culture

Black culture has always been highly interactive in both sacred and secular contexts. Rhetorical interplay characterized the work songs of slavery, animates the dynamics of folk preaching, and endures in street games such as playing the dozens. These exchanges enact what Geneva Smitherman calls "the traditional African world view," which asserts a "fundamental unity" of the spiritual and the material. Smitherman writes:

> Harmony in nature and the universe is provided by the complementary, inter-
> dependent, synergistic interaction . . . communities of people are modeled after
> the interdependent rhythms of the universe. . . . Balance in the community, as
> in the universe, consists of maintaining these interdependent relationships.   (75)

In some forms of black oral interaction, the author collaborates not merely
with another writer but with the audience of the discourse; as a result, the role
of author blurs with the role of audience. Both author and audience create the
work and are responsible for its success, for, in Leonard Doob's words, "there
is no sharp line between performers or communications and the audience, for
virtually everyone is performing and everyone is listening" (qtd. in Smitherman
108). This author-audience interchange occurs in at least three particular forms.
In communal collaboration the roles of author and audience are completely
indistinct. In call-and-response collaboration the roles of author and audience
remain distinct, and participation in each of these roles is limited to those
present. In historical collaboration the roles of author and audience remain
distinct, but participation in the roles is extended to those who preceded and
those who will follow the current author and audience. Each of these forms of
author-audience collaboration can apply to composition classrooms.

Communal Collaboration

In communal collaboration, the author and the audience meld into one. The
distinction between author and audience disappears because the attention of
the community focuses on the content of the discourse, not the persons creating
and listening to it.

During Slavery

With the entire community acting as both audience and author, black communal
collaboration began on American shores with the composition of spirituals. As
both slaves and white observers have explained, many spirituals were initially
composed through a collaborative process of spontaneous, synergistic exchanges.
Natalie Burlin elucidates this process:

> Minutes passed, long minutes of strange intensity. The mutterings . . . grew louder,
> more dramatic, till suddenly I felt the creative thrill dart through the people like
> an electric vibration . . . and then . . . came a "moan," sobbed in musical cadence.
> From somewhere in that bowed gathering another voice improvised a response
> . . . then other voices joined in the answer, shaping it into a musical phrase; and
> so . . . from this molten metal of music a new song was smithied out, composed
> then and there by no one in particular and by everyone in general.   (qtd. in
> Levine 159)

Clifton Furness portrays a group of slaves in another state engaged in a similar experience:

> Gradually moaning became audible in the shadowy corners where the women sat. . . . A rhythm was born, almost without reference to the words that were being spoken by the preacher. It seemed to take shape almost visibly and grow. I was gripped with the feeling of a mass-intelligence, a self-conscious entity gradually informing the crowd and taking possession of every mind there, including my own.
>
> . . . .
>
> A black man began to exclaim: "Git right—sodger! Git right—sodger! Git right—wit Gawd!"
>
> . . . .
>
> Instantly the crowd took it up, moulding a melody out of half-formed familiar phrases. . . . A distinct melodic outline became more and more prominent. . . . Scraps of other words and tunes were flung into the medley of sound by individual singers from time to time, but the general trend was carried on by a deep undercurrent, which . . . bore the mass of improvised harmony and rhythms into the most effective climax of incremental repetition that I have ever heard. I felt as if some conscious plan or purpose were carrying us along, call it mob-mind, communal composition, or what you will.   (qtd. in Levine 159–60)

Clearly, spirituals are, in Lawrence Levine's words, "product[s] of an improvisational communal consciousness" (160). Because spirituals developed communally, their language was shared by everyone and owned by no one; all distinctions between author and audience blurred during the original moment of composition.

During the Civil Rights Era

More recently, communal collaboration generated the civil rights songs that, in King's words, formed "the soul of the movement" (*Why* 61). Analyzing civil rights lyrics, Pete Seeger describes their typical composition:

> What it is—one person gets an idea for a song—usually borrowing an old tune —changing around the words, and then if it's a good idea, it'll be picked up by others and new verses added to it . . . until after a while you naturally can't say who composed the song.   (*WNEW's Story*)[2]

Interacting as equals, singers merge the roles of author and audience while shaping both tunes and lyrics.

Len Chandler explains the revision of "Which Side Are You On?" His original lyrics were:

> Come all you bourgeois black men
> With all your excess fat

> A few days in the county jail
> Will sure get rid of that.   (*WNEW's Story*)

On a march he heard a teenager sing:

> Come on all you people
> Worried about fat.
> A day of Route 80
> Will take care of that.   (*WNEW's Story*)

Chandler notes, "And I asked the kid that I heard do that . . . one of the kids on the march, where'd he get that verse . . . and he said, 'I don't know—I heard it somewhere and I don't know where it came from' " (*WNEW's Story*). In this collaborative effort, the community as a whole, rather than one identified person, altered the lyrics to fit a current circumstance. Providing a description of civil rights marchers performing communal collaboration, Seeger recalls,

> A picture I'll always keep in my mind . . . was after a day of marching . . . there was a gang of 50 young ones . . . waiting for supper. And singing at the top of their lungs. . . . and just making up verse after verse. If the spirit was real good, why a song could go on for five or ten minutes. Just as long as somebody could think of some verses for it."   (*WNEW's Story*)

These young activists acted as a community, creating verse after verse for each other. In this type of collaboration, no one can claim ownership or authorship because the community functions as both composer and audience.

Call-and-Response Collaboration

In call-and-response collaboration the roles of leader and audience remain distinct. However, the audience collaborates with the leader through discrete oral exchanges, causing the leader to adjust the arrangement, the delivery, and even the content of the discourse. Through this intensive communication the audience participates as coauthor.

In Sermons and Songs

This species of collaboration occurs throughout African-American folk culture, most notably in folk sermons. In *The Art of the American Folk Preacher*, Bruce Rosenberg comments that audience participation affects both the length and the quality of the sermon (104). As churchgoers offer verbal encouragement, preachers orchestrate their cadences to allow for congregational participation and then shift the homiletic content to reflect the churchgoers' responses to the developing sermons. Rosenberg describes two of Reverend Rubin Lacy's performances of the sermon "The Twenty-third Psalm"; in the first Lacy included an unusual illustration that he omitted from the second performance. Rosenberg attributes this change to the differing responses of Lacy's audiences (146).

The songs enlivening these worship services also exhibit call-and-response collaboration; as worship leaders initiate or "line out" the verses of a hymn, the congregation responds by repeating the verses or by creating its own lyrics (Rosenberg 16). Analyzing call-and-response collaboration, Smitherman classifies audience reaction into five categories: cosigning or agreeing with the speaker, encouraging the speaker, repeating the speaker's words, completing the speaker's statement, and acting "on T," powerfully acknowledging the truth of the speaker's words (107). Using several of these strategies while maintaining the role as audience, a congregation can effectively coauthor a sermon with its preacher and coauthor religious lyrics with its song leader.

In Civil Rights Lyrics and Oratory

Call-and-response collaboration shaped civil rights music. For certain songs the leader would call out a short verse and the audience would reply with a refrain. The volume and the enthusiasm of the refrain indicated to the leader the popular and unpopular topics for verses. An unnamed civil rights chant displays this call-and-response format:

LEADER: Pick 'em up and lay 'em down.
GROUP: Right. Right.
LEADER: Pick 'em up and lay 'em down.
GROUP: Right. Right.
LEADER: Pick 'em up and lay 'em down.
GROUP: Right. Right.
LEADER: All the way to Selma town.
GROUP: Right. Right.
LEADER: Oh, the mud sure was deep.
GROUP: Right. Right.
LEADER: Oh, the hills sure was steep.
GROUP: Right. Right.   (*WNEW's Story*)

At times an audience directly aided the song leader in composing verses. Chandler accounts for the formation of one verse of this modified military drill cadence:

There was a guy named Jim Letherer who had one leg. He said, "Make up a verse about me." And so I said:

LEADER: Jim Letherer's leg got left.
GROUP: Right. Right.
LEADER: But he's still in the fight.
GROUP: Right. Right.

LEADER: He's been walkin' day and night.
GROUP: Right. Right.
LEADER: Jim's left leg is all right.
GROUP: Right. Right.   (*WNEW's Story*)

As the Jim Letherer example illustrates, in call-and-response collaboration, direct intervention, as well as audience interest, can provide fuel for the engine of invention.

Call-and-response interplay also contributed to the oratory of King and other civil rights leaders. Especially when addressing primarily black audiences, King collaborated with his listeners through the call-and-response dynamic of the folk pulpit, arranging his rhythms to encourage audience responses and answering those responses. For example, in "I Have a Dream" he extemporaneously concluded with the famous "Let freedom ring" peroration. In an interview after the speech, King explained his spontaneity, "I started out reading the speech . . . just all of a sudden—the audience response was wonderful that day—and all of a sudden this thing came to me that I have used . . . and I wanted to use it here" (Garrow 283). King emphasized that the enthusiasm of his hearers influenced the content of his discourse and propelled him to add a rapturous and fitting conclusion to one of the best speeches of the century.

Historical Collaboration

Historical collaboration enables the contemporary author and audience to respond not only to each other but also to previous speakers and audiences from the same or different regions. As African-American folk culture carries discourse through time, orators and audiences refine the work of their predecessors by adapting it to contemporary experience. Both communal collaboration and call-and-response collaboration work within the framework of historical collaboration, much as the weft of a fabric operates within the threads of the warp.

In Sermons

Worshipers' responses to folk sermons influence the survival of illustrations, anaphoric series, and entire sermons. Several sermons still heard in churches and on the radio were delivered as early as the 1860s. For example, at least two sermons—"Dry Bones in the Valley" and "The Eagle Stirs Her Nest"—have been preached during slavery and proclaimed from black pulpits ever since. These widespread and highly durable sermons have been recorded and published numerous times by numerous preachers.[3] Ministers repreach these and other sermons and portions of sermons, eliciting the verbal approval of their congregations while deleting material that fails to spark any interest. Thus, as churchgoers engage in call and response, they not only shape the immediate content of a sermon but also determine its longevity.

In Civil Rights Lyrics and Oratory

"We Shall Overcome," the quintessential civil rights anthem, evolved through collaboration that lasted several decades. Begun before the turn of the century as a hymn called "I'll Be All Right," the song shifted to "I Will Overcome" when the Food, Tobacco, and Agricultural Workers Union of Charleston, South Carolina, adopted it as their anthem in the 1940s (Reagon 70–73). During a strike in 1945–46, workers emphasized union solidarity by changing "I Will Overcome" to "We Will Overcome" (Reagon 73–75).

Another metamorphosis occurred when members of the Charleston union sang "We Will Overcome" at the Highlander Folk Center in Tennessee. Highlander's Zilphia Horton reworked the hymn-turned-labor-song and included it in Highlander's music program (Reagon 76–77). Pete Seeger learned it from Horton, changed "We Will" to "We Shall," and composed the verses "The whole wide world around" and "We'll walk hand in hand" (Reagon 77–78). In 1959 police raided Highlander, took names, turned off the lights where people had congregated, and rummaged through the building. Sitting in the dark, Mary Ethel Dozier, a high school student, contributed a new verse, "We are not afraid," which, like Seeger's lyrics, became a lasting contribution to "We Shall Overcome."[4] Historical collaboration enabled singers of this tune to wed the authority of a religious tradition and a labor struggle to their own crusade for civil rights.

Displaying a highly fluid and intertextual sense of discourse, King also engaged in historical collaboration. He frequently repeated sermons and speeches, weaving old and new material together for "I Have a Dream" and practically all his other addresses. Like other masters of the black folk pulpit, he repeated passages that were well received by listeners (such as the "Let freedom ring" peroration, which he first used seven years before "I Have a Dream") and dropped those that met with silence.[5] He carried this technique into his writing as well; discourse lauded by his listeners spilled over into "Letter from Birmingham Jail" and virtually all his other essays, columns, and books.

Like King, Jesse Jackson uses historical collaboration, a practice that has confounded white critics unfamiliar with the historical collaboration of black folk culture. While campaigning for the presidency in 1988, Jackson and his audiences honed various themes that later emerged in his address to the Democratic convention in Atlanta, Georgia. Remarking on Jackson's method of composition, columnist William Safire derided Jackson's convention oration as a collection of "Jesse's Greatest Hits," including "I Understand" and "Your Patch Isn't Big Enough"—a criticism that could just as easily be applied to "I Have a Dream," "Letter from Birmingham Jail," and almost any of King's other addresses and treatises. What Safire cannot explain is why the method of composition he ridicules generates rhetoric far more memorable than that produced by the traditional methods of composition used by many other national politicians.

Implications for Teaching Composition

What are the implications of black oral culture for our teaching? Fundamentally, we must acknowledge that black folk communication can teach us something new about collaborative learning and collaborative writing. Once we accept the idea that African-American orality offers resources for literacy, we can develop a new heuristic that offers more effective classroom strategies. In this effort we must rely on students and faculty who have participated in the black folk community.

To use this new collaborative heuristic, we must heighten our sense of language as fluid, interactive, and intertextual. The collaborative system of black folk culture insists on more than one method of collaboration and insists on an analysis of the rhetorical situation to determine the appropriate method. Furthermore, the three collaborative strategies often work together within the same discourse. Many of the applications of this system require further study, but we offer some recommendations.

First, we can recognize the parallels between communal collaboration and group brainstorming. As in communal collaboration, group brainstorming can involve numerous participants composing on a roughly equal basis. Likewise, we can understand the parallels between call-and-response collaboration and peer editing; like call-and-response collaboration peer editing involves audience participation in a process largely directed by one person, either the call-and-response leader or the writer.

Second, we can broaden the range of our collaboration. Too often, we constrain collaborative invention to group brainstorming and collaborative revision to small-group peer editing. By screening a paper on an overhead projector, a teacher can promote collaborative revision through group analysis of the paper; call-and-response collaboration can work as a variation of group brainstorming.

Third, throughout the composition process we can heighten the intensity of our collaboration by using more than one collaborative strategy at a given stage of the composing process. A call-and-response-invention assignment after a communal-invention session both heightens and refines the student's inventive abilities.

Finally, we can use historical collaboration to assist students in locating themselves within an ongoing debate. Our students can use historical collaboration as they assimilate, subordinate, and identify other voices while adding their own words to a stream of language about a particular topic. Too often, we identify historical collaboration with plagiarism and, therefore, expel a productive collaborative strategy along with its negative counterpart. Without practicing plagiarism, our students can use historical collaboration to draw the power of past discourse into their prose.

In the face of Western culture's ideological enshrinement of the isolated author, black folk culture has preserved and refined its collaborative strategies through spirituals and sermons and has offered these strategies to American society through the songs and speeches of the civil rights movement. These procedures from a minority voice need to become the procedures of the majority voice as well. If we reject the ideology of solitary authorship, perhaps our students can learn to write speeches as powerful as "I Have a Dream" and can create rhetorical music as joyful as a spiritual while they smithy new songs from a molten metal of interactive discourse.

NOTES

[1]Gere, however, is currently studying collaboration among certain black female writers. The omission of black oral culture from models of collaboration may reflect a general conception of orality. Trained by Walter Ong, the early Jack Goody (especially his essay coauthored with Ian Watt), and others, composition theorists often conceive of orality as a sensibility that sharply contrasts with literacy. Even Mina Shaughnessy tended to look at oral culture as the source of obstacles to literacy. Despite the efforts of Sylvia Scribner and Michael Cole, Amy Shuman, and Shirley Brice Heath, many still see orality and literacy as disparate sensibilities (see, e.g., Farrell; Gilbert). While we do not deny that oral cultures present some obstacles to literacy, we claim that professionals make a serious mistake in studying oral cultures primarily to learn the obstacles they pose to literacy. Those who maintain that black orality inherently presents significant opposition to literacy cannot explain how Ned Cobb, an entirely illiterate Alabama farmer, could dictate an autobiography as eloquent and as valuable as any ever written in this country (see Rosengarten).

[2]This quotation and all other WNEW's Story of Selma quotations are used with the permission of Folkways Records and Rounder Records.

[3]For the origins of these sermons during slavery, see Lyell 135–36 and Levine 158. For "Dry Bones in the Valley," see Rosenberg 28; Cleveland, "Dry Bones in the Valley"; Franklin, "Dry Bones in the Valley"; and "Dry Bones." For "The Eagle Stirs Her Nest," see Rosenberg 28; Franklin, "The Eagle Stirs Her Nest"; and Cleveland, "The Eagle Stirring Her Nest." Versions of these sermons appear in Davis 136–42 and Rosenberg 155–62, 200–08.

[4]See Reagon 81–82 and MIA Newsletter. Produced by King's Montgomery Improvement Association, the Newsletter carried a firsthand, anonymous description of the events at Highlander when Dozier composed the verse "We are not afraid."

[5]Compare the "Let freedom ring" perorations at the conclusions of King's 1956 annual address and his 1963 "I Have a Dream" speech.

WORKS CITED

Bruffee, Kenneth. "Collaborative Learning and the 'Conversation of Mankind.' " College English 46 (1984): 635–52.

Cleveland, E.O.S. "Dry Bones in the Valley." The Eagle Stirring Her Nest. N.p.: n. p., 1946. 31–37. [Schomburg Center.]

———. "The Eagle Stirring Her Nest." *The Eagle Stirring Her Nest.* N.p.: n. p., 1946. 63–71. [Schomburg Center.]

Davis, Gerald. *I Got the Word in Me and I Can Sing It, You Know: A Study of the Performed Afro-American Sermon.* Philadelphia: U of Pennsylvania P, 1985.

"Dry Bones." Archive of Folk Culture, Library of Congress, tape 6685 B, 6686 B, 6687 A–D, 6688 A, B, 1942.

Elbow, Peter. *Writing with Power.* New York: Oxford UP, 1981.

Farrell, Thomas. "A Defense for Requiring Standard English." *Pre/Text* 7 (1986): 165–80.

Franklin, C. L. "Dry Bones in the Valley." Chess, LP 36, n.d.

———. "The Eagle Stirs Her Nest." Jewel, LPS 0083, 1973.

Garrow, David. *Bearing the Cross: Martin Luther King, Jr., and the Southern Christian Leadership Conference.* New York: Morrow, 1986.

Gere, Anne. *Writing Groups: History, Theory, and Implications.* Carbondale: Southern Illinois UP, 1987.

Gilbert, Janet. "Patterns and Possibilities for Basic Writers." *Journal of Basic Writing* 6 (1987): 37–52.

Goody, Jack, and Ian Watt. "The Consequences of Literacy." *Perspectives on Literacy.* Ed. Eugene Kintgen, Barry Kroll, and Mike Rose. Carbondale: Southern Illinois UP, 1988. 3–28.

Heath, Shirley Brice. *Ways with Words: Language, Life, and Work in Communities and Classrooms.* New York: Cambridge UP, 1983.

Jackson, Jesse. "Let's Find Common Ground." *New York Times* 21 July 1988: 12.

King, Martin Luther, Jr. Annual Address. Institute on Nonviolence and Social Change. Montgomery, 3 Dec. 1956.

———. "I Have a Dream." *A Testament of Hope.* Ed. James Washington. New York: Harper, 1986. 217–20.

———. "Letter from Birmingham Jail." *Why We Can't Wait.* By King. New York: Signet, 1964. 59–75.

LeFevre, Karen Burke. *Invention as a Social Act.* Carbondale: Southern Illinois UP, 1987.

Levine, Lawrence. "Slave Songs and Slave Consciousness." *American Negro Slavery.* Ed. Allen Weinstein and Frank Gatell. New York: Oxford UP, 1973. 153–82.

Lyell, Charles. "A Negro Church in Savannah." *The Negro American: A Documented History.* Ed. Leslie Fishel and Benjamin Quarles. Glenview: Scott, 1967. 135–36.

MIA Newsletter 7 Oct. 1959: 2. Box 106, 14, 5. King Collection, Boston University.

Ong, Walter. *Orality and Literacy: The Technologizing of the Word.* New York: Methuen, 1982.

Reagon, Bernice Johnson. "Songs of the Civil Rights Movement 1955–1965: A Study in Culture History." Diss. Howard U, 1975.

Rosenberg, Bruce. *The Art of the American Folk Preacher.* New York: Oxford UP, 1970.

Rosengarten, Theodore. *All God's Dangers: The Life of Nate Shaw.* New York: Avon, 1975.

Safire, William. " 'My Fellow Democrats.' " *New York Times* 21 July, 1988: 25.

Scribner, Sylvia, and Michael Cole. *The Psychology of Literacy.* Cambridge: Harvard UP, 1981.

Shaughnessy, Mina. *Errors and Expectations.* New York: Oxford UP, 1977.

Shuman, Amy. *Storytelling Rights.* Cambridge: Cambridge UP, 1986.

Smitherman, Geneva. *Talkin and Testifyin.* Detroit: Boston: Houghton, 1977.

Trimbur, John. "Beyond Cognition: The Voices in Inner Speech." *Rhetoric Review* 5 (1987): 211–21.

WNEW's Story of Selma. Folkways Records-Rounder Records, LP 5595, 1965.

Zebroski, James. "Soviet Psycholinguistics: Implications for the Teaching of Writing." *Linguistics and Literacy.* Ed. William Frawley. New York: Plenum, 1982. 51–63.

Rural Poverty and Literacy in the Mississippi Delta: Dilemmas, Paradoxes, and Conundrums

Anthony Petrosky

Mississippi is poor. In the Delta, one of the poorest places in the nation, the average income for a family of four is $7,500, and the largest source of money is the transfer of welfare payments. Teachers have a difficult time getting in touch with parents, because most of the families don't have telephones. The population is largely black, and so are the public schools. There were 264 kids, for instance, in the Ruleville Junior High School in Sunflower County, and only eighteen of those were white. Racism is still evident. The academies, for instance, still exist, and they are still all white. A number of people told me that employers pressure their white employees to send their children to these academies, even if they can't afford it or would like to send their children to the public schools, which are generally, from what I could learn, better staffed and better equipped than the private academies. And students in all the schools face the same problem: there's little work for anyone in the Delta, including high school and college graduates, so, to survive or raise families, most youngsters will have to leave.

As part of my work studying literacy and schooling in the Delta in 1988, I observed classes, talked with residents, and interviewed students, teachers, administrators, and state education officials.[1] Mississippi had recently undergone enormous mandated changes in education since it passed the School Reform Act in 1982 during Governor William Forrest Winter's term (1980–84). I was curious about its effects on literacy in a poor rural area like the Delta and skeptical, too, because I had experience with the largely negative effects of large-scale mandated change. So I asked to study two Delta districts, the Sunflower County schools and the Mound Bayou schools. They caught my attention because their students had performed well above state averages on their recent functional literacy examination, which is given in the eleventh grade before students can go on to the twelfth grade. Eighty percent of the Mound Bayou students had passed the examination in 1987 and 74% in the Sunflower schools had passed. This rate of success is impressive if you consider that about 50% of the black students in the state had failed the exam, and only about 70% of all students statewide had passed it.

These are also interesting school districts because of their histories. Mound Bayou was founded by a slave of Joseph Davis (brother of Jefferson Davis) after the Civil War and was incorporated before the turn of the century. It has always been a town of blacks, and it prides itself on its long tradition of offering quality education. Graduation there is the biggest day of the year, the day when families and relatives from all over the United States gather to celebrate their nieces and nephews, grandchildren and children. More than 80% of the parents have at least high school diplomas (only 45% of all the parents in the Delta are that educated), and around 62% of Mound Bayou's high school graduates go on to postsecondary education, and another 25% go into the military. Of its twelve hundred students, more than three hundred participate in a federal program of one kind or another, including the gifted and talented program, and 97% receive free lunches (the local phrase for federal welfare). All the teachers in Mound Bayou are black.

Sunflower County schools enroll twice as many students as does Mound Bayou; 75% of the teachers in Sunflower County are black, and, like Mound Bayou teachers, they pride themselves on the success of their students. About 50% of the high school graduates go on to postsecondary education, and, like Mound Bayou, more than 90% of the students get free lunches. The level of parental education in Sunflower County is considerably lower (30% to 40% have a high school diploma) than in Mound Bayou.

There's not much work for people, especially poor people, in either district, and, since the plantations turned to mechanization, sharecropping and farming jobs have disappeared. Although catfish farming has been steadily increasing and factories in the large towns like Cleveland employ some young people, there aren't many jobs for high school graduates. As a result, students know that they have to leave the Delta if they want to work and raise families. Such flight inevitably means a loss of community and close ties, especially for the Mound Bayou students who have been raised in the atmosphere of a close community. To survive, students must go on to postsecondary education or the military, and that means they have to leave the close-knit community that they are intimately a part of. To leave, they have to do well on tests, like the American College Test, which are used for admissions to Mississippi colleges and universities. A large part of the students in these two districts do well, and so their schools have been successful, which is quite an achievement for schools and teachers anywhere but especially so for these poor places, where even books and basic supplies are scarce. But this success-means-leaving bind presented problems for most of the kids I spoke with. Furthermore, so much of the curriculum had been directed to getting students up to snuff for the tests that almost all the instruction and the class talk were pragmatically geared to the testing, which had a strong effect on what went on in the classes, especially in the ways that the classroom language and methods may be said to mirror top-down administrative language. As we will see later, a very interesting use of authority, one that poses questions about its origins, dominated the recitation and drill that is the way classes are conducted in these schools, and there is a sense, I think, in which what happened in the classrooms can be said to mirror (on a smaller scale of course) the state's communication and policy procedures.

Classroom Talk

Let me now turn to a recitation from a junior high school English class in Sunflower County. Mrs. L., a veteran teacher, had taken her class to the library the week before this lesson. To get the effect of this exercise, imagine a cinder-block classroom with twenty-seven black students sitting in rows facing the front of the class. Handwriting charts form the border along the top of the blackboard, and above those are other charts that define such things as infinitives, active and passive verbs, and figures of speech. Mrs. L. is black, about 5′ 10″, and her loud, brassy voice rises and falls like a drill sergeant's when she asks questions and calls on students.

The class began with a question, "What's in the library?" After a pause the students answered in unison, "Books." She then asked, "How many sections are in the library?" The class responded with "Four." Then she shifted to what she referred to as "spatial representative learning" by telling everyone to take out a sheet of paper and draw a four-section diagram of the library. The kids had to pencil in such things as the magazine racks and the dictionaries. She put a master diagram on the board and asked them to tell her what to put where. Although the kids were clearly bored and unengaged, at times rolling their eyes when they caught my attention, they all raised their hands and answered her questions with a politeness and a deference that was at once admirable and frightening. The following dialogue took place about thirty minutes into the class. Mrs. L. was walking down the aisles and asking questions.

TEACHER: What kinds of books are on the back wall?
STUDENT: Periodicals.
TEACHER: No. Cox, what kind of books are on the back wall?
STUDENT: Fiction.
TEACHER: What else Misha?
STUDENT: Biographies.
TEACHER: If I wanted to know where George Washington was born, can I find that out from the encyclopedia?
CLASS (*in unison*): Yes.
TEACHER: How many kinds of encyclopedias can you think of?
CLASS (*in unison*): World Book. Book of Knowledge.
TEACHER: Dictionary. You all know what a dictionary is, right?
CLASS (*in unison*): Yes
TEACHER: Give me five things we use a dictionary for.
CLASS (*silence*)
TEACHER: Write that down. Look it up for tomorrow.
TEACHER (*after a brief pause*): Give me examples of special subject dictionaries.

STUDENT: Bible, sports.
TEACHER: Atlas is next. What is an atlas, Cannon?
STUDENT: Maps.
TEACHER: What's the Delta's shape? Take out a sheet of paper and draw the shape.
            (Five-minute pause while they draw)
TEACHER: Why is this the Delta?
STUDENT: Because it's shaped this way *(holds up his drawing)*.
TEACHER: Boy, am I learning a lot here. Are you learning a lot, Cannon?
STUDENT: Yes.
TEACHER: What are the two main highways in Mississippi?
CLASS *(in unison)*:   Fifty-five and twenty *(a few voices say fifty-nine)*
TEACHER: All that can be found in an atlas. *(The bell rings.)*
TEACHER: That's it for today. Go to the library. Look up what dictionaries are for. Keep your diagram. Think some more about it. We'll finish filling it in.

The next transcript is from an eleventh-grade English class in Sunflower County being conducted by "one of the best teachers," according to the principal. There were thirty students in the class, sitting at desks arranged in a horseshoe facing the front board, where Mrs. K. stood behind a lectern. They were reviewing *this, that, these,* and *those* in their grammar books. This review is ending as we pick up the transcript, and a review of double negatives, adverbs, and predicate adjectives is about to begin. Mrs. K. keeps her position in front of the class.

TEACHER: *Them* is unacceptable nonstandard what?
CLASS *(in unison)*:   English.
TEACHER: We're trying to correct our oral and written what?
CLASS *(in unison)*:   Speech.
TEACHER: This is supposed to help us with our what?
CLASS *(in unison)*:   Themes. *(After the students turned to the appropriate page, the next lesson began.)*
TEACHER: What does a predicate adjective do?
CLASS *(in unison)*:   Completes the linking verb and describes the subject.
TEACHER: The cake tastes delicious. *Delicious* is what part of speech, Oneida?
STUDENT: Predicate adjective.
TEACHER: Why don't we use *deliciously* Rob?
STUDENT: Because it's an adverb, and *delicious* describes the cake.
TEACHER: Right. Questions? All right, move to page 400. There's a rule at the top of the page, what does it say?
            (The class reads it aloud in unison.)

The next example is drawn from an eighth-grade English class in Mound Bayou. The students have been reading Richard Wright's *Black Boy* chapter by chapter, and this lesson concerns chapters 4 and 5. There were twenty-five students in the class, sitting at desks in rows facing the front, and the teacher, Mrs. P., sat on her desk with a book, asking questions.

TEACHER: What kinds of food did he eat?

CLASS (*in unison*): Bread and tea.

TEACHER: After he wrote the story about the Indian girl, who could he show it to?

STUDENT: A young lady next door.

TEACHER: That's right. He couldn't show it to his grandmother, because he was supposed to be praying, and Granny didn't believe in stories that weren't true. She thought they were the work of the devil.

(Seven kids are reading ahead, two are doing other work.)

TEACHER: Can you think of any way in which religion stifled his freedom?

STUDENT: Granny wouldn't let him read books.

TEACHER: Right. It's the first full paragraph on page 140. Granny didn't want him out on the streets or exploring the world.

These are not the same kind of recitations that I have observed in other districts in other states. Nowhere else have I heard responses in unison, and nowhere else have I seen such deference paid to teachers, although the grinding insistence on memorization echoes just about every recitation that I have observed. It seems that the oral religious tradition of call and response, in which questions with predetermined and well-known responses are put forth to a congregation and then the expected responses are brought forward in unison or individually, may be at work here. But, when teachers discussed this kind of teaching, they referred to it only as traditional, as the kind of teaching that has always gone on. I was struck by its similarities both to the top-down positioning of authority used by the state in its mandate-driven governance, through its 1982 School Reform Act, and to the authority vested in and implied by the national and state tests that it prepares students for. It may be easy to fault these teachers for their lack of methods that encourage "higher literacies" [2] but the teacher's success with their students on the standardized tests is an accomplishment that speaks to a solution (perhaps *their* solution but more likely, I think, coincidentally their solution) to the district's most pressing problem—getting students out of the Delta and into postsecondary education or the military. Isn't that solution an indicator of a sophisticated literacy at work in a large social and political sense?

There is also a sense in which these classroom exchanges—the recitations and drills, the posturing of control and authority, and the agreement to do these things—may be said to represent a concession to the technology of "basic skills," insofar as they seem to be grounded in notions of rote learning, as opposed, say, to notions of learning as generative. It seems, too, that the assessment technology has become the teaching method, especially as it is represented by recitations and multiple-choice and fill-in-the-blank exercises. And it seems possible that the language of this rural black culture (at least as it is represented by the call-and-response tradition) has been subverted to the language of the "basic skills" technology, perhaps simply because the fit of the call and response to that technology is so good. The students have learned the unspoken lesson of the technology; they automatically assume a submissive position in relation to teaching and learning.

But the picture is more complicated still. If the students allow themselves to be taken over by this technology, they succeed on the tests and get out of the Delta. But they don't learn the intellectual moves associated with generative acts like interpretive analyses and critical reading, those acts of mind and engagement that would allow them, for instance, to interpret texts or to frame ideas and problems from multiple perspectives or, for that matter, to shape and articulate their own perspectives. If they don't allow themselves to be taken over by the technology and rebel by not participating, which seems to be the only real option, they fail and go into the army (if they're lucky) or into the ranks of the unemployed, because there isn't anything else to do.

So what can the students do? What can their teachers do? They are, by all state and national standards, successful, and there is little reason to change. The system proceeds in one direction, and the strong relation of the instructional language to the testing technology (for whatever reasons) seems to work; a large percentage of students are able to leave the Delta, even though this means that they must leave their families and close community ties. The present system is predictable and effective; the communication in the classrooms can be seen as a welcome institutionalization of the state's authority and priorities. There is also a way, I think, in which the instructional language maintains existing class and socioeconomic order by allowing the students who do well the opportunity to leave the Delta, even though this causes them problems; this opportunity can be said to reinforce the values necessary to maintain the authority, the priorities, and the language that allow those values to exist in the first place. This cycle occurs within a context that places a high value on test performance, and it is arguable that the testing can produce positive change—change, perhaps, that would never have occurred if it were not for the testing.

School Reform: Mandates and Consequences

In 1982 Mississippi passed the School Reform Act, which reorganized the state department of education; appointed a nine-member state board of education and a state superintendent; developed compulsory school attendance; targeted dropout prevention; established a statewide kindergarten program to assist teachers in grades 1 through 3; instituted a performance-based accreditation system; developed an instructional management system; established a school executive management institute; instituted on-the-job performance evaluation for teachers; and established a statewide "basic skills" assessment program in grades 3, 5, 8, and 11 to accompany the state mandated functional literacy examination.[3]

The School Reform Act drastically changed education in the state, and almost all the teachers and administrators I interviewed thought that the mandates had brought about positive changes, especially in the focus on "basic skills" and functional literacy. The act, as policy for change, signals a central reliance on testing (as opposed to other alternatives for change, such as staff development and in-service education) to produce changes in teaching and curriculum. The two districts that I visited were successful at this; they manufactured their own objective-based tests to prepare for the "basic skills" assessment program. Teachers and administrators in Sunflower County and Mound Bayou talked about education in terms of improving test scores. Slogans and posters hung in the school hallways urged students to prepare for the "basic skills" and functional literacy exams. Such invocations make sense, of course; good scores reflect on everyone in the district, and these tests serve as the preliminaries for the ACT, which is used to determine admissions to state colleges and universities.

This single-minded emphasis on testing has been responsible for dramatic changes in the curriculum in so far as teachers now have clear-cut goals and objectives. As paradoxical as it may seem, the functional literacy examination, which has a composition component, has been responsible for introducing the teaching of writing in the high schools, for students must now take the exam in eleventh grade before they can go on to twelfth grade. I observed three high school writing classes in the Sunflower County schools, and the work was as impressive as the teacher (the classes were all taught by the same teacher). The students were writing autobiographical essays at the time I observed them, but they had written journals, poems, anecdotes, and stories earlier in the year. They worked in peer-editing groups, had individual conferences with their teacher, and wrote multiple revisions after talking with their teacher and other students about their work. While talking with their teacher, I learned that she had done postgraduate work at a National Writing Project satellite program at a college, and she was enthusiastic about how well her students had taken to regular, intensive writing. The students did well on the functional literacy test writing sample, with only three of her 145 eleventh-graders failing it (compared with 27% of the state's eleventh-graders who failed the writing sample and the 40% of the black eleventh-graders who didn't pass that part of the exam). But she also remarked on her concerns for the future of writing, because, although the functional literacy test mandated acceptable performance on a writing sample, the "basic skills" test (which was about to be phased in) proceeded from multiple-choice questions on grammar and usage, and, as she saw it, she was the only teacher in her building actually teaching writing. Everyone else on the English faculty taught, she said, directly from the grammar and usage textbook, which she abandoned a year ago. She was caught in a double bind: the administration had given her free rein to teach writing because the functional literacy examination tested writing, but now the "basic skills" assessment program was going to test grammar and usage in the traditional multiple-choice format, and she felt the pressure, because her students didn't do well on grammar drills, although they could correct their errors with a little help from her and other students. In addition, she felt isolated as a writing teacher; no one else in the building taught writing, and she didn't have the energy to convince them or to build a support system for herself.

I also observed an elementary mathematics teacher while she taught problem solving through writing, but outside of these two teachers, no one else seemed to offer writing or provide opportunities for students to talk and participate in class discussions. But, then, no one in the administration seemed to provide opportunities for teachers to participate in discussions, and there was little in-service training for teachers, mostly because the local districts and schools couldn't raise the money to supplement the eleven dollars a year for each certified teacher that the state budgeted for it, and curriculum decisions were mandated from the top down, rather than constructed by teachers.

These communication opportunities (or the lack of them) interest me; I think two of the issues concerning literacy in these schools relate directly to the kind of talk that goes on in classrooms and among teachers. The first issue has to do with the way the state's top-down communication and policy procedures are reproduced in the classrooms. The teachers and the principals I interviewed do not engage in policy decisions with other teachers and administrators or with district or state representatives. Most of what they do is enforce and learn how to enforce the state mandates. The communication is one-way. The transcripts of the class talk can also be read this way, I think, as examples of authority taking the position of the master. Academic conversations aren't encouraged in the classes, so there is very little opportunity for discourse to confuse authority, as it may, because only the authority is allowed to speak. These transcripts also have to be read in the context of the language of tests and the religious oral tradition of call and response, but these other influences contribute to the monolithic positioning of authority in these classes (whether purposefully or coincidentally), rather than to its confusion, dissipation, or reconstruction. And even though the functional literacy test has brought about a dramatic change in writing instruction in at least one high school, there remain questions about the source of that change. The mandates bring about change by focusing attention on given solutions, rather than on a process—a communication and policy process—of problems being identified, understood, and worked by those concerned with them. Although given solutions can produce environments where something like writing flourishes, they do so because the teachers have to make them flourish, not because they embarked on a course of discovery and change that they imagined.

The second issue concerning literacy in these schools has to do with the closeness of strong recitations and drills to testlike questions. About 90% of the classes I observed in English, science, and mathematics were conducted like the ones represented by the transcripts in this article. No discussions remotely resembled Socratic or great books inquiries; only two of the teachers taught writing, and neither one of them knew of other teachers who taught writing instead of or along with grammar drills. This state of affairs is puzzling, though, because these schools and students are successful on tests that represent important state and national goals, and their success is an indicator of sophisticated literacy, a literacy that has allowed teachers and administrators to read through all the mandates and prescriptions to the single most important thing they can do for their students.

These teachers are in a position to be caught in a paradox created by conflicting mandates and prescriptions. On the one hand, they are accountable for their students' success in a state and a nation that rely on and believe in standardized tests of "basic skills" to get students into colleges and universities. On the other hand, the teachers are increasingly accountable to the state, national, and professional prescriptions for "higher literacies" like writing that appear to subsume and challenge "basic skills" instruction and grammar drills. So there is a sense that these schools' successes in preparing students to do well on standardized tests, tests that determine which students leave the Delta and go on to postsecondary education or the military, may also be seen as their failures to provide students with opportunities to learn "higher literacies." "Basic skills" instruction, as it has been defined by tests and textbooks, proceeds from a technology of recitation and drill in manners that closely mimic testing situations, as the instruction in the classes I observed does. "Higher literacies" instruction, by contrast, proceeds primarily through generative acts like discussion, writing, and problem posing and solving. The situation in these districts puts in the foreground questions about the compatibility of these conflicting mandates and prescriptions and allows a challenge to the assumption that schools can respond to calls for education in "higher literacies" when the state and the nation continue to use tests of "basic skills" to get their students into colleges and universities.

The problem is further complicated by the language of the mandates and the testing. "Basic skills" instruction implies fundamentals, learning that may be necessary and prerequisite to anything higher (like "higher literacies"), and, in fact, all the administrators and all but two of the teachers I spoke with used these oppositional terms to represent learning as a series of building blocks. First, students learn the basics; then, once the foundation is secure, they learn the higher things. Pragmatically and traditionally, the basics have come to be associated with component skills. As in my writing-instruction example, students learn to identify parts of speech and to correct grammatical errors before they write; once they write, they begin with sentences and move on to paragraphs and then to multiparagraphed themes. Once they master these basic building blocks, the argument goes, they're ready to be creative and to do such higher learning as is required by acts of generative and interpretive language—to solve problems, for instance, that may be called ill-structured, problems for which there are no given answers or algorithms. Thus, the terms "basic skills" and "higher literacies" have created their own realities, forestalling discussions of their fundamentally different assumptions about teaching and learning and positioning the two different notions in a hierarchical relation to each other: "basic skills" stands for rote learning or learning component skills like the parts of speech before learning a whole process like writing; "higher literacies" stands for a problem-solving approach with the attention on whole processes. The language of *basic* and *higher* has allowed this positioning in a hierarchy, and it has allowed the hard questions of what these terms conceal and whose interests are served by their positioning to be largely unrealized.

I'm particularly interested in the metaphors at play here and the ways in which they neutralize each other by allowing a hierarchical positioning of what appear to be two incompatible ways of thinking about teaching and learning. I'm interested, too, in the ways such terms have allowed these institutions to segregate students, as they do, according to their mastery of "basic skills." Students who do not or cannot master rote learning receive more and more instruction in the rote learning they continually fail at; finally, the teaching and the testing are difficult to distinguish, and the students are unlikely ever to participate in the "higher literacies," because the assumption is that they cannot do so until they have mastered the basics. There's an endless cycle of teaching and testing concealed in these notions of "basic skills" and rote learn-ing, one that was clearly visible in the curricula of the schools I visited. Even more interesting is the preemption of "basic skills" from standing for any learning other than rote learning. Because of the cast of the language and its enactment in the districts' textbooks, tests, and curricula, it's impossible for *basic* to refer to, say, writing whole papers that say something to someone or interpreting texts in genuine discussions with other students. The visible activities of these two notions of learning, the ones represented by the language of *basic* and *higher*, are even different from each other. Students completing work sheets or partic-ipating in recitations like those I observed are not doing the same things as students writing stories or essays or engaging in discussions. But the metaphors of *basic* and *higher* allow the assumptions that one kind of learning proceeds from the other, when, in fact, not only are the visible acts of learning different, but their assumptions about teaching and learning as human activities are dra-matically and philosophically different. These differences further display them-selves in questions of how people learn. Do we, for example, learn the bill of rights by memorizing it or by, say, writing interpretive essays about it, in much the same way historians write interpretive essays about primary sources? My experience leads me to believe that we learn about the bill of rights by working with it the way a historian does and that memorization is frustrating, does not necessarily lead to an understanding of it, and is short-lived. The difference in learning here is all the difference in the world. Yet the language of the metaphors of *basic* and *higher* conceal these differences under a hierarchical positioning that allows "basic skills" and "higher literacies" to appear compatible and in a linear relation to each other.

Speculations and Cautions

One interesting paradox, I think, is that while much of the national debate on literacy proceeds from test results, little critical attention is being paid to those tests. Discussions often begin by assuming that such tests as the ACT or the

SAT are valid measures of all sorts of things, including student, teacher, and general educational success, for which they were never intended, and that huge national surveys like the National Assessment of Educational Progress are equally valid indicators of what students know and can do, when, in fact, these tests suffer from many significant problems and constraints.[4] The inherent difficulties and the expense of constructing alternative assessment procedures—such as direct observations, videotaping, and portfolio assessment of writing—have effectively entrenched paper-and-pencil multiple-choice testing.[5] Only recently have testing experts even begun to consider the effects of testing on teaching and the interrelations of assessment and instruction. In the Delta schools that I studied, the effects of testing and the mandates for change attached to the testing seemed to be more apparent than in any of the other districts I have studied.[6] As the situation was understood by students and teachers, scores on the ACT determine who will be able to leave the Delta for postsecondary education.

The contextual factors involved in this single-minded emphasis on testing and the kinds of teaching it seems to encourage pose another conundrum for anyone trying to understand the forces at play in the Delta schools. The history and the tradition of black rural language, at least as it is represented by call and response in formal instructional situations, fit all too well with the submissive positioning of students in the recitations. In addition, there is also the larger context of how language is used by the powers that be to create a social fabric within the educational system and the communities. Mississippi is a state with a history of master to slave relationships, of dominate to subservient, and the recitations have to be considered in the context of this history. It could be that the state administrators and legislators have enacted this history by providing teachers and local administrators with a policy for change that preempts conversation and dialogue. Teachers and local administrators aren't included in the discussions about their problems and their changes, at least not through any formal or ongoing staff development. This top-down communication system or policy is reproduced in the classrooms. Policy begets similar policy, whether it wants to or not, and all these contextual factors may be described as concentric rings, circles within circles, begetting more of the same at various levels of the educational institution.

This situation and proposals for how it may be changed are fraught with paradoxes and dilemmas. Should the state or the professions continue to encourage this kind of instruction, emanating as it does at least partially from the language of *basic* and *higher*, or should they encourage change and a curriculum that allows students opportunities to engage in discussions, problem posing and problem solving that seem to be integral to work in "higher literacies"? How could such encouragement happen? Are more mandates going to affect the situation in ways that may influence not only class procedures but the social and political contexts, so that teachers can decide instruction and policy or, at least, have a say? Or will more mandates allow class procedures to change just enough to make some superficial concessions to "higher literacies" while encouraging the underlying top-down lines of authority and communication? Is it possible, in other words, to teach the generative acts that I have been calling "higher literacies" or, at least, provide opportunities for them to occur, opportunities that imply, at the very least, two-way communication and collaborative learning in a context so heavily shaped by a top-down philosophy? Or is everything just fine as it is, the only problem being, as one principal put it, how to get more students up to speed on the tests? Finally, how can we begin to discuss the ethics of mandating or introducing work in "higher literacies" when the real priorities and goals are those implied by the "basic skills" tests that students must pass to go on in their education?

These are compelling questions, as confounded as they seem to be. Mississippi has already embarked on a course of action by its decision to emphasize certain kinds of testing in one-way communication and policy environments. But the state has not addressed the problems posed by the tension between the way these classes are taught and the ways they could be taught in order to attend to "higher literacies." They will have to attend to such literacies as soon as the state department of education moves to what its officials referred to, in a classic example of the evolution of *basic* to *higher*, as "the second phase of school reform": the phase that emphasizes "higher literacies" once the foundation has been formed through the basics.

NOTES

[1] This report was done as part of the grant work for the MacArthur Foundation-sponsored Higher Literacies Study directed by Rexford Brown from the Education Commission of the States. Although I refer to my observations and studies, Rexford Brown and I worked collaboratively with Sam Stringfield (then from Northwest Regional Laboratories) and shared our impressions, notes, and conclusions informally as colleagues and formally at the Aspen Conference on Higher Literacies in Aspen, Colorado, in July 1988.

[2] "Higher literacies" has always sounded strange to me, and I don't like the metaphor, especially as it allows us to continue talking about hierarchies, but it was the official language of the project. It was meant, I think, to stand for those acts of learning that we call interpretive and that occur through extended conversations and discourse, whether in English, science, mathematics, or history. "Basic skills" also implies a hierarchical positioning that conceals the incompatibility of these two views of teaching and learning. The often-expressed assumption that the higher builds on the basic represents a misunderstanding of the philosophical positions these two terms represent. Throughout this paper I put these terms in quotation marks because it is easy to slip into the ordinary language sense of basic and higher, and I like to keep at least my attention focused on the conundrum these terms pose.

[3] The functional literacy examination asks students to do such things as read paragraphs, directions, and schedules; balance checkbooks and calculate sums and distances; and write an essay. The "basic skills" assessment program is an objectives-based exam de-

veloped from teacher consensus on what were the crucial skills in subject areas by grades. The "basic skills" test is a multiple-choice exam, as is the functional literacy test, which also includes a holistically scored writing sample.

[4]There are numerous problems with large-scale paper-and-pencil multiple-choice tests like the ACT, SAT, and NAEP (National Assessment of Educational Progress), including the time constraints imposed on students taking the tests and the question of whether students are motivated to pay much attention to these tests. The fundamental problem has to do with the kinds of questions that can be posed in a multiple-choice format and the automatic exclusion of ill-structured problems for which there are no predetermined answers or algorithms for solving the problems. These ill-structured problems are referred to as generative throughout this paper; they put students in the position of having to come up with their own procedures and language, including their use of information and the kinds of knowledge usually tested as "basic skills," to work the problems. It's in this sense that ill-structured or interpretive work subsumes the kinds of skills emphasized in "basic skills" and returns them to being parts of larger problems, rather than problems in themselves, as they are largely represented on multiple-choice tests.

[5]Portfolio assessment usually implies some sort of evaluation based on a collection of student work, rather than on individual pieces of work or tests. Teachers often keep file folders of students' work and develop assessment criteria that allow them to consider all that a student has done in a concession to the long-term nature of learning and performance. Portfolios allow teachers to give consideration to the notion that a student's work can't be evaluated on a single sample, one of many performances, no matter how similar or diverse those performances are, because performances always occur in contexts, in situations like classrooms, where what a student does is always already related to what the instructor asks or teaches. The instructor, like the student, is also directly influenced by the contexts. In the language of test makers, student achievement can't be separated from instructor and program evaluation; the instructor and the program, including past instructors and any programs they represent, shape the kind of work that students do. Evaluations of students' work that don't take into consideration the kinds of instruction they have received cling to or, at least, perpetuate the illusion that students do what they do solely because of their achievement. Portfolios, especially for a subject like English, should include all the work the students have been asked to do over a period of time, including all teacher responses and commentaries, so that a person examining the portfolio would be able to see the kinds of work the students were asked to do, the kinds of responses their work received, and their achievement, then, in the light of the work they were asked to do. A folder of work sheets with red plus and minus marks would tell an evaluator, for instance, something different from a folder with few work sheets and a set of writing samples. Portfolio assessments could be done on the state and national level with matrix samples within state districts. This kind of assessment would yield useful information about not only students' work but also the kinds of things going on in their classrooms—the contexts for their work.

[6]Rexford Brown, Sam Stringfield, and I also studied schools in Pittsburgh, Pennsylvania, and in Toronto, Canada. Although we saw considerable recitation and drill in Pittsburgh, it almost always proceeded directly from workbooks, and the students never responded in unison or with the deference shown to the teachers in the Delta schools. It struck us that teachers would never get away with this kind of recitation in places like Pittsburgh; the students wouldn't allow it, because no tradition, either in the history or in the language, would encourage or permit it.

PROFESSIONAL CONTEXTS

Literacy and the Politics of Education
C. H. Knoblauch

Literacy is one of those mischievous concepts, like virtuousness and crafts-manship, that appear to denote capacities but that actually convey value judg-ments. It is rightly viewed, Linda Brodkey has noted, "as a social trope" and its sundry definitions "as cultural Rorschachs" (47). The labels *literate* and *illiterate* almost always imply more than a degree or deficiency of skill. They are, grossly or subtly, sociocultural judgments laden with approbation, disapproval, or pity about the character and place, the worthiness and prospects, of persons and groups. A revealing exercise would be to catalog the definitions of literacy that lie explicit or implicit in the pages of this collection, definitions that motivate judgments, political no less than scholarly, about which people belong in literate and illiterate categories; the numbers in each group; why and in what ways literacy is important; what should be done for or about those who are not literate or are less literate than others; and who has the power to say so. It would be quickly apparent that there is no uniformity of view, since the values that surround reading and writing abilities differ from argument to argument. Instead, there are competing views, responsive to the agendas of those who characterize the ideal. Invariably, definitions of literacy are also rationalizations of its importance. Furthermore, they are invariably offered by the literate, con-stituting, therefore, implicit rationalizations of the importance of literate people, who are powerful (the reasoning goes) because they are literate and, as such, deserving of power.

The concept of literacy is embedded, then, in the ideological dispositions of those who use the concept, those who profit from it, and those who have the standing and motivation to enforce it as a social requirement. It is obviously not a cultural value in all times and places; when Sequoya brought his syllabic writing system to the Cherokee, their first inclination was to put him to death for dabbling in an evil magic. The majority of the world's languages have lacked alphabets, though they have nonetheless articulated rich oral traditions in societies that have also produced many other varieties of cultural achievement. To be sure, there is ready agreement, at least among the literate, about the necessity of literacy in the so-called modern world; this agreement is reinforced by explanations that typically imply a more developed mode of existence among literate people. I. J. Gelb has written, for instance: "As language distinguishes man from animal, so writing distinguishes civilized man from barbarian," going on to point out that "an illiterate person cannot expect to participate successfully in human progress, and what is true of individuals is also true of any group of individuals, social strata, or ethnic units" (221–22). This argument offers a common and pernicious half-truth, representing the importance of literacy, which is unquestionable, in absolutist and ethnocentric terms.

However, if literacy today is perceived as a compelling value, the reason lies not in such self-interested justifications but in its continuing association with forms of social reality that depend on its primacy. During the Middle Ages, clerks were trained to read and write so that they could keep accounts for landowners, merchants, and government officials. Bureaucratic documentation was not conceived so that people could acquire literacy. Christian missionaries in nineteenth-century Africa spread literacy so that people could read the Bible; they did not teach the Bible so that the illiterate could become readers and writers. There is no question that literacy is necessary to survival and success in the contemporary world—a world where the literate claim authority to set the terms of survival and success, a world that reading and writing abilities have significantly shaped in the first place. But it is important to regard that necessity in the context of political conditions that account for it, or else we sacrifice the humanizing understanding that life can be otherwise than the way we happen to know it and that people who are measured positively by the yardstick of literacy enjoy their privileges because of their power to choose and apply that instrument on their own behalf, not because of their point of development or other innate worthiness. Possessing that understanding, educators in particular but other citizens as well may advance their agendas for literacy with somewhat less likelihood of being blinded by the light of their own benevolence to the imperial designs that may lurk in the midst of their compassion.

In the United States today, several arguments about the nature and importance of literacy vie for power in political and educational life. Sketching the more popular arguments may remind us of the extent to which definitions of the concept incorporate the social agendas of the definers, serving the needs of the nonliterate only through the mediation of someone's vision of the way the world should be. Literacy never stands alone in these perspectives as a neutral denoting of skills; it is always literacy for something—for professional competence in a technological world, for civic responsibility and the preservation of heritage; for personal growth and self-fulfilment, for social and political change. The struggle of any one definition to dominate the others entails no merely casual or arbitrary choice of values, nor does it allow for a conflating of alternatives in some grand compromise or list of cumulative benefits. At stake are fundamentally different perceptions of social reality; the nature of language and discourse; the importance of culture, history, and tradition; the functions of schools, as well as other commitments, few of which are regarded as negotiable. At the same time, since no definition achieves transcendent authority, their dialectical interaction offers a context of choices within which continually changing educational and other social policies find their justification. The process of choosing is visible every day, for better and worse, in legislative assemblies, television talk shows, newspaper editorials, and classrooms throughout the country.

The most familiar literacy argument comes from the functionalist perspective, with its appealingly pragmatic emphasis on readying people for the necessities of daily life—writing checks, reading sets of instructions—as well as for the professional tasks of a complex technological society. Language abilities in this view are often represented by the metaphors of information theory: language is a code that enables the sending of messages and the processing of information. The concern of a functionalist perspective is the efficient transmission of useful messages in a value-neutral medium. Basic-skill and technical-writing programs in schools, many on-the-job training programs in business and industry, and the training programs of the United States military—all typically find their rationalization in the argument for functional literacy, in each case presuming that the ultimate value of language lies in its utilitarian capacity to pass information back and forth for economic or other material gain.

The functionalist argument has the advantage of tying literacy to concrete needs, appearing to promise socioeconomic benefit to anyone who can achieve the appropriate minimal competency. But it has a more hidden advantage as well, at least from the standpoint of those whose literacy is more than minimal: it safeguards the socioeconomic status quo. Whatever the rhetoric of its advocates concerning the "self-determined objectives" (Hunter and Harman 7) of people seeking to acquire skills, functionalism serves the world as it is, inviting outsiders to enter that world on the terms of its insiders by fitting themselves to roles that they are superficially free to choose but that have been prepared as a range of acceptable alternatives. Soldiers will know how to repair an MX missile by reading the field manual but will not question the use of such weapons because of their reading of antimilitarist philosophers; clerks will be able to fill out and file their order forms but will not therefore be qualified for positions in higher management. Functionalist arguments presume that a given social order is right simply because it exists, and their advocates are content to recommend the training of persons to take narrowly beneficial places in that society. The rhetoric of technological progressivism is often leavened with a mixture of fear and patriotism (as in *A Nation at Risk*) in order to defend a social program that maintains managerial classes—whose members are always more than just functionally literate—in their customary places while outfitting workers with the minimal reading and writing skills needed for usefulness to the modern information economy.

Cultural literacy offers another common argument about the importance of reading and writing, one frequently mounted by traditionalist educators but sustained in populist versions as well, especially among people who feel insecure about their own standing and their future prospects when confronted by the volatile mix of ethnic heritages and socioeconomic interests that make up contemporary American life. The argument for cultural literacy moves beyond a mechanist conception of basic skills and toward an affirmation of supposedly stable and timeless cultural values inscribed in the verbal memory—in particular, the canonical literature of Western European society. Its reasoning is that true literacy entails more than technical proficiency, a minimal ability to make one's way in the world; that literacy also includes an awareness of cultural heritage, a capacity for higher-order thinking, even some aesthetic discernment—faculties not automatically available to the encoders and decoders of the functionalist perspective. Language is no mere tool in this view but is, rather, a repository of cultural values and to that extent a source of social cohesion. To guard the vitality of the language, the advocates of cultural literacy say, citizens must learn to speak and write decorously, as well as functionally, and must also read great books, where the culture is enshrined. In some popular versions of cultural literacy, English is regarded as the only truly American language and is, therefore, the appropriate medium of commerce and government. The economic self-interest that pervades the functionalist perspective frequently gives way here to jingoistic protectionism; cultural literacy advocates presume that the salvation of some set of favored cultural norms or language practices lies necessarily in the marginalizing or even extinction of others.

The argument for cultural literacy often presents itself within a myth of the fall from grace: Language and, by extension, culture once enjoyed an Edenlike existence but are currently degenerating because of internal decay and sundry forces of barbarism. People no longer read, write, or think with the strength of insight of which they were once capable. They no longer remember and, therefore, no longer venerate. The age of high culture has passed; minds and characters have been weakened by television or rock music or the 1960s. The reasons vary, but the message is clear: unless heritage is protected, the former purity of language reconstituted, the past life of art and philosophy retrieved, we risk imminent cultural decay. However extravagant such predictions appear to unbelievers, there is no mistaking the melancholy energy of contemporary proponents of cultural literacy or, if we are to judge from the recent best-seller lists, the number of solemn citizens—anxious perhaps about recent influxes of Mexicans, Vietnamese, and other aliens—who take their warnings to heart.

Arguments for cultural and functional literacy plainly dominate the American imagination at the moment and for obvious reasons. They articulate the needs, hopes, anxieties, and frustrations of the conservative temper. They reveal in different ways the means of using an ideal of literacy to preserve and advance the world as it is, a world in which the interests of traditionally privileged groups dominate the interests of the traditionally less privileged. Schools reflect such conservatism to the extent that they view themselves as agencies for preserving established institutions and values, not to mention the hierarchical requirements of the American economy. But still other arguments, if not quite so popular, reflect the priorities and the agendas of liberal and even radical ideologies struggling to project their altered visions of social reality, seeking their own power over others under the banner of literacy. The liberal argument, for instance, emphasizes literacy for personal growth, finding voice in the process-writing movement in American high schools or in the various practices of personalized learning. The liberal argument has been successful, up to a point, in schools because it borrows from long-hallowed American myths of expressive freedom and boundless individual opportunity, romantic values to which schools are obliged to pay at least lip service even when otherwise promoting more authoritarian curricula.

The assumption of a literacy-for-personal-growth argument is that language expresses the power of the individual imagination, so that nurturing a person's reading and writing abilities enables the development of that power, thereby promoting the progress of society through the progress of the individual learner. The political agenda behind this liberalism tends to be educational and other social change; its concern for personal learning draws attention to school practices that supposedly thwart the needs of individual students or that disenfranchise some groups of students in the interest of maintaining the values of the status quo. The kinds of change that the personal-growth argument recommends are, on the whole, socially tolerable because they are moderate in character: let students read enjoyable novels, instead of basal reader selections; let young women and young Hispanics find images of themselves in schoolwork, not just images of white males. Using the rhetoric of moral sincerity, the personal-growth argument speaks compassionately on behalf of the disadvantaged. Meanwhile, it avoids, for the most part, the suggestion of any fundamental restructuring of institutions, believing that the essential generosity and fair-mindedness of American citizens will accommodate some liberalization of outmoded curricula and an improved quality of life for the less privileged as long as fundamental political and economic interests are not jeopardized. Frequently, Americans do hear such appeals, though always in the context of an implicit agreement that nothing important is going to change. Accordingly, advocates of expressive writing, personalized reading programs, whole-language curricula, and open classrooms have been permitted to carry out their educational programs, with politicians and school officials quick to realize the ultimate gain in administrative control that comes from allowing such modest symbols of self-determination to release built-up pressures of dissatisfaction.

is one for what Henry Giroux, among others, calls critical literacy (226). Critical literacy is a radical perspective whose adherents, notably Paulo Freire, have been influential primarily in the third world, especially Latin America. Strongly influenced by Marxist philosophical premises, critical literacy is not a welcome perspective in this country, and it finds voice currently in only a few academic enclaves, where it exists more as a facsimile of oppositional culture than as a practice, and in an even smaller number of community-based literacy projects, which are typically concerned with adult learners. Its agenda is to identify reading and writing abilities with a critical consciousness of the social conditions in which people find themselves, recognizing the extent to which language practices objectify and rationalize these conditions and the extent to which people with authority to name the world dominate others whose voices they have been able to suppress. Literacy, therefore, constitutes a means to power, a way to seek political enfranchisement—not with the naive expectation that merely being literate is sufficient to change the distribution of prerogatives but with the belief that the ability to speak alone enables entrance to the arena in which power is contested. At stake, from this point of view, is, in principle, the eventual reconstituting of the class structure of American life, specifically a change of those capitalist economic practices that assist the dominance of particular groups.

For that reason, if for no other, such a view of literacy will remain suspect as a theoretical enterprise and will be considered dangerous, perhaps to the point of illegality, in proportion to its American adherents' attempts to implement it practically in schools and elsewhere. The scholarly right has signaled this institutional hostility in aggressive attacks on Jonathan Kozol's *Illiterate America*, the most popular American rendering of critical-literacy arguments, for its supposedly inaccurate statistics about illiteracy and in calculatedly patronizing Kozol's enthusiasm for radical change. Meanwhile, although critical literacy is trendy in some academic circles, those who commend it also draw their wages from the capitalist economy it is designed to challenge. Whether its advocates will take Kozol's risks in bringing so volatile a practice into community schools is open to doubt. Whether something important would change if they did take the risks is also doubtful. Whether, if successful, they would still approve a world in which their own privileges were withheld may be more doubtful still. In any case, one can hardly imagine NCTE or the MLA, let alone the Department of Education, formally sanctioning such a fundamental assault on their own institutional perquisites.

Definitions of literacy could be multiplied far beyond these popular arguments. But enumerating others would only belabor my point, which is that no definition tells, with ontological or objective reliability, what literacy is; definitions only tell what some person or group—motivated by political commitments—wants or needs literacy to be. What makes any such perspective powerful is the ability of its adherents to make it invisible or, at least, transparent—a window on the world, revealing simple and stable truths—so that the only problem still needing to be addressed is one of implementation: how best to make the world—other people—conform to that prevailing vision. At the same time, what makes any ideology visible as such and, therefore, properly limited in its power to compel unconscious assent is critical scrutiny, the only safeguard people have if they are to be free of the designs of others. To the extent that literacy advocates of one stripe or another remain unconscious of or too comfortable with those designs, their offerings of skills constitute a form of colonizing, a benign but no less mischievous paternalism that rationalizes the control of others by representing it as a means of liberation. To the extent that the nonliterate allow themselves to be objects of someone else's "kindness," they will find no power in literacy, however it is defined, but only altered terms of dispossession. When, for instance, the memberships of U.S. English and English First, totaling around half a million citizens, argue for compulsory English, they may well intend the enfranchisement of those whose lack of English-language abilities has depressed their economic opportunities. But they also intend the extinction of cultural values inscribed in languages other than their own and held to be worthwhile by people different from themselves. In this or any other position on literacy, its advocates, no less than its intended beneficiaries, need to hear—for all our sakes—a critique of whatever assumptions and beliefs are fueling their passionate benevolence.

WORKS CITED

Brodkey, Linda. "Tropics of Literacy." *Journal of Education* 168 (1986): 47–54.

Commission on Excellence in Education. *A Nation at Risk: The Imperative for Educational Reform.* Washington: GPO, 1983.

Gelb, I. J. *A Study of Writing.* Chicago: U of Chicago P, 1952.

Giroux, Henry A. *Theory and Resistance in Education: A Pedagogy for the Opposition.* South Hadley: Bergin, 1983.

Hunter, Carman St. John, and David Harman. *Adult Literacy in the United States.* New York: McGraw, 1979.

Kozol, Jonathan. *Illiterate America.* New York: Anchor, 1985.

The English Department and Social Class: Resisting Writing

James Thomas Zebroski

I am the son of a factory worker. I don't know precisely what my father did at work. For over thirty years, my father worked swing shifts (day turn, midnight turn, and four-to-twelve or afternoon turn) at a General Motors plant that employed over ten thousand workers. But only during the last five years or so before his retirement would he make any explicit mention of his workaday world.

My father's silence about his work paralleled his silence about the Polish language. My father knew and could speak Polish. He also, I later discovered, knew quite a bit of Russian and Slovak. If he had had degree initials—AB, MA, PhD—behind his name, his knowledge of languages would have been seen as the mark of a lettered man, a cultured man. As it was, my father never spoke Polish at home, nor did he so much as hint that he knew Polish, let alone Russian or Slovak. During my doctoral program I finally decided, after three years of putting it off, that I needed to take a series of courses in Russian so that I could gain access to materials on the work of Lev Vygotsky that were in the library but were in the Russian original. I brought my Russian textbook home over Christmas break to study vocabulary and discovered in the process that, as I read out the Russian words in my poor excuse for spoken Russian, my father already knew the meanings and the senses of the words in English in far more detail than the simplifying textbook gave.

My father's reasons for silence, both about his job and about his knowledge of Polish and Russian, did not involve shame or a belief that his work and his multilingualism were inferior. They weren't, and he knew that. Rather, I think my father kept quiet for the best of reasons, because he felt there would be a price to pay if his children knew their father's world too well. He had hopes for his children. Sometimes the price of hope is silence.

But my father wasn't the only silent one. I, too, have been silent, silent among my colleagues, silent about my origins and allegiances. And, again, it isn't that I am ashamed of who I am and where I have come from. In fact, the older I get, the surer I am that I have been lucky, blessed even, to live in or between two worlds, the world of the middle and upper classes that we name the university and the world of the working classes that is my family. My silence, like my father's, has arisen from my sense of how important these facts are and how dangerous they might be in the wrong hands.

Still, that makes these silences all too conspiratorial. It's not that simple. Tillie Olsen in *Silences* circles the territory of this essay. She says:

> Of the first generation. . . . A phenomenon of our time, the increasingly significant number of first (or second) generation of our people to aspire to the kinds of uses of capacity possible through the centuries only for a few human beings of privilege—among these, to write. . . . Marginal. Against complex odds. Exhausting (though exhilarating) achievement. . . . Coercians to "pass": to write with the attitude of and/or in the manner of, the dominant. Little to validate our different sense of reality, to help raise one's own truths, voice, against the prevalent. . . . [P]roblems being in the first generation of one's family to come to writing: its relationship to works of literature . . . the great unexamined.   (287 –88)

This essay pursues in more detail some of these "coercians to 'pass' " by examining the politics and the ideology of commonsense and everyday notions of style. Recently, scholars have been turning their attention to the ideology and the functions of United States schooling, to the ways in which institutions reproduce ruling ideology and reigning social relations through a multitude of discursive practices. Richard Ohmann and James Berlin have done important work in applying these and other approaches to the specific work of the English department and the field of composition. This essay extends the critique into the everyday life of the composition classroom, zeroing in on two specific questions:

1. How is it that, against my good intentions and best efforts to teach literacy in a progressive way, I may nonetheless function to impose the reigning ideology, to enact and support existing social relations, to silence the working-class student?
2. What can I do to resist functioning as an agent of the status quo?

One of the spots where reigning ideas and social relations are unwittingly and quietly reproduced is in the silent moment when the English teacher reads a student text. This reading is always an ideological and political act. To create meaning, the reader must evaluate; and the evaluative moment—no matter how long deferred or how positively worded or how complicated or how developmental—is both inevitable and political. We cannot escape the evaluative moment, so it seems especially important to problematize it, to think critically about it, to examine and even interrogate our own practices.

The Soviet theorist Valentin Vološinov begins with such evaluative moments. In his book *Marxism and the Philosophy of Language*, Vološinov argues that style is a political act. Like Eric Auerbach in his work *Mimesis: The Representation of*

Reality in Western Literature, Vološinov comes out of a philological, historicist tradition of language study that relates signifying practices to knowledge and power, all situated in a constellation of communities with class affiliations. For Vološinov, language reflects and refracts community. Style evokes and can help reproduce existing social-class relations.

Vološinov argues that language tends to range between two stylistic poles. The first style, which Vološinov calls a linear or monologic style, tends to be affiliated with the ruling classes. This monologic style draws hard, clearly demarcated boundaries between reported speech and reporting context, between speakers, between discourses. It tends to move toward purity and unity, in that this style is used most often to speak and write about officially sanctioned topics in officially approved ways.

In contrast, the pictorial or dialogic style tends to be more a mixture of popular and unofficial genres, full of voices of other people, full of reported speech. The dialogic style infiltrates boundaries and blurs established genres. It tends to mix texts and their authority. The result is often a hybrid language. English teachers recognize such hybrids and label them diction problems or lapses in straight thinking or plagiarism. Much of what English teachers have traditonally taught in composition courses is a respect for the sorts of discursive boundaries that the dialogic style breaks down.

Vološinov's theory suggests that our working-class students tend to prefer the dialogic style, while English teachers tend to inculcate and privilege the monologic style. We want to move students to purity. They want to enjoy mixture.

All of these tensions come together in the concept of good writing. We teachers are continually thinking about good writing, the concept we apply during the evaluative moment. We are all fairly clear about what good writing is. I know I think I am. But perhaps it is precisely when I am trying to help working-class persons improve their writing, to learn to produce quality texts, when I have their best interests at heart, that my most ideological and political act occurs. Where does my concept of good writing come from, after all, but from wide reading of elite literature and deep study of principles of composition that have been derived almost exclusively from the study of the writing processes of middle-class and upper-class people. So, as I stand there in the silent moment while my student patiently awaits my response, what do I do? Where lies my response and my responsibility? Recall the Tillie Olsen quotation: will this moment be the moment of "coercian to 'pass' "? Will I say, "Say it like this, and become one of us"?

Until I started thinking about such issues, I looked for the conventional qualities in student writing—purposefulness, some consideration of the audience, unity, development, fluency, graceful use of language. But now, as I look for these qualities, I reflect on the institutional and societal functions served by privileging them. Perhaps my search for purpose in student discourse contradicts my invitation to students to experience writing as heuristic, to let the writing discover its own purposes. Perhaps I am telling the student two contradictory things when I say, "Pursue the meaningful in your writing, search out the tensions and the problematic in your writing and life, but make sure everything in your final text is unified, make sure that everything fits." Maybe, I think to myself, unity is a code word for finding ways to make everyone fit. Also, I wonder about my preference for the voice that stands out, that says something in a fresh way, that avoids the cliché. Where does that voice come from? To whose benefit is it? Can everyone stand out? Should everyone?

To raise such questions about reading and the evaluative moment—one of the most commonplace and pervasive activities that takes place in the English department, in our classrooms, in our professional lives—is not to argue that our situation is hopeless. Nor is it to put forward a relativistic acceptance of all texts, for we recognize that relativism itself reinforces existing social arrangements. Rather, expression of doubt should sharpen our critical abilities, preparing us to recognize the limits of our situation, so that we may better resist that status quo, transforming, instead of reproducing, dominant social relations.

Let me return then, to my second question: What can I do to resist unwittingly becoming the agent of the status quo? Here are six strategies for resistance that I am currently using:

1.   I prize doubt. I try to make my felt sense of contradiction into the source of my writing. I search out and go after the contradictions by using literacy itself. I write in order to resist. This resisting writing becomes a record of my struggle, as well as a means of taking the struggle home to my classroom, to the English department, even to literacy conferences.

2.   I nurture in myself and in my students a healthy skepticism toward new advances generally and toward new advances in the technologies of literacy specifically. By asking one question—who may benefit from this?—I frame all current composition research and literary theory.

For example, in her research Linda Flower has argued that the concepts of writer-based prose and reader-based prose provide us with a tool for helping student writers revise their texts, distinguishing between texts used primarily to make meaning and texts used primarily to communicate meaning. Flower suggests that student writers need to learn to make their writer-based prose more reader-based. But who may benefit from such a way of viewing language? May writer-based prose be a way of saying, "This writer has little power, so we can attend to this text less closely, at least until the writer puts it our way—that is, in reader-based prose"? And do the powerful have to use reader-based prose? The works of Jacques Derrida are widely read by literary theorists. Can we characterize Derrida's writing as reader-based prose? It seems that the distinction between writer-based prose and reader-based prose, like several other current descriptors, has the potential for being a "coercian to 'pass.' "

Another example: What really happens in peer evaluation groups or during peer critique? When we ask students to share their texts and to write evaluations of those texts with suggestions for improvement, what exactly is being criticized? Is it possible that we are asking the students to do our dirty work by policing style, by enforcing the reigning monologic style that students may have trouble reproducing but that they are more likely to recognize in their reading? While I am not arguing against peer evaluations and group work, I do feel the need to think through the evaluative and ideological dimensions of such activities more carefully.

3.   I study up and try to get my students to do likewise. I take the phrase *study up* from Laura Nader, who criticized traditional ethnography for mostly studying down the social ladder, for going to the marginalized and the oppressed to find out in great detail how they create and sustain their everyday worlds. Nader argues, and I agree, that we need to do just as much, if not more, studying up, investigating how the power elites create and sustain their worlds. I like Shirley Brice Heath's *Ways with Words*, but perhaps it is time to complement that volume with a parallel in-depth study of how Wall Street financiers create community and use literacy. We need to match our vast literature on the life of oppressed communities with a critical study of life and literacy in oppressor communities. How do Exxon or the news media or the federal government use literacy and for what ends? What are the reading and writing practices of the powerful? And how about our colleges? We should be conducting ongoing ethnographic studies of the institutions in which we work and that are supposed to be such hotbeds of literacy. I make precisely this sort of writing research a theme of my composition courses.

4.   In all my courses, I put all these concerns on the table with my students. I make literacy and power a public issue in my classroom, the topic of investigation and inquiry. I see the students as a task force or investigative squad who work as a team to look into these issues locally. This strategy of resistance includes sending students out across campus and across the city to conduct interviews, to observe, to collect and analyze texts that come from these communities. Students write up their information in essays that are published and shared in a class book. This book becomes our textbook for several weeks as we read each paper and draw conclusions from the work as a whole.

5.   I seek out strange texts, texts that challenge my notions of good writing and bad writing. I look for texts that blur boundaries and speak many languages. I have already mentioned one text that speaks to me, Tillie Olsen's *Silences*. Obviously, anything that Studs Terkel writes fits this category; I have used his *Working* in many composition classes in which we have centered on that theme. Another that I'd highly recommend is Richard Sennett and Jonathan Cobb's *Hidden Injuries of Class*. This is an interesting text not only because the subject matter relates to what I have been discussing but also because the text is a hybrid that alternates between high sociological theory and the direct voices of

those in the working class. It is one of the few academic books that lets working-class voices speak, though the result of shifting between theoretic and everyday discourses, between monologic and dialogic styles, is at first startling and unsettling. Often, I find student texts that challenge all my ideas of good writing. Interesting student texts do not follow the maxims and advice ladled out in spoonfuls by the composition textbook and the teacher. The most structured of student texts often confuse the reader, while texts that break the rules of the parts and, instead, are arranged according to principles of flow work better. Texts that seem to fail also interest me. I suppose that interest explains my preference for Shaughnessy's *Errors and Expectations* over all the volumes I have so far come across that display examples of "good" student writing. Those good-writing examples always seem fake to me, set academic pieces, theme writing —high tech and glossy and slick but theme writing just the same. Shaughnessy's student texts are vibrant and alive with the world, for all their errors and blurrings and awkwardnesses. All these strange texts excite me because they include a diversity of voices, lots of reported speech, lots of boundary blurring. I put them forward as exemplars of Vološinov's dialogic-pictorial style and perhaps as models for a new sort of good writing. I find many such texts in working-class literature courses, which usually exist in English departments under the rubric of folklore courses.

6.   I try to democratically distribute narrative rights. Whom do we allow to tell stories? What kind of stories? How do we integrate narrative into our courses? How do we connect narrative with other writing? We English teachers have tended to reserve narrative for elite literature classes. Or maybe, as a developmental sop, we have let remedial writers briefly tell stories, but not too many and not for too long. We have marginalized narrative. We have dichotomized prose into narration versus exposition. We feel that our students should be devoting more time to exposition; they already know how to tell stories, and that certainly is not the sort of writing that later courses and jobs will demand of them. These two genres—narration and exposition—need to be blurred. We need to create assignments that integrate these two sorts of writing, assignments that demand that one form continuously illuminate the other. Narrative is accessible to our students and taps deep reservoirs of experience, experience that may be further reflected on in expository modes, if we must keep these distinctions. We need to encourage student narratives and our own.

As the six strategies reviewed here suggest, ideology influences not only the big actions, the big decisions. Ideology is not simply a matter of overt political indoctrination. It is not simply a matter of English departments teaching elite literature by using elite technologies of reading and in the process sifting out, alienating, and disposing of most working-class students. Reigning social relations can also be effectively reproduced or transformed in the most common-place, ordinary, everyday moments. One of these moments is the evaluative moment, that still, silent time when two universes collide, when two styles vie for dominion, when I, as teacher, decide either to give in to or refrain from making moves that coerce writers to "pass."

As the Old Testament shows us, momentous meetings do not always follow majestic portents and open displays of power. In the Book of Kings we are told that God did not appear to Elijah after the strong storm. Nor was God in the loud earthquake. Nor did God arise from the blinding fire. God, instead, appeared in the still, small voice. So, too, in my world, some of the most momentous meetings of minds and of classes happen when I hear and heed another still, small voice, when I listen for it in the silences and between the silences. When it speaks, I, too, cover my face with my mantle, not out of fear or passivity or surrender but out of awe.

WORKS CITED

Auerbach, Erich. *Mimesis: The Representation of Reality in Western Literature.* Trans. William Trask. Princeton: Princeton UP, 1953.

Berlin, James. *Rhetoric and Reality: Writing Instruction in American Colleges 1900–1985.* Carbondale: Southern Illinois UP, 1987.

Flower, Linda. "Writer-Based Prose: A Cognitive Basis for Problems in Writing." *College English* 41.1 (1979): 19–37.

Heath, Shirley Brice. *Ways with Words: Language, Life, and Work in Communities and Classrooms.* New York: Cambridge UP, 1983.

Nader, Laura. "Up the Anthropologist: Perspectives Gained from Studying Up." *Reinventing Anthropology.* Ed. Dell Hymes. New York: Pantheon, 1972. 284–311.

Ohmann, Richard. *English in America.* New York: Oxford UP, 1976.

Olsen, Tillie. *Silences.* New York: Bantam, 1978.

Sennett, Richard, and Jonathan Cobb. *The Hidden Injuries of Class.* New York: Vintage, 1973.

Shaughnessy, Mina P. *Errors and Expectations: A Guide for the Teacher of Basic Writing.* New York: Oxford UP, 1977.

Terkel, Studs. *Working.* New York: Avon, 1972.

Vološinov, Valentin. *Marxism and the Philosophy of Language.* Cambridge: Harvard UP, 1986.

Part Two

SPEAKING OUT
OF THE SILENCES

"Knowledge Is Power":
The Black Struggle for Literacy

Thomas Holt

More than a century ago, on a fall day in 1865, a group of black men—many of them recently freed from slavery, some of them having marched under arms with the Union army to destroy slavery—gathered at the Zion Church in Charleston, South Carolina. Their purpose was to protest the actions of another convention, one controlled by white Southerners, many of whom were former slave owners, most of whom had recently laid down their arms in the rebellion against the Union. At that white convention, a month earlier, a new constitution had been adopted for South Carolina, which in essence declared that blacks were now free from slavery but that they were not free citizens. They were denied basic civil rights; they were strongly discouraged from working at any job outside agriculture; they were denied any share in the basic services and resources of the state that whites enjoyed. In effect, the white convention had made blacks slaves again in all but name. At that time it seemed that the federal government and the northern white public were indifferent to what was going on. It was a bleak time for black Americans everywhere. So in South Carolina and in most of the other former Confederate states, black men met in conventions to petition the federal and state governments and southern white people directly to redress their grievances (Holt 9–26).

The South Carolina black men's convention passed a resolution on education:

> *Whereas,* "Knowledge is power," and an educated and intelligent people can neither be held in, nor reduced to slavery; Therefore [be it] Resolved, That we will insist upon the establishment of good schools for the thorough education of our children throughout the State; that, to this end, we will contribute freely and liberally of our means, and will earnestly and persistently urge forward every measure calculated to elevate us to the rank of a wise, enlightened and Christian people. Resolved, That we solemnly urge the parents and guardians of the young and rising generation, by the sad recollection of our *forced* ignorance and degradation in the past, and by the bright and inspiring hopes of the future, to see that schools are at once established in every neighborhood; and when so established, to see to it that every child of proper age, is kept in regular attendance upon the same. (*Proceedings* 9–10)

That resolution was adopted by a unanimous vote, and by their action those black South Carolinians expressed sentiments that were repeated in similar conventions throughout the South. Other resolutions passed by the South Carolinians emphasized that they expected no special treatment but were prepared to help themselves. They merely wished to be treated like other men, to have no obstructions put in their way, to be dealt with, they said, "as others, in equity and justice" (*Proceedings* 25).

But for them "equity and justice" required a state-supported system of universal education—schools for all regardless of color. The trouble was that universal education was not something the white ruling class in the South recognized as a right even for other whites, much less for blacks. Indeed, only during the preceding thirty years or so had education gained such recognition in many northern states. What these black Southerners proposed, then, was still a relatively radical innovation in the accepted litany of the rights of man.

How could this be? How could a people just emerging from slavery—if not slaves, still an oppressed, pariah class—take the lead on this issue? Slaves had not received the benefits of systematic education, and any effort to teach them the most rudimentary literacy skills was severely punished under most state laws. Free blacks in some parts of the South were allowed to have schools, but these were periodically shut down because of fear that the blacks were getting too uppity. And yet, here they were, free black men and former slaves, advocating the most modern of innovations in the relations between a state and its citizens—that the state was responsible for ensuring that its citizens had the means for functioning in the society. Here they were, articulating a thoroughly modern notion about the role of education in the life of the citizen: "Knowledge," they said, "is power."

It is possible—indeed, probable—that these phenomena express preexisting cultural values in the American black community, values that may well have had an African origin. We know that in Africa *griots*, the storytellers who functioned as historians of the clan, and other elders took responsibility for teaching young people as part of their socialization and preparation for adult responsibilities. We know that their instruction was not limited to crafts and skills, like carving and metalworking, nor even to religious or ritual knowledge and medicinal skills but that it included the history, values, and traditions of the family, of the clan, and of the nation. Education was intended to provide the young with a sense of one's place in that history and, thus, one's purpose in the world; a sense of obligation to kin and community, to one's ancestors and posterity. We know now that, contrary to earlier scholarship, a great deal of African culture survived in the Americas, especially when it involved cultural traits that were less dependent on material and economic life and more dependent on internally held values and beliefs. It is likely that African ideas about and valuation of education survived as well.

In the African villages, education served deeply social purposes. Traditionally and historically, for black Americans education has also served a profound social purpose; its goal is social, as well as personal, improvement—to uplift the people, to make conditions better. As James White, a black minister and Union army veteran who was a delegate to the Arkansas constitutional convention in 1868, expressed it: "The principle of schools, of education, is . . . to elevate our families" (Gutman 260). For White and his fellow black delegates, education was the key to social change; it emanates outward from the individual to the larger group—to families and communities and eventually to the nation. In this way education could change society. Knowledge was power.

Thomas Jones, a North Carolina slave who learned to read while hiding in the back of his master's store, provides eloquent testimony of the slave's idea of the potency of education. "It seemed to me," he said, "that if I could learn to read and write, this learning might, nay, I really thought it would point out to me the way to freedom, influence and real secure happiness" (Anderson 16). Unfortunately, Jones's secret attempts to educate himself also brought on him a severe and brutal whipping when he was discovered. But in a perverse way those beatings reinforced the slave's belief in the value of education. By the extraordinary efforts they made to keep blacks from learning, slave owners inadvertently acknowledged that learning was a powerful force in the world.

A few slave owners found it downright inconvenient to have illiterate slaves. Those masters who used their slaves as carpenters, millwrights, and similar skilled workers often found it useful to teach them to read and write and do simple arithmetic. So a few slave owners defied the law and educated their slaves in these basic skills. It was not that they changed their minds about slaves' being kept ignorant; they just figured it wouldn't endanger the system as a whole if *their* slaves were literate. The trouble was that there was no way to guarantee that *their* slaves wouldn't teach other people's slaves. As it turned out, their slaves could not be trusted to keep what they had learned to themselves. The record of slavery contains numerous examples of a literate slave passing on his knowledge, little though it may have been, to other slaves (Gutman; Holt 52–56; Webber 26–58).

A black woman named Deveaux in Savannah, Georgia—the heart of the old South—began a secret school for slaves in 1835 that she managed to keep open for the next thirty years. A few miles away, in Charleston, South Carolina—that breeding ground of secession—a black woman whom we know only as Miss L used a sewing class as a cover for the school she ran for slave children. Her students were cautioned always to keep a piece of sewing in their laps so that anyone coming on them wouldn't know that they were really learning to read and write. In Natchez, Mississippi, another slave woman, Milla Grandison, also taught a secret school. She had learned herself from her Kentucky master before being sold to a Mississippi slave owner. Slaves came to her hut every night and studied from 11 p.m. to 2 a.m. We have a good description of Grandison's school and her methods from a northern abolitionist.

Every window and door was carefully closed to prevent discovery. In that little school hundreds of slaves learned to read and write a legible hand. After toiling all day for their masters they crept stealthily into this back alley, each with a bundle of pitch-pine splinters for light. . . . Her number of scholars was twelve at a time, and when she had taught these to read and write she dismissed them, and again took her apostolic number and brought them up to the extent of her ability, until she had graduated hundreds.   (Gutman 261)

Grandison's students also discovered the power of knowledge in a dramatic way. A number of them wrote their own passes, which were required of slaves as they moved about on the highways, and used them to escape to Canada (Gutman 261–62).

Therefore, although most slaves were illiterate, legal interdiction could not altogether crush black efforts to become literate. Just as blacks maintained an invisible church, separate from the one that whites provided for them, they also maintained secret schools. These schools could be found in every major southern city and in countless rural communities and plantations. Their teachers were often barely literate themselves, but they passed on what little they knew to others in what one may call a chain letter of instruction. Because of these foundations established during slavery, this special form of slave resistance and revolt, Union officers and northern missionaries during and immediately after the Civil War found an educational infrastructure waiting for them in the South that provided the basis for constructing the postwar southern educational system.

Reconstruction

The traditional story of the heroic efforts of white northern missionaries who came south after the war to educate and minister to the newly freed slaves is a familiar one (see Jones; Morris). And heroic it truly was. But until now that story has neglected to chronicle the crucial contributions, financial and moral, that freed people themselves made to that effort. In fact, the former slaves themselves played the central role in building, financing, and operating the southern school system that emerged immediately after the Civil War. Impoverished former slaves voluntarily paid school tuition; purchased schoolbooks; hired, fed, boarded, and protected their teachers; constructed and maintained school buildings. They put their money, blood, sweat, and tears into those efforts. And sometimes they risked their lives to protect the schools and their teachers against the Ku Klux Klan and other violent white opposition. Their determination and devotion to their schools was legendary. As one government relief worker testified: "They will starve, and freeze themselves in order to attend school, so highly do they value the privilege of learning to read, write, and reckon . . ." (Gutman 261, 267).

One example of this determination comes to us from Richmond, Virginia, where Lizzie Parsons operated a school in 1868 in the Ebenezer Baptist Church.

All the parents had promised to contribute to what was called a fuel fund to buy wood to provide heat for the school. But 1868 was a brutally cold winter, and many of the parents were destitute. Parsons describes one such family she visited. The father had been thrown out of work; the household included four children and an invalid relative and her child. "The mother has striven in every way to get along without aid," Parsons testified, "till, at last, one of the children told me she had eaten nothing for two days. Yet they have never once failed to bring me their wood money." This family, on the brink of starvation, had kept faith with their commitment to support the education of their children (Gutman 271).

Schools like Parsons's sprang up almost everywhere immediately after Lee surrendered at Appomattox; some had appeared even during the war. This was before significant numbers of northern whites had come South, so the teachers were often former slaves or free blacks who had taught the secret schools during slavery. John Alvord, who was in charge of black education for the federal government, described the typical scene in these self-help schools:

> A cellar, a shed, a private room, perhaps an old school-house, is the place, and, in the midst of a group of thirty or forty children, an old negro in spectacles, or two or three young men surrounded by a hundred or more, themselves only in the rudiments of a spelling-book, and yet with a passion to teach what they *do* know; or a colored woman, who as a family servant had some privileges, and with a woman's compassion for her race—*these* are the institutions and the agencies [of black advancement]. (Gutman 270)

Self-help was essential to black education during the early years after the war, because state and federal efforts were either nonexistent, limited, or undependable. So the burden of supporting the schools fell on blacks themselves and on northern missionary societies. In South Carolina, for example, almost $107,000 was spent on black education for the fiscal year July 1866 through June 1867. For every $100 of this total, northern missionary societies contributed $61, and the federal government gave $23, but South Carolina's blacks themselves gave $16. Moreover, these figures do not include the value of the labor and in-kind contributions that blacks made. In Louisiana blacks set up a voluntary tax collection system to sustain public schools when the federal and state governments cut off their support for two years. In the last six months of 1867 alone, Louisiana blacks spent almost $29,000, while the government contributed less than $4,000. Blacks in Georgia organized statewide to form the Georgia Education Association, each member of which paid $3 in dues to join and an additional 25 cents a month to support black schools. Across the South in 1867 nearly half the schools in ten Southern states received financial support directly from black parents, above and beyond what they paid in state taxes. In six of those states (Delaware, Kentucky, Louisiana, Mississippi, Texas, and Arkansas), at least three of every four schools were partially financed by private funds collected from blacks (Gutman 269–293; Anderson 10–13).

These developments help explain the extraordinary emphasis that blacks placed on creating a modern educational system when they had the political means to influence state policies. By 1868 the so-called radical reconstruction had begun in the South. This was a period when blacks were allowed to vote and hold office throughout the South, and in many states they held the balance of power politically. In every state they used what power they had to ensure that a system of free public schools, open to all, was established. In most of the South this was the first time such a system had been attempted (Holt; Vaughn).

Postreconstruction

Just as black political empowerment had assured the growth of the southern public school system, black disfranchisement and suppression after 1876 ensured the virtual destruction of what blacks had built. Political power was returned to the same conservative white southerners against whom blacks had protested in 1865. The system in general was crippled, and all southerners—white, as well as black—received poor educations. But blacks were often denied schooling altogether. Nowhere did they receive the same quantity or quality of education as whites did (Rabinowitz).

At the end of the century, only 36% of southern black children four to fourteen years of age attended public school; in comparison, more than half of all southern white children attended school. Moreover, 86% of the blacks who did attend received schooling for less than six months a year. Southern states spent between two and five times as much to educate white children than to educate blacks. As late as 1910, the eleven southern states spent an average of $9.45 for each white public school student and $2.90 for each black child. Six years later, on the eve of America's entrance into World War I, the average was $10.32 for each white student but only $2.89 for each black (Anderson 148; Wright 10).

Any educator can appreciate the consequences of these budgetary discrepancies. In Jackson, Mississippi, the two black schools had class sizes averaging 75 and 125 students. In Atlanta, Georgia, the student-teacher ratio in black schools was sixty-five to one. An enduring irony of this situation was that blacks were paying taxes to support white education while receiving almost nothing in return (Grossman 247; Anderson).

Once again, blacks turned to self-help. This time their efforts were stimulated and seconded by the new philanthropic movement among such industrial capitalists as Julius Rosenwald, George Peabody, and John D. Rockefeller, Jr. They were the successors of the northern religious philanthropists of the reconstruction era. But theirs was a harder, more cynical, and self-interested brand of philanthropy. In time, blacks found themselves fighting for the right to education on two fronts—against southern whites who opposed any education at all and against the northern capitalists who wanted a brand-X education for blacks.

The causes of southern white hostility to black education were not difficult to discover. They didn't bite their tongues about what worried them about educating black people. A Virginia landowner put the question bluntly: "If we educate the Negro out of being a laborer," he said, "who is going to take his place?" The problem was, another added, "When they learn to spell dog and cat they throw away the hoe" (Anderson 96, 97).

If blacks were to receive any education at all, it had to be of a type that wouldn't change anything fundamental in the southern labor and social systems. Southern whites soon found support for their position from the so-called philanthropists, whose ostensible mission was to help blacks. Most of these men were wealthy northern capitalists who had earned and kept their fortunes by keeping a tight leash on the demands of labor. They could appreciate the need for a disciplined labor force. Unlike the religious philanthropists of old, they did not put much stock in egalitarian ideals.

William H. Baldwin, Jr., was one such man. Baldwin controlled the Southern Railroad and was on the boards of trustees of Hampton Institute and Tuskegee Institute. In those latter capacities he helped define what a safe education for blacks entailed. At a conference held in Capon Springs, West Virginia, called in 1899 to plan the course of development of black education, Baldwin had this to say:

> "The Negro and the mule is the only combination, so far, to grow cotton." The South needs him; but the South needs him educated to be a suitable citizen. Properly directed he is the best possible laborer to meet the climatic conditions of the South. He will willingly fill the more menial positions, and do the heavy work, at less wages, than the American white man or any foreign race which has yet come to our shores. This will permit the southern white laborer to perform the more expert labor, and to leave the fields, the mines, and the simpler trades for the Negro. (Anderson 82)

That was an era of depressed farm income, and men with money could exert a great deal of influence. John D. Rockefeller, Jr., was impressed by Baldwin's educational schemes and decided to underwrite the program. So he set up the General Education Board with a $1 million endowment. By 1909, he had given $53 million, and by 1921, $129 million. Rockefeller chose Wallace Buttrick to head the General Education Board, and Buttrick's ideas were much like those expressed by Baldwin. Under Buttrick's leadership the board's goal, he declared, was "[to train] the negro for the life that now is as shall make of him a producer—a servant. . . ." Buttrick was also of the opinion that, with the exception of Booker T. Washington, no blacks were yet qualified to run their own schools and fulfill those goals (Anderson 86; Spivey).

Therefore, the assistance from northern philanthropists came with strings attached: the kind of education they wanted to support would reinforce the southern system of inequality. James D. Anderson has demonstrated convincingly that, for the northern philanthropists, black education was intended to produce subservience, rather than service, and passivity, rather than power.

Blacks were forced to struggle not only against Southern whites who wanted to deny them any education at all but also against their Northern so-called allies who were advocating a system of education that undermined all that blacks had previously believed education stood for—that is, to uplift, not to keep down; to change things for the better, not to maintain the status quo; to educate for empowerment, not subordination.

Anonymous black men and women in countless communities across the South made their own humble witness for the right to an education that would matter, that would change things. The money contributed by the wealthy industrialists did provide the stimulus and the opportunity for their struggle, but in the end that money could not control the struggle.

In 1909 Julius Rosenwald, of the Sears Roebuck fortune, set up a Negro Rural Schools Fund, commonly known as the Jeanes Fund, which paid part of the salaries of county supervisors for black public schools. But there weren't many black public schools in the rural South, which is where most blacks lived. So the Jeanes teachers began organizing campaigns to raise money to build schools. Between 1913 and 1928, the Jeanes teachers helped raise about $5 million for school construction. By 1932 almost five thousand rural black schools capable of seating more than 600,000 students were built in 883 counties across fifteen southern states. These schools, which provided the core of the common school system for blacks in the rural South, came to be known as Rosenwald schools. But, in reality, Rosenwald's contribution was merely a supplement to the efforts of the local communities themselves, mainly the blacks. Altogether, Rosenwald contributed 15% of the total collected. Blacks themselves gave 17%, and local whites gave 4%. The balance, about 64%, came from public taxes, a great deal of which was collected from black taxpayers (Anderson 153).

This building campaign soon became a social movement. It belonged to the communities. It expressed their purposes, goals, and values. And so did the schools that they built. By making the success of these school-building campaigns dependent on the community, blacks checkmated the schemes of Baldwin, Rosenwald, and Buttrick to educate them for second-class citizenship (see Anderson 210–24).

A description has been preserved for us of one of these fund-raising rallies. It was held in Greene County, Alabama, in January 1925. Practically all the blacks in that county were tenant farmers who had been hard-hit by the boll-weevil infestation. They didn't have much money even in good times; now they were barely surviving. The idea of raising money to build a school seemed almost impossible. The chairman of the meeting was so full of despair that he spoke to the crowd with tears in his eyes. "We have never had a school in this vicinity," he said, "most of our children have grown into manhood and womanhood without the semblance of an opportunity to get an insight into life. . . ." (Note that the purpose of education is enlightenment.) The audience was deeply moved and fell silent. But at that moment an old man, who had been born in slavery, slowly drew from his pocket an old, greasy sack that contained all his life's earnings and emptied it on the table. "I want to see the children of my grand-children have a chance," he said, "and so I am giving my all." With that example of self-sacrifice, the rest of the audience—from whom it had seemed at first that $10 would have been a good collection—came up with a total of $1,365. When the total was announced, "they shouted and they cried and applauded. . . ." Eventually, they contributed labor and materials, as well as the money, to build a five-room school valued at $6,450 (Anderson 165).

Throughout the South came other stories like that one. In many places black farmers could not come up with the cash, but they found innovative ways to support the educational effort: they donated their labor and building materials. In Wood County, Texas, they planted a community crop of cotton—something like a "Victory Garden"—with the proceeds going to the school construction fund. In other places they called these donations their "Rosenwald Patch" (Anderson 171). Rosenwald got the credit, but the effort and the success belong to those anonymous black men, women, and children across the South who—like the old man in Greene County, Alabama—gave their all. By 1940 78% of southern blacks aged five to fourteen years were attending school, compared with 79% of southern whites. This dramatic turnaround helped lay the basis for the revolutionary changes that came to the South in the civil rights movement of the 1950s and 1960s.

Resistance to the policies of Rosenwald and Rockefeller and Baldwin and Buttrick also came from well-known black leaders like W. E. B. Du Bois, who argued powerfully against Booker T. Washington's Tuskegee idea during the early twentieth century. Resistance also came from students at Tuskegee, Fisk, Howard, and Hampton who, during the 1920s, went on strike against their school administrations and in many cases succeeded in getting new leadership. In the long run, all those struggles laid the basis for the student warriors during the civil rights movement in the late 1950s and early 1960s, because, next to the church, southern colleges were the most critical to the success of that movement.

Ironically, in time these same black colleges became unintended victims of the legal transformations that the movement achieved. The South's dual educational system had nurtured the generation that led the movement; but the idea of an integrated society that the movement aspired to has been used to attack the continued existence of that dual system. This is not a simple issue and should not be treated in a simplistic fashion; it is a poignant irony, nevertheless.

Education in the North

This history of black educational self-help in the nineteenth and early twentieth centuries must appear profoundly ironic to a late twentieth-century observer; in our time the black urban school has become a symbol for all the problems of modern education. Many people blame black parents for being insufficiently

attentive to their children's educational needs. Others even suggest that a cultural deficiency in black Americans makes them unappreciative of the value of
education: they don't try hard enough; they don't make sacrifices. But even this
brief review of the early struggles should make us skeptical of such interpretations.
Throughout our history black Americans have placed the highest value on
education and have made untold sacrifices to secure the right to an education
for themselves and their children.

What is the solution to our contemporary educational malaise? At this point
in the proceedings, we historians usually retire from the field. We are best
qualified to give the background of contemporary problems, but we have no
license to offer solutions. I do not pretend to answer that question. I can only
offer the assistance of the historian, which, at best, only helps us see contemporary problems more clearly, rather than provides the answers.

One thing is clear: blacks did not lose their hunger for education when they
left the rural South to come north during the early twentieth century. In fact,
educational opportunity was a major reason they came. The *Chicago Defender*
conducted a veritable crusade to encourage black Southerners to move north.
A headline from its 4 August 1917 edition declared: "Education Will Force
Open the Door of Hope behind Which Is Success" (Grossman 250). So you
see, it was the same traditional message: knowledge is power.

James R. Grossman's study of the southern black migration to Chicago provides ample evidence of the continued force of black aspirations for knowledge.
In Chicago of the 1920s, in vivid contrast with the situation today, the percentage of black southern migrant children attending school exceeded that of
foreign-born whites and matched that of native whites (92%). And in contrast
to white ethnic groups, black parents refused to take their children out of school
to put them to work. The black parents were committed to education, despite
the financial sacrifice (250–51).

But the Chicago experience also suggests how that enthusiasm for education
may have been dampened. Black students found few black role models among
the northern teachers of the early twentieth century. There were few black
teachers. One school with a 93% black enrollment had only six black teachers
out of forty; another school with 85% black enrollment had only two black
teachers out of thirty-three. There was no black principal in a Chicago school
until 1928. Some of the white principals openly expressed their disinclination
to hire black teachers, because of the awkwardness of interracial "intimacy"
among teachers, they said, or the "cocky" attitudes of the blacks (Grossman
254–55).

Many white teachers displayed overtly racist attitudes. They considered blacks
intellectually inferior. As one female principal of a 70% black elementary school
put it: "The great physical development of the colored person takes away from
the mental, while with the whites the reverse is true." The proof for this, she
claimed, could be found in the Bible in the last chapter of Ecclesiastes (Grossman
255).

Blacks were placed in special classrooms, called "subnormal rooms," within integrated schools. About three-quarters of the southern black migrants were classified as mentally deficient somehow. An elaborate scheme of classification was used, ranging from "feebleminded" and "defective" to "retarded" and "backward." By 1925 only one in eight such students made it back into the "mainstream" classes (Grossman 251–52).

Once again, the education that blacks received was not one intended to elevate, to uplift, and to empower but to make passive. According to a contemporary defender of this system, it was "designed for a type of child who has little interest in and is unable to learn academic work." The curriculum and the teaching that blacks received was consistent with the belief that black children were "less ambitious, less self-disciplined, and less intelligent." "Negroes," concluded the principal of one school, "need a curriculum especially adapted to their emotional natures" (Grossman 255).

The experiences of those students must have cast severe doubt on the traditional black belief that knowledge is power. Black Chicagoans found that schooling made little difference in their job prospects; they still received manual-labor jobs when they graduated. One truant black youth asked, "What work can I get if I go through school?" A contemporary survey of Pittsburgh during that period suggests that the answer to that question was discouraging. Despite their ambitions for white-collar employment, 56% of the graduates of a black girls' high school ended up as domestic servants, and for black boys the most likely white-collar position was as a clerk in a gambling establishment. A United States Office of Education study in 1940 concluded, with unintended irony, that higher educational attainment merely made blacks more "dissatisfied" with their jobs (Grossman 257–58).

We all know that a great deal has changed since the 1920s and 1930s. But it is equally clear that race still shapes the opportunities and the life chances of black Americans. A 1984 study has demonstrated that in 1959 a black man living in the same region of the country and with the same education and years of experience as his white colleague earned only 81% as much an hour as the white man. By 1979 things had improved, but the black man still earned only 88% as much as the white man (Farley).

By no means am I suggesting that education no longer matters. I believe that knowledge is intrinsically empowering in all kinds of ways, both overt and subtle. All I mean to suggest is that education, as a system and as we perceive it, does not stand off in pristine isolation from the main currents in the society. Throughout our history—through the cruelties of slavery, through the disappointments of reconstruction, through the brutal repressions of the years after reconstruction—through all those periods, black people have held on to the belief that literacy is one of the keys that will unlock the door. Like Thomas Jones, they believed "it would point the way to freedom, and really secure happiness"—not only for individuals but for the whole community (Anderson 16). But their ability to hold on to that faith depended on whether it was reinforced in their life experiences, in the classrooms, and in the society as a whole. It is in this sense, I think, that education must be relevant to the lives that people live.

I believe that there still is a great fund of enthusiasm for education in the black community. It is the fruit of a heritage of struggle. It is the legacy, sometimes written in blood, of "many thousands gone." We can tap into that fund of enthusiasm if we are true to that heritage, if we build on that legacy, if we—black and white—who take on the profound responsibility of educators also take their creed: offer our knowledge not as a means to conformity or submission but as a way to uplift, a way to change society for the better, a way to power.[1]

NOTE

[1]This paper was originally prepared for oral delivery. I acknowledge my profound debt to the published work on black education by James R. Grossman, James D. Anderson, and the late Herbert G. Gutman.

WORKS CITED

Anderson, James D. *The Education of Blacks in the South, 1860–1935.* Chapel Hill: U of North Carolina P, 1988.

Farley, Reynolds. *Blacks and Whites: Narrowing the Gap?* Cambridge: Harvard UP, 1984.

Grossman, James R. *Land of Hope: Chicago, Black Southerners, and the Great Migration.* Chicago: U of Chicago P, 1989.

Gutman, Herbert G. "Schools for Freedom: The Post-Emancipation Origins of Afro-American Education." *Power and Culture: Essays on the American Working Class.* Ed. Ira Berlin. New York: Pantheon, 1987. 260–97.

Holt, Thomas. *Black over White: Negro Political Leadership in South Carolina during Reconstruction.* Urbana: U of Illinois P, 1977.

Jones, Jacqueline. *Soldiers of Light and Love: Northern Teachers and Georgia Blacks, 1865–1873.* Chapel Hill: U of North Carolina P, 1980.

Morris, Robert C. *Reading, Writing, and Reconstruction: The Education of Freedmen in the South, 1861–1870.* Chicago: U of Chicago P, 1981.

Proceedings of the Colored People's Convention of the State of South Carolina Held in Zion Church, Charleston, November, 1865. Charleston: South Carolina Leader Office, 1865.

Rabinowitz, Howard N. *Race Relations in the Urban South, 1865–1890.* New York: Oxford UP, 1978.

Spivey, Donald. *Schooling for the New Slavery: Black Industrial Education, 1868–1915.* Westport: Greenwood, 1978.

Vaughn, William P. *Schools for All: The Blacks and Public Education in the South, 1865–1877.* Lexington: U of Kentucky P, 1974.

Webber, Thomas L. *Deep like the Rivers: Education in the Slave Quarter Community, 1831–1865.* New York: Norton, 1978.

Wright, Gavin. *Old South, New South: Revolutions in the Southern Economy since the Civil War.* New York: Basic, 1986.

Perspectives on the Intellectual Tradition of Black Women Writers

Jacqueline Jones Royster

In her 1974 essay "In Search of Our Mothers' Gardens," Alice Walker issued the scholarly community a challenge, as pointedly articulated in this passage:

> What did it mean for a Black woman to be an artist in our grandmothers' time? In our great-grandmothers' day? It is a question with an answer cruel enough to stop the blood. . . . How was the creativity of the Black woman kept alive, year after year and century after century, when for most of the years Black people have been in America, it was a punishable crime for a Black person to read or write? And the freedom to paint, to sculpt, to expand the mind with action did not exist. Consider, if you can bear to imagine it, what might have been the result if singing, too, had been forbidden by law. Listen to the voices of Bessie Smith, Billie Holiday, Nina Simone, Roberta Flack, and Aretha Franklin, among others, and imagine those voices muzzled for life. (233–34)

Walker paints a provocative image of the creative and intellectual impulses of African American women and raises questions that cut to the core of concepts like justice, equity, empowerment, and the actualization of potential. What she demonstrates through this milestone literary event is that—despite the bonds of slavery, despite laws that forbade basic literacy skills, despite incomprehensible barriers in all dimensions of their lives—black women were still bold enough to keep raising their voices. And, despite a myth that still dies hard, many of them wrote down their words. By doing so, they helped fashion a creative and intellectual authority, a garden that has yielded models of productivity and achievement for black women who are continuing to define and redefine intellectual possibilities.

Worth noting is the rarity of encountering the words *intellectual* and *black women* in the same sentence. The rarity, though, is not the fault of black women. It is the fault of entrenched systems of racism, sexism, and classism that do not permit justice, equity, or the freedom to see worth and value from whichever quarter they arise. Consequently, any analysis of the lives and the achievements of black women but clearly an analysis of their intellectual tradition must provide a conscious crediting of the effects of interlocking systems of oppression.

When we look with an informed eye at the ways in which black women have used writing over time, it should be immediately obvious that there was a struggle for basic literacy. All black people had to struggle for the right to learn, for the right to have access to the tools of learning, of empowerment, of privilege. Black women have had to struggle in desperation not just against racist and economic barriers but also against sexist barriers. Even so, a historical view of the ways in which African American women have used writing assures us that we are not looking at just a struggle for basic literacy. Over the centuries, there has been more going on in what black women write than just novice beginnings, practice, or five-finger exercises in thought and expression. In acknowledging a literacy continuum that distinguishes between the basically literate and those who accomplish stellar feats in using their literacy skills, we see that black women have gone well beyond the first spirals of hierarchical notions of literacy. They have established themselves not just as readers and writers but as master artisans and visionaries—that is, they belong to the central traditions of the literate world at its best.

In trying to establish a firm basis for making such an assertion, we can look synchronically at the diverse literary achievements of contemporary black women writers to identify connections across their lives and works, and we can look at the diverse literary achievements of black women historically. In addition, we can look diachronically at the resonating threads that speak to connections among current achievements, lives, conditions, and circumstances and their antecedents. With such information, we can begin to reconstruct a full image of our mothers' gardens—that is, the origins of the creative and intellectual authority of black women writers, as Hazel V. Carby has done in her pacesetting analysis, *Reconstructing Womanhood: The Emergence of the Afro-American Woman Novelist*.

The collective visions of writers like Gwendolyn Brooks, Alice Walker, Toni Morrison, Gloria Naylor, Paule Marshall, and Lorraine Hansberry have demonstrated that black women have a unique view and understanding of the human condition. They have chronicled lives, perspectives, and circumstances in ways that we have not known before. As evidenced by their receiving of prestigious awards and prizes in the literary world, black women writers are acknowledged as among the best writers in the United States, even in the world. They have a way with words, and both popular and scholarly critics have hailed these days to be a renaissance for black women writers.

In the tradition of scholarship, the acknowledgment of a renaissance carries with it an imperative to be mindful that nothing happens in a vacuum. The imperative dictates that we must search for origins, foundations, precedents, and foreshadowings, so that we have a substantive sense of what the renaissance is. These women did not spring forth from nothing and nowhere. Instead, they have been instrumental in continuing a creative trust, a tradition established by earlier black women writers. They join their predecessors in forming a continuous community of creativity and productivity from the 1700s to the present.

The voices of African American women have been a part of the American literary scene since the days of the black and unknown bards of spirituals and folklore, although they have not always been credited. As Louis Gates, Jr., and Ann Allen Shockley have pointed out, black women launched the African American literate tradition: Phillis Wheatley with the first volume of poetry in 1773; Ann Plato with the first book of essays in 1841; Harriet E. Wilson with the first novel in 1859; Frances Ellen Watkins Harper with the first short story during that same year; Frances Anne Rollins, using the pseudonym Frank A. Rollins, with the first biography in 1868; and so on. Over the centuries the voices of black women have been raised and, within marginalized contexts, occasionally have been heard, though categorized most often as minor voices, not major ones. This categorization was created and continues to exist in spite of a rising mound of evidence documenting the critical roles that black women have filled socially, culturally, and artistically.

Regardless of how others have seen them and their efforts, however, over the centuries black women have demonstrated systematically the central place that literacy has held in their lives. They have continued to write. They have articulated lives and conditions with courage, compassion, insight. They have offered to the world more than it has been willing to receive.

In essence, though, black women writers have for all practical purposes met the same fate as other women. They have been ignored, disregarded, marginalized, trampled, neglected, devalued, and forgotten. After all, as Mary Helen Washington contends,

> What we have to recognize is that the creation of the fiction of tradition is a matter of power, not justice, and that that power has always been in the hands of men—mostly white but some black. Women are the disinherited. (xvii–xviii)

For no one is that statement more true than for black women.

What does this perspective indicate about the intellectual capacities of black women or about them not just as creative beings but as intellectual beings who engage in activities that demonstrate the higher literacy skills of problem finding and problem solving? How have they contributed to the world of ideas and the progress of humanity in understanding ourselves and the universe? What is the tradition of black feminist thought?

To see and to understand the tradition of black women's intellectualism, we must enrich our definitions of *tradition*, *literacy*, and *intellectualism*, and then we must use this enriched vision to look again at the historical evidence of the ways in which black women have used their literacy. This framework can help us distinguish the significant threads and begin a thorough documentation of the nature of black women's intellectualism.

Tradition is defined by *Webster's Ninth New Collegiate Dictionary* as

> **1:** an inherited, established, or customary pattern of thought, action, or behavior (as a religious practice or a social custom) **2:** the handing down of information,

beliefs, and customs by word of mouth or by example from one generation to another without written instruction 3: cultural continuity in social attitudes and institutions 4: characteristic manner, method, or style.

Such definitions, however, do not go far enough in establishing what manner of circumstance a tradition is. What does it mean to claim a history? How are we empowered to see patterns and to assign value? By what manner and mechanisms are we authorized to count time or to credit experience?

Historically, the institutions of power and prestige have not afforded the experiences and contributions of black women the privilege of being considered for entry into a dialogue on historical or traditional values and contributions. The assumption was that there is no such history, no such tradition, no such value, and, of course, no such contributions. Consequently, the claiming of the status of tradition for black women's intellectualism is an act that goes radically against the tide. It is an act of empowerment. The power comes from having access to what Deirdre David terms "intellectual ancestry" (226). Emphatically, contemporary black women writers did not just spring forth; they evolved from prior communities of remarkably active women who created, preserved, nurtured, and passed along a rich legacy of habits of mind, spirit, and action.

The process of revealing the tradition of black feminist thought is a process of placing the historical events of black women's intellectually based activities within the meaningful scheme of their lives. It means coming to an understanding of their particular habits of mind, spirit, and action, and it means demonstrating that these particular events are recurrent, reflective, resonant and that there are echoes and reverberations throughout the totality of their experiences in this country.

At this point, we can place the definition of *tradition* against predominant visions of literacy. Too often, definitions of *literacy* are simplistic, referring generally to the ability to read and write as isolated activities. These definitions often do not take into account the complexities of the context in which literacy acts take place. Fortunately, the efforts of scholar-activists like Paolo Freire and Geneva Smitherman are bringing light to the dialogue, but threads recognizing the implications of narrow frames for concepts like literacy are not new. For example, during the struggle for women's suffrage and in response particularly to literacy requirements for the right to vote, Sojourner Truth said, "You know, children, I don't read such small stuff as letters, I read men and nations" (Lowenberg and Bogin 239). Truth could not read or write texts, but she did see that being unlettered does not automatically indicate an inability to think or to understand or to operate rationally. What her statement implies is that one set of tools for reading was not available to her, but other tools were, and she was able to use the available tools with power and authority.

From this point of departure, our visions of literacy can be enriched. As Jerrie Cobb Scott has conceptualized it, literacy includes at the core our ways of knowing, our multisensory ways of coming to awareness. It means developing the ability to gain access to information—for example, by being able to read, write, and see what is there and not there—and also developing the ability to use the information well, as in analytically and creatively finding and solving problems. It is more than deciphering and producing little letters on a page. Literacy is the skill, the process, the practice of "reading" and being articulate about "men and nations," which is more than just simplistic, isolated decoding and encoding skills.

Sojourner Truth was not literate enough to read "such small stuff as letters," but she was able to see what was there and not there, to grapple with complex situations, and to emerge as a rational and capable thinker. With the changing literacy demands of current cultural contexts, however, becoming literate does mean gaining the skills to read and to write; beyond that, it also means taking the power and the authority to know in multisensory ways and to act with authority based on that knowing. Knowledge is indeed power. In our day and time, literacy is indeed power. It allows us, as Mary Helen Washington weaves the notion throughout much of her analysis of black women writers, to write ourselves into being and, by doing so, to claim creative and intellectual power over information and experience. Like the claiming of a tradition, a move toward literacy is a political act.

Next is the pivotal centerpiece of black feminist thought, the concept of intellectualism. The politics of tradition claiming and the politics of literacy, with their ties to power and empowerment, often pale against the politics of claiming the self as an intellectual being. *Webster's Ninth New Collegiate Dictionary* defines *intellect* as

> **1a:** the power of knowing as distinguished from the power to feel and to will: the capacity for knowledge **b:** the capacity for rational or intelligent thought esp. when highly developed **2:** a person with great intellectual powers.

A contrasting view of intellectualism has been put forth by other scholars. Bell Hooks explains that the intellectual is a whole person, one centered in a life of the spirit, body, and mind and one who brings the possibility of wholeness and nonfragmentation to bear on experience, integrating intellect and passion. This more holistic view of intellectualism does not allow for the separation of analytical and creative thought from an ethical core or physical existence. This view takes into account what Lowenberg and Bogin explain as "psychic wholeness," from which a person is able to fashion an inner core that is capable of being used to "take soundings, establish directions, discern the self"—in other words, to operate as an intellectual being (8–14, 9).

The lives of black women in America are a testament to "psychic wholeness," to the way in which the experience of fragmentation, particularly the horrors and the remnants of the institution of slavery, can be defeated by persistence, resiliency, and an ability to remain whole. As Paula Giddings points out, black women were able to emerge from fragmentation, "whole, courageous, and loving." They were also able to emerge moving and shaking the world around them. If we start with the documentary evidence of the nineteenth century, text after text demonstrates that black women put their minds to the task of living lives after slavery, envisioning wide-ranging possibilities, creating multifaceted options, conceptualizing ways of reifying ideas and ideals, and putting thought into action.

If we examine the body of nineteenth- and early twentieth-century texts that are becoming available, we can easily see patterns emerging that highlight the tradition of black feminist thought. These women played critical roles as the interpreters and as the articulators of experiences. They had a penchant for contextualizing and centering pieces of the puzzle of black people's lives in the United States that did not fit. They had the capacity to imagine doable things within adverse circumstances. They were committed to putting thought into meaningful action, doing so in response to issues related to the abolition of slavery and racism and to education, economic opportunity, religion, lynchings, women's rights, the moral integrity of black women. Generally, they were the champions of truth, justice, and equality. They transmitted black American culture as mothers (actual and fictive), teachers, and social activists. They demonstrated a fully developed range of intellectual activity. In an adaptation of Joseph Williams's definition of critical thinking (Royster 3), they looked at the world, saw what was there and not there, were articulate about their visions of reality, and worked tirelessly to get things done that they thought would bring their ideals to life.

The validation for these assertions lies in the indisputable evidence of the lives of the women who set the standard. Fortunately, we know about their activities, their thoughts, and their feelings because they wrote them down. Some of them chose to express themselves through creative writing: Lucy Terry, Phillis Wheatley, Sarah Forten, and Harriet E. Wilson, each of whom wrote before 1860, and Frances E. W. Harper, Alice Dunbar Nelson, and Pauline Hopkins, each of whom were first published before 1900. Through poetry, short stories, plays, and novels, these early black women writers raised the banner of sociopolitical activism, condemning the injustice and the inequities of racist, sexist, and economic oppressions. They expressed themselves beautifully and insightfully on the misery and the misfortune of black people and on their strength and beauty. They used their writing to appreciate the people and the world around them, to discover personal identity by race and gender, to define and label relationships, to address sociocultural issues, to respond to power, and to offer solutions to pressing problems. From this body of texts, we have much to learn about black women's ways of knowing, thinking, and operating.

In their creative works, writers take on the facades of character, persona, and narrator, distancing themselves from their texts by the fact of the fiction-ness, regardless of the representativeness of the creative vision. In contrast, in their nonfiction works, writers have the privilege of speaking more candidly as themselves and not just as their creative-intellectual inventions. Fortunately, in documenting the tradition of black women's intellectualism, we have the advantage of a relatively large pool of nonfiction texts. Whether as creative writers or as writers of nonfiction prose, black women established their intellectual worth through persistent and courageous action. They spoke up and out, and they spoke often.

Like Sojourner Truth, several black women made speeches to carry the abolitionist message (see Quarles), but not all were unlettered, like Truth. The first black female public speaker was Maria Stewart in 1832 (see Giddings, *When and Where I Enter*; Quarles). A freeborn woman from Connecticut, Stewart was sponsored by the Afric-American Female Intelligence Society of Boston, one of the early black female literary societies (see Porter). Against societal norms, this organization boldly invited not just a woman but a black woman to speak before a mixed audience of men and women on the substantive issues of civil and women's rights. This act made Stewart the first American-born woman to give public speeches and to leave extant copies of the texts. According to Giddings, Stewart's speeches "articulated the precepts upon which the future activism of Black women would be based. Her ideas reflected both the fundamentals of the Victorian ethic and criticism of its inherent biases" (*When and Where* 50). Stewart was followed by Nancy Prince, Harriet Tubman, Sarah Parker Remond, Sojourner Truth, Frances Ellen Watkins Harper, Ida Wells-Barnett, Fannie Barrier Williams, and a continuing cadre of others (Lowenberg and Bogin 6).

Despite these individual achievements, however, literacy was still exceptional. The struggle for educational opportunities was constant. In the racist and sexist realities of the nineteenth- and early twentieth-century publishing world, there was a critical lack of systems and resources designed to nurture talent among women generally and black women in particular. As Anna Julia Cooper—who was born a slave but who became a scholar, an educator, a pioneer in the black club women's movement, and a social activist—wrote, "I constantly felt (as I suppose many an ambitious girl has felt) a thumping from within unanswered by any beckoning from without" (76). In *A Voice from the South*, published in 1892, Cooper appeals to American society to make, in her words, "not the boys less, but the girls more" (79). As a single text, *A Voice from the South* remains Cooper's most representative effort, and it stands today as one of the earliest and best historical resources for black feminist thought. It gives much sustenance to the contemplative mind and challenges any scholar who may question the historical depth of an intellectual tradition for black American women.

In a section of the book entitled "The Status of Woman in America," Cooper explains that even her black male contemporaries—who, she believed, should be more sensitive to the conditions of black women and more supportive of their efforts—would not admit a need for the voice of black women. She presents a long list of social and economic debates in American life from which black women are excluded. While Cooper identifies the political advantage of men, she also points out that

> politics, and surely American politics, is hardly a school for great minds. Sharpening rather than deepening, it develops the faculty of taking advantage of present emergencies rather than the insight to distinguish between the true and the false, the lasting and the ephemeral advantage. Highly cultivated selfishness rather than consecrated benevolence is its passport to success.   (137)

Her insightful argument is grounded in both a breadth and a depth of knowledge. Her words are rationally ordered and developed. Her language is powerful, and her images are compelling. Most of all, her insights are fired by her belief in her position. The book is her attempt to help a troubled nation see its problems more clearly and her attempt to offer solutions that she believed to be reasonable and productive.

In Cooper's estimation, "The world has had to limp along with the wobbling gait and one-sided hesitancy of a man with one eye" (122), with the bandaged eye symbolizing the feminine perspective. She speaks of black women as the "muffled chord," the "mute and voiceless note" (i), and she insists that they be heard:

> The colored woman, then, should not be ignored because her bark is resting in the silent waters of the sheltered cove. She is watching the movements of the contestants none the less and is all the better qualified, perhaps, to weigh and judge and advise because not herself in the excitement of the race. Her voice, too, has always been heard in clear, unfaltering tones, ringing the changes on those deeper interests which make for permanent good.   (138)

A Voice from the South, as the preeminent historical text in black feminist thought, is enlightening, but Cooper was not the only early standard-bearer of this intellectual tradition. Our visions of the history of black women's literacy and intellectualism can benefit even more from an examination of a wide-ranging body of early texts. The list of women who wrote speeches, essays, journals, biographies, autobiographies, and newspaper and magazine articles is an impressive one that includes, in addition to the names mentioned earlier, Charlotte Forten Grimké, Lucy Craft Laney, Fanny Jackson Coppin, Amanda Berry Smith, Mary Church Terrell, Josephine St. Pierre Ruffin, Nanny Burroughs, and Amy Jacques Garvey.

In producing both creative and nonfiction texts, these early black women writers passed on the intellectual torch. They demonstrated by their examples what it means to live a committed life, what it means to think and to act from the same body, to operate with reason, passion, and compassion. They gave evidence of the creativity and the productivity of an attitude that nurtures not only the notion of being thoughtful and rational but also the notion of the obligation to act in ways that make a positive difference in the lives of human beings.

A major dimension of their intellectual legacy is the notion of psychic wholeness. As a culture, we have reaped the rewards of this wholeness. We have benefited from their thoughts and actions, as evidenced, for example, by the number of their social, economic, and political programs that have changed, often in unacknowledged ways, the course of our modern lives. We have failed, however, to give credit to the quality of their intellectual, creative, and socially conscious vision.

At the 1851 Women's Rights Convention in Akron, Ohio, Sojourner Truth said:

> they talk about this thing in the head; what's this they call it? ["Intellect," whispered someone near.] That's it, honey. What's that got to do with women's rights or negro rights? If my cup won't hold but a pint, and yours holds a quart, wouldn't you be mean not to let me have my little half-measure full? (Lowenberg and Bogin 236)

Similarly, in *A Voice from the South*, Cooper urges the nation to forget about the problem of race and to concentrate on encouraging all members of the races to do their best. She says:

> God and time will work the problem. You and I are only to stand for the quantities *at their best*, which he means for us to represent . . . and so if a few are determined to be white—amen, so be it; but don't let them argue as if there were no part to be played in life by black men and black women, and as if to become white were the sole specific and panacea for all the ills that flesh is heir to—the universal solvent for all America's irritations. (171–72)

Today especially, we need the full potential of all our diverse citizenry, male and female, regardless of race, creed, color, cultural orientation, or background. What is certain is that, to take advantage of these wide-ranging possibilities, we must have the types of mental constructs that allow the envisioning of human diversity as a positive and productive fact of contemporary life. In the case of black women's literacy and intellectualism, the evidence speaks for itself. Black women have offered to this culture more than just a "half-measure." If we can right the injustice of their exclusion from intellectual domains, the process of our rectification may allow us to envision more productively other persons whom we now categorize as marginal, nontraditional, or illiterate.

Another of Cooper's statement in 1892 is all the more relevant for us almost a century later: "We need men and women who do not exhaust their genius splitting hairs on aristocratic distinctions and thanking God they are not as others" (33). At this critical point in our nation's history, we need people to recognize that difference and diversity constitute opportunities for richness and that the acknowledgment of any potential does not lessen the value of the whole but strengthens it.

WORKS CITED

Carby, Hazel V. *Reconstructing Womanhood: The Emergence of the Afro-American Woman Novelist.* New York: Oxford UP, 1987.

Cooper, Anna Julia. *A Voice from the South.* New York: Oxford UP, 1988.

David, Deirdre. *Intellectual Women and Victorian Patriarchy: Harriet Martineau, Elizabeth Barrett Browning, George Eliot.* Ithaca: Cornell UP, 1987.

Freire, Paolo. *Pedagogy of the Oppressed.* New York: Continuum, 1988.

Gates, Henry Louis, Jr. "Foreword: In Her Own Write." Cooper vii–xxii.

Giddings, Paula. Panelist. Forum on Black Women's Intellectualism. Spelman College. Atlanta, 24 Nov. 1986. Forum proceedings forthcoming. *Sage: A Scholarly Journal on Black Women.*

————. *When and Where I Enter: The Impact of Black Women on Race and Sex in America.* New York: Morrow, 1984.

Hooks, Bell. Panelist. Forum on Black Women's Intellectualism. Spelman College. Atlanta, 24 Nov. 1986. Forum proceedings forthcoming. *Sage: A Scholarly Journal on Black Women.*

Lowenberg, Bert J., and Ruth Bogin, eds. *Black Women in Nineteenth Century American Life: Their Words, Their Thoughts, Their Feelings.* University Park: Pennsylvania State UP, 1976.

Porter, Dorothy. "The Organized Educational Activities of Negro Literary Societies, 1828–1846." *Journal of Negro Education* 5.4 (1936): 555–76.

Quarles, Benjamin. *Black Abolitionists.* New York: Oxford UP, 1969.

Royster, Jacqueline Jones. *Critical Thinking Pilot Project: Summary Report.* Atlanta: Spelman Coll. Comprehensive Writing Program, 1987.

Scott, Jerrie Cobb. Coordinator. A Literacy across the Disciplines Workshop for Faculty and Administrators. Central State University. Wilberforce, Ohio, 28 Jan. 1988.

Scott, Jerrie Cobb, and Bing Davis. "A Picture Is Worth a Thousand Words: The Visual-Print Connection." *Dialogue: Arts in the Midwest* (Nov.-Dec. 1989): 19–21.

Shockley, Ann Allen. *Afro-American Women Writers, 1746–1933.* Boston: Hall, 1988.

Smitherman, Geneva. "Toward a National Public Policy on Language." *College English* 49.1 (1987): 29–36.

Walker, Alice. "In Search of Our Mothers' Gardens." *In Search of Our Mothers' Gardens.* New York: Harcourt, 1983. 231–243.

Washington, Mary Helen. *Invented Lives: Narratives of Black Women 1860–1960.* Garden City: Anchor, 1987.

Webster's Ninth New Collegiate Dictionary. 1986 edition.

Censorship and Spiritual Education

James Moffett

In addressing this subject, I wish to distinguish spirituality from morality and religion. Morality concerns good and bad behavior. As the root meanings of both *morals* and *ethics* indicate, these words derive from the customs of some group, an ethos, and too often tend to apply only to members of that group. As its root meaning suggests, religion aims to tie individuals back to some less apparent reality from which they have been diverted by, presumably, people and other attractive hazards in the environment. However divinely inspired, any religion partakes of a certain civilization, functions through human institutions, and is, therefore, culturally biased. Precisely because of this partiality and even partisanship, our devoutly Christian Founding Fathers refrained from making theirs the state religion and rightly forbade any theocracy.

Spirituality, by contrast, is the perception of oneness behind the plurality of things, peoples, and other forms; spiritual behavior is the acting on this perception. Thus, morality follows from spirituality, because the more that people identify with others, the better they act toward them. The supreme identification, of oneself with the One, brings about that reunion toward which religions work at the same time that it makes morality apply beyond the in-group to the world at large. So a spiritual education can accomplish moral and religious education but without moralizing or indoctrinating.

American schools have had to face directly the dilemma of *e pluribus unum* —a single curriculum for a pluralistic populace. In 1974 the most tumultuous and significant textbook controversy that North America has ever known broke out in Kanawha County, West Virginia. The textbooks teachers choose from today are limited by what happened there then. Ignoring the fundamentalist Appalachian part of its constituency, the district selected $450,000 worth of reading and language arts textbooks that fulfilled a state mandate for multicultural materials. Among these was a K–12 program that I had directed called Interaction.

By the time school started on 3 September, book protesters, stirred into action by a new school board member, had organized themselves for tough activist tactics borrowed from the labor movement. Led by fundamentalist ministers from the hills and hollows of the upper valley, they kept their children home from school and threatened other parents who did not, picketed mines until the miners struck, barricaded some trucking companies, demonstrated outside the board building in defiance of court injunctions, and on 10 September got city bus drivers to suspend service in sympathy.

The next day, the school board announced that it was withdrawing the books until a citizens review committee could report on them. But disruption escalated. At each of two picket points a man was wounded by gunfire. Cars were smashed, and a CBS television crew was roughed up. Extremist protesters fired on school buses returning from their rounds and even firebombed two elementary schools at night. Leaders of both sides were threatened and guarded. On 13 September, the safety of both children and adults seemed so much at risk that the super-intendent shut down all public schools for a four-day weekend, during which he and the school board slipped out of town. The whole county bordered on anarchy.

After delaying its climactic meeting for a week following a dynamite blast in its building, the school board voted 8 November on the recommendations of its citizens review committee. The majority of the committee members asked for the return of virtually all the books to the classrooms, and the minority rejected virtually all the books. The board decided to return all but the most controversial series and the senior high portion of Interaction, which were consigned to libraries. Protest activities abated when Governor Arch Moore finally allowed state troopers to reinforce county sheriffs, and they ended in the spring, after one of the ministers leading the revolt was sentenced to three years in prison for his part in firebombing a school.

The creek preachers have done me a great favor. They have made me think about the many ways we all suppress knowledge outside and repress it inside and about why we do so. Let me mention what these fundamentalists objected to in our books. In 1982 I interviewed three of the protest leaders in Kanawha County. I have studied carefully the criticisms that dissenting members of the citizens review committee wrote about particular selections in the disputed books. I have written an account and interpretation of the Kanawha County controversy as a book, *Storm in the Mountains: A Case Study of Censorship, Conflict, and Consciousness.* In trying to see more deeply by the light of this incendiary episode, I have honored most what meant most to the objectors, their religious beliefs and values.

In plain human terms the protesters feared losing their children. Books (like television) bypass the oral culture—hearth and ethos—and thus may weaken local authority and control. Perhaps all parents fear having their children men-tally kidnapped by voices from other milieus and ideologies. The rich range of ideas and viewpoints, the multicultural smorgasbord, of the books adopted in Kanawha County were exactly what fundamentalists don't want. They believe that most of the topics English teachers think make good discussion are about matters they consider already settled. The invitation to reopen such subjects through pluralistic readings, role-playing, values clarification, personal writing, and open-ended discussion can only be taken as an effort to indoctrinate their children in the atheistic freethinking of the Eastern-seaboard liberal establishment that scoffs at them and runs the country according to a religion of secular humanism.

In fending off other ethnicity, the book protesters objected again and again to selections by blacks and Chicanos, of whom there are few in West Virginia. However disguised as complaints about bad grammar and foul language, this objection has to be recognized as racism. But the real enemy is the outsider, the Other. Exclusion practically defines ethnocentricity, which is a failure to identify outside a certain reference group. Hence, bigotry and intolerance. About this censors may be extreme, but they are not unique. They are insisting, in fact, on a principle that public schools seem founded on—the transmission of culture. They are saying: "Those books are not passing on *our* heritage and values. They are indoctrinating our children with someone *else's* way of life." And, indeed, the educational goal of transmitting the culture always begs the question, "*Whose* culture?" America is and always has been a pluralistic nation.

The book protesters charged that our books attacked family, church, and state—authority in general. As the most exclusive social unit, the family is the heart of hearts of the culture. Hearth and ethos. Blood and soil. And so the pro-family movement serves as the nucleus for the New Right and its anti-Communist jihad.

Examples of works attacking the family were Gina Berriault's short story "The Stone Boy" and an excerpt from Oscar Lewis' anthropological study *The Children of Sanchez*, both of which the censors claimed presented parents as failures. This accusation has to be understood as part of an ongoing fight with schools about whether the family or the classroom should bear the blame for children who turn out badly and for society's ills in general.

All the programs denounced in Kanawha County contained modern poems that try to make Christ real to today's secular readers. One of the poems was T. S. Eliot's "Journey of the Magi." The reviewers there consistently branded these selections as mocking and blasphemous, though none of them were. As for attacks on the state, a couple of books in my own program contained interviews and trial transcripts that allowed students to hear what a number of participants in the Vietnam war had to say, including some involved in the civilian massacre of My Lai. The objection to these selections was that they were "not necessary for education" and seemed to be included only to make students "feel guilt and shame."

The issue of this Vietnam material was self-examination, which the censors chronically resisted. In fact, one of the set terms used throughout the censorship network in reviewing books is "invasion of privacy," a liberal-sounding objection that is invoked whenever, for example, students are invited to relate literature to their own experiences or to talk or write about their thoughts and feelings. One of the set terms used in the literature of psychological research on authoritarian or dogmatic personality is "anti-intraception"—fear of inwardness —something, incidentally, that women frequently attribute to men. Indeed, we shouldn't lay just at the door of conservative censors this preference for projecting onto others, instead of looking within, for self-exoneration over self-examination. As John Barth quipped in his novel *Giles Goat Boy*, "Self-knowledge is bad news."

"Know thyself" is the supreme tenet of spiritual education, already well-attested before Oedipus discovered that he was the culprit he sought. But this principle was never meant to carry a guilt trip. That is the negative view, based on a low self-concept—the master trait, by the way, that researchers find in the authoritarian or dogmatic personality. "Know thyself" pertains not simply to our personal makeup but to our transpersonal nature. It asks, "Who am I?" to whatever depth and height we can bear the answer. It is a cosmic voyage that should be the first-goal statement in every school district's curriculum guide, before that stuff about being good citizens and productive workers. Those results will follow as fallout from self-development.

It is not difficult to connect invasion of privacy with another of the most common objections in the censorship network—morbidity and negativity, which, if denied in oneself, become targets in books. Here are examples listed by one Kanawha County reviewer:

> "The Highwayman," Alfred Noyes—Girl shoots herself through the breast.
> "Lord Randall," traditional ballad—The main character is poisoned.
> "Danny Deaver," Rudyard Kipling—Poem concerning a military hanging.
> "The Tell-Tale Heart," E. A. Poe—A man cunningly contrives to kill
>   an old man whom he loves, carries this out, and dismembers the body.
> "To Build a Fire," Jack London—A man freezes to death.

On this basis, we could dismiss John Keats's "Ode to a Nightingale" as suicidal and Matthew Arnold's "Dover Beach" as nihilistic and proceed to eliminate not only tragedy but virtually all literature. Why avoid negativity within only to meet it in books?

And yet, the case that the censors make differs not a great deal from Plato's reason for banishing the poets. Dwelling on Barth's "bad news" just keeps you down. Why not keep fixed on the good news, gospel, the word of God? Indeed, another ancient spiritual dictum is "You become what you think." If you focus on the negative, you will become or remain negative. If you meditate on the divine, you will bring out your divinity.

Literary artists themselves, I wager, see their work as gospel, as good news, even though it may be wrought from the bad news of self-examination and other worldly realities, because they feel the transformative effect of the imagination. In its secular way literature tries to act as gospel. But if read shallowly, both holy writ and literature can be dangerous, because their rhetorical power and spellbinding stories can attach readers even more to surface forms than they already are.

As religious education was phased out of public schools in the last century, English education was phased in. Literature took over from scripture, literary criticism from biblical exegesis, textual performance from liturgical service. The syllabus is now the canon, the literature professor the hierophant. Has English teaching extended religious teaching in a secular way? If so, is that right? If not, should it? I think fundamentalists are right to hold out for spiritual education, but that cannot come about by controlling reading matter or by teaching morality and religion as such. The fundamentalists are right, too, that our secular society tends to censor out spirituality in its distrust of religion.

But education can be spiritual without manipulating minds, without teaching Spirituality 101, replete with textbooks, lectures, and mid-terms (open to qualified juniors and seniors only). In fact, I think schools will become spiritual to the extent that they reduce manipulation. Some of it—the overcontrolling of texts to read and subjects to write on and of the situations in which reading and writing occur—is designed to direct thought where adults think it should go. Some of the manipulation—the obsessive testing and the military-industrial managerial systems—is just bureaucratic self-accommodation. One way or another, in the name of "structure", youngsters are infantalized. The first step toward spiritual education is to put them in a stance of responsible decision making and in an unplanned interaction with other people and the environment. As part of this change, I would drop textbooks in favor of trade books, a syllabus in favor of a classroom library, and go strongly for individual and small-group reading. Any specific presenting and sequencing of texts, whether done in the editorial offices of amoral corporations or within the somewhat more sanctified walls of the faculty conference room, short-circuits the learning process and undermines the will of the student.

The solution to censorship may also be the way to a spiritual education. A single course of reading for a pluralistic populace doesn't make sense unless we really do want a cookie-cutter curriculum. If students are routinely reading individually and in small groups, negotiating different reading programs with the teacher, parents, and classmates, no family can object that their child is being either subjected to or barred from certain books or ideas. Teachers and librarians can point out thin or skewed reading fare in conferring with students and parents and can keep students and books constantly circulating.

Pluralism is central to this process, because spirituality depends on widening the identity. Every social system is a knowledge system and has limitations that must be overcome. Learning to think and rejoining the All both require expanding the frequency spectrum to which we can attune. Great books, yes, but youngsters need to experience *all* kinds of discourse and all kinds of voices and viewpoints and styles—hear out the world. Our heritage, yes, but we need to encompass *all* heritages, cross cultures, raise consciousness enough to peer over the social perimeters that act as parameters of knowledge. The Kanawha County imbroglio taught me that the same attachments to blood and soil, hearth and ethos, that Christ vividly enjoined us not to put before him work against intellectual understanding as well as spiritual development. As we identify, so we know. As we know, so we identify.

But our self and very life depend, we feel, on identifications with family, neighborhood, ethnic group, church, nation, and language. We have an investment in not knowing anything that will disturb such identifications. So we tend to limit what we are willing to know to what is known and accepted in our reference group. In my book *Storm in the Mountains* I call this not-wanting-to-know agnosis, partly to contrast it with *gnosis*, the esoteric term for direct and total revelation, but partly also to create an analogy with clinical states like anesthesia, amnesia, and aphasia. Just as our inner system may block sensory perception, memories, or abstraction, our acculturation may block any knowledge from within or without that threatens our identities. Agnosis is self-censorship.

Creek preachers aren't the only ones afraid of reading and writing. We all are, and that is the real reason that reading and writing have proved inordinately difficult to teach. Literacy is dangerous and has always been so regarded. It naturally breaks down barriers of time, space, and culture. It threatens one's original identity by broadening it through vicarious experiencing and the incorporation of somebody else's hearth and ethos. So we feel profoundly ambiguous about literacy. Looking on it as a means of transmitting our culture to our children, we give it priority in education, but, recognizing the threat of its backfiring, we make it so tiresome and personally unrewarding that youngsters won't want to do it on their own, which is when it becomes dangerous. This is an absurd state of affairs, but it is a societal problem going beyond schools alone to the universal fear of literacy—a fear based on ethnocentricity—and to the educational goal of transmitting the culture.

At bottom, this goal embodies a needless worry. By definition, culture is self-transmitting—caught, not taught. It is transmitted through every detail of our daily lives and our environment. It does not depend on books, but great books are great because they have passed into and shaped the culture even for those who never heard of them. This does not argue for neglecting great books, but if we pulled out all the stops on literacy, quit fearing it, and gave it to youngsters wholeheartedly for personal inquiry, we would produce a nation of real readers who would be far more familiar with great books than they are today. Over-controlling the content of reading, writing, and discussing has the same effect as censorship. Let's not castigate those bigots over there if we're doing our own version of the same thing.

One generation of teachers has somehow got to bring through one generation of students who will have thoughts we have not had before. It is clear that the nation's and the planet's problems cannot be solved by just thinking along the lines we do now, according to our heritage. These truly new ways of thinking will come from the same expanded consciousness that I have called spiritual. Practically, we must decondition ourselves, jump cultures, slip outside the cage of mere genetic and environmental inheritance. Transmit the culture, yes, but subordinate that to transcending the culture, which after all isn't doing very well right now, like the others. The world is warring right and left because the various cultures strive so intently to perpetuate themselves that they end by imposing themselves on each other. These lethal efforts to make others like oneself burlesque the expanded identity that would make possible real global unity. The secret of war is that nations need enemies to maintain definition, because differences define.

The exclusivity of cultures is so dangerous that each must build into itself the means of transcending itself. Actually, I think the deepest spiritual teachings in all cultures have tried to achieve this goal but, in doing so, seem subversive, which is why they had to go underground, where historians rarely find them. If schools took on the transcending of cultural conditioning, it would hardly mean more than fulfilling the already professed goal of teaching the young to think for themselves. But truly free inquiry has conflicted so much with the old goal of cultural transmission and identity maintenance that we have sabotaged our own noble aim. If we educate youngsters to transcend their heritage, they will be able to transform it and lead other cultures to do the same. The American way is to pioneer. If we don't transform our culture, we won't have a culture to transmit. So the practical way is, after all, the spiritual way.[1]

NOTE

[1]Parts of this article appeared in "Censorship and Spiritual Education," *English Education* 21 (1989): 70–87.

WORK CITED

Moffett, James. *Storm in the Mountains: A Case Study of Censorship, Conflict, and Consciousness.* Carbondale: Southern Illinois UP, 1988.

Caliban in the Composition Classroom

Donald Rothman

I begin with Caliban, a character who haunts me whenever I think about literacy and censorship, students and teachers, slaves and masters. I am concerned with him not from Prospero's point of view, perhaps not even from Shakespeare's, but from where I stand as a writing teacher and the director of a teacher education project working to improve writing instruction in our schools. Let me bring Caliban into this paper right away by quoting two passages from Shakespeare's *Tempest*:

> MIRANDA: I pitied thee,
> Took pains to make thee speak, taught thee each hour
> One thing or other. . . .
> CALIBAN: You taught me language; and my profit on't
> Is, I know how to curse. The red plague rid you
> For learning me your language! (1.2.355–57, 365–67)

> CALIBAN: Be not afeard; the isle is full of noises,
> Sounds and sweet airs, that give delight, and hurt not.
> Sometimes a thousand twangling instruments
> Will hum about mine ears; and sometimes voices,
> That, if I then had wak'd after long sleep,
> Will make me sleep again: and then, in dreaming,
> The clouds methought would open, and show riches
> Ready to drop upon me; that, when I wak'd, I cried to dream
> again. (3.2.133–41)

Caliban, in the presence of Miranda, his teacher, uses language to curse; but, in the ill-fated plot for his own revenge and liberation, he speaks what are, to me, the most beautiful lines in the play. Away from his master, where he feels a considerable sense of control, he expresses a profound appreciation of beauty, of himself, and of those around him. This diversity in language and thought can be said to anticipate what researchers like Geneva Smitherman, working in largely black schools in Detroit, and Eugene Garcia and Luis Moll, working in Hispanic schools in the Southwest, have found by recording students talking among themselves when teachers aren't present. The researchers have observed abundant evidence of sophisticated analytical thinking that contrasts sharply with what teachers report about these students' thinking and language skills.

Educators often ignore the inhibiting contexts in which we come to know these young people.

Caliban's speeches can serve as a metaphor for my students' writing and direct our attention to the importance of context in helping people learn to write. Our schools and universities often silence students who eventually internalize this institutionalized censorship. Much student writing resembles cursing: "Stay away! This wall will keep you from ever knowing me and will protect me from you." Much of the writing that teachers receive reveals nothing because it is a camouflage.

My goal is not to abandon us to cursing but to broaden the dialogue in which we ask students to participate. Specifically, students should be invited to enter into a conversation with writers around the world who have been banned, censored, exiled, and imprisoned because of their writing. Indeed, after writing their own histories as writers and talking about them in class, my students discover how much they have in common with these authors, especially those students who were punished for using Spanish on school grounds or were humiliated repeatedly into squeezing their summer vacations into five-paragraph essays. Our students must hear those who have put their lives on the line by writing; when they do hear, they will better understand the silences our schools have imposed on them. Once this censorship has been named, they are more likely to challenge those silences and to equip themselves to speak out against the global examples of the same oppression.

My belief in this dialogue comes not just from faith in a good idea but from the experience of working with basic writing students at the University of California, Santa Cruz, and with schoolteachers in the Central California Writing Project. These students and teachers have much in common, which is apparent when I ask both groups to write about their histories as writers. They always balk at first, claiming that they aren't writers. Once they acknowledge that one doesn't have to be famous to have a history (Brecht's poem "Questions from a Worker Who Reads" (252–53) helps make this point), a remarkable set of stories unfolds: an early love of words and scribbles turned into a nightmare of humiliation and regimentation in school; confessions about being driven to plagiarism, succumbing to alienation, and producing formulaic responses to inauthentic assignments.

Of course, there are exceptions. But the remarkable thing is how my freshmen tell the same story as the teachers I work with. They resent what happened to them; at the same time, they blame themselves for their weakness. Despite the evidence that we have a systemic problem, they see their inadequacies as writers, their reluctance to use writing as a way to affect those around them, as a personal failing, not as a result of censorship. Even the advanced undergraduates and graduate students I teach struggle with demons that confuse self-expression with egotism and public discourse with arrogance and presumption. Year after year, people proud to be living in a country with the bill of rights, with the first amendment, tell me they have never written an op-ed piece or a letter to the editor. They have never spoken at a public meeting. They do not feel that their literacy has liberated them at all. Quite the contrary, their writing is extracted from them like some tax or a pint of blood.

In helping students problematize their own literacy by examining their attitudes about reading and writing, I witness their intelligence and compassion. Certainly, they are writing, at least at first, for another potential master, one who claims to be interested in their freedom and in their role as citizens in a democracy. And they are wary of me, as they should be. But the class becomes a different sort of island once the students make assignments for each other and once drafts and revisions shape a collective purpose. When the class works, I am no longer the only one for whom students write. It is cause for optimism that, after many years of being silenced in many classes, students are still hungry to communicate with each other and with others in the world with whom they feel some alliance.

Like my students, serious teachers committed to education reform back off from the challenge to write to a public that is misinformed about education, because, they say, "Well, there isn't enough time." But underneath the time constraint is a deeply rooted fear: "I am not a writer." Or "I am not good enough to get anyone's attention." Or "I'm not sure enough about what alternative to propose." Or, just as likely these days, "I'll lose my job if I argue that compulsory patriotic observance like flag saluting is wrong or if I explain why the basal readers are stacked in my closet under spelling dittoes, despite the district's scope and sequence that depend on them."

Attached to these stories is the humiliation of silence in the face of injustice and sometimes, as in the English-only movement, subtle racism and oppression. When these teachers and my students begin to analyze this silence, to see it as more than their personal shame, we engage in learning that promises to create change.

What difference does it make if college students and schoolteachers see their own silences as personal debilities or the systematic exclusion of citizens from public discourse? As we read the Index on Censorship collection *They Shoot Writers, Don't They?*, edited by George Theiner, and listen to the voices of writers who have put themselves and their families at great risk by continuing to write, our own silences in this country take on new proportions. The context for our exploration of writing changes when we no longer ignore the question, "Why write?" but make it the center of our intellectual work. "Why write?" becomes our central concern, as we read essays, fiction, and even the morning newspaper together. In deepening our answers to this question, we turn to works that provide occasions for us to explore who we are as readers and as writers and who we want to become. We enhance our sense of potential as literate citizens.

We read Eduardo Galeano's "In Defence of the Word" (Theiner 188), in which he says:

> By writing it is possible to offer, despite persecution and censorship, the testimony of our time and our people—for now and for posterity. One may write in order to say, in a sense: "This is where we are, this is where we were; we are like this, this is what we were like." (199)

Galeano's insights resonate with our efforts to take our writing histories seriously, not just as autobiography but as cultural history as well.

In class we ask about our role in history, our sense of identity in our communities, our commitment to democracy. We read works of fiction to further our understanding of how our personal struggles with reading and writing are more comprehensible when seen in a context much larger than our classrooms. The colonial fiction we read exposes the naive belief that literacy in and of itself will be liberating. In fact, we see how writing is used to distort reality as often as it is used to reveal it. We measure our own temptations to lie in our writing against the lies of characters who write in Chinua Achebe's *Things Fall Apart* and J. M. Coetzee's *Waiting for the Barbarians* and *Foe*. Students come to recognize their own censorship (externally and internally initiated) once the experience is named through our reading of these books. "Read selfishly," I tell them. "Keep asking for answers to our questions." Through this route students find other writers, and they discover reasons for reading and writing that have little to do with winning my approval. The alliances that such literacy creates—alliances with characters, with other students in the class, and with other writers—are at the center of our motivation to talk, write, and revise. These alliances become empowering, helping us see that much depends on our resistance to censorship.

At the end of Achebe's book, a novel about the arrival of British missionaries in Nigeria and the consequent destruction of tribal life, the British commissioner considers the possibility of writing a chapter or at least a "reasonable paragraph" (148) about Okonkwo, the Ibo hero who takes his own life rather than face the degradation of living under British rule. Students observe that libraries are full of books about the Okonkwos of the world, books written by commissioners who know nothing about tribal life. We learn something about what can happen when someone else documents your life, pointing to Allan Bloom's book *The Closing of the American Mind* as an example of insensitive distortion of American students' lives. Students begin to see their papers as part of their own autobiographies and as chapters of our collective history. They see their authorship as connected to issues much broader than completing an assignment. They discover that no one else can tell their stories but that they need to feel part of a writing community to be willing to tell them.

The South African novelist J. M. Coetzee offers us another opportunity to examine our assumptions about literacy, writing, and power. *Waiting for the Barbarians* helps us realize how the fictions we construct about ourselves in writing can displace our apprehensions of reality. The magistrate in this novel, a liberal administrator for an unnamed empire, resists a plan to commit genocide against the aboriginal people surrounding his settlement and is promptly imprisoned. He suffers the torture that had hitherto been directed at the "barbarians." His suffering changes him, albeit modestly. And when, at the end of the book, he sits down to write about this outpost of "civilization," to document for future generations what he claims to know, he is appalled, as we are, by the lies he writes. Like Achebe's commissioner, he plans a book that will be a pack of lies.

We talk about these characters' abilities to write and their compulsions to lie, all within the context of a basic writing class designed to help students see their own writing as part of a world larger than our classroom. We challenge our reading to teach us something about the responsibility of the writer and of the literate student who perceives injustice and feels compelled to respond.

Students' essays and letters reveal not only their intelligence and desire to participate in global issues but also how their personal lives can be better understood if the context for exploration is broadened. Their writing eloquently describes how naming one's history and one's practice as a writer is made possible by the terms that novelists and other writers have used. Reading fiction that emerges from colonial struggles to find answers to the question "Why write?" leads to motivated, insightful, and compelling reading and writing. It also challenges the prevailing culture of our schools, where there is little interest in helping students analyze their own silences and enter into a dialogue with the world.

At the end of my course one quarter, a woman wrote an essay entitled, "There Is Someone Else." In this repudiation of solipsism, she discovers that one need not be special to write, that the term *writer* has been unjustly reserved for a small elite. She says:

> I have chosen writing as my method for speaking out. Through writing, we have the power to communicate with literate people throughout the world. . . . I have noticed through discussions with other students that a majority of people in the U. S. will not write because they feel they are unqualified. This is wrong. There is nothing specific which qualifies a person to write. Everyone is qualified to write, at least in the sense that every person has something to write about.

And a young first-year student, who was moved by our work together to publish a long article on censorship and textbooks in our local newspaper, wrote in an essay:

> How could a young, white, middle class American ever hope to reform the world he lives within, when he has never even experienced the social abuse and economic exploitation that has condemned the lives of so many others? A feeling of powerlessness overtook my views about writing at many points during the past quarter, until I made the discovery that I did share something in common with these writers

that I had put above myself: we all care about our life on this planet Earth and write out of the same desire to improve humanity. As so eloquently told by Galeano, "One writes in fact for the undernourished, those who cannot sleep, the rebels and the oppressed of this world."   (Theiner 189)

Fearing that his fellow students would idealize the censored writer and assume that being silenced endows one's words with special truth, he added this:

Having been struck down by the hand of dictatorship doesn't give anybody the unique understanding of our world's inequities or the special ability to successfully write for change, *only the impulse to feel one must* [emphasis added]. Today's college students have the same potential and ability to seek change in our nation [with a] free press as do those risking their lives to write.

He concludes:

I think what I'm really trying to say here is that I wish American college students would take the initiative to try to improve their world through the art of writing. I am in awe of the remarkable talent that I have been exposed to just in my small writing class. When I think of the potential for change that is being held in the hands of these fellow students I become frustrated. . . . I hope that no student ever believes that a writer who has put his life on the line to seek [a place] in the process of change has any more ability or potential than each and every one of us.

Here the act of writing about writers who have suffered greatly becomes a path to recognizing his own power and responsibility. While acknowledging the differences between his plight as a student writer and the suffering and anger of an imprisoned author, he recognizes his own obligation to make his views public. It is clear to me in reading these student papers that they are addressing an audience broader than me. They are speaking to a world larger than our classroom, and this expanded context invites and compels (with a different set of rules from those that shaped their school experience) powerful writing.

These are not the students Allan Bloom is listening to when he describes America's undergraduates. I suspect that, away from their master, his students are much more daring and even, like Caliban, smarter. Some of the students I teach write for the local newspaper, help organize conferences against racism, and volunteer in local literacy projects. I take pride in helping to make our writing class a place to nurture those activities.

What I have described of this class resembles the work I do with teachers in the Central California Writing Project. They have also begun to see that the strength of their voices, in Spanish and English, can be heard through the written word, despite painful histories that have silenced them as writers. They have found a powerful connection between their own writing and the political work they do fighting racism and supporting bilingual programs.

I have suggested that the students and the teachers I work with need to see their struggles with writing in a context much larger than our classrooms. When they read writers who have been explicitly censored, their works banned, their lives threatened, my students find more intelligible their own histories as writers and the pervasive sense of inadequacy that accompanies writing for them. And the examples from the colonial fiction that we read help us avoid the naive belief that literacy in and of itself will be liberating. In fact, we see how writing distorts reality, often with the effect of perpetuating great suffering.

In the process of reconfiguring our own writing histories and of exploring the reasons that writing makes sense in a democracy, we experience the kind of empowerment that curses alone do not provide. Caliban wants to speak again —but not Shakespeare's version this time. In *A Tempest*, Aime Cesaire's adaptation of Shakespeare's play for the black theater, we meet a Caliban who is implicit in Shakespeare but never realized. Like the earlier version, he has something to teach us about literacy.

> PROSPERO: Since you're so fond of invective, you could at least thank me for having taught you to speak at all. You savage . . . a dumb animal, a beast I educated, trained, dragged up from the bestiality that still sticks out all over you!
>
> CALIBAN: In the first place, that is not true. You didn't teach me a thing! Except to jabber in your own language so that I could understand your orders—chop the wood, wash the dishes, fish for food, plant vegetables, all because you're too lazy to do it yourself. And as for your learning, did you ever impart any of *that* to me? No, you took care not to. All your science and know-how you keep for yourself alone, shut up in big books like those.   (1.2)

And a bit later, Caliban continues:

> And you lied to me so much,
> about the world, about yourself,
> that you ended up by imposing on me
> an image of myself:
> underdeveloped, in your words, incompetent,
> that's how you made me see myself!   (3.5)

My commitment is to encourage the students and teachers we work with and all the other people for whom writing has become a form of punishment to write their own books or at least some chapters. They have been censored in ways that they come to recognize once the experience is named. And they produce moving and insightful work once they have the impulse to feel they must.

WORKS CITED

Achebe, Chinua. *Things Fall Apart*. London: Heinemann, 1958.

Brecht, Bertolt. *Poems 1913–1956*. Ed. John Willett. New York: Methuen, 1976.

Cesaire, Aime. *A Tempest: Adaptation for a Black Theater*. Trans. Richard Miller. Ubu Repertory Theater Publications. New York: Borchardt, 1985.

Coetzee, J. M. *Foe*. New York: Viking, 1987.

———. *Waiting for the Barbarians*. New York: Penguin, 1982.

Garcia, Eugene. "Effective Schools for Language Minority Students." *New Focus* Occasional Papers in Bilingual Education 1. *New Focus* (Winter 1987–88): 1–11.

Moll, Luis. "Some Key Issues in Teaching Latino Students." *Language Arts* 65 (1988): 465–72.

Shakespeare, William. *The Tempest*. Ed. Frank Kermode. The Arden Shakespeare. New York: Random, 1964.

Smitherman, Geneva. *Talkin' and Testifyin': The Language of Black America*. Boston: Houghton, 1977.

Theiner, George, ed. *They Shoot Writers, Don't They?* London: Faber, 1984.

Censorship, Identification, and the Poetics of Need

Deanne Bogdan

This paper grows out of my professional ethos in a number of ways. First, my writing on the censorship issue springs from a long-standing humanist perspective that has sanctioned the traditional civilizing force of literature to confer on the reader the power of moral choice ("Northrop Frye," "Sidney's Defence"). Such a perspective is consonant with an anticensorship stance. Second, I am a feminist practitioner of higher education who teaches graduate students, the majority of whom are women committed to taking responsibility for their own learning. Third, as a theorist in literature education, I have been concerned with the effect on curriculum of the challenge posed by contemporary literary theory to English studies as an institution, especially to the belief in literature and the literary response as the cornerstone of a liberal education (Batsleer et al.; Eagleton; Widdowson). This challenge has problematized the humanist argument against censorship. The generic defense of poetry—devolving on the intrinsic value of the aesthetic dimension of literature and on the presupposition that literature as literature provides its own educational reward when it is used as a conceptual framework for educational aims and objectives and for making decisions about what is to be taught—has the effect of making questions of literary content into questions of literary and artistic quality. Typical justifications for teaching the classics impute moral inviolateness to these works because of their richness, complexity, ambiguity, and so on. Within this context, censorship can be dealt with by appeals to such notions as organic unity and aesthetic distance, which subsume other values under aesthetic values. But growing awareness of the historically and socially constructed nature of the canon and of hegemonies hidden behind the veil of political interest renders the issue of curriculum choice based on artistic criteria more vulnerable to attack than in the past. Today the issue of whose interests are being served by the teaching of a particular work and under what conditions has become legitimated both within the academy and in the larger educational community of an increasingly pluralistic society.

My main question is shaped by the above context. Specifically, here I explore how what appeared to be a case of censorship as resistance to knowing can be understood as a performative utterance about the selection of materials to be studied within an acknowledged ideological bias. The relevance of such an inquiry into the right to literacy is that it brings into relief the points of contradiction at which the goal of empowering the reader, traditionally claimed by liberal humanist apologists for the educational value of literature, conflicts with assumptions about the pedagogical means to effect such empowerment if those assumptions cleave blindly and rigidly to faith in certain literary values that still remain unexamined in English classrooms. In embarking on this study, I expand the notion of censorship beyond its narrow connotation as the burning or banning of literature texts. Indeed, my intent is to conflate the censorship issue deliberately with that of the selection issue in order to underline the complex relations of the literary canon or syllabus (which books are read), the classroom treatment of literary response (how they are studied), the educational value of literature itself (why teach literature at all), and the powerful ideologies that propel our thinking about the problems raised by this interdependence.

In *Storm in the Mountains: A Case Study of Censorship, Conflict, and Consciousness*, James Moffett analyzes the school text censorship problem with the sophistication of a textual exegete who genuinely appreciates censors' objections. Taking censors seriously, not just politically but epistemologically, is something for which language arts educators are not renowned. Moffett's major contribution to the debate is his conception of *agnosis* as "the blocking of consciousness" (236) or resistance to knowing, "powerful prior mindsets" (172) that distort interpretations of a literary work because of preconceptions so strong that they "override almost any amount of contrary information given in the text" (171). Moffett recognizes that agnosis is universal and relative (everyone is afflicted with it to some degree). That human beings often opt for states of unknowing, consciously or not, is a phenomenon that Moffett rightly envisions literary education to be working against; that is, its prime educational function is surely to break down resistance to knowing. In "Ways of Teaching Literature" he asserts that literature is there not just to be understood but to be undergone (302). The notion of undergoing literature calls to mind the latin verb *patere*, to suffer. Through this "suffering" of the literary experience—through literature's imaginative, emotional appeal, as well as its intellectual import—the reader becomes liberated from psychological and social conditioning.

Moffett's book on censorship espouses a poetics of pluralism. If we know as we identify, Moffett avers, then educators should gradually widen the circle of identification through an increasing array of literary genres, authors, and subject matters, so that readers come to accept greater and greater kinds of difference in an ever-expanding consciousness-raising. Within this purview literature is a form of moral communication based not on role modelling virtue from literature to life but on developing an appreciation of moral ambiguity through textual complexity, which eventuates in a moral vision encompassing multiple viewpoints and centers of value. Ideally, students come to recognize in every voice one that resonates as part of themselves.

Literary experience, then, should produce in the reader what Henry James calls "the right '*quality* of bewilderment,' intense and striving" (qtd. in Nussbaum 528). For Moffett (*Storm*), reading literature causes readers to expand and to question what they know or think they know, pushing back "the defense perimeters of the mind" that place "parameters . . . on knowledge and understanding" (187). Agnosis, then, is on a collision course with what in the history of Western civilization has come to be known as the open mind, the very lifeblood of philosophy of education. "[L]et's suppose that everyone resists *some* knowledge. Some things we don't want to know," Moffett continues. But for him "[S]uch negative capability would seem to cut life off at its very roots" (182).

The fifteen-year history of feminist literary criticism corroborates Moffett's position. Each of feminism's three waves—reinterpretation, excavation, and theorization—seems to be the apotheosis of resistance to resistance to knowing. Feminist critics do not censor. Like Adrienne Rich and Annette Kolodny, they re-vision. They do not deny what is there. Like Elaine Showalter, Sandra Gilbert, and Susan Gubar, they foreground what has been eclipsed. They lack a critical tradition of their own; consequently, like Toril Moi and Chris Weedon, they appropriate male theorists to their project. And like Teresa De Lauretis, they interrogate their own ideology for racism and classism.

Applied to feminist criticism, the poetics of pluralism has succeeded in "add[ing] the variable of gender to a well-established tradition of [intellectual] inquiry" (Treichler 89). In this sense feminist criticism is compatible with the poetics of pluralism. Yet feminist criticism bears at least a dual relation to the poetics of pluralism. Inasmuch as feminist criticism has come into its own as a respected mode of interdisciplinary study, it makes an equal contribution to the existing storehouse of interpretive strategies. But feminist criticism also challenges the poetics of pluralism by calling into question the premises of a philosophy of reading that seems to accommodate a universal "we" or a unified reading subject. This is not to say that feminist criticism cannot or does not practice the willing suspension of disbelief or that it does not invoke polysemous meanings, multiple perspectives, and so on. That it emphatically does so needs no reiteration here.

But, as compared with other forms of criticism, feminist criticism is wary of hiving off imaginative re-creation of the text from the specificities of readers' lived experiences. Feminist criticism approaches literary reading from what I call a posttragedic stance. It is as though the feminist reader qua feminist reader has already undergone in life what the mainstream reader comes to literature to find out—that things are not what they seem, that language both says and does not say, that the reader has been betrayed by the gods. I am not referring here to individual cases of particular readers. Nor am I claiming that only women experience the tragedy of life or, conversely, that women readers do not derive values from literary reading other than the tragic. Rather, the feminist reader is already a critic by virtue of her feminist consciousness; agnosis is a well-nigh impossible state for her. Her gnostic vision is conferred on her a priori. She is a *connata*, one who knows already, one who has been forced into literacy by dint of her heightened somatic knowledge of androcentric reality. Divided consciousness thus becomes a precondition for feminist reading, and that fact so radically alters the relation between language and reality that mainstream/ malestream, the issue of conceptualizations of censorship, and the notion of agnosis become de facto problematic. Now that feminist criticism has come of age, it may be useful to reflect on how in its maturation process the negative capability of Moffett's agnosis can operate not as a death wish but as a life-force in the evolution of consciousness. When identity is fragile, sometimes maintaining it by "maintaining an enemy" (*Storm* 217), a condition Moffett regards as "a malady," may be necessary for self-preservation (193).

The Case of Judy and Her Sisters

The following study recounts my first experience teaching Women, Literature, and Education. A group of highly combustible, critically enlightened graduate students repudiated the poetics of pluralism and its consorts, the willing suspension of disbelief and literary context, in favor of what Lawrence Lipking calls "a poetics of need" (102). The students did so by refusing to analyze, delay gratification, accept bewilderment, defer moral judgment, engage aesthetic complexity, embrace a broad perspective, negotiate multiple points of view. In short, they insisted on taking literature personally and politically.

About halfway through the course I asked the class to look at just how the aesthetic mechanism intersects with female stereotyping in John Updike's short story "A&P." Instead of dispassionately considering nuances of tone, mood, voice, irony, ambiguity, verisimilitude, and the like (see Bogdan, "Literary Response," "Taxonomy")—all elements of what I had come to regard as a full literary response—they committed what I thought was critical heresy by ignoring the distinction between author and narrator, foreshortening aesthetic distance, and appearing arbitrarily to dismiss the work in a stock response to its sexist overtones. The notion of stock response has been with the literary establishment since I. A. Richards's *Practical Criticism*. According to Northrop Frye (*Well-Tempered Critic*), it is reaction by way of automatic reflex to the content of a work, which it judges "according to its moral anxieties. Stock response is apt to hanker after some form of censorship, for it cannot understand that works of literature can only be good or bad in their own categories, and that no subject-matter or vocabulary is inherently bad" (128).

One particularly gifted student, Judy, who in a mainstream course the previous year had written a paper cautioning against mere content analysis as a criterion for censoring any piece of literature and had with this same story skillfully traced the protagonist's development through the shifting subtleties of his sexist observations (see Bogdan, "Literary Response," "Taxonomy"), charged that within our feminist inquiry the literary response I was hoping for was, in fact, a stock response. Moreover, she challenged the very existence of the story in our course, asserting that over a span of thirteen two-hour meetings the class could not afford to learn how yet again sexism gets rationalized within a masculinist poetics. When queried about what should be done with such a piece, she replied—and several of her colleagues concurred—"I am not a censor, but burn the damned thing!"

Before considering whether Judy and her sisters were censoring, self-censoring, or positively exercising the power of choice, let us look briefly at what the students were reacting to. A rite-of-passage story, "A&P" concerns the events surrounding the presence of three teenage girls clad in bathing suits in a Massachusetts resort town supermarket. They are asked by the manager to leave for not being "decent," and the nineteen-year-old clerk who is the narrator quits his job as a protest against the way they're treated. Here is the opening paragraph:

> In walks these three girls in nothing but bathing suits. I'm in the third checkout slot, with my back to the door, so I don't see them until they're over by the bread. The one that caught my eye first was the one in the plaid green two-piece. She was a chunky kid, with a good tan and a sweet broad soft-looking can with those two crescents of white just under it, where the sun never seemed to hit, at the top of the back of the legs. I stood there with my hand on a box of HiHo crackers trying to remember if I rang it up or not. I rang it up again and the customer starts giving me hell. She's one of those cash-register watchers, a witch about fifty with rouge on her cheekbones and no eyebrows, and I know it made her day to trip me up. She's been watching cash registers for fifty years and probably never seen a mistake before.   (87)

This story was chosen for a number of reasons. I had been using it in my course in the philosophy of literature and literature education, as well as in conference workshops, to investigate the relation between moral and aesthetic values in literary response. Invariably, reaction to the story raises the issue of the tensions between form, content, authorial intention, artistic craft, and literary quality, on the one hand, and the ideologies of feminism and Emersonian individualism on the other. The story is fairly short, and I often used a taped reading that brought out its humor, generally encouraging a relaxed atmosphere. In the recent past I had noticed that the classes had been more or less divided in terms of their valuation of the story's effects along gender lines—the men being moved by the young protagonist's journey from innocence to experience, the women being irritated and sometimes angered by the concatenation of sexist images that the reader is forced to undergo along the way. I felt that a feminist criticism class probably afforded the optimum opportunity for exploring these issues. What I did not realize was just how powerfully experiential the confrontation of the personal and the ideological in reader response could be.

John Updike's "A&P" is an especially significant choice of text for a graduate class in education, in which a high proportion of students are teachers. The story is heavily anthologized in literature textbooks, partly because of Updike's insight into and ability to render the psychology of male adolescence. Within the ethos of literature education currently in the ascendant, in which sympathetic identification with characters who reflect the needs, desires, and attitudes of student readers is highly prized (witness the flourishing young-adult fiction industry), a story such as "A&P" is regarded by many English teachers as one to which students can easily relate (despite the temporal remoteness of New England in the 1960s) and thus one with which they are readily engaged. Actually, teenaged readers do not like the story much, as empirical studies have shown (see Vipond and Hunt; Beach). Yet that fact seems to set up the conditions for rich aesthetic and pedagogical rewards in striving to attain a full literary response, wherein personal, moral, social, and political values are played out dialectically (see Bogdan, "Literary Response," "Taxonomy," "In and out of Love").

Within the poetics of pluralism, mainstream readers of this passage, in pursuit of a literary interpretation of the story as a whole, are prepared to transcend their instinctive reactions to these images wrenched out of context. They follow out the narrative complexities and stylistic niceties of the central character's movement from innocence to experience, presumably emerging from the reading with a greater awareness of the human condition, recognizing, as Maxine Greene has put it, "Ah, this is just how things are, and I didn't know it!" (240).

The poetics of pluralism could also accommodate a feminist perspective in that the literary response could lead to a deeper understanding of gender relations. Here, the feminist reader would ideally be propelled beyond her negative stock response to a more refined set of moral discernments through attention to the story's literary richness. For example, she might accept the innocence/ experience archetype while still painfully aware of the patriarchal structure that allows the archetype to stereotype. More interested in the creation of new archetypes that signal the passing of innocence to experience by women in ways different from Updike's, she might, imbued with "the right '*quality* of bewilderment,' " nevertheless resist the temptation to negative closure of her response in this story. Using the strategies of literary criticism, she might note that the story's sexism devolves on fine discriminations of voice, on how the author modulates the protagonist Sammy's tone and attitude to create an ironical stance not only between Sammy and the reader and between Sammy and Updike but between Sammy and himself. By the end, she might even be able to see Sammy looking down at himself telling the story, with the sting of his sexism transmuted into the modality of tragic irony (Bogdan, "Literary Response," "Taxonomy").

That is precisely what Judy had done with the story in the other course. Why didn't she or her sisters do it in this one? What they did do—reject the exercise in the poetics of pluralism—is easy to dismiss as strident anti-intellectual ravings of an angry minority. I argue, rather, that their response was an act of literary criticism with an invisible history dating from Aristotle's sister, the apocryphal Arimneste, the mother of feminist criticism (Lipking), who was unabashed about taking literature personally and politically. Within Arimneste's poetics, the call "Burn it!" is less an act of censorship than the sword of discrimination carving out for women a literature of their own, responses of their own, and knowledge of their own, including the right to refuse to engage what they are already too painfully aware of. Judy and her sisters were simply renouncing, even for educational purposes, a story such as "A&P" in a women's literature course, where psychic nourishment was an educational value precluding reinforcement of a self-alienation already imposed on them by the literary-educational establishment. For them liberation from conditioning meant throwing off the oppression of having been schooled to identify against themselves (Fetterley). There was neither the time nor the stomach for revisiting the old wounds.

It is hard to imagine any teacher or academic committed to the spirit of free inquiry—particularly in English studies, where the expansive power of inhabiting other lives and other worlds through sympathetic identification has been paramount—vilifying the poetics of pluralism or regarding agnosis positively. How can one quarrel with a deep-browed humanism that simultaneously recognizes the limitations of human consciousness and envisions overcoming them? I certainly endorse the poetics of pluralism as the life-enhancing outcome of literary education, and I celebrate the merits of literature as a means of achieving that goal. Mind expansion is difficult to argue with. Who in education would consciously espouse blinkered perception as an educational objective? Moreover, I recognize that it is precisely literature as "an *alien* structure of the imagination, set over against us, and strange in its conventions and often in its values" (Frye, *Stubborn Structure* 77) that makes it especially valuable as a destabilizing mechanism in divesting the reader of entrenched habits of mind.

The poetics of pluralism is predicated on conceptions of literariness as the interplay between processes of identification and the Russian formalists' conception of *ostranenie*, the "making strange" of reality (Hawkes 62) crucial to the kind of suffering through that affords correspondences between self and other, thus "calling something into existence that was not there before" (Plato 557). But sometimes the actuality of time, place, student body, and educational context—in this case the need of a feminist criticism class of students to preserve their identity—preclude magnanimity as a first priority. The poetics of pluralism is contingent on a certitude of identity that comes with being in power, rather than out of power, individually and collectively. When readers are feeling out of power, as is often the case for students in a feminist criticism class, the first priority may be the consolidation of identity, an objective that puts psychic safety and comfort ahead of the destabilization wrought by further instances of *ostranenie*.

In their desperation to proclaim the expressly political mandate of feminist criticism, Judy and her sisters recall Virginia Woolf in *Three Guineas*. When asked to contribute to a building fund for a women's college, she wrote:

> No guinea of earned money should go to rebuilding the college on the old plan; just as certainly none could be spent upon building a college upon a new plan; therefore the guinea should be earmarked "Rags, Petrol, Matches." And this note should be attached to it. "Take this guinea and with it burn the college to the

ground. Set fire to the old hypocrisies. Let the light of the burning building scare
the nightingales and incarnadine the willows. And let the daughters of educated
men dance round the fire and heap armful upon armful of dead leaves upon the
flames. And let their mothers lean from the upper windows and cry, 'Let it blaze!
Let it blaze! For we have done with this "education"!' " (35–36)

Here, as in the response to "A&P", militance is no impairment to intelligence,
as Moffett (*Storm*) would have it, but epistemological revolution. Constance
Penley, quoting Shoshana Felman, applies it to the learning process as the
productive nature of miscognition, "a means of access to 'information hitherto
unlearnable' " (134).

For Arimneste, Woolf, Penley, Felman, and Judy and her sisters, feminist
criticism is not just another literary "approach." To quote Judith Fetterley, "At
its best feminist criticism is a political act whose aim is not simply to interpret
the world but to change it by changing the consciousness of those who read
and their relation to what they read" (viii). This means changing what, how,
and why they read. On the face of it, such a mandate does not encourage the
refusal to read. Feminist criticism shares with the poetics of pluralism a commitment to tolerating difference and can be served by pluralism in the best of
critical and political worlds—that is, one in which aesthetic pleasure does not
depend on a forced "immasculation" of the female reading subject (Fetterley;
Schweickart). This kind of psychic bifurcation—brought about through unconscious identification with male values, one of which is misogyny—reinforces
the divided consciousness a woman already brings to the reading experience.
(Not since Plato has reading for pleasure been deemed an activity for consenting
adults.)

Feminist criticism holds no monopoly on the desire to change the regulatory
nature of reading androcentric texts; certainly, critical pedagogy also espouses
that mandate for the reading of literature. But a feminist theory of reading
reconceptualizes literature as moral communication by questioning the grounds
of literary importance in terms of a genderized divided consciousness. Under
the gaze of a woman reading with the passion of her subjectivity, a subjectivity
formed by self-conscious awareness of her posttragedic quality of bewilderment,
literary taxonomies topple, aesthetic categories dissolve, and "strong writers turn
pale" (Lipking 107). A poetics of need builds a literary theory by taking literature
personally and politically and, through it, embraces a tolerance of difference
akin to the poetics of pluralism in that the goals of both are the goals of literature
as moral communication—not as a role model for behavior but as a scrupulous
"self-consciousness of reading, speaking, and listening to one another" (de Lauretis 8) or, as Jacqueline Rose has put it, a "self-subversive self-reflection" (18).
But whereas the self-reflection of pluralism conceives of difference in terms of
equality, a poetics of need does so in terms of oppression that is entrenched
and often invisible.

Yet such a poetics, still in the writing, is not systematic. Women readers participate in a host of diverse practices that write the story of their bewilderment. In so doing, they act as both *connatae* and as in*connatae*. As *connatae* they continue to unearth lost authors, deliberately misread found ones, and steal the language through puns and neologisms. As *inconnatae*, those bewildered by unanticipated painful discrepancies between appearance and patriarchal reality, sometimes they just say no as a kind of civil disobedience—expressing their refusal in the hyperbolic rhetoric of book burning. The immolation of John Updike's story by Judy and her sisters was not resistance to knowing and not an inability to see alternatives but, rather, the conscious suppression of alternatives for their own good. This might be construed by a poetics of pluralism as at least a case of self-censorship. However, I would defend their cry "Burn it!" as a self-empowering choice to enact a poetics of need. The framework of feminist criticism is, after all, engaged and emergent; no literary theory "builds from the ground up on women's own experience of literature, on women's own ways of thinking," except through "masculine modes" (Lipking 87). And the road to self-subversive self-reflection is arduous enough without "the accumulation of depression and despair" (Ruthven 87) that can come from studying male-authored texts in images-of-women criticism, though most courses in women's literature do practice this kind of investigation. Theoretically, there is no reason why research into sexual stereotyping in literature should not enrich the understanding of aesthetic mechanisms, literary conventions, the history of taste, and feminism itself. But feminist criticism is an instrument of what Antonio Gramsci has called counterhegemony. Through it women, especially at the graduate level, live out their self-transformations. Within this context, as K. K. Ruthven points out, it is difficult to simply "academise material which many women feel cannot be handled 'objectively' because it touches too raw a nerve" (71–72). The "polysemous bliss" (87) promised by the poetics of pluralism can be threatening to women who fear that their theorizing can only be reactive to the law of the father. One way of giving the lie to daddy is to refuse to theorize, a refusal that "could in itself be to create a theory" (Meese 144).

Hence the call "Burn it!" To brand this action an instance of censorship would be to detain Judy and her sisters in the double bind of the educated woman, eloquently articulated by Jane Roland Martin in her critique of R. S. Peters. According to Martin, for a woman to be educated along the lines of Peters's rationalist model, innocent as it is of the qualities of affect, she would have to undergo a double immasculation, not unlike the female reader of "A&P." For both Martin's educated woman and Judy and her sisters, "To be unalienated they must remain uneducated" (104). We can change the ideal of the educated person by supplanting Peters's model with Martin's. The remedy for the feminist reader-critic is less sanguine, as Martin herself acknowledges; to engage the logical structure of her oppression, she must submit to the androcentric order of symbolic thought and language itself (100–01). Ways of crossing this double cross (Meese) tend to be radical. I submit that Judy and her sisters staged their defiance of the poetics of pluralism through the mind and the voice of their own readerly bodies—the site of their literal and metaphorical appropriation (Meese 120) as the ground, the material cause of the male hero's individuation process.

Identification, Need, and the Selection-Censorship Problem

In making inferences about the significance of Judy and her sisters to the relation between feminist criticism-pedagogy and the selection-censorship problem, we must understand the context in which this story was vehemently rejected by the students. I have recounted the surrounding circumstances in some detail elsewhere (Bogdan, "From the Inside Out," "Judy and Her Sisters"); but here it suffices to sketch out the constellation of forces that predisposed the students to act as they did. This course was being offered for the first time. While women's literature and feminist critical strategies had been used in other disciplines, this was the first forum for focusing on the literary as such within a feminist purview. I was a part-time instructor, new to feminism, and I strongly identified with the students, some of whom were personal friends, whose counsel I had sought in drawing up the syllabus and whose advice I continued to solicit as the course progressed. These were women (and one man) whom I regarded as equals in every way. From the beginning, the question of whether to read male authors at all was a political one on which we disagreed. I believed that it was historically, aesthetically, and pedagogically correct to include male-authored literature primarily as a way of raising consciousness about images of women and theories of representation; conversely, the students felt that time and psychic space were too precious for such ruminations, however critically enlightening.

The pedagogical dynamics of the first half of the course had put into the foreground issues of pedagogical style and authority. The students had been feeling out of power for a number of reasons. In the first place, a series of guest lecturers had overwhelmed them with the performance mode of teaching. In addition, my having had to honor a speaking engagement abroad necessitated my absence from the class just when the students' confidence in themselves and in the collegiality of the course needed reinforcement. Bereft and recalcitrant on the evening of my return (the occasion of this account), they simply occupied the space when given the chance. Intending to present a taxonomy of responses and respondents that I had developed from the literary theory of Northrop Frye (Bogdan, "Taxonomy"), I played my taped reading of "A&P" to provide some common ground from which to discuss the orchestration of possible interpretations. To avoid a wholly direct pedagogy, I encouraged the class to respond freely after listening to the tape before I filled in the gaps according to the tenets of the taxonomy.

In terms of what transpired, there was doubtless a much wider range of response than I remember now or was aware of then; but my theoretical construction was certainly rendered futile and irrelevant. I had hoped to demonstrate just how the dialectical working through of the sexist biases in the story, by way of inducing the "right '*quality* of bewilderment,' " could ultimately neutralize the story's offensiveness. In the face of the call to "burn the damned thing," I lost any hope of moving my students from engagement to detachment in a single evening. Indeed, since then I have come to suspect that the polarization of these two states masks a false dichotomy in modes of literary knowing, a dichotomy that trivializes the intuitive and privileges the ratiocinative, that denigrates readers' tacit knowledge in favor of critics' "objectivity." While there is always somewhere to go in criticism, one can only be where one is. This truism is often ignored by pedagogical zealots in hot pursuit of critical dialectic. Though I did not understand why or how, I felt that something other than censorship, self-censorship, or literary naiveté was going on there and that not only was it something that had to be recognized but also it was something I needed to honor. Perhaps the right quality of bewilderment was beginning to induce post-tragedic consciousness.

What conclusions may be drawn from the above for the educational value of literature? From Philip Sidney to Northrop Frye, defences of poetry have assumed the salutary educational effects of imaginatively inhabiting other worlds and other lives through sympathetic identification. Indeed, I would hazard that every school guideline for literature on this continent is replete with claims for the power of literature to educate by vicarious experience. But there is rarely an acknowledgement that literature has imaginative limits, that it sets up the intellectual and emotional territory framing moral choice, or that identification cuts both ways—that it can be alienating, as well as uplifting. If educators continue to enlist the educational value of literature on the basis of its capacity for culturing the emotions through sympathetic identification, they might look to feminist criticism to see what happens when we stop pulling our ideological punches.

It can be argued that protection from discomfiting emotional experiences in reading literature is no grounds for exclusion, that, through discussion of the issues confronted in strong works, students erode their resistance to knowing, thereby becoming initiates of the poetics of pluralism by broadening their spheres of identification and sharpening their critical faculties. This is what I take Frye to mean when he speaks of transferring the imaginative energy from literature to life (*Educated Imagination* 55). I agree with this and have written in favor of a pedagogy of critical inquiry to mitigate the current romance between many literature educators and engagement with the text as a transparent window on reality (Bogdan, "Censorship and Selection"; Bogdan and Yeomans). I believe, too, that students should examine the evidence, not throw it out. But that begs the question of the shaping power of identification and the practical problem of text selection. If literature is to be undergone, as well as understood, and if psychic nourishment and socialization are held up in literature education as values equal to those of critical judgment and aesthetic appreciation, the poetics of need must at times displace the poetics of pluralism. As Ruthven rightly asks,

"[W]hat can you do with an offensive text once you've exposed it? . . . Whether acknowledged or not, censorship is inevitable in the compiling of a feminist syllabus, especially if one of the criteria for selection is that the work should instill a positive sense of feminine identity" (73).

There are many things one can do with a misogynist text once it has been exposed. For example, I have recently developed, along with Judy and one of her sisters, several approaches for teaching "A&P" in the secondary schools (see Bogdan, Millen, and Pitt). Here we have undertaken three tasks: to apply some of the feminist criticism of the Anglo-American school to bring to consciousness and to help students deal with the images of women in this story; to explain some of Julia Kristeva's main ideas in posing the question of whether and how "A&P" is an open or closed text; and to use the theory of Michel Foucault (see Diamond and Quinby) to relate the story to issues in popular culture. But this does not answer Ruthven's point about censorship and identification. Sometimes the poetics of need should predominate. When it does, when issues of identity and identification are paramount, the line between censorship and choice becomes blurred by the belief that the right to read is an obligation to read. To read or not to read is not an abstract principle that operates in a vacuum. The case of Judy and her sisters underlines the delicate balance between the power of literary naming and the self-determination of the reader. In theorizing the complexity of the relation between censorship and choice, we may find it useful to dwell on the passage in Plato's "Symposium" referred to earlier about the creative function of poetry in bringing into being forms that never were (557). Sometimes it is important first to close down alternatives, to use negative capability as a way of calling things out of existence for a while to make way for new growth.[1]

The case of Judy and her sisters raises the question of the developmental nature of the poetics of need. Does a poetics of need, defined by the imperatives of identity and identification, turn on a conception of lack? Does need merge into pluralism once it becomes positive rather than negative? I am not sure about the usefulness of such questions. Categorizing according to positive or negative values cannot capture the richness of most feminist criticism: for example, in the feminist critique of Romanticism, in which some of the most exciting scholarship has been concerned in part with the complexities of women's negative and positive relationships with male Romantic poets (see Homans on Dorothy Wordsworth, *Women Writers* 41–103, and her *Bearing the Word* 40–67). I hesitate to view feminist criticism in terms of evolution or progression, for valuations of greater or less maturity or sophistication reinforce stereotypes about shrillness and ax grinding. That all intellectual inquiry is politically interested and that all knowledge is partial are important lessons to be taught by a poetics of need. Yet feminist criticism is in a sense developmental in that it does have a history; it is described in terms of waves, one of its most recent waves being its concern with the hegemonies embedded in its own practices of eclipsing issues of race and class. It seems reasonable to assume that feminist androcentrism and ethnocentrism (a variation, perhaps, of posttragedic divided consciousness) might be in some sense developmental, that its present location in multiple centers of value is related to its having achieved some distance on itself. I find this an interesting matter. At the symposium Women Writing across Borders, which took place at the Ontario Institute for Studies in Education in June 1988, aesthetician Gisela Ecker said that feminist criticism can and should deploy any number of strategies along a continuum of anger to play. Though some applauded her inclusiveness, others thought that the deconstructive approaches she was advocating, especially for women marginalized within feminist criticism, was a luxury they could ill afford.

The developmental assumptions of the poetics of need point up rich correspondences between feminist criticism and a Freirean pedagogy of the oppressed, particularly with respect to classroom implications of the elevation of identification over reason (Scahill 96) in the acquisition of literacy skills. Perhaps the psychological-epistemological question of whether Judy and her sisters are suffering from agnosis is less important than the moral-political question of whether they should have been made to suffer "A&P" at all. Surely the operative word is, again, *patere*, what can and should be literally tolerated by students in any given educational situation. A poetics of need recognizes the developmental value that education places on building individual, social, and political identity through identification. So does every literature curriculum guideline, and that developmental mandate blurs the fine line between censorship and selection far more than is comfortable for most educators.

Whether it is feminist, nationalist, pluralist, or consumerist, the bias inscribed in every literature curriculum makes it problematic to speak of the educational value of literature as self-evident, intrinsic, ideologically neutral, or morally inviolate in unqualified terms. As Michael Ryan writes:

> The practice of knowing is itself already a form of bias because it entails selecting and excluding more often than not, according to historically determined institutional norms of what *should* be studied and known. . . . Education . . . enables knowledge, and education, . . . necessarily produces bias. (142)

Rarely is that bias made incarnate, as with Judy and her sisters, but their exclusion of "A&P," I think, is codependent with teachers' inclusion of the widest possible range of authors, genres, and subject matters in the literature curriculum. If this codependence is acknowledged, the poetics of need may, in fact, become inseparable from the poetics of pluralism. In one respect it already has in the form of feminist criticism as a kind of polyvocality (see Martindale; Moffett, *Storm*) that celebrates rather than dreads, evades, or merely tolerates difference. Such a criticism, simultaneously deconstructive and creative, taking "itself apart as it takes others into itself" (Meese 127), is made possible through "an affirmation of woman's prophetic double stance" (Aiken 298) as a reader wholly conscious of both her marginality and her privilege. By asking women's questions of texts, questions bespeaking mutuality and interdependence, readers can perpetually rewrite those texts so that ultimately, it is hoped, the selection-censorship dilemma may become a nonissue in the future of education.

Logically, censorship defined as political bullying, as the imposition of one person's or group's values on others by impeding knowledge, is a separate question from the question of text selection raised by the poetics of need. This is also the case in practice. Educators do recognize the difference between restricting access to materials and being sensitive to the cultural climate of the school and to the importance of psychological readiness for some literary works. Yet, in view of the educational authority vested in a curriculum, the "logic of classi-fication" (Moffett, *Storm* 205), the dialectic between inclusion and exclusion in choosing what is to be taught, problematizes the notion of appropriateness. When this issue is made even more complex, as it is by feminist challenges to aesthetic distance, formalist conceptions of literary evidence, the uncritical acceptance of dominance and of humanism, the case of Judy and her sisters becomes a rich one for justifying the educational value of literature in the most personal and political terms.

To render the notion of appropriateness problematic is only a first step in resolving the selection-censorship issue, which, within my formulation, is pri-marily epistemological. In the real world, teachers and administrators must make logical arguments in defence of particular books, write rationales for the teaching of literature itself (in the face of other competing aspects of the language arts curriculum, such as writing process and media literacy), and deal with the political consequences of every decision they make; those decisions are taken up more and more concretely as formerly disenfranchised minority groups become aware that what and how students read affect their literacy and help shape their values and form their identities. I conclude this essay not by offering strategies, advice, or principles for how to proceed but, rather, by using the case of Judy and her sisters as a heuristic for further contradictions about the relation between censorship-selection, identification-identity, and the poetics of need-pluralism.

In the past three years the focus of the discussion in my course in women's literature and feminist criticism has shifted from the question of whether to read male authors to the question of the heterosexist, white, middle-class bias of the course; to the relevance of feminist criticism to the material reality of women's lives; to the constructive and constructed nature of female subjectivity. In 1989 I introduced journal writing as a formal component of the course requirements and began the year with the feminist critique of Romanticism. Despite the equally heterogeneous composition of that class, the dynamics of the group were much less tumultuous than those of the class with Judy and her sisters in 1986. I suggest that the reason has to do with the combination of using journal writing as a means of integrating engagement and detachment, on the one hand, and the psychological distance created by starting with subject matter safely removed in time, on the other, though I am not attributing a cause-and-effect relation to these factors. Both became significant in opening up a kind of sacred space for addressing the life-giving and life-threatening questions that reading and writing about literature engender for students in feminist criticism.

At the same time, in my many discussions with Judy and her sisters about the implications for learning in that initial course offering, I have come to wonder whether the integrative function of journals and the psychic security of historicizing, doubtless invaluable within the educational project of feminist criticism and in mitigating the emotional intensity of direct confrontation, might attenuate the benefits of such confrontation. Neither Judy nor I, for instance, are conscious of having had a learning experience equal to that recounted in this paper, not just in terms of what we were forced to undergo on that fateful February evening but in terms of the tough reexamination of our beliefs it has precipitated for our lives since then. For example, I have since dismantled and reassembled my taxonomy in the light of feminist, Marxist, and deconstructionist literary theories (see Bogdan articles in Bogdan and Straw). Undisplaced extremity is a powerful condition of learning; making strange may be more educationally profitable than making nice. One thing is certain: throughout all that pain, no one ever seemed to stop thinking. Alienation can be transformative. In this sense the educational value of literature *is* intrinsic, self-evident, and morally inviolate. Plato had one thing right—literature influences, and it influences powerfully. That this influence is not empirically measurable in terms necessarily persuasive to all is to my mind a blessing; if it were, the subversive role of literature traditionally claimed by its apologists would be seen for what it is—a vehicle for transformation, as well as enculturation—and the literature curriculum would consequently be sanitized into a parody of itself. That is precisely what is happening now throughout the Western world, where the raising of consciousness seems to have become ironically counterproductive, incurring either the ire of those who know or the fear of those who prefer not to know. Increasingly, it has become difficult to speak, to take a position without offense to what is other. Yet, as has been acknowledged, the mortification of feeling induced in the case of Judy and her sisters proved to be personally cathartic and educationally gratifying.

The above constitutes a state of undecidability that I will not attempt to resolve, especially when literacy scholars underscore the importance of individual, social, and political identities in learning to read and write. But problematizing the problem is better than thinking it a simple matter. Educational values themselves (as they are generally conceived by liberal, enlightened educational bodies), even when those values include such objectives as eroding sexist and racist stereotypes, call forth the paradox of education's dual aim to enculturate and to transform simultaneously. This paradox is nowhere more apparent than in the task of justifying and implementing the literature curriculum, which purports both to lead students out of themselves and whatever security the culture has succeeded in providing, on the one hand, and into an awareness of how that security is controlled and manipulated by language itself, on the other. In a culture as diverse as that of multicultural Toronto, where in a single school there can be represented sixty-two nations and fifty-four first languages, one student's imaginative heaven is bound to clash sooner or later with another's imaginative hell. How to maximize this reality, not defend against it, is one of today's major challenges to literature education. To meet this challenge, those who draft official guidelines for the teaching of literature need a consistent philosophy of literature education, a philosophy in which rationales for teaching literature do not collide with arguments against censorship. Such a philosophy would have to take into consideration methodological questions, along with the selection-censorship problem, the how as well as the what of teaching literature through a definition of literary literacy that encompasses both a poetics of need and a poetics of pluralism, both the pedagogy of engagement and that of detachment (Bogdan, "Joyce, Dorothy, and Willie"). But even a theory of literary literacy cannot solve the problem of what is to be read by whom and under whose aegis. The options for such decisions range from the adoption of a single literary text for the seventh grade (as is now the case in one Canadian province) to the abolition of the literature curriculum altogether in favor of class libraries (Moffett, *Storm*). In view of the premises of this chapter, a narrower range of identification is more consonant with the poetics of need, and a wider range is more consonant with the poetics of pluralism. The literature curriculum needs to accommodate both, so that literary literacy signifies the feeling of coming to know the truth about oneself and the world (engagement) and getting distance on that feeling (detachment).

I do not claim that even attaining such a goal will be a panacea in the selection-censorship issue. But awareness of the political context of the engaged reader is a logically and psychologically prior question in the respecting of readers' individual, collective, and imaginative identities. If cultural literacy is to be more than a body of shared meaning that binds a society together (Hirsch), if it is to be truly emancipatory, it must acknowledge patterns of dominance and control of the culture and provide for recognition of those patterns as part of its educational mandate. Within those patterns of dominance, the overarching question becomes that of agency, the transformational effects of induced alienation notwithstanding. It is too easy to cloak these realities under the humanist-pluralist hieratic mantle. True transformation occurs only when people transform "the structures by which they are formed" (Reither 7). For the poetics of need to be equal to the poetics of pluralism, the literature curriculum may have to adopt an affirmative-action policy, giving pride of place to identities now marginalized (see Zita). At the same time, the curriculum must guard against the kind of chauvinism that would result in making the plays of Shakespeare museum pieces accessible only to an elite who are fortunate enough to be privy to the cultural legacy of a poetics of pluralism. This is a dilemma that teachers of literature must face; in the process of doing so, however, they must surely take comfort in the knowledge that Shelley's dictum in his *Defence of Poetry* about the educational value of literature has come into its own: no longer are poets "the *un*acknowledged legislators of the world" (line 80, emphasis added).[2]

NOTE

[1]The author is indebted to James Garrison for this reference and for its application to the thesis of the paper.

[2]This is an expanded and edited version of "Judy and Her Sisters: Censorship and the Poetics of Need," which first appeared in *Proceedings of the Philosophy of Education Society 1989*, edited by James M. Giarelli, and published by the Philosophy of Education Society and subsequently revised as "A Case Study of the Selection/Censorship Problem and the Educational Value of Literature," published in *Journal of Education*. The author acknowledges the support of a grant from the Social Sciences and Humanities Research Council of Canada for this article and thanks Helene Moglen and K. Judith Millen for their comments and suggestions in drafting this version.

WORKS CITED

Aiken, Susan H. "Women and the Question of Canonicity." *College English* 48 (1986): 288–301.

Batsleer, Janet, et al. *Re-writing English: Cultural Politics of Gender and Class*. London: Methuen, 1985.

Beach, Richard. "The Creative Development of Meaning: Using Autobiographical Experiences to Interpret Literature." Bogdan and Straw 211–35.

Bogdan, Deanne. From Meditation to Mediation: Breaking out of Total Form." Bogdan and Straw 139–65.

———. "A Case Study of the Selection/Censorship Problem and the Educational Value of Literature." *Journal of Education* 170.2 (1988): 39–57.

———. "Censorship and Selection in Literature Teaching: Personal Reconstruction or Aesthetic Engagement?" *Ethics in Education* 8.2 (1988): 7–9.

———. *From the Inside Out: On First Teaching Women's Literature and Feminist Criticism*. Popular Feminism Papers of the Centre for Women's Studies in Education 6. 4 May 1987. Toronto: Ontario Institute for Studies in Education, 1987.

———. "In and out of Love with Literature: Response and the Aesthetics of Total Form." Bogdan and Straw 109–39.

———. "Joyce, Dorothy, and Willie: Literary Literacy as Engaged Reflection." *Philosophy of Education, 1989*. Proc. of the Forty-Fifth Annual Meeting of the Philosophy of Education Society. San Antonio. 14–17 Apr. 1989. Ed. Ralph Page. Normal: Illinois State UP, 1990. 168–82.

———. "Judy and Her Sisters: Censorship and the Poetics of Need." *Philosophy of Education, 1988*. Proc. of the Forty-Fourth Annual Meeting of the Philosophy of Education Society. San Diego. 25–28 Mar. 1988. Ed. James Giarelli. Normal: Illinois State UP, 1989. 66–77.

———. "Literary Response as Dialectic: Modes and Levels of Engagement and Detachment." *Cuadernos de Filologia Inglesa* 2 (1986): 45–62.

———. "Northrop Frye and the Educational Value of Literature." *English Studies in Canada* 8 (1982): 203–14.

———. "Reading and 'The Fate of Beauty': Reclaiming Total Form." Bogdan and Straw 167–95.

———. "Sidney's Defence of Plato and the 'Lying' Greek Poets: The Argument from Hypothesis." *Classical and Modern Literature* 7.1 (1986): 43–54.

———. "A Taxonomy of Literary Response and Respondents." *Paideusis: Journal of the Canadian Philosophy of Education Society* 1.1 (1987): 13–32.

Bogdan, Deanne, K. Judith Millen, and Alice Pitt. "Approaches to Gender in Teaching John Updike's 'A&P.' " *Critical Approaches to Teaching Literature in the Secondary School.* Ed. Emrys Evans. Sydney, Austral.: St. Clair (forthcoming).

Bogdan, Deanne, and Stanley B. Straw, eds. *Beyond Communication: Reading Comprehension and Criticism.* Portsmouth: Heinemann, 1990.

Bogdan, Deanne, and Stephen Yeomans. "School Censorship and Learning Values through Literature." *Journal of Moral Education* 15 (1986): 197–211.

de Lauretis, Teresa. "Feminist Studies/Critical Studies: Issues, Terms, Context." *Feminist Studies/Critical Studies.* Ed. de Lauretis. Bloomington: Indiana UP, 1986. 1–19.

Diamond, Irene, and Lee Quinby, eds. *Feminism and Foucault: Reflections on Resistance.* Boston: Northeastern, 1988.

Eagleton, Terry. *Literary Theory: An Introduction.* Oxford: Blackwell, 1983.

Ecker, Gisela. "Anger and Play: Strategies of Feminist Writing." Women Writing across Borders, Ontario Institute for Studies in Education. Toronto, 20 June 1988.

Felman, Shoshana. "Psychoanalysis and Education: Teaching the Terminable and Interminable." *Yale French Studies* 63 (1982): 21–44.

Fetterley, Judith. *The Resisting Reader: A Feminist Approach to American Fiction.* Bloomington: Indiana UP, 1981.

Frye, Northrop. *The Educated Imagination: Six Talks for Radio.* Toronto: CBC, 1963.

———. *The Stubborn Structure: Essays on Criticism and Society.* London: Methuen, 1970.

———. *The Well-Tempered Critic.* Bloomington: Indiana UP, 1963.

Gilbert, Sandra, and Susan Gubar, eds. *The Norton Anthology of Literature by Women: The Tradition in English.* New York: Norton, 1977.

Gramsci, Antonio. *Selections from the Prison Notebooks.* London: Laurence, 1971.

Greene, Maxine. "Toward Possibility: Expanding the Range of Literacy." *English Education* 18 (1986): 231–43.

Hawkes, Terrence. *Structuralism and Semiotics.* Berkeley: U of California P, 1977.

Hirsch, E. D., Jr. *Cultural Literacy: What Every American Needs to Know.* Boston: Houghton, 1987.

Homans, Margaret. *Bearing the Word: Language and Female Experience in Nineteenth-Century Women's Writing.* Chicago: U of Chicago P, 1986.

———. *Women Writers and Poetic Identity: Dorothy Wordsworth, Emily Bronte, and Emily Dickinson.* Princeton: Princeton UP, 1980.

Kolodny, Annette. "Dancing through the Minefield: Some Observations on the Theory, Practice, and Politics of a Feminist Literary Criticism." Showalter 144–67.

———. "A Map for Re-reading: Gender and the Interpretation of Literary Texts." Showalter 46–62.

Kristeva, Julia. *Desire in Language: A Semiotic Approach to Literature and Art.* Ed. Leon S. Roudiez; trans., Thomas Gora, Alice Jardine, and Leon S. Roudiez. New York: Columbia UP, 1980.

Lipking, Lawrence. "Aristotle's Sister: A Poetics of Abandonment." *Canons*. Ed. Robert Von Hallberg. Chicago: U of Illinois P, 1984. 85–105.

Martin, Jane Roland. "The Ideal of the Educated Person." *Educational Theory* 30.2 (1981): 97–109.

Martindale, Kathleen. "On the Ethics of 'Voice' in Feminist Literary Criticism." *Resources for Feminist Research/Documentation sur la recherche féministe* 16.3 (1987): 16–19.

Meese, Elizabeth. *Crossing the Double-Cross: The Practice of Feminist Criticism*. Chapel Hill: U of North Carolina P, 1986.

Moffett, James. *Storm in the Mountains: A Case Study of Censorship, Conflict, and Consciousness*. Carbondale: Southern Illinois UP, 1988.

———. "Ways of Teaching Literature." Bogdan and Straw 301–17.

Moi, Toril. *Sexual/Textual Politics: Feminist Literary Theory*. London: Methuen, 1985.

Nelson, Cary, ed. *Theory in the Classroom*. Urbana: U of Illinois P, 1981.

Nussbaum, Martha. " 'Finely Aware and Richly Responsible': Moral Attention and the Moral Task of Literature." *Journal of Philosophy* 82 (1985): 516–29.

Penley, Constance. "Teaching in Your Sleep: Feminism and Psychoanalysis." Nelson 129–48.

Plato. "Symposium." *Plato: The Collected Dialogues including the Letters*. With an introduction and prefatory notes. Ed. Edith Hamilton and Huntington Cairns. Bollingen Series 71. Princeton: Princeton UP, 1961. 526–74.

Reither, James. "Teaching Reading and Writing: Texts, Power, and the Transfer of Power: Or, What If They Had a Revolution and Nobody Came?" *Inkshed: Newsletter of the Canadian Association for the Study of Reading Writing* 8.4 (1989): 3–13.

Rich, Adrienne. *On Lies, Secrets, and Silence: Selected Prose, 1966–1978*. New York: Norton, 1979.

Richards, I. A. *Practical Criticism*. New York: Harcourt, 1929.

Rose, Jacqueline. "Femininity and Its Discontents." *Feminist Review* 14 (1983): 5–21.

Ruthven, K. K. *Feminist Literary Studies: An Introduction*. Cambridge: Cambridge UP, 1984.

Ryan, Michael. *Marxism and Deconstruction: A Critical Introduction*. Baltimore: Johns Hopkins UP, 1982.

Scahill, John H. "Educational Policy Studies." Rev. of *Teachers as Intellectuals: Toward a Critical Pedagogy of Learning*, by Henry A. Giroux. *Educational Studies* 20.1 (1989): 91–97.

Schweickart, Patrocinio P. "Reading Ourselves: Toward a Feminist Theory of Reading." *Gender and Reading: Essays on Readers, Texts, and Contexts*. Ed. Elizabeth A. Flynn and Patrocinio P. Schweickart. Baltimore: Johns Hopkins UP, 1986. 31–62.

Showalter, Elaine. *A Literature of Her Own: British Women Novelists from Bronte to Lessing*. London: Virago, 1977.

———, ed. *The New Feminist Criticism: Essays on Women, Literature, and Theory*. New York: Pantheon, 1985.

Treichler, Paula. "Teaching Feminist Theory." Nelson 57–128.

Updike, John. "A&P." *Pigeon Feathers and Other Stories*. New York: Knopf, 1962. 187–92.

Vipond, Douglas, and Russell Hunt. "Point-Driven Understanding: Pragmatic and Cognitive Dimensions of Literary Reading." *Poetics* 13 (1984): 261–77.

Weedon, Chris. *Feminist Practice and Poststructuralist Theory*. Oxford: Blackwell, 1987.

Widdowson, Peter, ed. *Re-reading English*. London: Methuen, 1982.

Woolf, Virginia. *Three Guineas*. 1938. New York: Harcourt, 1966.

Zita, Jacquelyn. "From Orthodoxy to Pluralism: A Postsecondary Curricular Reform." *Journal of Education* 170.2 (1988): 58–76.

On Teaching Convicts

Maurice Laurence, Jr.

Education within a prison is a way of providing hope in the face of despair. By deciding to work inside the walls, the prison educator shows convicts that their lives, condemned by others, have value. Those, including educators, who work in prisons give inmates the daily care and guidance they find in no other place. Yet the society that scorns these inmates and desires to let them die, abandoned and forgotten, simultaneously accuses the prison system of being callous and harsh to inmates. Prison educators often work with convicts who are ill-housed and ill-clothed in a situation where there are too few staff people to meet the challenge of educating a large number of inmates.

When convicts feel most condemned and scorned, the prison educator shows them that they deserve the literacy instruction and job training that can provide some hope of avoiding destitution. In many cases the message falls on deaf ears. The prison educator meets these inmates when their lives have caught up with them, when the chips on their shoulders have become millstones around their necks. They are strangers to happiness angered by their vulnerability. Kindness is foreign to many of them, and the promise of a better life is something they can scarcely afford to believe in.

It is no secret that many convicts have difficulty with reading and language skills. The following case is typical of many.

He is a black male, uncertain about what grade he reached in school or even how old he was when he left school. Even when he was in school, he did not attend regularly or pay attention to what was happening in class. His father was not around much, and his mother was too preoccupied to keep track of what he was or was not doing. He cannot name four men who have been president since 1950. He does not know how many weeks there are in a year. He does not comprehend why we need child labor laws or why we should pay taxes. He does not know how an eye and an ear are alike. He cannot read such common words as *find, answer,* and *neighbor.* The meaning of such words as *domestic* and *tranquil* escape him. He has worked in construction and is grateful when taught the word *danger,* because he had often seen signs like that without knowing what they meant. He hopes to return to his construction job when he leaves prison. He hopes he can stay away from the alcohol and the drugs that led to his arrest. Since being in prison, he has been attending Alcoholics Anonymous meetings and is surprised to learn that Alcoholics Anonymous also exists in the community to which he will return.

Illiteracy, while not the cause of the arrest of inmates like him, is one symptom of the cultural disintegration and the psychological conflict that have led to their transgression of the law. The reasons for the difficulties vary, and the prison teacher must be aware of the social and emotional history of the person being evaluated to make effective use of the results of educational testing. In some cases, the person has not had the cultural opportunities for consistent and adequate instruction in language skills. In other cases, the opportunities were there, but the person's state of mind prevented making use of them. The person fell into truancy and delinquency.

These persons most often reach prison when they become involved in crimes against property or with offenses involving the drug code. The stay in custody is typically about 2½ years. Despite the overcrowded conditions, for many inmates prison is the first time they have led a life in which meals appear on a regular schedule or someone cares whether they are attending school, not to mention learning something.

The difficulties of their present lives are compounded by the uncertainty of the future. Many inmates, after leaving prison, find themselves destitute. They find it difficult to find a job and to keep it, to get the money needed to buy a decent meal or a place to live. I was told by one convict, who had recently returned to prison from the street, what it was like to worry about the twenty-five cents needed to buy a newspaper. He would go to small restaurants when the waitresses changed shifts so that he could order a meal from one waitress and tell the second waitress that he paid the first.

One of our prison chaplains has told me that, when he visits the wards of the city hospital, he finds many ex-convicts there. The life on the street, the exposure to the elements, the lack of food, the alcohol, the drugs have finally taken their toll. At twenty-five many of these inmates have a mask of bravado. At forty-five they have a life of regret. The inmate spoken of in the previous paragraph had a malignant tumor. He came back to prison to prepare for his death. In prison he enjoyed a few months of relative serenity and then was released to his family. A few months later the illness had taken him.

Whoever undertakes to teach convicts must never for an instant forget that those entering prison lose their personal property and their freedom. Most people in our society remain tight-lipped about their sorrows. Convicts, who often have known nothing of happiness, have immensely greater reason to be guarded about expressing themselves. They fear that their vulnerabilities will cause others to take advantage of them. They live in an institution where their heartfelt sentiments are often ridiculed and where their spoken desires are answered with verbal slaps. They deny the emotional reality of their desperation. It is common for prisoners to say that they are not worth the effort needed to educate them. It is common for them to drop out of school at the first sign of success. Such words and actions express a self-condemnation as cruel as any condemnation imposed by the courts.

Inmates ask for sympathy but then make life difficult for anyone who tries to help them. Most of them first try to use the teacher by asking for extra paper, pencils, envelopes, file folders, paper clips, and pens. Dictionaries and calendars are among the items most commonly stolen from the prison classroom. "Why do you keep asking me for these things?" I asked one of my students. "Because you keep on saying no," he told me.

Challenges come at deeper levels, too. Take the example of a thirty-year-old black convict, typical of many on the receiving end of such labels as *manipulator* and *con man*. He rejected my invitation to come to school and told me he was going to commit suicide. After our conversation he watched me walk back across the prison yard to the school and called out to me from the window of his cell, "Hey, man, thank you anyway."

Eleven days later, as I stood at the bars of his cell, he asked me to shake his hand. "Why do you want me to come to school? I've lived a fast life, man. You be wasting your time. A month from now I'll probably be dead." Then, noticing the weak and apprehensive halfheartedness of my grip, he said, "Shake my hand for real, man." His touch seemed dirty; after shaking his hand, I only wanted to wash my own.

A week afterward he came to the school, and I tested him. He could not read and could barely write. He had trouble reading a clock face. Anything beyond simple addition and subtraction was too much for him. What became of that man, or why he let me test him, I do not know.

The guilt that many inmates carry around inside is overwhelming. One inmate told me that, after he raped a woman, he wore the same clothes for a week afterward. He hoped that doing so would help the police recognize him. When the police finally came to his door and put handcuffs on him, he felt relief. Later, during his first release, when he walked down the street of his neighborhood, he felt like a leper. Parents pulled their children inside. He found the world outside the prison walls confusing and lonely. Afraid he would rape again, he asked to come back to prison.

For such persons, progress in school only intensifies the realization that opportunities in the past were missed. The commitment to pursue an education is a statement of trust in the value of one's own life. One inmate told me that it didn't matter whether he went to school or not. He had twenty years to serve, and he would probably kill himself before they passed. In contrast, one inmate said, "I want to learn because I'm going to live a long time." That man had a short sentence and a great deal of hope.

The task of the prison educator is essentially one of teaching convicts the meaning of hope and the happiness that can derive from hope. It is a lesson that many inmates have never had the opportunity to learn. As teachers, we must help them not to get out of prison but to live more productively, even while in prison. Some inmates have hope of a long life after a short sentence, but many more live with the thought of suicide during a long sentence. Prison is the only life available to them. As educators, we must help them find some meaning and value in their daily existence behind the concrete walls.[1]

NOTE

[1]The author thanks Max Day, Boston Psychoanalytic Society and Institute, for suggestions that made it possible to write this paper.

The Rhetoric of Empowerment in Writing Programs

Harriet Malinowitz

For people who are relatively powerless in society—such as workers, people of color, and women—there can be a contradiction in the idea that writing is a tool of empowerment. In traditional writing courses, students have been taught rhetorical patterns that define, describe, analyze, classify, tell what happened, show causal relation, and argue to convince an audience; yet teachers usually haven't acknowledged that these rhetorical techniques are taught within a social context that systematically repudiates their authentic use. For example:

> Workers can be fired for describing, defining, or analyzing their experiences in the workplace because the result is likely to be the argument of unionization.
>
> People of color are defined and described primarily by white people in the media and the academic disciplines, and are classified by them in business, industry, health care, education, and government, from the Moynihan Report to our welfare and legal systems.
>
> Women in most states still can't legally classify a rape as such if it occurs in marriage, and narrating an experience of sexual harassment on the job will more likely lead to public humiliation for the narrator than justice for the perpetrator.

Recent trends in writing pedagogy veer away from the use of rhetorical modes and formulaic paragraph arrangements. The new process theorists of the past fifteen to twenty years focus on the internal dynamics of composing, emphasizing its essentially recursive quality and techniques such as prewriting, freewriting, drafting, revising, and problem solving. Old buzzwords like *thesis statement* and *topic sentence* have been supplanted by a content-oriented vocabulary, including *thinking, meaning, ideas,* and *transactions*. To make instruction more student-centered and to make students feel more empowered in their capacity for personal expression, teachers sometimes try to restructure authority arrangements in the classroom. The process people define writing as something other than just the acquisition of writing *skills*; they try to take a more holistic view of the writer in the world and of the meaning at the root of the writing act.

Writing process theory has brought us a long way from the alienating dogma of the five-paragraph theme and has been indisputably pivotal in the evolution of composition studies. At the same time, its focus needs to be broadened if its intentions are to be fully realized. It is artificial to search for meaning and to reconfigure power when the goals and the arrangements of the classroom are not related to the power relationships that exist outside the classroom, including the social roles of teachers and administrators and the bureaucracies of schools and literacy programs. For the process people, as well as for the traditionalists they have been deposing, there is a schismatic sense of concern with what Paulo Freire calls the world and the word. The world is brought into writing classrooms as an adjunct in the development of students' writing processes, instead of writing's being seen as part of a larger process, a process of engagement in a dialectic with history and culture. The process approach, like its product-centered antecedents, draws no necessary connection between students as people who write and think in a classroom and people who live in a sociopolitical universe. The process people do link form to content; but the process that students are expected to negotiate is often personal and individualistic, and the context, instead of being the ideologically and materially complicated real world, is frequently, as the introduction to one textbook in the vanguard of this school asserts, "the writing workshop" (Brannon, Knight, and Neverow-Turk 1). James Berlin calls the field of apolitical writing process theory "cognitive rhetoric," one that "rest[s] secure . . . in its scientific examination of the composing process," yet one that he believes is "eminently suited to appropriation by the proponents of a particular ideological stance, a stance consistent with the modern college's commitment to preparing students for the world of corporate capitalism." According to this school of thought, says Berlin, "the structures of the mind correspond in perfect harmony with the structures of the material world, the minds of the audience, and the units of language" (480–82).

Like most academics and professionals, process theorists and teachers tend to be middle-class, and they are most often white. Like members of most dominant groups in society, they have the privilege of presuming their experiences to be normative or universal and to view education as culturally neutral; diversity in race, class, and gender is often boiled down to the image of the classroom as a benevolent melting pot of experiences and perspectives. These ideas, which I believe arise more from self-perpetuating naivete and apoliticism than from a conscious desire to strangle students' writing powers, nevertheless engender an intellectual vigilantism, in which the insiders—that is, the students who demographically most resemble their teachers—swim, while the outsiders sink. The problem is that writing instructors see themselves as purveyors of technique, in which meaning has an important role; yet the real context of the writer may be invisible to them. As Adrienne Rich says, "For young adults trying to write seriously for the first time in their lives, the question 'Whom can I trust?' must be an underlying boundary to be crossed before real writing can occur" ("Teaching Language" 64). Process classes often pretend that class peers are the intended audience of student writing, but it is still understood that anything not accessible to a white, middle-class teacher may be seen as the product of a process gone awry. What the field of writing pedagogy needs, especially that part concerned with nontraditional students, is a shift from student problems, attitudes, and fears as the sources of scrutiny to a serious questioning of teacher ideology.[1]

A good example is something that happened a few years ago, when I was a new adjunct instructor in a developmental writing program. A group of us who taught different sections of the same course met to create a recommended list of novels or full-length works of nonfiction that could be used as a content addition to the course. Each of us was responsible for writing synopses of a few books of our choosing. When we met a few weeks later to pare down the list, all books written by nonwhite authors were eliminated for one reason or another. Maya Angelou's *I Know Why the Caged Bird Sings* was rejected as being "strongly antiwhite." Zora Neale Hurston's *Their Eyes Were Watching God* was considered a poor choice because her use of "dialect" might overrun everything we were trying to teach our students about correct usage. Winnie Mandela's *Part of My Soul Went with Him*—a book about her life and that of her husband, jailed African National Congress leader Nelson Mandela—was deemed too "inaccessible," as were *Down Second Avenue: Growing Up in a South African Ghetto* by Ezekiel Mphehlele and *The Woman Warrior* by Maxine Hong Kingston. Such books as Eudora Welty's *One Writer's Beginnings* and Carson McCullers's *Heart Is a Lonely Hunter* remained on the list.

I'd heard rumors that the department had been accused of racism. It was clear from the discussion of the book list that both a wish to redress the department's image and the personal anxieties of individual instructors were in play. The six of us in the meeting were all white, but most students in the program were people of color. One of the instructors in the meeting said that Maya Angelou's problems with white people made her "uncomfortable" and that she could not teach the book "because of its consistent attitude throughout the story." Others agreed, adding that they were afraid their students might understand more of these books than they did. Finally, the department's reputation was alluded to, and it was agreed that the best way to steer clear of any further misunderstandings was to use only white (thus, safe and teacherproof) texts in the classroom. This was a program that claimed a commitment to "writing as process" and "writing as a social act"; but the instructors' own processes and social perceptions unfortunately remained unanalyzed, including their process of trying to socialize the largely nonwhite worker-student body into white, middle-class reality.

In his introduction to *Freire for the Classroom*, an anthology of essays on liberatory teaching, Ira Shor proposes that teachers join students in creating a critical pedagogy that is "*participatory, critical, values-oriented, multicultural, student-centered, experiential, research-minded, and interdisciplinary*" (22). Most of these items are priority areas for process theorists. The difference between theories of politically liberating pedagogy and writing process goes back to the gap between the word and the world. Shor's "desocializing model for teacher education" is one in which teachers ground themselves in ethnography and cross-cultural communication, in an understanding of inequities in society, in the history of egalitarian movements that have been socially transforming, and in models of community change (24–25). Process pedagogy at its best makes writing possible, enabling students to achieve some academic and social legitimacy; at its worst it so neglects student writers' realities that it becomes simply another setup for failure. In any case, process theory ignores the paradox it presents for nontraditional students by, on the one hand, urging them to find their voices and the tools to name their perceptions and experiences while, on the other hand, ignoring the dangers that can arise when these tools are used in the real world and proposing no ways to overcome the voicelessness and passivity that the larger society delegates to them. Generating a pedagogy that is not political, writing process theory can implicitly impart to such students the rules of false expression—fostering, in the words of several Marxist educators, the "reproduction of subordinate consciousness." Even attempts to decenter authority in the classroom are ineffectual as long as they fail to acknowledge the dissonance, confusion, and outright resistance that result for students who are simultaneously interacting with the larger institutions that contain the classroom and that directly refute such arrangements. The reorganization of authority in the classroom can't be just a way of encouraging students to write; to make any real sense, the reorganization must also be a model for using language to reshape authoritative structures in the world.

To engage in this collaboration sincerely, teachers must be willing to give up some of their own power. To give up power does not mean to make oneself neutral, inconspicuous, ignorant, unavailable, irresponsible, or value-free. Rather, it means to investigate the social foundations and the limits of one's own process of making meaning, recognizing that this construction is political, as well as technical. As Henry Giroux says,

> illiteracy as a social problem cuts across class lines and does not limit itself to the failure of minorities to master functional competencies in reading and writing. . . . As a part of the larger and more pervasive issue of cultural hegemony, illiteracy refers to the functional inability or refusal of middle- and upper-class persons to read the world and their lives in a critical and historically relational way. . . . Fundamental to [the struggle toward literacy] is the need to redefine the nature of teachers' work and the role of teachers as transformative intellectuals. (12, 24–25)

In this context, to give up power means to question the assumptions that have delimited one's worldview or, put simply, to engage in consciousness-raising. The women's movement has probably offered the best model for this process, starting in the late 1960s, when women gathered together and discussed the truths about their lives. As similar personal problems surfaced again and again and surprising commonalities among women's experiences were more fully understood, these narratives were alchemized from confessions into sociopolitical parables and gave birth to the feminist maxim that the personal is political. Later, in the 1970s, awakened by Third World women who challenged the white, middle-class foundations of contemporary feminist theory and activism, some white women within the movement went back to consciousness-raising. This time they attempted to confront honestly their own racism, to discover how it functioned in their personal lives and in the alternative institutions they were creating, and to learn much of what they did not know about the lives of women of color. The realization that they were reproducing in another form the subordination that feminism sought to eradicate was enormously disturbing to many white women, yet, for those who were interested in building a viable and global movement, the challenge became a galvanizing force toward growth.

In 1979 four feminists, two black and two white, published a set of consciousness-raising guidelines for women's groups that were working on the issue of racism (Cross et al.). They began by asserting that theoretical and analytical discussion alone was not sufficient to bring about meaningful change in social, human relationships. Their suggested topics for discussion ranged from early memories and childhood experiences to contemporary feminist issues. Some of the questions were the following: "What did you learn at home about Black people and people of color?" "What kind of contact did you have with people of different races? Were they adults, children, playmates?" "In what ways was race used by you or your friends as a subject of so-called teenage rebellion?" "If you were growing up during the 50s and 60s, what kind of information did you get about Black people through the media?" (Cross et al. 54–56). The questions guided discussions that have taken place in women's groups around the country through the 1980s and that have given us important insights into how we have come to see ourselves and others as people in the world. Just as the early days of feminism opened up the idea that we are not just people but women, so does racism consciousness-raising open up the idea for white people that we are not just generic people. For teachers, as well as activists—and it is a Freirian precept that to teach really is to be an activist—dispensing with the facile notion of global humanness and confronting the politics of difference must be the first part of any liberatory process. The second part might be called divestiture; having recognized difference, one must be willing to help break the monopolistic hold of one's (or one's group's) experience on mass consciousness.

Liberating education is not just an idea; it is a practice with a history. Here are a few instances of educational practice in which the *process* that teachers and learners collaborated in was the transformation of their own lives.

The Highlander Folk School began in the early 1930s in Tennessee. Highlander, a name derived from a popular term for Appalachian, was founded and led by Myles Horton, who wanted to create a school for mountain people in a time when most of the local population was on relief. Modeled on the folk school tradition that had begun in nineteenth-century Denmark, Horton's pedagogy was unabashedly partisan and aimed to provoke imaginative leaps from actual to possible social conditions. Horton promoted the idea of adult education as worker education, and he tapped an incipient revolutionary consciousness by using the conditions of the students' lives as the source material of learning. Most worker-education programs then, as now, emphasized basic skill-focused literacy and the acquisition of pragmatic job-related knowledge, but Highlander taught literacy in the context of music, dance, poetry, and the theater arts— all steeped in the principles of collective organizing. Highlander worked with unions and farmers' organizations, often educating on the picket line. The school openly violated Tennessee's jim crow laws and worked to open the labor movement to all working people. Among the creative fruits of the Highlander community was an early incarnation of the song "We Shall Overcome."

By the end of World War II, as unions expanded their membership, literacy skills were cultivated at Highlander through the making of posters and leaflets and the writing of news releases and shop papers; students also learned about parliamentary procedures, public speaking, and community relations. In the 1950s and 1960s the school's focus shifted to the civil rights movement and in the 1970s to community organizing around regional issues.

As Highlander evolved, many of its middle-class educators discovered that traditional academic methods had no value where people struggled daily to meet the most basic material needs. At the same time they discovered that within the struggle for food and jobs lay the foundations of the educational process. Mutual learning centering on the most critical problems and conflict situations in students' lives, what Freire has called "dialogic learning," was the key to Highlander's success. As Horton once wrote in a letter:

> The tie-in with the conflict situations and participation in community life keeps our school from being a detached colony or utopian venture. But our efforts to live out our ideals makes possible the development of a bit of proletarian culture as an essential part of our program of workers' education. (Adams 517)

The Citizenship Schools, started in the racially segregated Sea Islands of South Carolina in 1954, represented another program spearheaded by Highlander, though the schools later ended up under the auspices of the Southern Christian Leadership Conference (Graves 3). The Citizenship Schools were initiated by Esau Jenkins, a bus driver who wanted to create a literacy program that would enable black people to register to vote. Highlander provided critical start-up support, and by 1963 the Southern Christian Leadership Conference reported that more than four hundred schools had been started across the South, with an estimated 100,000 students who had learned to read and write through the program (Adams 513).

Asked to explain the success of this program when other literacy projects had failed, Horton said:

> It isn't a kind of mass education gimmick that you can plunk down anywhere and it works. That's why they couldn't get people to come to those state-financed literacy programs. It wasn't that people wanted to read and write because it was a good thing. They wanted to read for a purpose. That's why so many programs don't work; they are based on the thought that everybody if given a chance would learn to read and write. It's obviously not true . . . you must start where people are. That means their perception of where they are, not yours. . . . In the case of the Citizenship School, the basis was their everyday experiences and their ambition, their goal, which was voter registration. The content comes from what the people want to learn.   (Graves 4)

Another successful, internationally celebrated literacy program that read the world and, consequently, helped people read the word was the national literacy crusade in Nicaragua. Begun in 1980, less than a year after the dictator Somoza was ousted by the popular Sandinista revolution, and staffed largely by young students, the crusade brought the Nicaraguan illiteracy rate down from fifty percent to twelve percent in five months of intensive work and spawned numerous adult education programs that still continue. Since then, local adult literacy programs have steadily continued to build on the crusade's groundwork. The crusade was mounted as a tangible tool of empowerment, most tellingly in that it was accompanied by a revolution in health care and the government's arming of the people with weapons to defend themselves. As Myles Horton said, "The purpose of education is to serve whatever system it's part of" (Graves 5). The system the Nicaraguan literacy crusade was avowedly serving was a revolutionary one, a system that had not been given to the people but, rather, had been claimed by them. Roberto Saenz, one of the crusade's planners and later vice-minister of adult education in Nicaragua, said:

> It is a political project with pedagogical implications, not a pedagogical project with political implications. There are no neutral projects, not in Nicaragua, not in the United States, not anywhere. Every social project carries with it an ideology—in order to maintain a system, to reproduce a system, or to sustain a process of profound change.   (qtd. in Hirshon 7)

In September 1980 the National Literacy Crusade of Nicaragua received UNES-CO's first prize for "distinguished and effective contribution on behalf of literacy" (Hirshon 215); the country ranked third in literacy in Latin America, only after Cuba (which had undergone a similar national literacy effort) and Argentina. By contrast, as Jonathan Kozol has amply documented, the United States, a country with incomparably greater economic resources, ranks forty-ninth among the 158 member nations of the United Nations in its literacy level, with more than 60 million people—more than one-third the adult population—being illiterate. Estimates indicate a fifty percent illiteracy rate by 1990 (4). Kozol says: "Illiteracy in any land as well-informed and wealthy as the USA in 1985 is not an error. It is not an accident" (89). Pointing out that at one time "laws throughout the nation made it a crime to teach black people how to read and write" (93), Kozol demonstrates that our history has institutionalized literacy as a ruling-class privilege and that only a radical shift in national priorities and consciousness, not superficial panaceas, will alter the devastating trend, as happened in Cuba and Nicaragua.

Two educational programs in which I played a part have presented important alternatives in learning. One was a women's studies program at a large state university in the late 1970s, when I was a graduate student in creative writing. A chance encounter with a women's literature seminar drew me to my first penetrating look at the social context that encompassed me as a woman, the literature I had always loved, and, inevitably, the literature I wrote. I continued to take and to audit feminist literature, history, and theory courses. Not only was the content of the courses central to my own living but the form was different. Students were involved in policy and planning, in hiring faculty, in proposing courses, and in shaping course content. The instructors had had nothing in their graduate training or professional experience that specifically prepared them to teach this discipline; many of the ground-breaking classics of the field were being published while we sat in our classrooms, collaboratively digging our own way. As the boundaries of what we felt we needed to know expanded, so did our networks; our courses began to overlap with and at times consolidate with those in other "special studies" programs, like African-American studies and labor studies. These were the programs that the university considered the most expendable, indulgent frills, the first to be reduced or axed in budget cuts; and yet, because of the unusual level of involvement and passion they ignited, they were the only programs students actively fought to keep.

Around this time, May 1979, Adrienne Rich gave a commencement address at Smith College in which she posed some of the fundamental questions about the purposes and sources of education that women's studies sought to answer:

> Suppose we were to ask ourselves simply: What does a woman need to know to become a self-conscious, self-defining human being? Doesn't she need a knowledge of her own history, of her much-politicized female body, of the creative genius of women of the past—the skills and crafts and techniques and visions possessed by women in other times and cultures, and how they have been rendered anonymous, censored, interrupted, devalued? . . . [D]oesn't she need an analysis of her condition, a knowledge of the women thinkers of the past who have reflected on it, a knowledge, too, of women's world-wide individual rebellions and organized movements against economic and social injustice, and how these have been fragmented and silenced? . . . Without such education, women have lived and continue to live in ignorance of our collective context, vulnerable to the projections of men's fantasies about us as they appear in art, in literature, in the sciences, in the media, in the so-called humanistic studies. I suggest that not anatomy, but

enforced ignorance, has been a crucial key to our powerlessness.   ("What Does a Woman" 1–2)

Years later, Rich's questions come back to me manifested in new forms through my work in a college program housed in a labor union. The Institute of Applied Social Science is a Hofstra University branch campus at District 65 (now a United Auto Workers affiliate), a historically progressive union that Martin Luther King, Jr., once called "the conscience of the labor movement." The institute is a small (about 140 students), fourteen-year-old enterprise founded to empower workers to shape the conditions of their lives. Many of the students had been out of school for twenty years or more, got high school equivalency diplomas in mid-life, and began college, often to their surprise, when their children were fully grown; the median student age is thirty-nine. As Barbara Joseph, director of the program, explained:

> People come to the institute because ordinary people who work finally have a chance to be validated. It isn't that they need approval from faculty and leadership—it's that they have to have their reality recognized by themselves collectively as co-students and by a curriculum that addresses their experience, the conditions of their lives, their hopes, their visions, and their ability to create the conditions that they want and need for themselves, their families, and their communities. Empowerment is a very important issue in our school. Empowerment comes from dealing with people at their basic level of need, and that need for education is demonstrated over and over again.

The students' writing and reading skills are at varying levels of proficiency, but a significant number of the students begin the program in need of developmental work. The basic writing courses at the institute have been taught in a variety of ways; I have taught the same course differently at different times. But the important feature that distinguishes them from basic writing courses I have known elsewhere is the fact that they are nested in a context that draws on, rather than draws away from, the students' real experiences: their lifelong disjointed experiences as outsiders in academe, where writing performance has always loomed as the most notoriously vulnerable front line, and their experiences as social outsiders, denied credit for their roles as actors in history. Most students start the program with an adult education seminar that introduces them to andragogy, an essentially Freirian concept in which adults are seen as active learners through their own initiative, rather than as the obedient receptors of didactic teaching. Through discussions and written journals, the students' past experiences with infantilizing, paternalistic schooling constitute the primary text of the course, which then becomes a backdrop for their theoretical reading. Students critically rethink the nature of their education, gaining confidence as they proofread the past with new eyes and see their "failures" as acts of resistance and survival, a healthy response to an intellectually abusive society. Most students say that the course becomes a spur to self-realization and self-direction, affecting not only their relations to school but also their relations to work, family, and community life. Because of this effect, they bring to the basic writing class and to their other classes the beginnings of that sense of self infused with conviction that is the primordial feature of all real writing: a voice. As they continue in their other courses—studying the history and the culture of working people, the relations of groups in society, the theory and the practice of social transformation—that voice further crystallizes into what Adrienne Rich calls the "outsider's eye," which can be "her real source of power and vision" ("What Does a Woman" 6).

Mina Shaughnessy writes that "a person who does not control the dominant code of literacy in a society that generates more writing than any society in history is likely to be pitched against more obstacles than are apparent to those who have already mastered that code" (13). When writing, including the tools of mastering the code, is integrated into a curriculum in which the outsider's vision is nourished, students become owners, rather than renters, of language. To own language, one must own some piece of reality that feels worth describing. This is the beginning of exploring a writing process.[2]

NOTES

[1]For a working definition of the nontraditional student, I use a modified version of a description developed by Bruce Carmel, Maureen McDonogh-Kolb, and Adam Haridopolous. Nontraditional students often possess at least some of the following traits: they are working-class, people of color, and older than conventional college age; they speak English as a second language or a nonformal dialect of English; and they are the first or among the first in their families to attend college.

[2]Several parts of this paper draw on some collaborative thinking with Deborah Mutnick, Sheila Smith-Hobson, and Barbara Henning. The entire paper benefited from the editorial advice of Sara Cytron. Many thanks go to them all.

WORKS CITED

Adams, Frank. "Highlander Folk School: Getting Information, Going Back and Teaching It." *Harvard Educational Review* 42 (Nov. 1972): 497–520.

Berlin, James. "Rhetoric and Ideology in the Writing Class." *College English* 50 (1988): 477–94.

Brannon, Lil, Melinda Knight, and Vara Neverow-Turk. *Writers Writing.* Upper Montclair: Boynton, 1982.

Cross, Tia, Freada Klein, Barbara Smith, and Beverly Smith. "Face to Face, Day to Day—Racism CR." *But Some of Us Are Brave.* Ed. Barbara Smith, Gloria Hull, and Patricia Bell Scott. Old Westbury: Feminist, 1981. 52–56.

Freire, Paulo, and Donaldo Macedo. *Literacy: Reading the Word and the World.* South Hadley: Bergin, 1987.

Giroux, Henry. "Literacy and the Pedagogy of Political Empowerment." Freire and Macedo 1–27.

Graves, Bingham. "What Is Liberating Education? A Conversation with Myles Horton." *Radical Teacher* May 1979: 3–5.

Hirshon, Sheryl. *And Also Teach Them to Read.* Westport: Hill, 1983.

Joseph, Barbara. Interview. *Building Bridges: Community Labor Report.* Prod. Mimi Rosenberg. WBAI, New York. 12 Nov. 1987.

King, Martin Luther, Jr. Speech at District 65's thirtieth anniversary meeting, Madison Square Garden, 23 Oct. 1963. *Dr. Martin Luther King, Jr., Speaks to District 65 DWA.* District 65 Wholesale-Retail Office and Processing Union, n.d.

Kozol, Jonathan. *Illiterate America.* New York: Anchor, 1985.

Rich, Adrienne. "Teaching Language in Open Admissions." *On Lies, Secrets, and Silence: Selected Prose 1966–1978.* By A. Rich. New York: Norton, 1979. 51–68.

———. "What Does a Woman Need to Know?" *Blood, Bread, and Poetry: Selected Prose 1979–1985.* By A. Rich. New York: Norton, 1986. 1–10.

Shaughnessy, Mina. *Errors and Expectations.* New York: Oxford UP, 1977.

Shor, Ira. *Freire for the Classroom: A Sourcebook for Liberatory Teaching.* Portsmouth: Boynton, 1987.

Literacy and Citizenship:
Resisting Social Issues

David Bleich

There is reason to think that students want to write about what they say they don't want to write about. They want a chance to write about racism, classism, and homophobia, even though it makes them uncomfortable. But what I think makes them most uncomfortable is to surrender the paradigm of individualism and to see that paradigm in its sexist dimensions. This discomfort is what Caroline Le Guin discussed at the 1988 CCCC meeting in St. Louis as the classroom manifestation of "resistance" to social and political thinking. Here I present a few examples of this resistance with the aim of showing both the eagerness of students to speak out on these issues and the ease with which they fall back on the clichés of the individualist perspective. My material further suggests how individualism is a form of sexist ideology; this implies a confirmation of Gerda Lerner's claim that "[s]exual dominance underlies class and race dominance" (209). Thus, material in this essay suggests that student resistance to discussing social issues may be ultimately traced to the influence of sexist ideology. I hope my account of these experiences is helpful to those wishing to introduce literacy in its social contexts by showing how clichés and conventionalized usages are not failures of literacy competence but failures of political and social motivation.

Here is an unusual instance of a student writing a "private" seven-page essay for his instructor in response to the work of a classmate and to a group discussion of her work:

> But this class is no longer enjoyable for me as when it first was. Do you understand Stephanie [the teacher]? All my other classes I'm Joe, just Joe. But in English L162, I'm Joe who used to be poor! I hate having to feel sorry because I make everyone else sorry or feel bad!

Joe was led to write that essay in part because of the following remarks given in Mary's essay responding to Rebecca Harding Davis's "Life in the Iron Mills":

> I found myself identifying with both sets of characters. By sets I mean the rich and the poor. Personally, I probably identified a little more with the rich just because I don't feel sorry for the poor. . . . I always feel like if they wanted to

they could work and improve their situation. . . . It's not that I have anything against poor people; I just feel that they have just as much of a chance as anyone else to improve their situation as it seems like many times they aren't trying.

The foregoing remarks by Mary—a member of Joe's study subgroup, which worked together for the whole year—led to a group discussion in which other students, in addition to Mary, issued the familiar opinion that the poor are to be blamed for their poverty. Similarly, on the topics of racism and homophobia, members of the class often expressed the views that AIDS is the fault of homosexuals and that blacks bring on racism with their own behavior. In short, many in this class subscribed to the belief that social injustice is usually the fault of the victim, though individual victims of crimes are never to be blamed. Important exceptions to this last view are rape victims. Women as a class are not blamed for rapes. But each time there is a *case* of rape, men (and some women every now and then), often police, raise the question of whether the crime was provoked. In this case the sexist ideology is *disguised* by attention to individual cases. The fact that blaming the victim is individualized to conceal the sexist protection of the quintessential sexist criminal suggests both the link between sexism and individualism and the underlying role of sexism in ideologies of domination.

In his essay to Stephanie, Joe detailed that he was the fifth of seven children in a family headed by the mother, who sometimes lost her job and who had difficulty getting credit enough to send Joe to college. He recounted how clothes were passed along and how other boys in gym class humiliated him because of his subpar gym shoes: "At the same time they made fun of my shoes they made fun of me." He described how he wanted to cry and did cry and felt humiliated because the boys saw he was going to cry and mocked him for being a "sissy."

Following his two-page narrative with commentary, Joe directly addresses the opinions given by Mary:

> My anger is kindled by this fucking declaration! She sees her father as successful now but once he was poor and uses him as representing the whole poor social class. I'm glad he succeeded; he must be a fucking exception since most poor people are still poor. By her remark, I get the impression that I and my family are lazy and don't try to improve our situation. Right. I want to be poor for the rest of my fucking life! What a joke! . . . The only choice I had was to get any job to help my mom pay the bills to keep me and the rest of my family alive. . . . I spit on those remarks [in which] people claim that everyone can make it if they try. God! If only a rich person can understand the pain of not knowing what the future will be and the day-to-day trials poor people sacrifice themselves to just to be able to live until tomorrow. I am not poor anymore, but I still have the understanding that I don't have choices and chances I wish I did.

Joe continues for a while before reaching the conclusion, cited above, that he is sorry to be in this class. He sympathizes with Stephanie, who, from her feminist perspective, reported different forms of condescension from men. Nevertheless, he, after sitting in this class for six months, has been goaded to this angry pass.

> But this class (I guess because I've learned how to analyze, pinpoint and describe feelings) has become hurting to me. When I walk in, it's as if I am playing the role of a poor person again. . . . it's different than when I first had the class. Everyone seemed to be people, but now I "see" middle-class, rich, and I start to analyze their speech, writing, and even what they look like!

It seems that Joe is also angry at having learned to analyze speech and writing, at having learned to announce his feelings, thoughts, and opinions to such a forceful and convincing degree that other people are also sorry and sad. Should we believe his claim that this result, this spontaneous piece of writing in which key aspects of our course and of sexism and classism emerge with conviction, is something for which he is actually sorry?

Of course, we should believe his claim, but why? I think the key to the matter is that the ideology of individualism—which protects rich, white, heterosexual men—is what Joe has no means of rejecting, partly because he participates in it since he is male, white, and heterosexual and partly because, historically, Western civilization has suppressed other kinds of social ideology. In his seven angry pages, Joe does not consider his father or other men partly responsible for his childhood struggle. His anger is focused exclusively on the rich, and even then he clearly announces his own wishes for a pair of Nikes or Air Jordans. He seems to want to characterize himself as "Joe who used to be poor," rather than as "Joe who is poor," since he writes that "most poor people are still poor." There is some attention to Stephanie's perspective, but in thinking about what he would do if someone said that men don't cry, he observes, "I would punch in their fucking face and crush in their neck." The word *fuck* appears repeatedly in this writing. Doesn't this usage tie him into other sexist values? Doesn't the usage suggest, at least through the extremely defiant tone of the discourse, a defense of manhood, a declaration that his manhood can (must?) live through the humiliation of poverty?

The question I am thinking about is this: When Joe says he would like to be just plain Joe, as he was at the beginning of the course with his condition of economic anxiety not known, isn't this his acceptance of the ideology of individualism, the belief that people are "equal," regardless of substantive differences in social class; the belief that the equality of one person to the next is somehow "deeper" than politics, deeper than gender, race, and class? Joe is angry in this excessive way not simply because he is poor and because others think it's his fault but also because he was made to realize that the ideology of individualism no longer protected his dignity in this course, and he found himself claiming an alliance with the feminist views of the teacher. This suggests that sexist values are more entrenched and recalcitrant than classist values, as Gerda Lerner claims.

Sexist values are also more firmly entrenched than racist values. To see this, consider the work of Tina, the only black student in this class of 140 students. Like most black students living and working in extreme minority situations, Tina was circumspect for the first semester of this course. One of her subgroup colleagues notices this with some annoyance as he points out in one of his analytical essays that her essays frequently begin with aloof—obviously false—disclaimers, such as, "I have never really thought about my ethnic background because it never came up in conversation" and "I can't recall ever speaking to someone of a higher class than myself." Sam, Tina's critic, then goes on to point out how her strong feelings and opinions finally emerged, and he shows just what they are. Sam, however, takes both the disclaimers and the strong feelings seriously, and he wonders, in writing, about the "contradictions" in Tina's work. He even writes: "Is Tina really a chicken that will bend to the will of anybody, just to avoid getting hurt? Perhaps this is why Tina never admits to knowing anything or fails to express how she feels on a number of occasions." Sam's essay, I assume, was deliberately provocative, and it succeeded in ways that my essay assignments did not.

First, Tina writes:

> I could be real mean and tell you that I think your whole analysis of me is BULLSHIT! and leave it at that but you would try to analyze this blanket statement and probably come up with one thing ANGER! Yes this paper made me angry not because it is wrong but because it might have some truth to it.
>
> Jumping right into it now. To tell you the truth, the reason that I don't usually express my feelings is because I tend to say unkind things that offend people and make them feel bad. . . . My parents often tell me that I have a smart mouth. . . . My friends are constantly asking me why I'm such a smart-ass.
>
> You are exactly right about class [as in *classy* or social class] in the aspect that you think I wanted to fit in but at the time I didn't consciously realize it. But to me class is more than nice expensive clothes. Class is an attitude or an air about people that they exude. . . . Class is power, prestige, opportunities.

Tina responds, so far, with force and dignity to Sam's critique. Notice, however, that, while she takes on the matter of class as the collective issue it is, her address to the matter of her circumspection is answered on a purely personal level—that is, her wish to say strong things is attributed not to the fact that she participates in collective complaints but to the fact that she, personally, has a "smart mouth." With this in mind, consider how she writes about race:

> In my essays on race I didn't contradict myself. I understand that since we are different people we interpret things differently. . . . You said that I stated "I don't think that there is much difference in the races, people are people and they are all capable of the same feelings. I think ethnic background may affect ideology, but other than that there is no difference." When you point out this statement it is a true fact to me. Sure I obviously notice what skin color a person has, and

I acknowledge that fact, but after I get to know a person I really just look past the skin and into the soul. . . . I sort out who I want to be friends with by their inner self and not their outer covering.

Tina explains that ideology is responsible for stereotyping—the current euphemism for minority bashing—but her strongest statement of principle, that in the citation, says practically the same words that every white student uses to protest his or her lack of racism—the reference to "their inner self and not their outer covering." The reference to an outer covering and an inner essence tends to conceal from us the fact that interracial relations, like intergender and interpersonal relations, require the informed and respectful recognition of fundamental differences between individuals and groups. Just as Joe's language suggests the ideal of an inner equality among persons, regardless of class differences, Tina's language uses that same ideal about race differences.

Like Joe's language, Tina's language indirectly permits hegemony to masculine values. In one of her essays, Tina complains about how the black man is portrayed (though in that same essay she complains of Zora Neale Hurston's portrayal of Delia in "Sweat" as the "dumb Black woman"). She elaborates on this complaint in response to one of Sam's points:

When you say that it is the way the black man is portrayed that really got to me you are exactly right. I am sick and tired of people dishing [talking in a bad way about] all over my brothers [black men]! It is a proven fact that the black male is the most discriminated against person in society. I know the reason for this too. It is because people feel threatened by black men, because black men are strong willed and plus they are stereotyped as being no good, or in gangs, or mean as hell. But do you realize that these characteristics could be talking about anybody of any race. . . . I also want to know why you don't feel qualified enough to voice an opinion? You don't have to be black to see the discrimination of stereotypes especially in relation to black men.

It is noteworthy that black men come off well. Perhaps this is because Tina is speaking to an all-white audience. Yet I wonder why she complains so strongly of Mrs. Breedlove's treatment of Pecola in Toni Morrison's novel *The Bluest Eye* and why she shows so much sympathy with Cholly Breedlove's missing a father, in spite of what he does in his own role as a father. I wonder why she does not recognize that Hurston and Morrison are advocates of women as much as or more than they are advocates of blacks. I think it is because sexism provides the ideology through which racial differences can be minimized and sometimes overlooked. When Tina sympathizes with black men and when Joe wants designer track shoes, these are indirect paths toward identification with the hegemonic group (men for Tina, the rich for Joe), rather than ways of opposing the hegemony. When asked with which social group she identifies herself, Tina wrote, "college students."

I will not offer an extended example of the corresponding issue with homophobia; in another essay ("Homophobia and Sexism as Popular Values") I discuss at some length the founding of homophobia on sexist values. (For a more extended treatment of this issue, read Suzanne Pharr's book *Homophobia: A Weapon of Sexism*.) But I offer a few considerations. I heard at a recent meeting a speaker claim something I also thought was true at the time—namely, that with regard to homophobia the students "close ranks" and express a common disgust for homosexual behavior. In some sense this is true, since neither gays nor lesbians tend to speak up against such a virulent majority. However, distinctions should be made, at least on the basis of what happened in the class I'm discussing here. About 30 men either advocated or agreed with other advocates of gay bashing and of the extermination of gays. Yet, while many women also expressed physical disgust at lesbian behavior, no women advocated either gay bashing or the extermination of gays. My explanation for this gender difference is that, because the men are the hegemonic group, their excess and their tolerance and advocacy of violence serve the perpetuation of the hegemony; in today's homosexual ways of life, power over women is not a value, even though the traditional masculine tropes of power often play a role in gay relations. Here, too, male students seeking a more civil point of view still do not go beyond the individualist perspective; gays can do what they want, as long as they don't approach me. Women, on the other hand, seem more ready to accept the classes of gays and lesbians and are not as afraid as men are of being approached.

I don't know that I need statistics to persuade you that the majority of students will write, "It is what is inside that counts as long as you are a good person," as their final answer to issues of gender, race, and class. Part of the reason for this majority view is that religious values collaborate with the ideology of individualism and with sexism to censor the full capability of what people can say and write.

By "religious values" I mean the belief in the "savability" of the individual human soul. In religious thinking, the individual soul is an ultimate unit that makes the doctrine of salvation possible. There are only two social categories in religious thought—the single person and the total human race. Salvation depends on an individual act—of confession, of contrition, of declaration of faith, for example. Eligibility for salvation is *granted* by a masculine priesthood to each person one at a time and never to groups *recognized as such*. When there is no priesthood, individuals choose salvation *by themselves*. In this way religious ideology supports individualism.

In class, in response to the issues of homophobia, about a fifth of the class of 140 students cited religion as the reason for the rejection of gay and lesbian behavior; religious teaching rejects it either as intrinsically wrong or as wrong because it implies a change in what is understood to be a "family." The gay or lesbian styles of living are thought to be in violation of "natural" mores of sex and family. Students do not see that these ways of sex and family, when understood to be a necessary way of life, necessarily protect only the class of heterosexual men who use and abuse the family structure to maintain social hegemony. This power motive renders traditional sex and family "necessary, natural, and right."

The ideal of the nuclear family, as opposed to the extended or communal or ethnic family, permits the overvaluation of the individual child and the individual soul. Following religious ideology, parents and society teach children to be "good inside" before they teach children social and political responsibility and communal or ethnic consciousness. Social consciousness, in religious terms, is so vague as to be practically useless: "Do unto *others*. . . ." Most students have no language to identify these others in real social and political terms. Because of this double gap in language and social awareness, students resist the introduction of social and political issues. They become either excessively defensive and obscene, like Joe, or inattentive to their own interest, like Tina. Unwittingly, they fall back on the only ideology they learned—individualism —and feel an unaccountable personal and social frustration.

The issue of what students want to write about is, therefore, complicated by the matter of how ideology determines what people want. In the process of teaching language and literacy, we teachers are bringing in new language to the classroom. This new language urges on us new values and makes us all somewhat uncomfortable. However, I don't think we have a choice anymore; the discomfort of studying language with and for other people and other interests is far less than the suffering created by learning language as isolated individuals.

WORKS CITED

Bleich, David. "Homophobia and Sexism as Popular Values." *Feminist Teacher* 4.2-3 (1990): 21–28.
Lerner, Gerda. *The Creation of Patriarchy.* New York: Oxford UP, 1986.
Pharr, Suzanne. *Homophobia: A Weapon of Sexism.* Inverness: Chardon, 1988.

Part Three

LITERACY AND ITS ENEMIES, ILLITERACY AND ITS FRIENDS

Language, Logic, and Literacy

Keith Walters

The reputed consequences and promised blessings of literacy are legion.[1] For society at large, increased literacy means at least a chicken in every pot, lower levels of unemployment, improved competitiveness for our nation in the world's markets, and greater participation of citizens in the democratic process. For individuals, literacy brings "more" and "better" chances of improving one's lot in life, whether seen in economic, social, or intellectual terms. Unfortunately, because of the nature of public discourse in our culture, little serious discussion of how to realize these putative benefits ever occurs. Yet, while little agreement exists about the paths that might lead us to those benefits, a high degree of agreement exists among most members of the society and many researchers that the majority of these possible benefits are bound up somehow with relationships between language, logic, and literacy. Put in a slightly different way, the growth of literacy, whether stated in historical or developmental (that is, individual) terms, is usually assumed to entail—and perhaps be contingent on—the increasingly "logical" use of language at all levels—syntax, argument structure, and reasoning.

This essay examines some of these relationships by looking at the ways in which various researchers have understood them. Doing so forces us to challenge our assumptions about these relationships, not because they are necessarily false or invalid, but because they are in need of great qualification if they are to help us understand, evaluate, and foster literacy in this or any culture. I undertake this critique because I contend that a major enemy of literacy remains a misunderstanding of its nature—what it can and cannot, or should and should not, be expected to do for individuals, groups, or societies as well as how these changes might be brought about, given the sociohistorical contexts in which the changes will occur.

Although this misunderstanding may be conscious and even malevolent on the parts of some, it results in most cases from a willingness to select some subset of our culture's general beliefs about literacy and elevate them to the status of universally valid truths. Hence, a poorly articulated constellation of beliefs, our society's ideology of literacy, becomes the standard by which the Other—other groups, other cultures, other times—is judged and always found wanting. This problem occurs even among those of us who write about literacy. As Raymond Williams notes:

It is genuinely difficult for someone who has spent a working life with print, and has had access, through it, to writing in societies quite unlike his or her own, to take seriously the idea that the conditions the reader shares with those available writers . . . are socially specific conditions, which cannot be simply read back as the central truths of all active writing and reading.   (4)

In other words, those of us who have reached the stage that C. A. Perfetti terms "hyperliteracy"[2] cannot help but project our own experiences, values, and ways of knowing and doing as they relate to literacy on others whose experiences and situations might be quite different from our own. When examining what has been written about the relationship between language, logic, and literacy, we repeatedly see one or more of these defined only from the perspective of the hyperliteracy of the researcher, thereby impeding a clear understanding of the relationships that may exist among the phenomena themselves.

Certainly since the time of Lucien Lévy-Bruhl's *Les fonctions mentales dans les sociétés inférieures*, published in 1910, and its English translation, *How Natives Think*, published in 1926, a commonplace among Westerners has been that "undeveloped" or "primitive peoples" think in a different way from those who are "developed" or "civilized." For Lévy-Bruhl, the thought of primitive peoples was not "alogical" or "antilogical" or even a simpler, more basic model of "civilized" thought; it was, instead, something different, "prelogical" or indifferent to what we see as logical contradictions. However, these differences in ways of thinking were not exactly "either/or" because Lévy-Bruhl acknowledged that this kind of "prelogical" thought continued to exist in "civilized" societies, especially with respect to issues such as religion. As C. Scott Littleton points out, Lévy-Bruhl was interested in this problem because what he saw as the facts about these two types of thinking stood in direct contradiction to the assumption of unilineal cultural evolutionism almost universally accepted among intellectuals at the time. Lévy-Bruhl's work was roundly rejected by generations of anthropologists for several reasons, including, Littleton notes, the fact that he had too quickly divided the world into us and them, with all of "them" exactly alike, an outlook very much against the spirit of the times in anthropological circles. Although not concerned explicitly with literacy, Lévy-Bruhl can be taken as one of the early examples of what many call "Great Divide" or "Great Leap" theories of accounting for differences across cultures—in this case, differences in ways of thinking.

While many bases for dividing the peoples of the world into groups can be found, literacy has certainly been a convenient and common one, at least since the appearance in 1963 of Jack Goody and Ian Watt's seminal essay "The Consequences of Literacy." Although not the first to focus on literacy as a significant axis of differentiation, Goody and Watt have influenced the discussion of literacy and its nature in the last twenty-five years perhaps more than any other writers because of the way they chose to lay out the problems associated with understanding the phenomenon. Numerous important researchers working in a variety of fields—including the classics, literature, rhetoric, and cognitive psychology—have subscribed to a view of literacy not too unlike that usually ascribed to Goody and Watt's essay. Stated in its strongest form, this theory claims that literacy and more particularly alphabetic literacy of the kind used for Western languages causes cognitive changes to the extent that literate people (that is, those literate in a language using alphabetic script) simply think differently—that is, more logically—than those from cultures without alphabetic literacy—an idea that many Westerners find appealing, no doubt because it "explains" what they perceive to be the superiority of Western culture.

Not surprisingly, this approach to literacy has come under serious attack from many quarters. Because of its length and detail, Brian Street's work is a good introduction to many of the criticisms that have been made of "Great Leap" theories. In some ways more interesting than the criticisms raised by Street are those found in Goody's own more recent work on literacy. Since publishing the original essay with Watt, Goody has been continually "refining" his ideas, as he puts it, although some readers probably see his refinements as retractions.

By 1968, for example, in his introduction to *Literacy in Traditional Societies*, Goody had acknowledged that the word *implications* would have been a better choice than the word *consequences* for the title of the original essay. In his 1987 book, *The Interface between the Oral and the Written*, Goody states that he currently prefers the word *writing*, rather than *literacy*, as a referent for his interest. At least half a dozen times during the course of this book, he explicitly criticizes his earlier work, including his essay with Watt, noting that it had placed too much importance on the alphabet as the apex of writing systems (e.g., 40, 64, 76) and on the uniqueness of classical Greek and Western achievements (e.g., 56, 64). In fact, Goody states:

> Our initial emphasis had been too much on the tradition of western humanism and the problems to which it gave rise. We certainly gave greater weight than we should to the "uniqueness of the West" in terms of modes of communication, a failing in which we were not alone. . . .   (xvii-xviii)

Thus, a major problem has been the privileging of the researcher's own cultural past, assigning it a place of undue preeminence. Further, Goody goes to great lengths to explain how and why he and Watt had been trying to avoid the simple dichotomous theories of others. The refinements Goody sees over time in his work are probably clearer on rereading these works, especially on rereading them in reverse chronological order, than on first reading. Further, if readers have misunderstood or misapplied his work, Goody must bear some of the responsibility, for, as Street points out, Goody's "language, the texture of argument, and the treatment of the ethnography tend to override [his own] warnings" about the limitations of what he is saying (5).

Yet, while Goody has been narrowing the scope of his claims—especially as to the advantages of one script over another, the "consequences" that differences in script may have, and the relationship of these to logic—other researchers, such as Walter J. Ong and David Olson, have, at least until recently, continued to subscribe to some strong version of the "Great Leap" theory, defining the relationship of language and logic to literacy in such a way that they fall prey to many of the fallacies from which Goody has tried to distance himself.

I do not deal with the work of Ong in great detail here, except to note that he, perhaps more than any other commentator on literacy, is better known to teachers of language, writing, and literature, no doubt because of his important works on literary criticism and the history of Western rhetoric. Further, his work on literacy, especially the often reprinted "Literacy and Orality in Our Times" and *Orality and Literacy: The Technologizing of the Word*, has been readily accepted by many in these fields. Consequently, it should be of great interest that Ong, like Goody, has recently sought to separate himself from "[the] people out there who fit [the] recipe for reductionists" (Ong, "Comment" 701). In response to an article by Patricia Bizzell, in which she notes that humanists like Ong and Eric Havelock, a classicist, "tend to dichotomize non-literate and literate states of being . . ." (142), Ong acknowledges that "although we can isolate certain general traits which differentiate literate cultures from oral, these general traits never occur without admixtures of specific differences" ("Comment" 701).

However, much as Goody notes that "the general trend of [the] research [since the Goody and Watt essay] is to strengthen rather than lessen the case for emphasizing the social and cognitive effects of writing" (*Interface* xviii), Ong contends, "By no means do all changes in culture identifiable after the introduction of writing reduce to the shift from orality to literacy. But an astonishing number of them relate massively to this shift (and later to the shifts to print and to electronic processing of the word)" ("Comment" 701).

In other words, Ong, like Goody, appears to distance himself from the strongest form of "Great Leap" accounts of the significance of the coming of literacy, although he has no means given up faith that the distinction between "orality" and "literacy" is still the most significant axis for differentiating cultures.

As with Goody, some of the blame for what Ong or others might see as misinterpretation and misuse of his work must be placed at the feet of the author himself. Prior to Ong's recent comments, many and perhaps most of his readers, regardless of disciplinary training or knowledge of the research that had been done on literacy, had believed Ong to be a proponent of a "Great Leap" theory of literacy and its ramifications; no doubt, a number of these readers will continue to place Ong among those who hold such views (see, e. g., Daniell, "Against the Great Leap," and, in this volume, "The Situation"). "Reductionism is unreally simplistic, relationism is complex," writes Ong ("Comment" 701). No student of literacy would disagree; however, many of Ong's readers do not find the complexity of "relationism" reflected in his texts.

Yet to recant or modify earlier readings of his work is the Canadian psychologist David Olson, whose views on literacy have appeared in a series of papers beginning with his influential article "From Utterance to Text: The Bias of Language in Speech and Writing."[3] (See also Hildyard and Olson; Olson, "Language," "Cognitive Consequences"; Watson and Olson.) Olson sees literacy as what he terms "essayist literacy," logic as the syllogism and syllogistic thinking, and language as language appropriate for writing the essay. He contends that the essay represents the unambiguous fixing of meaning in the text and that the task of the writer since the rise of the British essayist technique of John Locke and those who followed him has been "to write in such a manner that the sentence was an adequate, explicit representation of meaning, relying on no implicit premises or personal interpretations" ("From Utterance" 268). As Olson would have it, writers of well-written essays manage to enter Karl Popper's third world of objective knowledge (see Stubbs); they transcend the bounds of natural languages, managing to reach that formal semanticist's nirvana where all propositions can be translated unequivocally into the predicate calculus (see Keenan; Kempson). Although Olson admits that "explicitness of meaning . . . may be better thought of as a goal rather than an achievement" ("From Utterance" 275), he is among the most extreme of those who link the conventions of a particular literate form—in his case, the essay—with logical thought as represented in written language.

As with the views of others who take such strong positions, Olson's views have not stood unchallenged. Two critiques of Olson's work deserve special attention, Brian Street's book and Martin Nystrand's convincing essay, "The Role of Context in Written Communication." Nystrand begins with the contention that "the writer's problem is not just being explicit; the writer's problem is knowing what to be explicit about" (197) and then explains three fallacies he sees in what he terms "the doctrine of autonomous texts" found in Olson's work. The first of these fallacies is a confusion of "situation of expression with context of use" (200). Because written texts are usually produced privately, without immediate feedback from the intended reader, researchers have often contended that written texts necessarily involve explicit, "decontextualized" language. Nystrand points out that, "unlike speech, where situation of expression and context of use are concurrent, written texts are produced for a context of eventual use" (200). In other words, the putative explicitness of written texts is perhaps less a function of their being written than of their being composed for use at some future time.

A second fallacy underlying the doctrine of autonomous texts Nystrand terms "confusing fullness of meaning with explicitness of text." Here, Nystrand notes that elaboration and complication of texts are not coterminous. Using the example of a tax code, he demonstrates that making the text more explicit may meet the needs of readers highly knowledgeable in the subject, such as tax lawyers, but it only confuses low-knowledge readers, such as general taxpayers. "A well-written text communicates not because it says everything all by itself but rather because it strikes a careful balance between what needs to be said and what may be assumed" (201).

The third fallacy present in this doctrine is the use of autonomy as the basis for distinguishing spoken and written texts. Nystrand states that adherents of this doctrine typically offer "a skewed comparison," juxtaposing the most spoken of oral genres, "casual chatter," with the most written of literate genres, "literary composition," ignoring the myriad intervening genres in which oral and written strategies and practices overlap, interact, and ultimately give rise to new genres.[4]

As interesting as Nystrand's critique of the doctrine of autonomous texts is his analysis of Olson's own text. Contrasting the structure of argument with the structure of communication, Nystrand demonstrates that Olson, as a highly skilled thinker and writer, respected all the conventions of not merely the genre in which he was writing but also the particular academic journal for which he was writing, thereby meeting both the expectations of the journal's editors and its readers. Consequently, Olson's essay, whether viewed from the perspective of format or structure, "functions [successfully] not because it is independent of its context but because it is so carefully attuned to this context" (201). Nystrand's discussion illustrates that the definitions Olson assigns to language, logic, and literacy and the interrelationships he assumes to hold among them are not so simple and transparent as he argues.

To Nystrand's critiques, others can be added. If, as Olson contends, meaning is (or even can be) unequivocally fixed in the text, one may ask how so many readers of the works of Goody and Ong could, in the eyes of those authors, misinterpret the meaning of their texts. A second criticism focuses on the impoverished model of reasoning and persuasion that Olson appears to hold. Although his privileging of logical proofs over all others is in line with much of the earlier Anglo-American philosophical thinking about language and how it should operate, it ignores the realities and complexities of practical reasoning and persuasion, as discussed by Stephen Toulmin and Chaim Perelman. It likewise fails to acknowledge other possible models; one can argue, for example, that persuasive discourse in Arabic is based on a model in which logical, pathetic, and ethical proofs all have an acknowledged role to play, not because Arab culture is less "literate" or its rhetoric less "logical" than Anglo-American culture and logic, but because the culture and its rhetorical practices have, like our own, developed in the context of particular linguistic, social, and historical circumstances (cf. Walters).

It is not surprising that Olson, trained as a psychologist, focuses on syllogistic reasoning as he does and ultimately equates logic with the syllogism. As Goody points out (*Interface* 216–17), interest in "higher mental functions" and ways of reasoning across cultures has largely been the domain of cognitive psychologists, and the syllogism has long been the "litmus test" for separating those who can think abstractly from those who cannot. Yet, as Jane Hill notes, the ability to reason with syllogisms seems to be a product more of formal schooling than of language structure or, one may add, mere access to literacy. Citing the work of J. F. Hamil and Klaus Galda, Hill states that "careful probing of apparently 'illogical' responses to syllogistic problems by speakers of non-Western languages will almost invariably reveal the respondent has changed the major premise and that the reasoning does follow appropriately from this changed form" (21). She later adds, "When the background cultural knowledge which speakers can be presumed to share is incorporated into the structure of argumentation, it can be shown that the vernacular logical system which governs argument is highly rule-governed and 'logical' " (21). An especially relevant example of this kind of behavior can be found in Beth Daniell's reading of the work of Alexander Luria with illiterates and neoliterates in Uzbekistan in the 1920s, research often cited as evidence of the differences between literate and nonliterate individuals with respect to logical thought (e.g., Ong, *Orality* 49–57; Farrell, "IQ" 476). Work such as that of Hill and Daniell is surely a blow to those who link language, logic, and literacy by means of a particular form and product of literate discourse, such as the syllogism or the essay.

A very different approach to the problem of ways of reasoning across cultures and the influence that literacy may have on these ways is the work of Sylvia Scribner and Michael Cole. Seeking to replicate the findings of Luria earlier this century, Scribner, Cole, and a team of researchers went to Liberia to study the Vai, an ethnic group many of whose members have access to literacy in one or more of three scripts of different kinds, acquired in different ways and used for different purposes. After initial studies, Scribner and Cole gave up on the possibility of finding "general cognitive effects" of literacy, focusing, instead, on isolating specific cognitive skills that correlated with the particular scripts mastered and the contexts for learning them. The work of Scribner and Cole stands as a landmark in our understanding of the nature of literacy.

In his recent work, however, Goody, who had collaborated with Scribner and Cole on one study, offers a critique of their research based on the distinction between what he terms mediated and unmediated effects of literacy. As Goody sees it, Scribner and Cole, working in the paradigm of experimental psychology, were naturally searching for unmediated effects of literacy—that is, correlational (if not causal) relationships between individuals' acquisition of literacy or literacy in a particular script and their cognitive abilities. In contrast, Goody, given his training and interests as an anthropologist, is ultimately concerned with the mediated effects of literacy on societies in which those who become literate use literacy in novel ways and for novel purposes. It is far less likely that these effects can be, as Goody puts it, "mocked up" and tested by using the methods of experimental psychology (*Interface* 227). Similarly, Hill points out, "the relationship between language and nonlinguistic knowledge and behavior is highly complex, and world view cannot simply be 'read off' linguistic structures" (16), as has often been the case in discussions of the effect of language or literacy on logic.

Having considered the work of researchers who focus on literacy in some general sense or on logic in trying to understanding the relationship between these and language, let us turn to two researchers who focus on language itself as a way to understand the relationship between language, logic, and literacy:

Thomas Farrell on what he sees as the importance of mastery of the standard language and E. D. Hirsch, Jr., on cultural literacy. Based largely on the work of Havelock, Ong, and Luria ("Standard" 477), Farrell's work is especially interesting because he contends that the mastery of the code of standard English enables one to think logically, logic again being equated with syllogistic reasoning and the kinds of questions asked in the verbal sections of standardized tests.[5] In contrast, he argues that some dialects of English, most notably dialects of Black Vernacular English, and by extension their speakers, are intrinsically less logical because the surface structures of their dialects do not correspond to those of "standard English" in certain crucial cases. As Farrell puts it:

> I am suggesting that the development of abstract thinking depends on learning (1) the full standard deployment of the verb "to be" [[6]] and (2) embedded modifications and (3) subordination. Historically these are the three features of language that developed as the ancient Greeks moved from oral to literate composing, which resulted in the development of abstract thinking. IQ test scores reveal that black ghetto children have not developed the power of abstract thinking, and they do not speak standard English. The hypothesis, then, is that the mean IQ scores of black ghetto students will go up when they learn to speak and write standard English. ("IQ" 481)

Farrell appears to think that "conferring these linguistic forms is equivalent to conferring a mental construct which he believes is now absent in the minds of these speakers" (Walters, Daniell, and Trachsel 859). John Baugh reviews some of the responses to Farrell's hypothesis and others like it that are based on the mastery of the surface structure of the standard dialect, demonstrating the numerous problems with such approaches to the relationship between language and logic; like nearly all linguists, Baugh argues that such arguments are necessarily flawed.

Like Farrell, Hirsch is concerned with language and thinking, but his argument seems to be that students are unable to think because they have nothing to think with; they lack a mastery of the standard language and "the whole system of widely shared information and associations" (103) ostensibly represented by his list of "what literate Americans know." In fact, the list is an amalgam of names, places, dates, and even expressions, many of which teachers of English as a second language would simply call idioms.

Hirsch apparently believes that one cannot use the English language, or at least not the standard variety of American English, well without having the body of knowledge he and his colleagues have collected. Here I admit that I might not score especially high on a test of cultural literacy as defined by Hirsch. In other words, I do not recognize all the entries in his list; more seriously, I may not know the right things about the items that are familiar. Most important, however, is the fact that I, like many of this culture's hyperliterate, do not know many of the things that literate Americans are supposed to know. This observation leads me to argue that Hirsch is attempting to define what will be at best a second culture for some—perhaps the majority—of us. In fact, Hirsch acknowledges this situation (21), yet he does so without treating any of the issues involved in learning or teaching a second dialect, language, or culture or the frequently encountered resistance to any of these.[7]

The problems with Hirsch and his limited view of literacy do not stop here. He refuses to deal with the consequences—not merely the implications—of the normative character of all descriptions (see Haas on the normative use of linguistic descriptions). Despite his admission that intellectuals consciously create a national culture, choosing selectively and judiciously, Hirsch fails to acknowledge his own active role in this process or to take the responsibility for it, arguing that he is only describing, not prescribing (xiv). Protestations to the contrary, Hirsch is more than an amanuensis in sheep's clothing. Having criticized what he terms "the shopping-mall school" (see Powell, Farrar, and Cohen), Hirsch gives Americans a shopping-mall culture. The dictionary version of the appendix, *The Dictionary of Cultural Literacy* (Hirsch, Kett, and Trefil), is in many ways a *USA Today* of American intellectual life. Certainly Thomas Jefferson's name is there, but that he owned slaves, agonized over the fact, and could bring himself to free them only in his will is not mentioned; instead, Jefferson is characterized as "a champion of political and religious freedom" (246). Thanks to the difficulty of reaching consensus; the homogeneity in age, class, education, and experience of those whose opinions have been sought; and the very nature of Hirsch's endeavor, our culture has been defined by an exceedingly small minority of the intellectual community so that it is denatured and devoid of any serious conflict or vitality.

There are other problems.[8] While acknowledging that the contents of the list will change, Hirsch seems to ignore what these cultural lags, as Goody and Watt characterize them, ultimately mean or how they will be dealt with in the list. If Uncle Tom's name is on that list, when will Rosa Parks's name get there?[9] Hirsch's acknowledgment that his compendium will become the basis for a series of exams represents functional literacy at its worst, "dominated," as Michael Katz puts it, "by rote memorization, routine drill, and passive, unquestioning acceptance of everything said by the teacher or written in the textbook" (209). Apparently, Hirsch looks forward to such a day, contending that if this body of knowledge, linked intimately with a knowledge of the conventions of use for the standard language, is conferred on those who do not have it, the ability to think critically and "full citizenship" in a society blind to class, ethnic, regional, or sex differences must surely follow:

> As the universal second culture [of Americans], literate culture has become the common currency for social and economic exchange in our democracy, and the only available ticket to full citizenship. Getting one's membership is not tied to class or race. Membership is automatic if one learns the background information and the linguistic conventions that are needed to read, write, and speak effectively. (22)

Hirsch, Kett, and Trefil appear unaware of the irony in their statement that "Cultural literacy is shallow; true education is deep" (xv).

An exceedingly different perspective on language and what needs to be passed on as part of cultural heritage comes from Alice Walker in her comments about language. In defending her decision to use the language that she did in the opening pages of *The Color Purple*—and here she is speaking about both the explicitness of the language and the fact that it was unmistakably Black Vernacular English—Walker, like many before her, states:

> For it is language more than anything else that reveals and validates one's existence and if the language we actually speak is denied to us, then it is inevitable that the form we are permitted to assume historically will be one of caricature, reflecting someone's literary or social fantasy.   (58)

Yet, as she notes:

> [O]f course our language is suppressed because it reveals our cultures, cultures at variance with what the dominant, white, well-to-do culture perceives itself to be. To permit the language to be heard . . . is to expose the depth of the conflict between us and our oppressors and the centuries it has not at all silently raged. (63)

In many ways Walker, like Hirsch, is talking about the survival of a culture—but a first, not a second, culture that she contends must and will survive, not merely for its own sake, but as a necessary, if often unacknowledged, part of that second, larger culture of which Hirsch has such a simplistic view. She speaks for the many whose cultures, first or second, are poorly represented in the appendix to *Cultural Literacy* or the accompanying dictionary.

I began by noting that one of the enemies of literacy is a failure to understand its nature and its possibilities. Having surveyed some of the approaches that researchers have taken with respect to the relationships that may obtain among language, logic, and literacy, I would add that another of its enemies is surely defining it—or some component of it—in such a way that it excludes vast segments of those who want it, need it, or indeed already have it but, for a variety of reasons, use it in different ways from the hyperliterate, those of us who have the luxury of spending our lives talking and writing about it.

Our own educations have encouraged us to proceed in this direction. Frank Smith, himself a psychologist, notes in his introduction to papers from the 1982 Victoria conference, which brought together researchers from many disciplines to talk about childhood literacy before schooling:

> Although it is widely accepted that education and its institutions are primarily sociocultural in origin and purpose, educational research during the past two or three decades has turned almost exclusively to psychology for theoretical support

of its practices and solutions to its problems. . . . The persistent underlying conviction is that if reading and writing are analyzed into component elements of
basic skill and knowledge which are presented and rehearsed under appropriate
conditions of incentive and reinforcement, then every relevant factor has been
attended to. From this perspective, learning is essentially a series of inevitable
psychological processes.   (v, viii)

Thus, what we might term "a psychological bias" has permitted us to attribute
to our own experiences a false universality. It not only has encouraged us to
seek exceedingly psychological accounts for what goes on (or fails to go on) in
the classroom but also has led us to accept and to promulgate impoverished
notions of language, logic, and literacy.

Consequently, discussions of language that occur in school are usually couched
in terms of right or wrong, rather than appropriate or inappropriate, and even
less discussion of the protean contexts of language use, whether for spoken or
for written language, and the shifting standards of appropriateness for each takes
place. Logic, for the purposes of schooling, is still often reduced to efforts to
teach or to test the syllogistic thinking of multiple-choice tests. Similarly, school-
based notions of literacy frequently appear to have, at best, tenuous links to
the uses of literacy in life outside school, as work by ethnographers (e.g., Shirley
Brice Heath) and sociolinguists (e.g., Sarah Michaels) has demonstrated.

Efforts to replace our traditional psychological bias with some other bias, be
it anthropological or sociolinguistic, would not solve our problems. Nor are our
problems likely to be solved by reaching some consensus. In fact, the conflicts
evident among the researchers at the Victoria conference (see, esp. the papers
by Frank Smith, Hillel Goelman, and Antoinette Oberg for commentary) witness the unlikelihood of any philosophical, methodological, or pedagogical consensus on these issues. What is needed, instead, is a learning to live with the
tensions and the contradictions in our own goals and practices, not by ignoring
them or minimizing them, but by encouraging and even celebrating them as
we, the hyperliterate, charged with the task of educating the next generation,
seek to understand the nature and the challenge of that task.

In concluding the introduction to *Local Knowledge*, Clifford Geertz comments:

> To see ourselves as others see us can be eye-opening. To see others as sharing a
> nature with ourselves is the merest decency. But it is from the far more difficult
> achievement of seeing ourselves amongst others, as a local example of the forms
> human life has locally taken, a case among cases, a world among worlds, that the
> largeness of mind, without which objectivity is self-congratulation and tolerance
> a sham, comes. If interpretive anthropology has any general office in the world,
> it is to keep reteaching this fugitive truth.   (16)

Surveying much of the current public and academic debate about literacy, I am
forced to conclude that there is too little of our seeing "others as sharing a
nature with ourselves," "ourselves" as "a case among cases," and the hyperli-

teracy that we so privilege, that so defines the core of our being, as a literacy among literacies.

As a consequence of our failures, many suffer, not merely those whose language, logic, and literate practices we dismiss, but also, as Geertz eloquently and rightly notes, we ourselves, who spring so quickly to defend our practices on the grounds of largeness of mind, objectivity, and tolerance. We have much to learn from those whose worlds and experiences are exceedingly different from our own. Confronting those worlds and those experiences should force us to face and examine our own assumptions, as individuals and as members of this culture, about the relationship of language and logic to literacy. Doing so will no doubt help us as we seek to understand what a right to literacy means, to whom it is to be offered, and on what conditions.

NOTES

¹This essay is a revised and expanded version of a talk presented at the MLA Right to Literacy conference in 1988. Revisions have taken into account a number of works unpublished at the time of the conference, including works by E. D. Hirsch Jr., Joseph F. Kett, and James Trefil (*Dictionary*); David Olson ("Mind"); and Walter J. Ong ("Comment"). I wish to thank Beth Daniell, Andrea A. Lunsford, Beverly Moss, and Jonathan Tamez for helpful comments on drafts of this paper. I, alone, remain responsible for errors of fact or interpretation.

²In his discussion of asymmetries between speech and print, C. A. Perfetti distinguishes four hypothetical observation points: beginning literacy, intermediate reading, adult skilled reading, and hyperliteracy. This last point is characterized by a stage in which "print experience has exceeded speech experience," "speech experiences have become more like print," and "speech is slightly more similar to print than print is to speech," a "reversal of [the original] asymmetry" (359).

³There may be evidence of such an effort in Olson's "Mind, Media, and Memory," especially in his review of the major positions in the literature on literacy (423–24; see also the comments of Derrick de Kerckhove and Charles Lumsden, "General Introduction" 5). Despite his apparently having traded one dichotomy for another equally questionable one (namely, given/interpretation), Olson appears to be moving away from his earlier adherence to the "Great Leap" theory that took literacy as its major axis.

⁴Similar critiques of much of the literature on speech-writing differences or the oral-written continuum can be found in Shirley Brice Heath ("Protean") and more recently in Deborah Tannen "Commingling." Douglas Biber's recent work offers novel ways of analyzing the putative differences between spoken and written language. Among the new genres that blend characteristics traditionally associated with speaking and with writing is human-computer interaction, as described by Kathleen Ferrara.

⁵The major sources here include Thomas Farrell's original article ("IQ"); the responses submitted to *College Composition and Communication* by Karen Greenberg, Patrick Hartwell, Margaret Himley, and R. E. Stratton; and the reply by Farrell ("Reply").

⁶Despite the discussion of the use of the verb *to be* in Farrell's article, the replies it

prompted, and his response, readers may still come away without an understanding of the linguistic facts. Contrary to Farrell's implication, no language—to my knowledge—can be said to be "without the verb 'to be' " ("Reply" 473). Although no surface manifestation of this verb occurs in simple declarative sentences in many languages, this verb manifests itself overtly in the surface structure of interrogative and negative sentences as well as a host of other kinds of structures in these same languages. Thus, the issue at stake when Farrell writes about "the standard forms of the verb 'to be' " ("Reply" 473) is not the "presence" or "absence" of the verb; it is, instead, the question of whether this verb is overtly marked in one particular sentence type, simple declarative sentences. These facts about linguistic typology leave Farrell caught between a rock and a hard place, especially since such languages include Russian, the language of Lev Vygotsky and Alexander Luria, as Hartwell notes (463); Arabic; Hebrew, the language of the Old Testament; and Aramaic, the language in which Jesus of Nazareth orally delivered his teachings. Yet, Farrell comments:

> (While abstract thinking develops in literate languages such as Russian which do not have the standard forms of the verb "to be," it strikes me as highly unlikely that a metaphysics of the stature of those developed by Plato, Aristotle, Thomas Aquinas, Etienne Gilson, or Jacques Maritain will ever be developed in a language without the verb "to be.") ("Reply" 473)

[7]Although the concept of resistance has recently become popular in discussions about the teaching of writing, thanks largely to the work of Henry Giroux on schooling in America, quantitative sociolinguists have long dealt with a related phenomenon. Since William Labov's 1966 New York City study, it has been clear that while working-class speakers are aware that their way of speaking is stigmatized by the upper classes and equally aware of how those upper classes speak, working-class speech persists. The reasons for the persistence of this and other kinds of highly "stigmatized" patterns of speech have been the subject of much discussion, as the work of Labov and Martha Laferriere demonstrates. One can only wonder how Hirsch's program of cultural literacy will overcome these obstacles.

[8]See, e.g., Morris Shamos, who contends that "scientific literacy for all is an empty goal" (14), and Bizzell, who offers other criticisms of *Cultural Literacy*.

[9]Interestingly, Rosa Parks's name appears in *The Dictionary of Cultural Literacy* (Hirsch, Kett, and Trefil), which had not been published when this paper was first delivered, although her name did not appear in the appendix to *Cultural Literacy*. A quick perusal of *The Dictionary* reveals a common culture that is far less male-dominated and far more darkly complexioned than that of the original appendix. Such a rapid shift in the content of cultural literacy and the failure of the creators of *The Dictionary* to comment on it are particularly noteworthy, given their arguments for the conservative nature of cultural literacy (see, esp., xiv–xv).

WORKS CITED

Baugh, John. "Language and Race." Newmeyer 64–74.
Biber, Douglas. *Variation across Speech and Writing.* Cambridge: Cambridge UP, 1988.

Bizzell, Patricia. "Arguing about Literacy." *College English* 50 (1988): 141–53.

Daniell, Beth. "Against the Great Leap Theory of Literacy." *Pre/Text* 7 (1986): 181–194.

de Kerckhove, Derrick, and Charles J. Lumsden, eds. *The Alphabet and the Brain: The Lateralization of Writing.* Berlin: Springer-Verlag, 1988.

———. General Introduction. de Kerckhove and Lumsden 1–14.

Farrell, Thomas J. "IQ and Standard English." *College Composition and Communication* 34 (1983): 470–84.

———. "Reply by Thomas J. Farrell." *College Composition and Communication* 35 (1984): 469–78.

Ferrara, Kathleen. "Register Variation: 'Terminal Talk' as an Emergent Language Variety." New Ways of Analyzing Variation 18. Duke University, Durham, 26 Oct. 1989.

Galda, Klaus. "Logic in Non-Indo-European Languages: Yucatec Maya, a Case Study." *Theoretical Linguistics* 6 (1979): 145–60.

Geertz, Clifford. *Local Knowledge: Further Essays in Interpretive Anthropology.* New York: Basic, 1983.

Giroux, Henry. *Theory and Resistance in Education: A Pedagogy for the Opposition.* South Hadley: Bergin, 1983.

Goelman, Hillel. "The Discussion: What Was Said." Goelman, Oberg, and Smith 201–13.

Goelman, Hillel, Antoinette Oberg, and Frank Smith, eds. *Awakening to Literacy.* Exeter: Heinemann, 1984.

Goody, Jack. *The Interface between the Oral and the Written.* Cambridge: Cambridge UP, 1987

———. Introduction. Goody, *Literacy* 1–27.

———, ed. *Literacy in Traditional Societies.* Cambridge: Cambridge UP, 1968.

Goody, Jack, Sylvia Scribner, and Michael Cole. "Writing and Formal Operations." 1977. Goody, *Interface* 191–208.

Goody, Jack, and Ian Watt. "The Consequences of Literacy." 1963. Goody, *Literacy* 27–68.

Greenberg, Karen. "Response No. 1." *College Composition and Communication* 35 (1984): 455–60.

Haas, W. "Introduction: On the Normative Character of Language." *Standard Languages: Spoken and Written.* Ed. W. Haas. Manchester: Manchester UP, 1982. 1–36.

Hamil, J. F. "Transcultural Logic: Testing Hypotheses in Three Languages." *Discourse and Inference in Cognitive Anthropology: An Approach to Psychic Unity and Enculturation.* Ed. Marvin D. Loflin and James Silverberg. The Hague: Mouton, 1978.

Hartwell, Patrick. "Response No. 2." *College Composition and Communication* 35 (1984): 461–65.

Heath, Shirley Brice. "Protean Shapes in Literacy Events: Ever-Shifting Oral and Written Traditions." Tannen, *Spoken and Written* 91–117.

———. *Ways with Words: Language, Life, and Work in Communities and Classrooms.* Cambridge: Cambridge UP, 1983.

Hildyard, Angela, and David Olson. "On the Comprehension and Memory of Oral vs. Written Discourse." Tannen, *Spoken and Written* 19–33.

Hill, Jane. "Language, Culture, and World-View." Newmeyer 14–36.

Himley, Margaret. "Response No. 3." *College Composition and Communication* 35 (1984): 465–68.

Hirsch, E. D., Jr. *Cultural Literacy: What Every American Needs to Know.* Boston: Houghton, 1987.

Hirsch, E. D., Jr., Joseph F. Kett, and James Trefil. *The Dictionary of Cultural Literacy.* Boston: Houghton, 1988.

Horowitz, Rosalind, and S. Jay Samuels, eds. *Comprehending Oral and Written Language.* San Diego: Academic, 1987.

Katz, Michael. "Critical Literacy: A Conception of Education as a Moral Right and Social Ideal." *The Public School Monopoly: A Critical Analysis of Education and the State in America.* Ed. Robert B. Everhart. Cambridge: Ballinger, 1982. 193–223.

Keenan, Edward. "Logic and Language." *Daedalus* 102.3 (1973): 185–94.

Kempson, Ruth. *Semantic Theory.* Cambridge: Cambridge UP, 1977.

Labov, William. *The Social Stratification of English in New York City.* Washington: Center of Applied Linguistics, 1966.

Laferriere, Martha. "Ethnicity in Phonological Variation and Change." *Language* 66 (1979): 603–17.

Lévy-Bruhl, Lucien. *Les fonctions mentales dans les sociétés inférieures.* Paris: Alcan, 1910.

———. *How Natives Think.* 1910. Trans. Lilian A. Clare. 1926. Princeton: Princeton UP, 1985.

Littleton, C. Scott. "Introduction: Lévy-Bruhl and the Concept of Cognitive Relativity." Lévy-Bruhl, *How Natives Think* v–lviii.

Luria, Alexander. *Cognitive Development: Its Cultural and Social Foundations.* Cambridge: Harvard UP, 1976.

Michaels, Sarah. "Narrative Presentations: An Oral Preparation for Literacy with First Graders." *The Social Construction of Literacy.* Ed. Jenny Cook-Gumperz. Cambridge: Cambridge UP, 1986. 95–116.

Newmeyer, Frederick, ed. *Language: The Socio-Cultural Context.* Cambridge: Cambridge UP, 1988. Vol. 4 of *Linguistics: The Cambridge Survey.* Cambridge: Cambridge UP, 1988.

Nystrand, Martin. "The Role of Context in Written Communication." Horowitz and Samuels 197–214.

Oberg, Antoinette. "The Symposium: What It Meant." Goelman, Oberg, and Smith 214–21.

Olson, David. "The Cognitive Consequences of Literacy." *Canadian Psychology/Psychologie Canadienne* 27 (1986): 109–21.

———. "From Utterance to Text: The Bias of Language in Speech and Writing." *Harvard Educational Review* 47 (1977): 257–81.

———. "The Language of Instruction: The Literate Bias of Schooling." *Schooling and the Acquisition of Knowledge.* Ed. R. Anderson, R. Spiro, and W. E. Montague. Hillsdale: Erlbaum, 1977. 65–89.

———. "Mind, Media, and Memory: The Archival and Epistemic Functions of Written Text." de Kerckhove and Lumsden, *Alphabet* 422–41.

Ong, Walter J. "A Comment about 'Arguing about Literacy.' " *College English* 50 (1988): 700–01.

———. "Literacy and Orality in Our Times." *ADE Bulletin* 58 (Sept. 1978): 1–7.

———. *Orality and Literacy: The Technologizing of the Word.* London: Methuen, 1982.

Perfetti, C. A. "Language, Speech and Print: Some Asymmetries in the Acquisition of Literacy." Horowitz and Samuels 355–69.

Powell, Arthur G., Eleanor Farrar, and David K. Cohen. *The Shopping Mall High School: Winners and Losers in the Educational Marketplace.* Boston: Houghton, 1985.

Scribner, Sylvia, and Michael Cole. *The Psychology of Literacy.* Cambridge: Harvard UP, 1981.

Shamos, Morris. "The Lesson Every Child Need Not Learn: Scientific Literacy for All Is an Empty Goal." *Sciences* July–Aug. 1988: 14–20.

Smith, Frank. Introduction. Goelman, Oberg, and Smith v–xv.

Stratton, R. E. "Response No. 4." *College Composition and Communication* 35 (1984): 468–69.

Street, Brian. *Literacy in Theory and Practice.* Cambridge: Cambridge UP, 1984.

Stubbs, Michael. *Language and Literacy.* London: Routledge, 1980.

Tannen, Deborah. "The Commingling of Orality and Literacy in Giving a Paper at a Scholarly Conference." *American Speech* 63 (1988): 34–43.

———, ed. *Spoken and Written Language: Exploring Orality and Literacy.* Norwood: Ablex, 1982.

Walker, Alice. *Living by the Word: Selected Writings 1973–1987.* San Diego: Harcourt, 1988.

Walters, Keith. "On Written Persuasive Discourse in Arabic and English." Unpublished essay, 1987.

Walters, Keith, Beth Daniell, and Mary Trachsel. "Formal and Functional Approaches to Literacy." *Language Arts* 64 (1988): 855–68.

Watson, Rita, and David Olson. "From Meaning to Definition: A Literate Bias on the Structure of Word Meaning." Horowitz and Samuels 329–54.

Williams, Raymond. *Writing in Society.* London: Verso, 1983.

Literacy and Knowledge

Deborah Brandt

The relation between literacy and knowledge is deep and abiding. Desire for knowledge contributes to the allure of literacy. Knowledge of God or self or duty or truth has variably been the driving promise behind literacy movements in this and other societies, just as the fear of an uncontrollable spread of knowledge explains the many efforts in history to suppress the contagion of literacy. Knowledge is at the heart of literacy's value and power, its fundamental goal and most tangible product.

Likewise, literacy has shaped the forms and meanings of knowledge in literate cultures.[1] As many have observed, without the literate technology of print, what we know and how we know it would be inconceivably different. The invention of alphabetic writing and, subsequently, print meant that people could devote less mind space to memorizing and recapitulating knowledge from the past. Literacy allowed a new form of knowledge: cumulative, critical, idiosyncratic, and anonymous.

But while the effects of literacy on knowledge are well recognized, it is worth considering the effects that print-based knowledge is now having on our understanding of literacy and our ability to imagine solutions to literacy problems. In a 1984 essay Anthony Smith points out that, when print made knowledge portable and reproducible—that is, objective—those qualities became the essence of our definition of knowledge. Print, he writes, "imposed a standardized system, for ever, upon the task of communicating knowledge" (183). To be authoritative, knowledge has to be authored—that is, inscribed.

But it is equally true that the qualities of print-based knowledge have now come to infuse conceptions of literacy. As texts make knowledge removable from contexts of human interchange, literacy, too, is imagined and described in terms of social, cognitive, and linguistic decontextualization. As texts stabilize and standardize the image of knowledge, so is literacy identified with standardization. With the growing textualization of knowledge in advanced literate cultures has come a growing textualization of our definitions of literacy.

My aim here is, first, to trace this equivalence of literacy with textuality and then to take issue with it. I look specifically at the work of the influential educational psychologist David R. Olson to show how, in his formulation, the ability of literate technology to transform knowledge comes to stand in for literate knowledge itself. Olson identifies literacy with a deliberate shift away from a knowing how and a knowing who (that is, orality and oral knowledge) toward a knowing that (that is, literate knowledge and literate orientation). My second aim is to show how this characterization is incompatible with the social and cognitive acts of reading and writing. Studies that focus on how people actually accomplish reading and writing reveal that know-how and know-who figure centrally in the work. Process-centered perspectives on reading and writing compel a reformulation of the nature of literacy because what they show is that the forms of knowledge literacy is credited with transforming and even destroying are actually the forms of knowledge by which it is practiced and passed.

The equivalence of literacy with textuality is apparent in the theories of many leading scholars, including Jack Goody, Eric Havelock, Walter Ong, and, perhaps most blatantly, E. D. Hirsch. But Olson makes an interesting study because he applies his theory of literacy most comprehensively to educational issues. Olson articulates the transition that children make as they leave the emotionally charged, familiar, and essentially oral world of the home to step into the literate realm of the school, where even oral language serves primarily to reinforce an orientation to knowledge-bearing texts ("Language of Instruction"). Olson says the transition requires a dramatic repudiation of the interpretive habits of everyday discourse in favor of the new and different demands of the text.

As Olson explains, everyday talk at home is interpersonally based: the status of the speaker is intertwined with the message and, thereby, interwined with the meaning of the message. Children learn language initially not in terms of what words say but in terms of the actions and results that words bring about. But this interpretive procedure fails in the presence of written discourse, particularly school textbooks, in which the social relationship of writer to reader and the relation of writer to message are irrelevant to the making of meaning. As a form of archival language, textbooks appear as a series of disembodied assertions—impersonal, detached, and message-focused. Learning to read these texts, as Olson describes it, is learning how to take them on their own terms ("Writing").

In various essays Olson describes this interpretive shift as an ascendancy of the logical function of language over the rhetorical or social function, the rise of the what over the who ("From Utterance to Text"). In other essays he sees the interpretive shift as a difference between the casual meaning of oral discourse and the literal meaning of written discourse ("Some Social Aspects of Meaning"; Olson and Hildyard, "Writing and Literal Meaning"). In spoken exchanges, Olson says, we tend to privilege the world at the expense of words: we adjust our interpretation of someone's spoken words to what we know about the world and what we think the speaker means to say. That results in casual meaning. But in written discourse the reverse is more typically true. We privilege language over the world and align our understanding of what a text means with our understanding of what a text says. Semantic relations must transcend social relationships. This process results in what Olson calls literal meaning.

Olson's descriptions of literate orientation emphasize parallel transitions from home to school and from utterance to text. Learning to read and learning to go to school are metaphors for each other. Both require unmooring oneself from local social groundings in the world of pragmatic action to handle decontextualized symbols in decontextualized circumstances. To be a reader and to succeed in school, one must be willing and able to enter the house of language-on-its-own.

It is clear that—like Goody, Ong, and others—Olson undertakes to characterize the nature of literacy by working backward from the nature of texts. Look closely at what makes texts textual, he says, and there you find the stuff of literacy. Texts not only make literates, in his estimation, but make them in their own image. To be literate one must be like a text—decontextualized, abstract, literal, and anonymous. The kind of knowledge that texts keep and render is the kind of knowledge, Olson says, that one must apply in writing and reading them. And because texts are purely language, literate knowledge, in Olson's view, is basically metalinguistic: knowledge of language as an object of knowledge.

Olson reinterprets in individual, cognitive, and contemporary terms what has been accepted as the cultural effect of mass schooling. With the rise of the school, the responsibility for passing knowledge moved away from the hand-to-hand, mouth-to-mouth relationships of parent to child and craftsman to apprentice and into the codified written text. Text-based knowledge came to be perceived as everything that craft-based knowledge was not: not practical, not contextual, not communal, not, in Walter Ong's terms, close to the human lifeworld. But in Olson's interpretation of this shift, we see how a model of literate learning becomes a model for literacy learning. Becauses texts serve as the primary sustainers of knowledge, they come to be treated by Olson and others as the primary sustainers of literacy. And that's where I think big problems lie.

The biggest problem with this characterization, to put it in terms familiar from composition studies, is that it puts product over process.[2] And it does not jibe well with descriptions of readers and writers in action. In a well-known set of studies on composing processes, for instance, Linda S. Flower and John R. Hayes describe a group of writers whose methods of writing seem to embody what Olson describes as a literate orientation ("Cognition of Discovery"). The attention of these writers was distinctly text-centered. They concentrated almost exclusively on the what of the discourse, rather than on the who. They were concerned primarily with features and conventions of written texts and were literal in their treatment of meaning. They said what they meant, meant what they said, and moved on. Their approach could be described as abstract and decontextualized. But they were also the weakest writers in the study. And this pattern holds true in every expert-novice study of writers and readers that I know. What appears to Olson as a profile of the literate orientation turns up, in process accounts, as a profile of writers and readers in trouble. In contrast to the poor writers in the Flower and Hayes study, the experts were enmeshed

in an immediate, dynamic, and particular context, focusing considerable attention on the unfolding relation between self and other and keeping themselves
immersed in the pragmatic event of composing.

As process studies have established, the central concern in writing and reading
is not "What does that say?" or "What do I make that say?" but more broadly,
"What do I do now?" The work of reading and writing is not merely and not
mostly encoding and decoding texts or managing semantic meaning. Rather, it
is finding and maintaining the broad conditions that will keep an act of writing
or reading going. The trick for writers and readers is not how to make a text
make sense but how to make what they are doing make sense. The essence of
literate orientation is knowing what to do now.

We see this time and time again in the comparisons between expert and
novice writers and readers; the difference is in how much time and attention
the experts give to establishing and maintaining a working context in which to
write or read, a set of conditions from which the event of writing or reading,
including the language, can gather sense. Flower and Hayes have called this
context "current meaning," which, they say, "may be a distant cousin to the
meaning formulated in a finished text" ("Images" 122). This is not a textual
context or a text world; it is, rather, a here-and-now, off-the-page sense of what
is going on. Good writers and readers are marked not by an ability to go it alone
with language but by an awareness that there is more to writing and reading
than just the language. From a process perspective we see that literacy is a
context-making ability, not a context-breaking ability.

According to expert-novice reports, experts are doing more and different
things as they write and read than novices do: more inferencing, more testing,
more planning, more revising, more connecting, more focusing on purpose and
point to drive the process, and so on. This difference may be summed up by
saying that effective writers and readers read an evolving text not for literal
meaning or for casual meaning but for what-do-I-do-now? meaning. Understanding textual language is understanding what it means for things on your
end, understanding what a text is saying about what you need to be doing. As
Olson would have it, literacy requires untangling language from people, laying
aside reliance on pragmatic events for meaning, coming to terms with the fact
that the words on a page are working independently of you. That, Olson says,
is the hard realization that literacy requires. But, in fact, the requirement is the
reverse. Becoming literate is not learning how to handle language divorced from
action but coming to understand the action that written language relates to,
coming to realize that written discourse is about what people do with it and
that what appears before you on a page has everything in the world to do with
what you're supposed to be doing.

This insight into how literates act in the presence of print helps distinguish
the form and the basis of literate knowledge from the form and the basis of
textual knowledge. Text-based knowledge as an object of knowledge may be
physically decontextualized, literal, propositional, logical, conceptual, semant-

ically rendered, visually and conventionally standardized, and essentially anonymous. Text-based knowledge, historically, may have contributed to the loosening of communal bonds, the destruction of craft apprenticeship, and the rise of, among other things, science, modernization, abstraction, and social alienation. But when we are looking at text-based knowledge, we are looking at a result, a repercussion, an aftermath of literacy—not an image of literacy, not a cause of it, not a requisite for it, and not a realistic model of literate orientation or literacy learning. Literate knowledge—that is, knowing how to read and write—is a knowledge embodied in a doing, a knowledge in which what is made is not separated from the making of it. In that sense, literate knowledge resembles craft knowledge, know-how, knack. And, like craft knowledge, literate knowledge must be passed—hand to hand, mouth to mouth—by people who know how. Because reading and writing know-how is passed person to person, it is, by necessity, local, communal, practical, and, to overhear readers and writers in action, astonishingly ad hoc.

Ethnographer Shirley Brice Heath and historian Harvey J. Graff, among others, have demonstrated how these contextual aspects of literacy work in large-scale cultural arrangements. Heath has documented how the meanings of oral and written language are of a piece with a social group's orientation to time and space and with their habits of problem solving, child rearing, and story telling. Graff likewise traces the historical implications of literacy's ties to social context, seeing literacy practices and their meanings in constant flux as they relate to changing cultural, ethnic, economic, and educational configurations, including systematic inequities.

Studies of reading and writing processes, though focused on the local sites of individuals accomplishing acts of reading and writing, corroborate in crucial ways these ethnographic and historical perspectives. Writers and readers in the act show us how here-and-now social involvement is not merely the cultural impetus for literacy but its interpretive underpinning as well. For writers and readers in the act, literate language, like oral language, derives its meaning from local contexts of practical action—namely, the here-and-now, intersubjective actions of writing and reading. Written language can find meaning only in relation to this ongoing context, a context more of work than of words. Hence, while the move from the oral to the literate may require a new level of symbolic reflectiveness, it preserves the connections among context, language, and knowledge that pertain in oral language use. It requires a deepening understanding of how literate language refers to the pragmatic work of writing and reading. Knowledge of that relation is embodied not in the features of textuality but in the social texture of lived experience.

I end by briefly addressing an important issue in which the textual-knowledge versus literate-knowledge tension is, to me, especially apparent. It has to do with home language difference as a factor in literacy success and failure in school. Children who do well in school tend to live lives outside of school that are richly dependent on literacy. They belong to households where reading and writing connect members to the world and to each other in tangible and often pleasurable ways. They have ample access to people who know how to read and write and who show them how. They experience literacy as a means of social connection and collectivity, as something that is associated with people, places, and time. Yet, according to many researchers, including Olson, the cause of their success in school is more narrow. Olson, for instance, attributes their success to a textual orientation that, he says, is carried in the talk of their social group: an orientation that favors detachment toward language, a tendency to treat it opaquely, as worthy of interpretation and manipulation in its own right. This booklike talk, Olson says, leaves these children sitting pretty when they meet the exotic, decontextualized language demands of the school. The same analysis is used, in reverse, to explain school literacy failure. Children from social groups who use talk primarily to maintain social solidarity and context-resonant meaning are at risk as readers and writers because their language orientation is deemed antitextual. It does not go by the book. To meet the demands of school, Olson says, these children need to learn a different, decontextualized orientation to language; that, he says, is the first step in becoming literate.

This analysis is, to me, an example of the textualizing of literacy, an analysis that assumes that the text is the picture of literate orientation. It is also an analysis in which what may be a surface outcome of a long-standing ease with print is treated as the essence of literacy and even the requisite for literacy. This analysis validates decontextualization as both the ostensible aim and the means of literacy learning in school. Worse, I think, it excuses inequity in a climate already steeped in inequities. For mainstream children, language use rooted in rich social networks of family, community, and local culture is seen, rightly, as the foundation for their success. But for African-Americans and other American subgroups, these same language connections are treated, wrongly, as their greatest liability. While we need, as many have advocated, a school more tolerant of nonstandard language, we also need definitions of standard literacy that are themselves less narrow and exclusionary, definitions in which context resonance and social solidarity, for instance, are appreciated as aspects of literate orientation. That depends on finding new ways of imagining what literacy is and where it comes from, focusing less on outcomes and more on the acts of writing and reading. We need to reconcile in more realistic ways cognitive models of literacy with social models, differentiate textual knowledge from literate know-how, and, above all, recognize that what sustains literacy isn't a what but a who.[3]

NOTES

[1]For a useful history of Western literacy, see Graff. For particular discussions of the relationship of literacy and knowledge, see Eisenstein; Ong; and Goody, especially the chapter titled "Alternative Paths to Knowledge in Oral and Literate Cultures."

²For an introduction to the process perspective in composition pedagogy and research, see Brannon; and Hairston. For discussions of the relevance of process perspectives to understanding literacy, see Brandt.

³Some of the material in this article appeared in slightly different form in Brandt, *Literacy as Involvement*.

WORKS CITED

Brandt, Deborah. *Literacy as Involvement: The Acts of Writers, Readers, and Texts*. Carbondale: Southern Illinois UP, 1990.

Brannon, Lil. "Toward a Theory of Composition." *Perspectives on Research and Scholarship in Composition*. Ed. Ben W. McClelland and Timothy R. Donovan. New York: MLA, 1985. 6–25.

Eisenstein, Deborah. *The Printing Press as an Agent of Change*. New York: Cambridge UP, 1979.

Flower, Linda S., and John R. Hayes. "The Cognition of Discovery: Defining a Rhetorical Problem." *College Composition and Communication* 32 (1981): 365–87.

———. "Images, Plans, and Prose: The Representation of Meaning in Writing." *Written Communication* 1 (1984): 120–60.

Goody, Jack. *The Interface between the Written and the Oral*. New York: Cambridge UP, 1987.

Graff, Harvey J. *The Legacies of Literacy: Continuities and Contradictions in Western Society and Culture*. Bloomington: Indiana UP, 1986.

Hairston, Maxine. "The Winds of Change: Thomas Kuhn and the Revolution in the Teaching of Writing." *College Composition and Communication* 33 (1982): 76–88.

Havelock, Eric A. *The Literate Revolution in Greece and Its Cultural Consequences*. Princeton: Princeton UP, 1982.

———. *The Muse Learns to Write: Reflections on Orality and Literacy from Antiquity to the Present*. New Haven: Yale UP, 1986.

Heath, Shirley Brice. *Ways with Words: Language, Life, and Work in Communities and Classrooms*. New York: Cambridge UP, 1983.

Hirsch, E. D., Jr. *Cultural Literacy: What Every American Needs to Know*. Boston: Houghton, 1987.

Olson, David R. "From Utterance to Text: The Bias of Language in Speech and Writing." *Harvard Educational Review* 47 (1977): 257–81.

———. "The Language of Instruction: The Literate Bias of Schooling." *Schooling and the Acquisition of Knowledge*. Ed. Richard Anderson, Rand Spiro, and William E. Montague. Hillsdale: Erlbaum, 1977. 65–89.

———. " 'See! Jumping!' Some Oral Antecedents of Literacy." *Awakening to Literacy*. Ed. Hillel Goelman, Antoinette A. Oberg, and Frank Smith. Exeter: Heinemann, 1984. 185–200.

———. "Some Social Aspects of Meaning in Oral and Written Language." *Social Foundations of Language and Thought*. Ed. David R. Olson. New York: Norton, 1980. 90–110.

———. "Writing: The Divorce of the Author from the Text." *Exploring Speaking-Writing Relationships: Connections and Contrasts*. Ed. Barry M. Kroll and Roberta J. Vann. Urbana: NCTE, 1981. 99–110.

Olson, David, and Angela Hildyard. "Writing and Literal Meaning." *The Psychology of Written Language: Developmental and Educational Perspectives.* Ed. Margaret Martlew. New York: Wiley, 1983.

Ong, Walter. *Orality and Literacy: The Technologizing of the Word.* New York: Methuen, 1982.

Smith, Anthony. "On Audio and Visual Technologies: A Future for the Written Word?" *The Written Word: Literacy in Transition.* Ed. Gerd Baumann. Oxford: Clarendon, 1984. 171–92.

The Situation of Literacy and Cognition: What We Can Learn from the Uzbek Experiment

Beth Daniell

Discussions of literacy are bound up in subtle and complex ways with assumptions about what it means to read and write. Most Americans take for granted the cognitive, social, and economic benefits of literacy, while, similarly, many academics extend the notion to conform to their own particular experience with texts. As Keith Walters and Deborah Brandt point out in their contributions to this volume, however, such attitudes are often narrow, even ethnocentric. Culturally laden definitions of literacy, especially those concerning the relation of literacy and thinking, can in fact become powerful enemies of literacy and of attempts to foster literacy in a pluralistic, democratic society.

In this essay I examine some recent and some not so recent scholarship involving literacy and thought in order to demonstrate that identifying literacy with particular ways of thinking privileged in our culture keeps us from reading the ways in which persons in other groups think about and use literacy. Regarding our own literate and cognitive customs as transhistorical, we fail to recognize social and political influences and constraints on both literacy and thought, thereby labeling the discursive practices of others in terms that indicate deficiency or inferiority. From this attitude come pedagogies, insensitive to the felt needs of learners, that actually prevent human beings from using reading and writing to create meaning in their own lives. I argue, in short, that the use of language and literacy generally tells us more about the social and political relations in a particular situation than it does about cognitive development.

The not so recent work that I examine here is Alexander Luria's report on research in 1931 and 1932 among the indigenous Turkic-speaking Muslim people of Uzbekistan in the Soviet Union. Luria's account of this work, which for a variety of reasons remained unpublished for almost forty years, appeared in the United States in 1976 as *Cognitive Development: Its Cultural and Social Foundations*. A student of Lev Vygotsky,[1] Luria designed this project in order to study the cognitive effects of social and cultural change. Vygotsky and Luria hypothesized that, as the revolution with its attendant collectivization and modernization reached traditional populations in outlying provinces, fundamental changes in thought processes would occur, and so Luria set out to document them.

During the time of Luria's project, the Uzbek peasants being collectivized were also receiving literacy instruction, and Luria makes note of the degree of literacy attained by the subjects he discusses.

Recent scholars who believe, along with Eric Havelock, Jack Goody and Ian Watt, and David R. Olson, that literacy causes profound changes in the thought processes of human beings often refer to Luria's research as they argue for one or another of the cognitive consequences of literacy. Of this group no one seems to place more confidence in Luria's account of the Uzbek experiments than Walter J. Ong. Like others who think that literacy brings about a mental great leap, Ong sees literacy primarily as a technology that fosters abstract thinking. In a 1978 essay titled "Literacy and Orality in Our Times," Ong says that writing is "an absolute necessity" for the analytical, sequential, abstract thought that he apparently takes to be the end point of cognitive development (2). Most of us agree when Ong asserts that writing is "absolutely essential" for "certain noetic operations which a high-technology culture takes for granted" (2). Some remain skeptical, however, when he claims that "[w]ithout writing, the mind cannot even generate concepts such as 'history' or 'analysis' " and that writing is "essential for the realization of fuller human potential and for the evolution of consciousness itself" (2).

In his 1982 book *Orality and Literacy*, Ong devotes chapter 3 to showing how the thought and language of orality differ from the thought and language of literacy. Ong lists, among other characteristics of orality, "additive rather than subordinate" (37), "aggregative rather than analytic" (38), "empathetic and participatory rather than objectively distanced" (45), and "situational rather than abstract" (49). In the eight pages (49–57) in which Ong explains that oral thinking is situational and not abstract, he draws almost exclusively on Luria. In short, Ong finds in the Uzbek research empirical evidence for his own contention that literacy causes fundamental changes in human cognition.

The respect that Ong has earned among scholars in both literature and rhetoric has made his ideas on literacy particularly accessible and influential in English studies. Indeed, his theoretical statements on literacy have been used as the basis of various explanations of and proposals for student performance and educational reform (e.g., Lanham, "Composition," but cf. Lanham, "Rhetorical Paideia"; Lazeree; Comprone; Vavra; Welch). The most widely disseminated statement is Ong's own "Literacy and Orality" article. Here, Ong uses his orality-literacy dichotomy to interpret the behavior of an inner-city black student in a college English class. Because "Literacy and Orality" neglects the social, political, and economic conditions in which this student lives, the essay gives the impression that the "primary orality" of this young man's home culture is sufficient explanation for "classroom responses" that Ong sees as inappropriate. Regardless of his intentions, Ong's application of broad cultural and historical theories to contemporary individuals and groups seems to many merely to provide justification for the status quo. Probably the best-known application of Ong's orality-literacy theory is Thomas J. Farrell's 1983 article "IQ and Standard

English," an essay that evoked many strong responses, including the charge of racisim (Greenberg, in Greenberg et al. 460).

Ong's commitment to the notion of literacy as a cognitive activity causes him to choose evidence, including Luria's data, selectively and thus to neglect the social and political aspects of literacy and of research concerning literacy. Privileging the relation of literacy and thought over the relation of literacy and its sociopolitical context lets us continue to assume that literacy shapes thought in the same way for all persons, regardless of specific circumstances. Our students, including the young man described in Ong's "Literacy and Orality," can ill afford a literacy separated from their particular histories and immediate concerns. To challenge the view that literacy triggers inevitable cognitive changes, I reexamine Ong's reading of Luria's experiment. I begin with an alternative reading of Luria that privileges the social and political and contextualizes Luria's work. Crucial to this reading is an account of the ideology and theory of the Uzbek experiment.

In an essay on Soviet literacy campaigns, Ben Eklof sums up this context with the term *Stalinist literacy* (138). Just how accurately this term applies to literacy in the central Asian republics in the early 1930s is not clear, though the kulaks (land-owning peasants) in the cotton-growing areas of Uzbekistan were being forcibly deported during this period (Conquest 189). Well before the 1917 revolution, the Bolsheviks and others had identified illiteracy with the exploitation of the people by the Tsarist government. One of the first goals of the revolution was therefore to bring literacy to the masses, but civil and economic upheaval in the 1920s delayed systematic implementation. According to Eklof, Stalin co-opted the literacy campaigns, incorporating them into his top-down plans to modernize the economy (138, 142). Under Stalin, literacy became, like massive industrialization and forced collectivization, a tool in the creation of a centralized state, rather than a means to human liberation. Another function of Soviet literacy campaigns was the Russification of indigenous peoples. Perception of this goal often stirred resistance—in the western provinces so much that literacy workers were often attacked, sometimes even killed (Eklof 140).

Luria's *Cognitive Development* makes no mention of Stalin's methods and aims or of the attitudes of the native population toward collectivization or other moves to modernize the region. Nor does Luria discuss the increasing Communist party control during the 1920s and 1930s on psychology or explain that after the Uzbek expeditions this sort of developmental research fell into disfavor, with accusations against him and Vygotsky of reformulating "bourgeois" theories and insulting national minorities (Joravsky 123; on the ethnocentrism charge, see Cole xiv; cf. Valsiner 117–65, 284–308).

Although Luria offers a little more detail in *The Making of Mind* (60–62) than in *Cognitive Development* about his subjects' attainments in literacy, he tells us virtually nothing about their literacy instruction. We don't know, for example, whether literacy classes were voluntary or what the relationship was—

linguistically, culturally, and politically—between teachers and students. It is fair to assume that instruction was in Uzbek, not Russian, and that the script was based on the Latin alphabet (Valsiner 285–86). However, according to Frierman, neither dialect nor orthography issues were altogether settled by 1931, so it is not clear whether the peasants were being taught in their native rural dialect or an urban one or whether they were using the script based on vowel harmony or the simplified script that became official in 1934.

While such issues are important to consider in studying research on literacy, Luria does not discuss them, because literacy was not the focus of his experiments. For Luria, literacy was only one measure of the degree of modernization the Uzbek subjects had attained (but cf. Wertsch 33–40). Committed to building a Marxist psychology, both Luria and Vygotsky believed that as the social structure changed, so would the mind. *Cognitive Development* is, therefore, replete with conclusions that those who have been collectivized perform better on developmental tasks than do independent farmers. The collective activists, in fact, do better than independent farmers even when the collective activists are identified by Luria as illiterate.

Ong includes in his reading of the Uzbek experiments neither the intellectual nor the political background of Luria's research, apparently not considering the possibility that these conditions may have skewed the research design or its conclusions. Rather, in *Orality and Literacy* Ong deals with the complexities of the situation by means of one sentence and one phrase. The sentence: "In an elaborate framework of Marxist theory, Luria attends to some degree to matters other than the immediate consequences of literacy, such as 'the unregulated individualistic economy centered on agriculture' and 'the beginnings of collectivization' (1976, p. 14)" (50). More important, isolating literacy and research from context, Ong dismisses Vygotsky's theory of the relations of language, society, and individual thought with the phrase "elaborate Marxist scaffolding" (50). Ong thus glosses over Luria's Marxism and also over the distinction between Marxist theory and Stalinist totalitarianism.

In *Orality and Literacy* Ong uses Luria's research to make five points about the differences between "situational" oral cognition and "abstract" literate cognition; I discuss only three in this essay. First, literates accepted the premises of syllogism-type questions; illiterate subjects, by contrast, rejected premises unfamiliar in their experience and therefore gave answers that, as Ong explains, "would not fit . . . into pure logical forms" (52). Second, literates classified drawings of familiar objects by using abstract principles ("they are all farming tools") while illiterates categorized according to the function of the objects in practical situations ("if you're going to saw, you need a saw, and if you have to split something you need a hatchet") (52, 51; *Cognitive Development* 72, 55). Third, unlike literates, illiterates showed "difficulty in articulate self-analysis" (54); that is, literates were able, as Luria phrases it, to "distinguish psychological features" (*Cognitive Development* 159), but the illiterates were unable to talk about themselves in these terms.

In one series of tests, Luria's experimenters presented the Uzbek peasants with syllogism problems like "In the Far North, where there is snow, all bears are white. Novaya Zemlya is in the Far North and there is always snow there. What color are the bears there?" and "Cotton can grow only where it is hot and dry. In England it is cold and damp. Can cotton grow there?" (*Cognitive Development* 100–16). When some of the Uzbeks refused to accept the experimenters' premises as facts and responded with "I don't know what color the bears there are, I never saw them" and "We speak only of what we see; we don't talk about what we haven't seen" (*Cognitive Development* 111, 109), Luria concludes that these people cannot use syllogistic thinking. Ong is more tolerant of such responses, explaining that to the oral mind such questions seem either patently silly or completely uninteresting (*Orality and Literacy* 52). Neither Ong nor Luria seems to consider the possibility that such responses were examples of elaborate communal leg pulling aimed at the city-slicker academics from Moscow.

Similarly, neither Ong nor Luria considers that such responses could index healthy skepticism or veiled resistance. Luria tells us that the "experimental sessions began with long conversations (sometimes repeated) with the subjects in the relaxed atmosphere of a tea house—where the villagers spent most of their free time—or in camps in the fields and mountain pastures around the evening campfire" (*Cognitive Development* 16). But how do we know that the villagers and farmers really were relaxed? Perhaps the rapport that Luria describes did in fact exist, but Luria's book, instead of documenting it, only claims it. Considering the history of colonial exploitation of central Asia by Russia, the well-known violence of the revolution and the civil war, and the deportations of those resisting collectivization, I have little reason to share the trust that Luria assumes between his researchers and his subjects. In social research, Jack D. Douglas tells us, informants as well as experimenters always have an agenda. But Ong's reading questions neither Luria's research methods nor the Uzbeks' forthrightness.

Sometimes, in answer to the syllogism questions, Luria's peasants gave answers like "From your words, I would have to say that cotton shouldn't grow there. But I would have to know what spring is like there, what kind of nights they have" and "To go by your words, [the bears] should all be white" (*Cognitive Development* 111, 114). Luria continues to see such responses as evidence of faulty thinking, labeling them with comments such as "reference to lack of personal experience" and "refusal to draw conclusions" (*Cognitive Development* 111). Ong, at this point, posits another explanation: " 'To go by your words,' " he says "appears to indicate awareness of the formal intellectual structures. A little literacy goes a long way" (*Orality and Literacy* 53). Well, perhaps.

The peasant who gave this last "To go by your words" response is, it is true, "barely literate" (*Cognitive Development* 114). But Luria tells us that when presented with the white-bears syllogism, another peasant—"Ishnakul, age sixty-three, collective farmworker, *illiterate*, one of the most respected people in the village"—replied, "If you say they are white from the cold, they should be white there too" (*Cognitive Development* 114, emphasis added). This response merits no discussion from Ong, even though the two answers are reported on the same page in *Cognitive Development*. Ong credits only one answer as indicating movement toward abstract thought, the one from the literate speaker, while Luria classifies the two answers together because both speakers were active in the collective. If literacy per se were making the cognitive changes in these peasants, wouldn't responses so similar come from persons with the same degree of literacy? As I see it, these phrases—"From your words," "To go by your words," and "If you say they are"—reveal little about "awareness of the formal intellectual structures"; instead, they appear to indicate that the peasants feel they must respond to the questions asked by the strangers from Moscow, although they do not want to be held responsibile for the truth value of the premises.

Just as Ong's belief in the cognitive effects of literacy causes him to ignore the sociopolitical context of Luria's research and thereby gloss over the inconsistencies between his own thesis and Luria's report, so too it causes him to concentrate on "formal intellectual structures" rather than on the semantic content of the experiment. For example, one chapter in Luria's *Cognitive Development* titled "Generalization and Abstraction" reports the results of classification tests. Many of these problems focused on farming-related items—ears of grain, buckets, wheels, logs—items familiar to the rural Uzbeks of course, but also objects meaningful in a society trying to glorify the worker and to convince people to farm collectively. Another group of questions had to do with tools—axes, saws, knives, hatchets, hammers and sickles. Reading for form, not content, Ong misses the fact that the language of the research project encodes the ideological symbols of the Russian Revolution.

Ignoring these symbols further impoverishes the reading of the Uzbek research because tools index the theoretical framework of Luria's empirical study. Luria's project, as I have noted, was based on Vygotsky's theory of language, which, according to Michael Cole and Sylvia Scribner, was based, at least in part, on Engels's theory of tools. According to Engels, human beings use labor and tools to change nature and, in doing so, change themselves. What Vygotsky did was to extend Engels's concept of tool use to include signs (Cole and Scribner 7; cf. Valsiner 123–25). Reacting against the deterministic behaviorist theories of early psychology, Vygotsky set out to show that "the individual modifies the stimulus situation as a part of the process of responding to it" (Cole and Scribner 14). Thus, both tool and sign have a "mediating function" (Vygotsky 54). The tool transforms the outside environment; the sign transforms, first, other persons and then the user (Vygotsky 55).

Vygotsky believed that all "higher functions"—by which he meant voluntary attention, logical memory, formation of concepts—"originate as *actual* relations between human individuals" (57). The social "interpersonal process" later becomes an individual "intrapersonal" one (57). According to Vygotsky, speech and writing are both tools and signs and at the same time products of the ongoing transformation of individuals by their environment and of social relations by individuals.

It seems almost predictable, then, that Luria's project has to do with tools, symbols of the revolution and emblems of the theory of language and learning out of which he is working. Of course I don't believe that Luria's researchers purposely framed the test questions to express the ideology explicitly; according to Luria, the questions were consciously structured to contain information familiar to their rural subjects. Nevertheless, the semantic content of the questions is consistent with the ideological and theoretical underpinnings of the project. Ong's reading fails to consider the possibility that Luria's "elaborate Marxist scaffolding" goes beyond Soviet cant, that indeed the theory offers an explanation for the results in a way that Luria's account only hints at.

Synthesizing the theories of Vygotsky and Mikhail Bakhtin,[2] Caryl Emerson explains that both see the word as socially acquired. According to Emerson, Bakhtin believes that the words of others are "authoritative . . . distanced" and can be acquired sometimes only by "reciting by heart"; in other situations the words of others become in the retelling "internally persuasive," that is, "one's own" (Emerson 255). This is similar to Vygotsky's argument that words are first used as tools to change the external environment before they are used internally as signs to transform the self. This process, I suggest, is precisely what is going on in the responses of the Uzbek peasants. Some of them are using or attempting to use the words of others before this authoritative, distanced language has become internally persuasive—before these words, these ways of speaking, carry much internal meaning.

For example, in the last chapter of *Cognitive Development* Luria reports on the changes in self-analysis and self-awareness that accompany social change. This section plays an important role in Ong's reading; in his theory, consciousness of self is a function of literacy (*Orality and Literacy* 179). Luria elicited responses from his informants by asking, "What sort of person are you?" "What are your shortcomings?" "Are you satisfied with yourself or would you like to be different?" (150). When illiterate peasants from outlying districts were asked such questions, they answered by saying: "I have only one dress and two robes, and those are all my shortcomings" (148); "I was a farmhand; I have a hard time and many debts, with a measure of wheat costing eighteen rubles—that's what troubles me" (149); "How can I talk about my character? Ask others; they can tell you about me. I myself can't say anything" (149).

In *Cognitive Development* Luria explains such responses with terse comments like " 'Shortcomings' understood as things that are lacking" (148); "Question understood in terms of external conditions of life" (150).[3] Ong's comments in *Orality and Literacy* are similar: "Self-evaluation modulated into group evaluation (we) and then handled in terms of expected reactions from others" and "Judgement bears in on the individual from the outside, not from within" (55). Sometimes Ong is more sympathetic, as when he introduces one peasant's response by commenting, "Another man . . . responded with touching and humane directness" (*Orality and Literacy* 55). These subjects' expressed desire for respect from their cultural group is seen by both Luria and Ong as evidence of a lack of self-differentiation, not as attempts to preserve some traditional identity in the face of forced social change.

Those subjects who are considered cognitively developed enough to be able to "distinguish psychological features" turn out to be collectivized according to Luria and literate according to Ong. But, again, Ong misses the content. Whether collectivized or literate, those peasants who "distinguish psychological features" remark on either the improvements in their lives brought about by the revolution or the changes that the revolution will now make possible (*Cognitive Development* 155–59). To Luria's questions, they gave answers like these: "Before, I was a farmhand, I worked for a boss and didn't dare talk back to him; he did with me as he pleased. Now I know what my rights are" and "Before I didn't know anything about freedom, and now I do. Before I worked a lot for others and couldn't get a pound of bread for my family, but on the farm I'm living better. I have things to give to others, and I even got married this year" (*Cognitive Development* 157).

Like new converts to any religion, these peasants testify in the accepted code to a change-for-the-better life: I once was lost but now am found, was blind but now I see. Whether sincere or expedient, these speeches tell us little about logical, abstract, or analytical thinking or about literacy. They tell us, instead, about the apparently universal conversion experience and reveal a typical trope of revolutions: self-analysis and vows of self-improvement. The peasants whom Luria credits and Ong accepts as having achieved independent thought appear to be those who accept the discourse of the revolution and try to use its authoritative words.

In my reading, the Uzbeks' responses emerge as verbal attempts to interact with a new and unfamiliar power structure. If the answers the Uzbek peasants gave to Luria's experimenters are psychological data, they are also political maneuvers. On the one hand, then, it seems that there is little for us to learn from this research about the cognitive effects of reading and writing. Both Ong and Luria, for different reasons, give explanations that fail to take into account the situational and discursive events that mediate the differences that Luria's research does, in fact, document. On the other hand, there are some things that the Uzbek experiment can teach us about language, literacy, and thought. We learn from this research, for example, that human beings demonstrate their affinity for specific social groups by demonstrating their facility with the language peculiar to those groups. Like the freshmen whose papers David Bartholomae analyzes in "Inventing the University," Luria's peasants recognize some of the features of the language of authority and attempt to use those features, but, as outsiders, they do not necessarily use them felicitously.

In oral cultures, Ong asserts, thought means not analyzing but rather stitching together formulaic expressions and clichés—that is, the commonplaces ("Literacy and Orality" 2). But Bartholomae claims that all the students in his study, including the most literate, used these culturally accepted concepts, statements, and methods of argument as a way of appropriating the authority to speak in a situation marked by an unequal distribution of power (148–49). Writers of the low-rated papers drew commonplaces from their neighborhoods, while the successful writers used the commonplaces of the academic discourse community. The writer of the best essay, who "approximates the specialized language of what is presumed to be a more powerful and more privileged community" (157), based her analysis on two different commonplaces, one dealing with the subject—"creativity is using old things in new ways" (149)—and one offering a way of discussing the assigned topic—the ploy of setting oneself against "some more naive way of talking about [the] subject" (153). Similarly, I believe, collectivization and literacy instruction taught some of the Uzbek peasants not only the surface language but also some commonplaces of another social order, one with a different worldview.

Bartholomae implies what Vygotsky teaches and what Luria's work demonstrates: All reading and writing and all thought are socially acquired and culturally constituted. Ong says that for the black student described in "Literacy and Orality" who came to class without a textbook "even though the class was engaged in an analytic discussion of a text," education means "identification, participation, getting into the act, feeling affinity with the culture's heroes, getting 'with it'—not in analysis at all" (4). The most literate among us, I submit, have become so by identifying, participating, getting "with it." Our consciousness evolves not so much from the fact that we read and write as from what we read and what we are allowed to write. Our language, our literacy, and our thought are shaped by the worldview that we partake of and by our proximity to those who shape that view. Perhaps independent thought is, after all, best defined as the kind of thinking that a given culture rewards by calling it independent, not a kind of thinking that exists apart from the social realm.

In addition, we learn from Luria's research that literacy, whether our own or that acquired by the Uzbek peasants, cannot be separated from the politics of its production and distribution. The kind of thinking that both Ong and Luria call "abstract" includes accepting culturally privileged taxonomic categories and the premises of the syllogism, itself a peculiarly Western form, not a universal one. We learn from the Uzbek experiment that both thought and literacy are situational and that part of the situation is always power. Ignoring the power relations of the situation while assuming the capacity of literacy to automatically bestow culture-specific cognitive patterns reifies literacy and separates it from the concerns of the learners. The rigid, decontextualized—and oppressive—pedagogies that result hinder rather than advance the right to literacy.[4]

NOTES

[1]Technically, Luria and Vygotsky were colleagues and collaborators at the Institute of Psychology at Moscow University and at several other institutions from 1924 until

Vygotsky's death in 1934. In the preface to *Cognitive Development*, Luria calls Vygotsky "my teacher and friend" (vi); *The Making of Mind*, Luria's intellectual autobiography, makes it clear that Luria regarded all his work as an elaboration and refinement of Vygotsky's theoretical positions.

²Much of what in "The Outer Word and Inner Speech" Caryl Emerson attributes to Bakhtin she now ascribes to Vološinov (private conversation, 24 May 1989). The part of this article that I rely on here is from Emerson's reading of "Discourse in the Novel," an essay clearly Bakhtin's in *The Dialogic Imagination* (259–422). See Morson and Emerson.

³Cf. Valsiner 297–98. In discussing Luria's findings on self-awareness, Valsiner points out, "The Russian term used by Luria—*nedostatok*—can be applied *both* to external lack of something in terms of material goods, and to deficiences of one's character or personality." In *The Making of Mind* Luria says that the interviews were carried out in Uzbek (63), but nowhere that I am aware of does he discuss language as a methodological problem; in other words, there is no discussion of the shades of meaning of the Uzbek word finally translated, through Russian, as *shortcomings*. Ong does not discuss the problem of language in regard to this research.

⁴John Trimbur and Jim Zebroski read earlier versions of this paper and made helpful substantive comments and suggestions. Denise Boerckel, Andrea Lunsford, and Art Young gave sensitive, critical readings of this version. Research for this essay was supported by a National Endowment for the Humanities summer stipend.

WORKS CITED

Bakhtin, Mikhail. *The Dialogic Imagination: Four Essays*. Ed. Michael Holquist. Trans. Caryl Emerson and Michael Holquist. Austin: U of Texas P, 1981.

Bartholomae, David. "Inventing the University." *When a Writer Can't Write: Studies in Writer's Block and Other Composing-Process Problems*. Ed. Mike Rose. New York: Guilford, 1985. 134–65.

Cole, Michael. Foreword. *Cognitive Development: Its Cultural and Social Foundations*. By A. R. Luria. Cambridge: Harvard UP, 1976. xi–xvi.

Cole, Michael, and Sylvia Scribner. Introduction. *Mind in Society: The Development of Higher Psychological Processes*. By L S. Vygotsky. Cambridge: Harvard UP, 1978. 1–14.

Comprone, Joseph. "An Ongian Perspective on the History of Literacy: Psychological Context and Today's College Student Writer." *Rhetoric Review* 4 (1986): 138–48.

Conquest, Robert. *The Harvest of Sorrow: Soviet Collectivization and the Terror-Famine*. New York: Oxford UP, 1986.

Douglas, Jack D. *Investigative Social Research: Independent and Team Field Research*. Beverly Hills: Sage, 1976.

Eklof, Ben. "Russian Literacy Campaigns, 1861–1939." *National Literacy Campaigns: Historical and Comparative Perspectives*. Ed. Robert F. Arnove and Harvey J. Graff. New York: Plenum, 1987. 123–45.

Emerson, Caryl. "The Outer Word and Inner Speech: Bakhtin, Vygotsky, and the Internalization of Language." *Critical Inquiry* 10 (1983): 245–64.

Farrell, Thomas J. "IQ and Standard English." *College Composition and Communication* 34 (1983): 470–84.

Frierman, William. "Language Development in Soviet Uzbekistan." *Sociolinguistic Perspectives on Soviet National Languages: Their Past, Present and Future.* New York: Mouton, 1985. 205–33.

Goody, Jack, and Ian Watt. "The Consequences of Literacy." *Comparative Studies in Society and History* 5 (1963): 304–45.

Greenberg, Karen, et al. "Responses to Thomas J. Farrell, 'IQ and Standard English' (with a Reply by Thomas J. Farrell)." *College Composition and Communication* 35 (1984): 455–78.

Havelock, Eric. *The Literate Revolution in Greece and Its Cultural Consequences.* Princeton: Princeton UP, 1982.

Joravsky, David. "The Construction of the Stalinist Psyche." *Cultural Revolution in Russia, 1928–1931.* Ed. Sheila Fitzpatrick. Bloomington: Indiana UP, 1978. 105–28.

Lanham, Richard. "Composition, Literature, and the Lower-Division Gyroscope." *Profession 84* 1984: 10–15.

———. "The Rhetorical Paideia: The Curriculum as a Work of Art." *College English* 48 (1986): 132–41.

Lazeree, Donald. "Literacy Theory and Departments of English." Introduction. Forum on Literacy, MLA Convention. Washington, Dec. 1984.

Luria, A. R. *Cognitive Development: Its Cultural and Social Foundations.* Ed. Michael Cole. Cambridge: Harvard UP, 1976.

———. *The Making of Mind: A Personal Acccount of Soviet Psychology.* Ed. Michael Cole and Sheila Scribner. Cambridge: Harvard UP, 1979.

Morson, Gary Saul, and Caryl Emerson, eds. *Rethinking Bakhtin: Extensions and Challenges.* Evanston: Northwestern UP, 1989.

Olson, David R. "From Utterance to Text: The Bias of Language in Speech and Writing." *Harvard Educational Review* 47 (1977): 257–81.

Ong, Walter J. "Literacy and Orality in Our Times." *ADE Bulletin* 58 (1978): 1–7. (Rpt. in *Profession 79* 1979: 1–7. Rpt. in *Journal of Communication* 30 (1980): 197–204. Rpt. in *The Writing Teachers' Sourcebook.* Ed. Gary Tate and Edward P. J. Corbett. New York: Oxford UP, 1981. 36–48. Rpt. in *Pacific Quarterly* 7.2 (1982). Rpt. in *Composition and Literature: Bridging the Gap.* Ed. Winifred Bryan Horner. Chicago: U of Chicago P, 1983. 126–40. Rpt. in *A Sourcebook for Basic Writing Teachers.* Ed. Theresa Enos. New York: Random, 1987. 45–55. Rpt. in *The Writing Teachers' Sourcebook,* Ed. Gary Tate and Edward P. J. Corbett. 2nd ed. New York: Oxford UP, 1988. 37–46.)

———. *Orality and Literacy: The Technologizing of the Word.* London: Methuen, 1982.

Valsiner, Jaan. *Developmental Psychology in the Soviet Union.* Bloomington: Indiana UP, 1988.

Vavra, Edward A. "Comment and Response: Four Comments on 'Grammar, Grammars, and the Teaching of Grammar'." *College English* 47 (1985): 647–49.

Vygotsky, L. S. *Mind in Society: The Development of Higher Psychological Processes.* Ed. Michael Cole, Vera John-Steiner, Sylvia Scribner, Ellen Souberman. Cambridge: Harvard UP, 1978.

Welch, Kathleen. "Classical Rhetoric, Literacy and the Teaching of Writing: Ong, Orality, and Composition." Conference on College Composition and Communication. Seattle, 17 March 1989.

Wertsch, James V. *Vygotsky and the Social Formation of Mind.* Cambridge: Harvard UP, 1985.

In Praise of the Local and Transitory

Kathryn Thoms Flannery

Recent historical and ethnographic studies of literacy make it difficult to continue to argue that learning to read and write will necessarily lead to socioeconomic advancement, political enlightenment, or more humanized behavior. And yet, such arguments for literacy persist not only in best-selling books about the sorry state of education in the United States and in the pronouncements of politicians but also, and perhaps most important, in our own discussions of what we understand our mission as teachers of English to be.[1] Teaching a recent graduate-level introduction to literacy studies, I was struck by how deep-seated is the need to see ourselves as liberators. The members of the class, already high school teachers or college teachers or preparing to be teachers, were confronted with readings that undercut their faith in the fundamental goodness of their calling, readings that required them to reassess their faith in the inherent value of reading and writing.

I was not prepared for how wrenching such a reassessment would be for my class or for me. Much of the recent work in literacy studies suggests how powerless teachers are to alter the uses to which literacy will be put or to affect how and to whom the rewards for literacy achievement will be distributed in our culture (cf. Graff; Heath, "Functions and Uses"; Ogbu). In fact, much of this work suggests the extent to which literacy instruction is likely to be not purely liberatory but in the service of domesticating or hegemonic forces in a given society (cf. Freire, Galtung). To see ourselves in such terms—as at least potentially in complicity with, rather than in clear opposition to, classist or racist or sexist forces—is to meet the enemy and find that it might just be us.

Once we have done so, once we can no longer accept the sense of literacy and our relation to it as benign, we find ourselves at ground zero, from which we need to build alternative practices—not merely alternative definitions of literacy but alternative conceptions of what it might mean to be a teacher of reading and writing. I suggest an alternative way of thinking about our practice, an alternative to the seduction of the liberatory model. I do not intend to propose a new, universally applicable model. Indeed, I argue that any global, universalizing claims ought to be suspect from the start. Rather, I detail here what sense we might make of Shirley Brice Heath's compelling project in the light of Michel Foucault's call for the tactical use of subjugated, local knowledges (see Heath, *Ways with Words*; Foucault, "Two Lectures"). Such a reading offers not another simple answer to a humanly complex problem but ways to ask better questions about our practice.

When my graduate class read Heath's *Ways with Words*, they thought at first that they had found the alternative they had been looking for: a positive, constructive, effective practice that was within our grasp as teachers; a pedagogy that would lead to real social, political, and economic change; a practice that would allow us to maintain our positive images of ourselves as teachers. But the students' enthusiasm was dampened when they came to Heath's account of the demise of her project. I focus on that moment in her book not because it is a place where hope for change is dashed—I don't think it has to be that—but because I think that it points to a different way to consider our practice.

Heath lived and worked for nearly a decade, beginning in the late 1960s, in what she calls the Piedmont Carolinas, primarily in two communities, "Roadville" and "Trackton." She was, as she describes herself,

> both ethnographer of communication focusing on child language and [also] teacher-trainer attempting to determine whether or not academic questions could lead to answers appropriate for meeting the needs of children and educators in that regional setting.   (1)

This double role is particularly important. Heath can be seen as both a producer of knowledge—someone who acknowledges as knowledge that which would generally go unnoticed in traditional characterizations of literacy[2]—and as someone who attempts to make use of that knowledge in her own practice as a teacher. In so doing, she makes that knowledge available to others, to be used—potentially, at least—in their terms. Thus, the classroom teachers with whom Heath worked became "learning researchers, who used knowledge from ethnographies of communication to build a two-way channel between communities and their classrooms" (354). As Heath emphasizes at several points in her account, the teachers were able to develop learning materials from their own and from their students' experiences as language users in their home communities. The teachers were able to mesh classroom materials with the lives of their students. The students themselves became "ethnographers of their own home habits and those of the classroom," learning to " 'code switch' between systems" of language use, thus bridging the gap between home and school (354–55).

But when Heath, the participant-observer, left, "the methods used by [the] teachers . . . all but disappeared" (356). Conditions had changed that had helped to make possible what Heath calls "productive innovations in philosophies, methods, and materials" (356). The desegregation crisis that had mandated change was diffused, and the autonomy that teachers had exercised to effectively address the crisis was replaced by greater bureaucratization, by programmed teaching generated not by teachers but by administrators and "experts." This is a discouraging moment in Heath's account. Those of us who have worked in the public schools and any of us who have had to deal with our own versions of the bureaucratic behemoth know how helpless one can feel to make a difference in the curriculum, much less in the larger community.

One way to respond to Heath's account at this point is to throw up our hands and say, "Well, the system has to change." Or "If we could only get the bureaucrats to see the value in projects such as Heath's, more people could do that sort of work." I don't want to discount the importance of changing the system so that teachers and students become the primary shapers of classroom practice. I believe that doing so represents an essential goal to work toward. But I suggest that—when we make that move, when we move to the level of system—too often either we paralyze ourselves ("How can *I* do anything, after all, to change anything as complex as the educational system?"), or we run the risk of substituting our own version of bureaucracy, of "totalizing system," as Foucault calls it, for that presently in place (*Archaeology of Knowledge* 39). In other words, we run the risk of becoming the thing we oppose.

To escape this double bind, we need to see Heath's project as important because it is local, specific, and necessarily temporary. The aim should be not to institutionalize Heath's project but to support, wherever possible, the proliferation of other local, specific, and necessarily temporary projects. Heath's account of her work is knowledge we can use, but it is knowledge of a certain sort. I turn now to Foucault to offer some language for thinking about this knowledge of a certain sort.

I am guided here by Paul Bové's argument in *Intellectuals in Power*, in which he articulates his sense that "Foucauldian inventions" might serve as "chemical baths for materializing local instantiations of power in ways that enable decentralized struggles against such power and for greater autonomy and self-determination" (306). Foucault is not reducible to a method; he does not offer a liberatory rhetoric (as much as some readers may want him to have done so). Rather, his work can lead us to ask difficult questions about our practice, about its affiliations, about its institutional origins, about its transformations into something other than what we might have hoped it could or would be.

In "Two Lectures," published in France in 1977, Foucault discussed the work in which he had thus far been engaged: "some brief notes on the history of penal procedure . . . some observation on sophistry" and the like. In one sense, "none of [this work] does more than mark time." It is, in Foucault's words, "repetitive and disconnected, it advances nowhere" ("Two Lectures" 78). In ordinary terms, work that does not at least point to a whole, to a complete picture, work that does not seem to take us somewhere is work that is useless, ineffectual. But, Foucault suggests, such work "could be justified by the claim that it is adequate to a restricted period [of time]" (79) and that its adequacy, in fact, is tied to its discontinuity, its refusal in a sense to posit a whole or a telos. If one understands the "inhibiting effect of global, *totalitarian theories*," as Foucault offers it, for example, in *Discipline and Punish* (80); if one understands how unitary theories work to cancel out the other, to silence the voices that do not fit, to erase the parts of the picture that detract from the balance of some idealized whole, then local and fragmentary knowledges that challenge the wholeness of global theories become of critical importance.

The sorts of knowledges Foucault is concerned with—what he calls "subjugated knowledges"—are of two kinds. One he labels "historical contents," that which is otherwise hidden by our procedures of knowing (for example, what a traditional or monumental history of the Elizabethan period might bury or disguise about the uses to which ordinary people might put the literacies available to them; what a social historian such as Natalie Zemon Davis would say, as opposed to what a literary historian writing on Sidney or Shakespeare might say, about the effects of printing in the sixteenth century). The emergence of such historical contents "allow[s] us to rediscover the ruptural effects of conflict and struggle that the order imposed by functionalist or systematising thought is designed to mask" (Foucault, "Two Lectures" 81–82).

The other sort of knowledge Foucault calls "naive knowledges," that which is "located low down on the hierarchy, beneath the required level of cognition or scientificity"—what, for example, "the psychiatric patient" or "ill person," or nurse knows that is "parallel and marginal to the knowledge of medicine" ("Two Lectures" 82)—or, more to our purposes, what the people in Roadville and Trackton knew or what our students know about the workings of language in their lives that would normally exist silently and unrecognized next to school English as a subject. This second sort of knowledge Foucault describes further as

> a popular knowledge (*la savoir des gens*) though it is far from being a general commonsense knowledge, but is on the contrary a particular, local, regional knowledge, a differential knowledge incapable of unanimity and which owes its force only to the harshness with which it is opposed by everything surrounding it— that it is through the re-appearance of this knowledge, of these local popular knowledges, these disqualified knowledges that criticism performs its work.   ("Two Lectures" 82)

The two kinds of subjugated knowledges, the buried knowledges of erudition and the disqualified naive knowledges, go hand in hand to suggest the outlines of a history of struggle—not, it is important to emphasize, to complete some deficient history, to fill in the blanks, but, rather, to provide tools for present use. Paul Bové, reading especially Foucault's later work, would rather call such histories "fictions" to further emphasize the extent to which Foucault attempts to distinguish his own researches from a historical empiricism or from the desire to house the past (or the present) within some full account and thereby domesticate it. Bové calls these fictions "anarchic tools for others to do with as they want," and, as such—as uncontrolled tools—they violate the seamless wholeness of global ways of knowing (300).[3]

But here is the tricky part. Foucault is careful to say that his genealogies of subjugated knowledges are not offered simply as new pieces to fill out some incomplete puzzle. We cannot just insert a few common folk to fill out our picture of Elizabethan England or chronicle the language use of the working class to develop a more complete linguistic map of America or peer over the shoulder of one more writer to say for sure what constitutes *the* writing process. Foucault's notion of the local and the transitory, the knowledge that seems to go nowhere, is designed to resist the tendency to lock in our understandings of the world and the tendency to refuse to allow the world to be other than our understandings. The subjugated knowledges are opposed to systematizations, opposed to the sort of discourse that would posit a picture of the whole, opposed to canon and to unitary theories of anything, in order to honor productivity, difference, change ("Two Lectures" 84).

Once we have seen the inhibiting limitations of global and totalizing pictures of literacy, once we have been alerted to the local and the particular, our practice necessarily changes. That is one of the most exciting parts of Heath's work, that she calls attention to the local and the particular not only in the students' lives but in the teachers' lives as well. Teachers and students learned to attend to what would otherwise go unnoticed and unvalued. And in noticing and valuing, they were able to connect, however briefly, school literacy with home literacies in such ways that students who might otherwise fail could succeed, but where the concept of success itself had changed, had opened out to include the formerly excluded.

To continue Heath's project read through a Foucauldian lens requires the sense that no ethnography can ever be complete, that, as Heath suggests, communities change—slowly, to be sure, but change nonetheless. So what a teacher and students learn about their language this year should not preempt what that teacher and other students will learn next year. But perhaps Foucault offers something other than just a vision of the phoenix as the metaphor for teaching. It may be that ethnography as a system of inquiry was itself "adequate to a restricted period" (to redeploy Foucault's characterization of his work), but that new conditions and new students require some other tactical use of other knowledge attentive to the local, the decentered, the different. It may be, in other words, that ethnography in its uncritical forms, in its proliferation institutionally, runs the risk of taking on the characteristics of the canonical, of forgetting that it is not a more complete picture of but one (albeit powerful) writing of culture (cf. Clifford).

But what is the alternative? It should be clear from Foucault's argument that one cannot say, in the abstract, what a new tactical use ought to be. But one can say that work from several different quarters under the large umbrella of literacy studies seems to provide us with the sort of knowledge we can use tactically: knowledge that points to the "multiplicity of values, uses and consequences which characterize writing [and reading] as social practice[s]" (Scribner and Cole 70) and thereby undermines a unitary theory of literacy, a unitary approach to teaching and learning. As Sylvia Scribner and Michael Cole argue, "recognition of the multiple meanings and varieties of literacy also argues for a diversity of educational approaches, informal and community-based as well as formal and school-based" (81).

Such a valuing of multiple literacies and multiple educational approaches, however, cannot be taken as another version of pluralism, if by pluralism one means that differences are entertained as long as they converge on some common goal and can thereby be centrally controlled or managed. In pedagogical terms such pluralism often means that, as teachers, we allow diversity in the classroom as long as it does not threaten our own authority, our own control over the production and transmission of knowledge—that is, as long as we continue to decide what counts. The radical import of Foucault's work is that it forces us to imagine a multiplicity that might dislodge our comfortable intellectual and institutional certainties.

The point is that, if we do recognize multiplicity in its most radical form, we cannot institutionalize the content, the specifics, or the pedagogies of literacy learning. This does not mean we are barred from action. I am not advocating a quietistic patience with things as they are. In fact, I argue that we don't have to wait for systems to change (they will change as we do) or feel compelled to institute systems (there is a tendency toward systematization of knowledge we may rather resist). Acting on what we do know and learning more as we act, we need to lend ourselves to the proliferation of contents, specifics, and pedagogies, especially as they work to make possible greater autonomy and self-determination. We cannot determine ahead of time the results of our knowledge, but we need to work in concert with others—with students, with other teachers, in the community—to make knowledges available for their use, to be used for their own ends, so that new knowledges can be made in ways we do not fully understand and cannot control.

NOTES

[1]One version of the liberatory model much discussed in the popular and academic press is E. D. Hirsch's *Cultural Literacy*. In this paper, however, my interest is not in reviewing any particular version of a commonplace view, something I have already done elsewhere (see "Concepts of Culture"). The fact that the view is commonplace and— despite recent work in history, anthropology, critical pedagogy, sociolinguistics, and social psychology—remains so seems to make it all the more difficult for us to practice a critical pedagogy.

[2]Mariolina Salvatori, of the University of Pittsburgh, suggested this way of reading Heath's project—the acknowledging as knowledge.

[3]Henry Giroux also has been drawn to Foucault's discussion of subjugated knowledges, seeing in it a starting point for understanding "how curriculum and schooling have been constructed around particular silences and omissions." Such understanding, which Giroux joins to a concept of emancipatory authority and a feminist notion of solidarity, might lead, he suggests, to a "pedagogy that is both empowering and transformative" (100).

WORKS CITED

Bové, Paul. *Intellectuals in Power: A Genealogy of Critical Humanism.* New York: Columbia UP, 1986.

Clifford, James. Introduction. *Writing Culture: The Poetics and Politics of Ethnography.* Ed. James Clifford and George E. Marcus. Berkeley: U of California P, 1986. 1–26.

Davis, Natalie Zemon. "Printing and the People: Early Modern France." *Literacy and Social Development in the West: A Reader.* Ed. Harvey Graff. Cambridge: Cambridge UP, 1981. 69–95.

Flannery, Kathryn T. "Concepts of Culture: Cultural Literacy/Cultural Politics." *Farther Along.* Ed. Hephzibah Roskelly and Kate Ronald. Portsmouth: Boynton, 1990. 86–100.

Foucault, Michel. *The Archaeology of Knowledge.* Trans. Alan Sheridan. London: Tavistock, 1972.

———. *Discipline and Punish: The Birth of the Prison.* New York: Vintage, 1979.

———. "Two Lectures." *Power/Knowledge: Selected Interviews and Other Writings, 1972–1977.* Ed. Colin Gordon. New York: Pantheon, 1980. 78–108.

Freire, Paulo. *Education: The Practice of Freedom.* London: Writers, 1976.

Galtung, Johan. "Literacy, Education and Schooling." *Literacy and Social Development in the West: A Reader.* Ed. Harvey Graff. Cambridge: Cambridge UP, 1981. 271–85.

Giroux, Henry. *Schooling and the Struggle for Public Life: Critical Pedagogy in the Modern Age.* Minneapolis: U of Minnesota P, 1988.

Graff, Harvey J. *The Legacies of Literacy: Continuities and Contradictions in Western Culture and Society.* Bloomington: Indiana UP, 1987.

Heath, Shirley Brice. "The Functions and Uses of Literacy." *Literacy, Society, and Schooling: A Reader.* Ed. Suzanne De Castell et al. New York: Cambridge UP, 1986. 15–26.

———. *Ways with Words: Language, Life, and Work in Communities and Classrooms.* Cambridge: Cambridge UP, 1983.

Ogbu, John U. "Literacy and Schooling in Subordinate Cultures: The Case of Black Americans." *Perspectives on Literacy.* Ed. Eugene R. Kintgen, Barry Kroll, and Mike Rose. Carbondale: Southern Illinois UP, 1988. 227–42.

Scribner, Sylvia, and Michael Cole. "Unpackaging Literacy." *Perspectives on Literacy.* Ed. Eugene Kintgen, Barry Kroll, and Mike Rose. Carbondale: Southern Illinois UP, 1988. 57–70.

Bloomsday: Doomsday Book for Literacy?

C. Jan Swearingen

> The essential characteristic of the first half of the twentieth century is the growing weakness, and almost the disappearance, of the idea of value.
>
> [T]he surrealists have set up non-oriented thought as a model; they have chosen the total absence of value as their supreme value. [M]en have always been intoxicated by licence, which is why, throughout history, towns have been sacked. But there has not always been a literary equivalent for the sacking of towns. Surrealism is such an equivalent.
>
> Writers do not have to be professors of morals, but they do have to express the human condition. And nothing concerns human life so essentially, for every man at every moment, as good and evil. When literature becomes deliberately indifferent to the opposition of good and evil it betrays its function and forfeits all claim to excellence.
>
> [S]uch easy morals in literature, such tolerance of baseness, involve our most eminent writers in responsibility for demoralizing little country girls who have never left their villages and have never heard the writers' names.
>
> Simone Weil,
> "The Responsibility of Writers"

Simone Weil's appraisals can be extended to the manner and the tone of many current literary theorists and pundits of literacy. Academics of the right and the left have begun to resemble one another in the disdainful and sometimes autocratic attitudes they manifest toward students, the classroom, and texts. Despite substantial ideological and theoretical differences, the two extremes— here exemplified by the irresistibly homophonic duo Harold Bloom and Allan Bloom—propound views that are equally elitist in tone. An often derisive dogmatism in the manner of their pronouncements undermines the forms of literacy that are taught at the college level: the articulation of self, the exposition and free exchange of views and ideas, and the disciplines of textual analysis and interpretation. Some elements in this curious state of affairs are not new. The 1930s saw many left-wing poets and bohemian artists turn to embrace ideologies of a reactionary right. T. S. Eliot struck a template that was emulated by many New Critics during the Dulles years, when New Criticism, alongside McCarthyism, came of age. Walter Ong has distilled Marxist appraisals of the staunchly back-ward-looking stance embodied in the New Criticism that held sway in English studies through the mid-1960s:

> Marxist criticism . . . maintains that the self reference of the New Critics is class-determined and sycophantic: it identifies the "objective" meaning of the text with something actually outside the text, namely the interpretations it imagines to be the ones supported by the sophistication, wit, sense of tradition and poise of what is essentially a decaying aristocracy. (162)

A similarly recherché appeal to fading aristocracy and dying classicism is embodied in the recent rhetoric of Allan Bloom, William Bennett, and, in smaller measure, E. D. Hirsch. Bennett derided a Duke instructor's comment that there is no such thing as literary excellence, because all standards are arbitrary, as "curricular debasement" that Bennett repeatedly charges is brought about by a "standard kind of left-wing political agenda" consisting of "a coalition between Marxism and feminism." Bowing to such "trendy lightweights," he intoned, marked "the closing of the Stanford mind." "For a moment a great university was brought low by the very forces universities came into being to oppose—ignorance, irrationality, and intimidation." Stanford's President, Don-ald Kennedy, deftly identified the contradiction in Bennett's remarks: "Bennett would use the privilege of his bully pulpit to bully rather than to engage the issues" by debating the topic (Bennett and Kennedy qtd. in "Colleges Losing Credibility" and McCurdy).

The roots of New Criticism in Romanticism provide a second insight into the ivory towerism represented by Allan Bloom's and William Bennett's calls for a return to classical texts and classical rigor. "The romantic quest for 'pure poetry,' sealed off from real-life concerns" (Ong 161), is often seen as a quest for authenticity of self and voice, goals that do not seem to be wholly at odds with the ideologies of cultural pluralism, multiple perspectives, and epistemo-logical indeterminacy propounded by the current academic left wing. But there are aristocratic nuances in this stance as well. The romantic quest for purity, autonomy, and authenticity of voice can also be seen as derived from "the feel for autonomous utterance created by writing and, even more, the feel for closure created by print" (Ong 161). The New Critics, in a continuity with this tra-dition, "assimilated the verbal art work to the visual object world of texts rather than to the oral-aural event world" (Ong 160). New wave critical theories remain bound to the materials and technology of the written text as an artifact. "Semiotic structuralism and deconstructionism generally take no cognizance at all of the various ways that texts can relate to their oral substratum." Instead, they tend to focus on texts developed during the eighteenth and nineteenth centuries, the "late typographic point of view" (Ong 164), when the fascination of writers turned more and more to inward and self-contained dynamics, perfect materials for psychoanalytic criticism, New Criticism, and deconstruction alike.

Notions of self-consuming artifacts spawn self-absorbed theorists impatient with the epistemological naïveté of undergraduates.

Among the many ironic reversals suggested by the theme of the friends and enemies of literacy, I first thought the neoconservatives—Allan Bloom, William Bennett, E. D. Hirsch—represented particularly deserving recipients of a critique. I began to compose my invective. The New Right is an enemy of literacy because it is turning back the clock, ignoring the cultural and pedagogical advances that have been achieved in the past two decades by sneering at substantive reforms in curricular content and pedagogical methods as mere trendiness or as an unseemly politicizing of curriculum. Allan Bloom is a particularly good example of the seductive appeal of reactionary thinking that exploits a misrepresentation of the past it ostensibly admires. The version of classicism he espouses is quite different from the classical texts he so adulates. Socrates, Aristotle, the Stoics, and Cicero were deeply concerned with politics, ethics, and pedagogy in their own pluralistic cultures (see Nussbaum). What Allan Bloom laments is not the classical era but the passing of a more recent era in which these classics were read, contemplated, and discussed in seminar rooms totally—and rightly, in his view—removed from the babel of the streets. Here I began the ascent to my own righteous, Parnassian tone. Bennett, Hirsch, and Bloom are wolves in classical sheepskins. Their calls for a return to the past are dangerous because they espouse, explicitly and with no evidence of shame, a resuscitation of the elitism, racism, and sexism of long-gone eras in which few were educated. The appeal of Allan Bloom and William Bennett is far from negligible not only outside but inside academia as well—another cause for alarm. They appeal to those who believe that only the best and the brightest (and the richest) should enter the sacred groves of academe. Hirsch anticipates questions of cultural and gender bias in The List. But he can be exonerated only slightly because the explanation he gives is a mystifyingly limp appeal to what Allan Bloom terms mob rule. Hirsch explains that the literatures of minority races and cultures and of women are not on The List because the list represents a tribal consensus. It is just such a tribal consensus, I fear, that permits Bloom to appeal to the basest kind of mob thinking when he contends that, if women had been home with their children instead of pursuing careers out of frivolous vanity, all these problem students would vanish.

There are more than a few problems with the neoconservative vision of past culture and civility marketed by the academic right wing. The past that is the object of the nostalgia is a past in which only a fraction of today's college population ever entered universities. The ranks of the college-bound have increased 400% since the 1950s and 3,000% between 1870 and 1940 (Nussbaum 22). The image of a stronger and smarter America in 1950, 1920, or 1890 is an image of and for a small, privileged elite. In 1890, only half of the five-to-nineteen-year-olds were in school at all. One in six of the eighth-graders finished high school. Many schoolteachers were single young women who made $300 a year and stopped teaching when they married. Hirsch applauds the traditional classical curriculum in Latin, Greek, English, modern languages, history, mathematics, physics, biology, and geography, whose renewal was recommended by the 1893 "Report of the Committee of Ten on Secondary School Studies" but fails to mention how few of the students in that era completed high school. At the turn of the century, elementary school teachers outnumbered high school teachers twenty to one (Pattison 711). That gap has been reduced but not without creating a new set of problems. The demographics surveyed in C. P. Snow's *Two Cultures* still hold for higher education when America is compared with Europe and Britain. America has elected to educate a larger percentage of students to a higher grade level. One result is populist democratization and decentralization. An equally important result is bureaucratization. For better and worse, education has become a "vast, civic industry" (Pattison 711). Compounding the problems, immigrant student populations make new demands on already overburdened educational systems, demands that are unpopular among the middle-class taxpayers who underwrite public education. The frequently begrudging and critical attitude of this group toward education is only fed by Allan Bloom's and William Bennett's seductive absolutes. The recent influx of Asian, Middle Eastern, and immigrant Hispanic students has added to the diversification of the college-student population and has brought with it an additional expansion of contents and appropriate pedagogies.

Still, the rhetoric of absolutes sells better than the careful thought that the same rhetoric ostensibly propounds. Recent defenders of civilization denounce, pronounce, and speak in categorical absolutes, rather than in the carefully qualified musings characteristic of Socratic inquiry. All too often, they manifest ignorance of and arrogant disdain toward the voices and the experiences of women and cultural minorities that have recently been incorporated into the literary and historical canons. Bennett defends himself by saying that he is just trying to get people to think about the issues. This, I thought, would be the last point in my line of attack: while the pronouncements of the right espouse democratic traditions, the manner in which they are delivered belies the democratic concepts of values, decision making, and discourse. Why does Allan Bloom, in propounding a pristine form of classical inquiry and questioning, speak so consistently in the imperative mode, unqualified even by the conventions of academic prose? He begins few phrases with *perhaps, most,* or *some.* Boldly declarative and imperative sentences march like armed forces through his prose; the republic is overridden by the imperial regime.

As it turned out, however, my attack on the academic right as, ironically, an enemy of literacy could not remain so satisfyingly simple. Recently published wartime writings by Paul deMan and Martin Heidegger prompted academic avant-garde reactions to examinations of the ties between their theories and their political actions. Stanley Corngold alleges that

> when deMan in his late work gives texts the properties of persons who entrap, coerce, kill, disfigure, and mutilate readers, he conjures a personality beyond Good

and Evil of the type of Neitzsche's New Man as he was received in deMan's youth by George, by D'Annunzio, by Benn. This is the "new philosopher," whose goal is "to prepare great ventures and over all attempts of discipline and cultivation by way of putting an end to that gruesome dominion of nonsense and accident that has so far been called 'history.' "

. . . I believe that deMan's critical work adheres to and reproduces, in literary theoretical masquerade, his experience as a collaborator. His later writings impose images, attitudes, and ideas of the systematic and threatening application of excessive violence to persons; and this, not the "aestheticization of politics," defines the totalitarianism to whose empirical realization he once actually contributed. (931)

Charges such as Corngold's that the sources of critical theory had or should have any political connections and consequences provoked voices of disdain as the dons of deconstruction manned the barricades to defend their dead ancestors. In impassioned apologetics they bashed not only their enemies but a few cousins as well.

Hermeneutics is often explicitly a reaction against various recent language-oriented theories in the name of pre-linguistic "experience" or "life." . . . [It assumes] the existence of stable monological texts of determinable meanings, meanings controlled in each case by the intentions of the author and by the text's reference to a pre-linguistic "real world out there." . . . "Soft" phenomenology . . . is derived, also somewhat sentimentalized and simplified, from the rigours and complexities of Husserl, Heidegger, and others of the founding fathers of phenomenology. (Miller 1104)

J. Hillis Miller's defense of Heidegger as a founding father—an odd defense for an antifoundationalist—draws some of its potency from an implicit attack on any reader naive and sentimental enough to locate things in a "real world out there." It could almost be a part of Allan Bloom's jeremiad lamenting the loss of rigor in the ivory tower occasioned by pandering to relevance. It harmonizes with William Bennett's response to Stanford curriculum reformers who promoted canon reforms based on real-world concerns, such as social justice and relevance. Miller denounces Ricoeur's conceptualizations of reading, meaning, and understanding as simpleminded, sentimental, "soft." Only hopelessly backward readers, Miller intimates, could find gazing at an illusory reality more appealing than the rigorous study of disruptions in the linguistic fabric. Corngold recalls Nietzsche on this point; the new philosopher is beyond good and evil, beyond "that gruesome dominion of nonsense and accident that has so far been called 'history' " (931). Miller asserts: "Ricoeur's basic presuppositions are mistaken. There is no such thing as an 'experience of being in the world and in time' prior to language. All our 'experience' is permeated through and through by language. . . . By taking no account . . . of what deMan [and others] say . . . Ricoeur has detached his work from the real action these days in narrative theory" (1104, 1105). The real action, that is, issuing forth from deMan, Derrida, Harold Bloom, Miller, and a group Miller designates as their "brilliant younger associates" (1105). No soft hermeneuts these, but hard rigormaniacs of the sort William Bennett admires. "There is *no such thing* as an 'experience of being in the world and in time' prior to language" (1105; emphasis added).

Though already overbashed, Harold Bloom should make a cameo appearance, particularly after his provocatively titled *Ruin the Sacred Truths*. The veritable magus of misreading, Bloom applauds the critical act of "strong" readers as a misreading. You have to be strong to be wrong. But if every reading is inevitably a misreading, whence Bloom's criteria for "strong" readers? Do these criteria, like the wife of Cain, magically appear from a land east of Eden? What do strong misreaders do, once they have learned their craft? Wayne C. Booth offers an irreverent answer:

> Critical discussion is not pointless; indeed it is our main task to revitalize it. It is best kept alive by recognizing that it is finally validated only in the individual who deconstructs what he reads, and then offers his own creation, an inevitable misreading. Nobody who is anybody these days tries to solve by the end of the book the problems raised at the beginning.   (244)

Programmatic misclosure is precisely one of the theory-induced relativisms that Allan Bloom and William Bennett think has gone too far in current academic fads. That many rank-and-file English teachers agree with Bloom and Bennett on this point helps explain the otherwise disturbing appeal of neoconservative absolutes within academia. Many decidedly nonnaive educators ask, how can students who have not yet learned to read as naive or sentimental readers jump in at the level of problematizing such reading? How can anyone learn to problematize something that has not yet been known or imparted? If we do impart traditional modes of reading and writing, do we do that only to hastily snatch them away? What have been and what will be the consequences, for literacy, of giving "texts the properties of persons who entrap, coerce, kill, disfigure, and mutilate readers" (Corngold)? It is our presentation of texts to students that gives them this or other senses of their properties. Writing classrooms are full of students who are mute because they have never come into contact with the cultural conventions of post-Cartesian, post-enlightenment, or post-Romantic conceptions and practices of self and voice. Dogmatic pronouncements of the entrapment of the reader by the text are themselves coercive and entrapping, mutilating and silencing. To announce to students that there is no such thing as accurate reference because there is no reality unmediated by language can be an arrogant pedagogical act, a verdict that would be accepted, I believe, by a large number of writing and literature teachers. The avant-garde critical-theory mandarinate—despite its claims to epistemological subtlety, sometimes linked with political correctness—has in its manner and dogmatism manifested a scandalous disregard for the epistemologies and voices that students bring with them to academia. It is one thing to challenge and to teach through questioning; it is another to use the classroom as a platform for propounding epistemologies and ideologies whose dogmatism cuts off question, discussion, thought itself.

It has not been a quiet year in Lake Wobegon. As I have attempted to demonstrate, the bullies of the left and the bullies of the right have shown themselves to be bullies in equal measure, as Donald Kennedy said, using their "bully pulpit to bully rather than to engage the issues" by debating the topic. That is the problem, and that is why both groups, despite their differences, have been enemies of literacy. It is also why we must ask who profits from the marketing of literacy on both sides and who remains watching, still disenfranchised, on the sidelines? To whom are such visions of literacy addressed? Who will or can buy these carefully crafted products? Who will begin to emulate them? Literacy has become a commodity and ceases to be regarded as the critical, crucial reality it is for large numbers of people who still "live in the world and in time," people who yearn to enter history, not to deny it.

The Allan Blooms, William Bennetts, and E. D. Hirsches have been decried by the academic avant-garde for profiteering, drawing personal gain from the recent hysteria about literacy that, the liberals charge, they helped create. It is neither uncomfortable nor unexpected for a traditionalist like Allan Bloom to defend traditional hierarchies of content, salary, and rank and to promote the orthodox conservative notion of education of, for, and by a homogeneous elite. That is precisely why he and his kindred are denounced by the academic left wing. However, the liberal physicians may need to heal themselves, for is it not contradictory when exponents of a (politically) liberal and (epistemologically) radical left wing speak and write in a tone that conveys disdainful contempt not only toward the misguided classical nostalgia of the Allan Blooms and the William Bennetts but also, more problematically, toward the naive reader and the epistemologically soft?

More than two decades ago, Kenneth Burke characterized the manner and the sensibility of the literary professorial elite as "comic primness, or prim irony," which he defined as "an attitude characterizing a member of a privileged class who somewhat questions the state of affairs whereby he enjoys his privileges; but after all, he does enjoy them and so in the last analysis he resigns himself to the dubious conditions in a state of ironic complexity that is apologetic but not abnegatory" (126). That description accounts for some versions of academic neoconservative indifference to political realities and motives—it's in bad taste, not for polite company. But Burke provides an account of a slightly different mode of avoidance that illuminates parallels between the absurdist iconoclastic left and the neoconservative right. "A deliberate cult of the irrational, the Absurd, would obscure the perception of [economic and political] conditions, even suggesting that there is a certain bad taste or literary crudeness in the mere mention of them; but a 'dialectical' way of deriving these same absurdities can be 'rational' " (259). Who today most promotes and profits from the blurring of realities that Burke defines here—the neoconservative marketeers of neo-classical curricula or the radical-left cultists of the irrational and the absurd? Both groups eschew and obscure mention of the conditions, and the state of affairs that hold for basic or advanced literacy. Students and teachers of basic literacy suffer from this state of affairs.

Perhaps the dogmas of epistemological relativism and semantic indeterminacy, particularly in view of their bombastic delivery system, will be more effective in waking up the slumbering freshman than were the dogmas of correct diction, cohesion, and effective argumentation. But caution is in order. Bombardiers, however politically correct or pedagogically well-intentioned, run the risk of perpetuating the dependency and the passivity of the disenfranchised.

> Every woman adores a Fascist,
> The boot in the face, the brute
> Brute heart of a brute like you.
> You stand at the blackboard, daddy,
> In the picture I have of you.   (Plath)

Sylvia Plath's woman may be extended to any group of marginalized, underlings, or lessers. Students can be edified or brutalized for their own good in ways they come to consider normal or even enjoyable. For inculcating and perpetuating abusive pedagogical psychopathologies, the Allan Blooms of the right and the Harold Blooms of the left are equally culpable. Neoconservatives, who like to think of themselves as edifiers, should consider the patronizing elements in that stance; the academic avant-garde needs to consider the nuances in its manner that are brutal and brutalizing in other ways. It is not so much the aestheticization of politics, the turning away from the political and the social and into theory, that is most problematic. The imposition of an epistemologically sophisticated critical language—laced almost obsessively with images of "the systematic and threatening application of excessive violence to persons" (Corngold) that entrap, mutilate, kill, scar, blind, and disfigure—is troubling not just because of the nature of such language but also because of the manner of its dissemination. Teachers of literature, literacy, and literacy theory walk a fine line when they claim that they are liberating students by reciting tales of their exploitation and marginalization. The air of violence and rarefied mystification transmitted by recent metaphors of language use and interpretation can prolong the dependency of student on teacher.

While not always pedagogical in their treatments of the reformist roles that should be played by deconstruction and other postmodern theories, recent appraisals of the relation between literacy and theory acknowledge that deconstruction and postmodernism should turn to an examination of their potentials as agents of change. Jonathan Culler calls for a reappraisal of the end-stopped stance that has been adopted, somewhat defensively, by proponents of deconstruction. He proposes rethinking "the conception of oppositional criticism," because "the desire to be in opposition may frequently run counter to the attempt to produce change" (788). Gayatri Spivak's reconfiguration of deconstruction in the service of reading defines similarly forward-looking roles for recent theory (*Master Discourse, Native Informant*). Henry Sussman calls for disarmament in the theory-praxis wars dividing literary and literacy theorists while defending an honorable role for some elements of deconstructionism in dismantling kitsch and pat answers to the complex problems that have been defined within the current literature of literacy (3–62). The acknowledgment that some branches or practices of literary theory manifest an unwarranted disdain for praxis is a notable advance. Though perhaps slight and long overdue, such acknowledgments advance the possibility of rapprochement through explicit acceptance of its desirability. Pedagogies that can both clarify and deepen, that focus and expand, can begin to harmonize and affirm the relations between the best that has been thought and said and the newer voices only recently encouraged by our reading and writing curricula. The criteria defining *best* and *quality* for old and new literatures and literacies are receiving welcome and needed scrutiny. The January 1990 issue of *PMLA* is devoted to black literature, rhetoric, and culture. Gender, culture, ethnicity, and cross-disciplinary methodologies are given prominence in MLA's second edition of *Introduction to Scholarship in Modern Languages and Literatures* (Gibaldi). Composition and rhetoric are forging solid bases for renewed partnerships with literary studies at both the departmental and the national scholarly level.

Out of scrutiny and the necessary deconstruction that such scrutiny demands are emerging broader understandings of quality, exemplarity, and cultural redefinition. Repressive tolerance and pluralism (Sussman 228) are beginning to be superseded by qualitative tolerance and selective pluralism. As Gayatri Spivak observes: "It seems we wish constantly to adjudicate greatness and it constantly escapes us. Yet we must assume it exists. We cannot have a straight answer about greatness and that is the good thing about it" ("Forum" 47). Without such conscious movements out of the zero degree long since reached in both no-exit deconstruction and intolerant traditionalism, the value and the possibility of literacy will be further eroded, sustaining a tolerance for baseness and brutality encouraged by the manner of eminent theorists and defenders of culture alike and the concomitant demoralization of those students who, like Simone Weil's "little country girls," have never left their villages or heard such theorists' names.[1]

NOTES

[1]The preconference version of this manuscript, entitled "Bloomsday for Literacy," was published in *Freshman English News* 17 (1988): 1, 2–5. Portions of that manuscript appear here, with thanks to Christina Murphy, editor of *Freshman English News*.

WORKS CITED

Bloom, Allan. *The Closing of the American Mind.* New York: Simon, 1987.

Bloom, Harold. *A Map of Misreading.* New York: Oxford UP, 1975.

———. *Ruin the Sacred Truths: Poetry and Belief from the Bible to the Present.* Cambridge: Harvard UP, 1989.

Booth, Wayne C. *Critical Understanding: The Limits of Pluralism.* Chicago: U of Chicago P, 1979.

Burke, Kenneth. *A Rhetoric of Motives.* Berkeley: U of California P, 1969.

"Colleges Losing Credibility because of Faculty 'Trashing,' Official Says." *Dallas Times Herald* 5 Feb. 1988: A4.

Corngold, Stanley. Letters. *Times Literary Supplement* 26 Aug.–1 Sept. 1988: 931.

Culler, Jonathan. "GRIP's Grasp: A Comment." *Poetics Today* 9.4 (1988): 783–89.

deMan, Paul. *Wartime Journalism, 1939–1943.* Lincoln: U of Nebraska P, 1988.

Gibaldi, Joseph, ed. *Introduction to Scholarship in Modern Languages and Literatures.* 2nd ed. New York: MLA, forthcoming.

Heidegger, Martin. *Heidegger et le nazisme.* Trans. Victor Farias. Paris: Verdier, 1987; Philadelphia: Temple UP, 1989.

Hirsch, E. D., Jr. *Cultural Literacy: What Every American Needs to Know.* Boston: Houghton, 1987.

McCurdy, Jack. "Bennett Calls Stanford's Curriculum Revision 'Capitulation to Pressure.' " *Chronicle of Higher Education* 27 Apr. 1988: A2.

Miller, J. Hillis. "But Are Things As We Think They Are?" *Times Literary Supplement* 9–15 Oct. 1987: 1104–05.

———. "NB Debate between Tzvetan Todorov and J. Hillis Miller." *Times Literary Supplement* 17–23 June 1988: 676–755.

Nussbaum, Martha. "Undemocratic Vistas." *New York Review of Books* 5 Nov. 1987: 20–26.

Ong, Walter. *Orality and Literacy: The Technologizing of the Word.* New York: Methuen, 1982.

Pattison, Robert. "On the Finn Syndrome and the Shakespeare Paradox." *Nation* 30 May 1987: 710–19.

Plath, Sylvia. "Daddy." *A Book of Women Poets from Antiquity to Now.* Ed. Willis Barnstone and Aliki Barnstone. New York: Schocken, 1980. 537.

Spivak, Gayatri. "Forum: Who Needs the Great Works?" *Harper's* Sept. 1989: 43–52

———. *Master Discourse, Native Informant: Deconstruction in the Service of Reading.* Cambridge: Harvard UP, in press.

Sussman, Henry. *High Resolution: Critical Theory and the Problem of Literacy.* New York: Oxford UP, 1989.

Weil, Simone. "The Responsibility of Writers." *The Simone Weil Reader.* Ed. George Panichas. New York: McKay, 1977. 286–89.

The Ideology of Illiteracy: A Bakhtinian Perspective

Charles Schuster

Let's begin with a straightforward statement—namely, that all of us engaged with this text are literate. The basis for establishing ourselves as literate, when we cannot even agree what the term *literacy* means, is constituted by our ability to generate and process language, to write and read, to make sense of texts. But literacy also has something to do with intuitive understanding, with shared boundaries of meaning, with making sense of each other through verbal and written interaction—factors that are too often ignored in discussions of literacy. I shall want shortly to return to this notion of socially constituted meaning making, but for now I want to critique two more accepted views of literacy. One holds that literacy is bound by notions of educational praxis; the other argues that literacy is an outcome of intellectual power and training.

Certainly, I would agree that literacy, whatever we precisely mean by it, can be promoted through educational and intellectual development. Illiteracy flourishes in the dark; its tumorous growth thrives on neglect, poverty, ignorance, privation. Too little public and private energy and money have been concentrated on this problem, leading to what Jonathan Kozol calls *Illiterate America*. Kozol opens his book with a statistical indictment of illiterate America:

> Twenty-five million American adults cannot read the poison warnings on a can of pesticide, a letter from their child's teacher, or the front page of a daily paper. An additional 35 million read only at a level which is less than equal to the full survival needs of our society.
>
> Together, these 60 million people represent more than one third of the entire adult population.
>
> 15% of recent urban high school graduates read at less than 6th grade level.
>
> The U. S. ranks 49th among 158 member nations of the U.N. in its literacy levels.
>
> 47%—that is nearly half—of all black 17-year-olds are functionally illiterate. (4–5)

Kozol's analysis strongly suggests a conspiracy theory of capitalism: he posits an America that maintains illiteracy in order to maintain itself politically, socially, economically. Illiterates are a submissive work force, a neo-slave population in twentieth-century America.

Even if we grant this appalling state of affairs, defining the problem as educational and political does not allow a meaningful solution. That is, if a third of America is illiterate, then apparently what is needed is a massive political and economic mobilization. Through a domestic peace corps, sixty million people could be taught to read and write. End of problem. That this solution oversimplifies is obvious: it addresses the issue in the wrong terms. Illiteracy is not just the ability to read and write; if it were, we could eliminate it through educational outreach, repeated viewings of Sesame Street, a proliferation of book mobiles. Literacy, however, does not consist exclusively of the ability to encode and decode written texts, although that is certainly part of its meaning.

Perhaps the problem is not educational deprivation but intellectual limitation; Robert Pattison seems to think so. Pattison defines literacy as "a combination of variables—individual and cultural awareness of language and the interplay of this awareness with the means of expression" (7). "Reading and writing," he tells us, "may be parts of literacy but do not constitute the whole" (7). For Pattison, literacy is not just the ability to process words; more important it is the ability to use language critically and intellectually to synthesize judgment and form original perspectives.

Pattison describes three kinds of illiteracy: the illiteracy of "The Wild Boy" (10) who lacks language altogether; the illiteracy of Gracie Allen, who purports to understand words on a purely literal level and thus operates only on the surface of language; and the illiteracy of Agamemnon, who appears to function within a language community but who is in some intellectual and psychological sense "unconscious and egoless" (15). This last kind of illiteracy chiefly concerns Pattison, for it is the most common and can occur "in high places" (17). Agamemnon, according to Pattison, "is a robot, and even though he is a character from an age that had not yet adopted reading and writing, he may more justly be called illiterate because of his insensitivity to speech, thought, and their relation to action" (16). Pattison attributes this insensitivity to a lack of brain development and inadequate educational training.

Pattison's model of illiteracy, however, carries unfortunate implications. His Agamemnon is not really illiterate. His insulting of Chryseis, his naive belief in false dreams, his bumbling actions—all point not so much to a basic illiteracy as to a basic stupidity, just as the persona of Gracie Allen represents, in a comic sense, a basic ingenious stupidity. Pattison works hard to erase this unfortunate characterization by describing language processing in terms of underdeveloped cranial hemispheres, but the inescapable conclusion is that by any outside evaluation Agamemnon and Gracie Allen are—pun intended—dumb. If their brains functioned better—that is, if they were smarter or were made smarter through a growth in critical intelligence—they would become literate.

I propose an alternative model for illiteracy, one that develops a social-constructionist view derived from the work of the Russian critic Mikhail Bakhtin. As a starting point, I nominate a different model for the illiterate—not the Wild Boy or Gracie Allen or Agamemnon but another player in the tragedy of the Trojan War, Cassandra.

Cassandra, of course, speaks language. She is beautiful, intelligent, thoughtful. From Apollo she learned the gift of prophecy but, because she refused the god's amorous advances, she is cursed by him so that her prophecies are never believed. Cassandra foretells the Greek invasion and warns against the Trojan horse, all to no avail. Thus Cassandra speaks to the Trojan hierarchy, but they cannot hear her. Articulate and prescient, Cassandra is struck dumb through the very act of speaking. The more she reveals her incisive predictions and native intelligence through language, the stupider she becomes, or, at least, the more stupid she is perceived to be by Priam, Hector, Paris, and the other Trojan leaders. For Cassandra, meaning becomes meaninglessness. Her ultimate rape by Ajax and her murder at the hands of Aegisthus underscore her powerlessness, her role as a victim of forces beyond her control.

Kozol's illiterates might be able to learn how to read and write if we funded libraries, night schools, and community centers. Agamemnon might be able to learn how to be smarter through a long and painstaking education. Gracie Allen and even the Wild Boy of Aveyron might be able to learn language use in some fashion with intensive tutelage. They are potentially educable. Cassandra's situation, however, is hopeless. She cannot learn anything that will allow her to communicate what she knows, what she feels to be certain. She is doomed to a solipsistic existence, despite the power of language that she possesses. Because of Apollo's curse, Cassandra no longer functions within a community of utterance. Her speech genres exist in some separate sphere of meaning and, thus, no longer intersect with those around her. In a sense, only by being struck dumb could she ever hope to become a functioning, literate member of Greek society. Her literacy is and always will be illiteracy.

Cassandra's predicament mirrors that of many individuals as well as whole classes in American society—intelligent, knowledgeable, informed individuals who cannot participate interactively in meaning making through language. We label these people "illiterate." From a Bakhtinian point of view, illiterates today are cursed not by Apollo but by dominant cultures within society to endure a state of alienation wherein speaking, listening, reading, and writing become meaningless activities. In the view that I am promoting here, literacy is the power to be able to make oneself heard and felt, to signify. Literacy is the way in which we make ourselves meaningful not only to others but through others to ourselves.

For Bakhtin and V. N. Vološinov, a key member of his circle, language is not just a social construct; on the contrary, language constructs us socially. Vološinov states, "It is not experience that organizes expression, but the other way around—*expression organizes experience*. Expression is what first gives experience its form and specificity of direction" (*Marxism* 85). In this view, language is primal. All that we see, do, and experience—all that we are—is filtered and organized through language; it permeates all our ideas, actions, and basic understandings of the world around us. If we grant this epistemological view of language, illiterate people are not just marginalized; they are excluded from understanding themselves and their place in the world. They lack much of the power necessary to organize experience, to make themselves both heard and understood in society at large.

To state this is to overstate the matter—but only slightly. Illiterate people are not completely absent from the dominant culture and society, although Ralph Ellison has shown us how invisible many of them are. That they are not completely absent is a result of the ways in which their illiteracy is defined. The illiterates I am describing—mainly poor whites, blacks, and Hispanics, economic and social outcasts—are not illiterate within their own cultures. In their communities, they possess the power to speak and be heard and often the power to write and be read.

Once they move outside those communities, however, their particular brand of illiteracy becomes felt. Literate at home, they become illiterate at work, illiterate in society at large. They are Dr. Jekyll and Mr. Hyde, only in this case the dark transformation is not located within the individual but is imposed from outside by a dominant society that defines them as other.

Language, after all, is the ligature that binds person to person, individual to culture, human to the world of humanity. It is the connective that binds *I* to *you* because language is always addressed to the other. As Vološinov reminds us:

> The *word is oriented toward an addressee,* toward *who* that addressee might be . . . *the word is a two-sided act.* It is determined equally by *whose* word it is and *for whom* it is meant. As word, it is precisely *the product of the reciprocal relationship between speaker and listener, addresser and addressee.* Each and every word expresses the "one" in relation to the "other." . . . A word is a bridge thrown between myself and another. If one end of the bridge depends on me, then the other depends on my addressee. A word is territory shared by both addresser and addressee, by the speaker and his interlocutor. (*Marxism* 85–86)

This concept of "addressivity" is a central one to Bakhtinian theory. Language does not exist in isolation; it is always addressed to a listener who is another user of language. As we speak or write, we are always addressing the other who is simultaneously responding to us—otherwise words would, quite literally, fail us. Every meaningful use of language simultaneously engages both self and other: we speak and conceive of ourselves as being listened to; we write, and the reader is created within the written word, within ourselves. An addressee enters into the territory of the utterance—shaping it, giving it evaluative accents, permeating it with an appropriate tone and style, forming it from within. Words are shared archipelagoes of social interaction, linked beneath the surface by history, by shared values, by mutual responsiveness. For Bakhtin, this idea of responsiveness is crucial:

> The listener and his response are regularly taken into account when it comes to everyday dialogue and rhetoric, but every other sort of discourse as well is oriented toward an understanding that is "responsive." . . . Responsive understanding is a fundamental force, one that participates in the formulation of discourse, and it is moreover an *active* understanding, one that discourse senses as resistance or support enriching the discourse. (*Dialogic Imagination* 281)

This active responsiveness is precisely what is missing for those branded as illiterate. Through acts of social, political, and economic exclusion by the dominant culture, they have been denied genuine listeners, denied response on the part of those whom they are purportedly addressing. Like Cassandra, they use language with no effect. In view of their powerlessness to be understood, their inability to influence or signify, it should come as no surprise that they both define themselves and are defined by others as illiterate. Indeed, they are illiterate.

This is not to say that they cannot speak or write words, sentences, phrases. For Bakhtin, there is a crucial difference between a word as it appears in a dictionary or in a sentence and a word as it appears in an utterance. A word in a dictionary is not a word at all but a mirage, having the appearance of a word but no body or spirit. Likewise, the sentence, as opposed to "the utterance," is a grammatical unit, a typesetter's convention. Sentences, like individual words, are neutral, grammatical categories. They contain words, but "like the word, [the sentence] has no author. Like the word, it belongs to *nobody*" (Bakhtin, *Speech Genres* 84). Thus the sentence "has no capacity to determine directly the responsive position of the *other* speaker, that is, it cannot evoke a response" (*Speech Genres* 74).

The actual word exists in an interactive medium—spoken or written. "Verbal discourse" says Vološinov, "is the skeleton that takes on living flesh only in the process of creative perception—consequently, only in the process of living social communication" ("Discourse" 109). In his notes from 1970–71, Bakhtin states:

> Everything that pertains to me enters my consciousness, beginning with my name, from the external world through the mouths of others (my mother, and so forth), with their intonation, in their emotional and value-assigning tonality. I realize myself initially through others: from them I receive words, forms, and tonalities. . . . Just as the body is formed initially in the mother's womb (body), a person's consciousness awakens wrapped in another's consciousness. (*Speech Genres* 138)

This quality of social interaction, of shared consciousness, is what distinguishes an utterance from a sentence (see also Stacey, esp. 62–71). An utterance necessarily exists within a social setting. An utterance creates and completes a meaning that is oriented toward another individual or socially constructed reality. *Utterance* is the term Bakhtin chooses to describe language that conveys meaning, that creates expression. Sentences are inert; utterances are interactive, intertextual, transformative.

Let me be deconstructive for a moment and consider how I wrote this essay. After several tedious false starts, some lasting as long as three and one half pages, I was stuck. I had not yet found a way to conceive of this essay. What I did was apply the method that I have elsewhere termed "situational sequencing"—that is, I placed myself within a context of readers who shared my interest in literacy. I imagined this essay being read and responded to by literacy specialists. I had no specific idea what it meant to write to literacy specialists. Although unsure, I assumed that I could engage in a communicative utterance, that they and I would share certain speech conventions, verbal routines, political and disciplinary values.

In imagining my audience, I also imagined myself interacting with them. I thus created an addressee toward whom my utterance oriented itself—a voiceless addressee, it is true, but one who read attentively, sympathetically, questioningly, thoughtfully, empathetically. This constructed addressee was, for me, enabling: it allowed me to choose words that were framed within utterances, not sentences, for those words were engaged responsively with a reader even before I wrote them. If my language was not so engaged, then my utterances would have undergone an ontological shift back to sentences—which is precisely what I had before—sentences that contained meaning but that were not aware of themselves within this mirrored network of responsiveness and addressivity, of utterance and speech genre. Ultimately, were I to speak to literacy specialists more often, I would not have to engage in the artificial step of constructing a situation for my discourse; that situation, that ideological state of multiple rejoinder, would operate as a formative principle in my language. This shared context of mutual responsiveness is what is lacking among those we characterize as illiterate: other than their own politico-racial-socioeconomic class, they have no audience, no ability to construct one, and, thus, they cannot operate from a position of mutual responsiveness. No matter how much they try, they cannot conceive of themselves as participating in the literacy event of writing and reading this essay, because they lack the prior experience of creating responsive addressees beyond their own social class structure.

ʻGiven this problem, illiterate people inevitably engage in mock conversation when their words are directed to the dominant society that surrounds them. As mock speakers, they use words and sentences that are directed toward mock listeners. Utterance is impossible, for speaker and listener do not exist within the same ideological plane, the same social purview. Illiteracy is an outcome of this isolation, for, as Bakhtin informs us, "addressivity, the quality of turning to someone, is a constitutive feature of the utterance; without it the utterance does not and cannot exist" (*Speech Genres* 99). Illiterate people are embedded within a language use that won't allow them to transform sentences into utterances that reach beyond their own communities. For them the condition is existentially insufferable: since their language cannot be directed toward an other, it is impossible for them to constitute a self. They possess a self only within the ghettoized communities that they seek to escape; and, once they escape those communities, they have no self at all.

Bakhtin's discussion of utterance and addressivity should be considered within the context of his analysis of speech genres, which he describes as socially defined and accepted conventions that organize forms of utterance. Anecdotes, letters, formal and informal greetings, business memorandums, the romantic novel— these are speech genres. Not only do we create these speech genres as we speak and write, but they also create us, for they establish the accepted forms that shape our utterances. These speech genres represent forms accreted over time by society, naturalized through social usage. Moreover, speech genres take on particularized definition within specific speech communities. Thus the speech genres within the business community are not identical to those within the academic community or to those used by black teenagers or young, male, blue-collar workers. Not sharing in the values of the dominant culture, not participating in meaningful linguistic exchange with that culture, illiterate people find themselves on the margins of the dominant-culture speech genres. Excluded from engaging in meaning making in society, they can choose either to violate speech genres as an act of verbal rebellion or imitate them without hope of succeeding at communication.

If I offer a dire picture of illiteracy, it is because the situation is dire. The only opportunity I see for eliminating illiteracy in America is social transformation in which persons discover a means to engage one another meaningfully through language—not as antagonists, not on the basis of class differences, not through racism or sexism or commodification but through a shared identification of self with other. To be effective, this ideological alteration must be initiated largely by the dominant classes within society, for only they have the power to create speaking subjects out of individuals currently considered illiterate. Bakhtin tells us that "understanding is imbued with response," that the act of understanding requires that "the listener becomes the speaker" (*Speech Genres* 68). For Bakhtin, the concept of addressivity merges with the concept of alterity: the more there is of the other, the more there is of the self, but only if the other can be addressed and held in genuine relation to the self. The condition of human otherness, of alien people and alien words, does not just threaten the self—it constitutes the self. Viewed in this way, literacy is, as it should be, an essential act of community. Unless we can become a literate society, we are no society at all, for in losing the other, what we really lose is ourselves.

WORKS CITED

Bakhtin, Mikhail M. *The Dialogic Imagination: Four Essays.* Ed. Michael Holquist. Trans. Caryl Emerson and Michael Holquist. Austin: Texas UP, 1981.

——. *Speech Genres and Other Late Essays.* Trans. Vern W. McGee. Austin: Texas UP, 1986.

Kozol, Jonathan. *Illiterate America.* Garden City: Anchor-Doubleday, 1985.

Pattison, Robert. *On Literacy.* Oxford: Oxford UP, 1982.

Schuster, Charles. "Situational Sequencing." *Writing Instructor* 3 (1984): 177–84.

Stacey, Michelle. "Profiles: At Play in the Language (Allen Walker Read)." *New Yorker* 4 Sept. 1989: 51–74.

Vološinov, V. N. "Discourse in Life and Discourse in Art (Concerning Sociological Poetics)." App. 1. *Freudianism: A Critical Sketch.* By Vološinov. Trans. I. R. Titunik. Ed. in collaboration with Neal H. Bruss. 1976. Bloomington: Indiana UP, 1987. 93–116.

——. *Marxism and the Philosophy of Language.* Trans. Ladislav Matejka and I. R. Titunik. Cambridge: Harvard UP, 1973.

Part Four

CREATING AND SUSTAINING LITERACY

Toward a Social-Cognitive Understanding of Problematic Reading and Writing

Glynda Hull and Mike Rose

All about us we hear news of a literacy crisis in America: the technicians who cannot read manuals, the unemployed workers who must struggle to fill in the blanks on a job application, the fathers who fail to decode the printed stories in their children's primers—all sorts of people, young, old, of varied races whose facility with written language is sufficiently poor to impair their functioning day to day. Associated with these reports—sometimes sensibly, sometimes not—is America's other population, one that we know intimately: that significant stratum of students (variously termed remedial, nontraditional, developmental, underprepared, nonmainstream) who enter higher education but are not prepared for the writing and reading tasks that they encounter.

Such students listen to teachers talk about sentence and paragraph structure; they fill in blanks in workbooks; they sit before material written in a language that is formal, complex, and strange. And they try to write. The small body of research that exists on what happens as such students try to write suggests that, for them, composing is a slow, often derailed process that proceeds by rules and strategies that are often dysfunctional. But that is about the extent of our knowledge. Teachers receive these students' essays and try to evaluate them and make inferences about what the students learned or didn't learn, what their cognitive capacity is, whether or not they're fit for the institution that already classifies them as marginal. And teachers do so with a limited knowledge of the complex cognitive and social processes that produced the writing they read.

Clearly, we need further information on what it is that cognitively and socially defines an underprepared student as underprepared. What kind of knowledge does an underprepared student bring to the classroom? How is the teacher representing the writing process and the writing task? How is the student representing the teacher's discussion of the writing process and the writing task? What occurs between the two in the classroom as they attempt to negotiate a common understanding of the task, and in what ways might that interaction further define the student as remedial? What happens when the student sits down to write? Researchers have few answers to those questions; not a lot of research has addressed them.

We are conducting a research project on remediation at the community college, state college, and university level that, we hope, will provide some information on what it is that cognitively and socially defines an underprepared student as underprepared. The writing and reading classes we chose to study are those considered to be the most remedial in each of the institutions we visited. Students in these classes are very much at risk to succeed, and, in some ways, they present profound challenges to the stated mission of the institutions that enroll them.

We focus here on a piece of writing produced by Tanya, one of the students in a basic reading and writing class—close in level to an adult literacy program—in the urban community college we studied.[1] Tanya is nineteen years old, never finished high school, grew up in the inner city. We tutored her over a four-month period. We asked her, in the instance we focus on here, to write a paper that was more difficult than any she had done so far, one closer to the school-based writing tasks she would eventually confront if she moved closer to her goal of becoming a nurse's aide or a licensed vocational nurse. To meet her interests, we provided a simple case study written by a nurse, "Handling the Difficult Patient." The author gives a first-person account of her experiences with an ornery patient in a hospital. The nurse begins by sympathetically describing the patient—very ill, hooked to an intravenous tube, gaunt. She then details how she introduced herself and received a response of anger and rejection: "You're killing me, you XXX!" The next nine paragraphs of the article were marked up by Tanya and figured prominently in the piece of writing she did for us. Those nine paragraphs follow.

Case Study of a Difficult Patient

"Oh, this is going to be a great day," I said to myself. "Just be patient, kind, and understanding. Maybe he only needs some TLC to alleviate his fears. He really seems more frightened than anything." With these thoughts, I began to care for him as skillfully as I could.   [paragraph 4 of original text]

The day was exhausting. No matter what I did and no matter how gently I handled him, it was all to no avail. Sometimes the verbal abuse pounded and grated until it became almost physical. My nerves were frazzled; 3 P.M. just didn't come soon enough.   [5]

In giving the evening nurse my report, I tried to provide a fair assessment of the situation and to prepare her for the ordeal that lay ahead. She was willing to give it a try, but if he proved too difficult, she said, she wouldn't remain on the case.   [6]

My thoughts were similar, but deep down I really wanted to help him. What was the right approach?   [7]

The next morning there was no night special to report. She had left the case, and the report she sent to the Registry of Nurses was so descriptive that it would be almost impossible to find a replacement. My second and third days were as terrible as the first. By the fourth day, the evening nurse decided she wouldn't take the abuse any longer and also left the case. To say I felt abandoned was an understatement; even the doctor didn't have any advice.   [8]

The turning point came on my fifth day. I was attempting range of motion exercises with the patient. Despite his cursing, I explained the purpose of the therapy and told him I was doing it as gently as possible. He continued to object, and at one point I said, "I hope you understand that I'm doing this to help you." He growled sarcastically, "Oh, sure, girlie! You're doing this for me, are you? And I suppose for free, too."   [9]

Well, five days of total frustration were enough. I was extremely hurt and angered. Retaliation had never been one of my methods, but this time it flowed out naturally.   [10]

"You're right," I said. "I am getting paid for what I'm doing, but here's the difference: I have pride in my profession, and I earn my pay by giving my patients the best nursing care I possibly can. But I can give the minimum, too. I can sit here most of the day and still collect my 35 bucks at the end of the shift. If that's what you want, the choice is yours. So make up your mind fast, because I'm not taking any more of your abuse."   [11]

Then I stopped what I was doing, picked up the newspaper, and proceeded to read it. I felt terrible about speaking that way to a patient. Never before had this happened. My confidence in my ability to keep calm was as shaky as my hands were. The patient was asleep when I left at 3 P.M.   [12]

We asked Tanya to write a summary of the article, explaining to her that a summary is a short version of a reading that reports its main points. It is "what you would tell someone who hadn't read the article if they asked you, 'Tanya, what was that about?' " To gain some access to Tanya's composing process, we used a stimulated-recall procedure; that is, we videotaped Tanya as she wrote, recording the emergence of her text on the page (Rose). We then played the videotape for her to prompt her to recall what she was thinking as she wrote. The summary that Tanya wrote follows. After the whole process, we talked to her about her reading. We were satisfied that she had a general idea of what a summary is and that she understood the case study she had read.

Tanya's Summary of the Case Study

Page 1
1 The Handling About
2 difficult patient

3 this something telling about
4 a nurse ~~to~~ who won't to
5 help a patience.
6 She was a special night nurse,
7 this man had a stroke and
8 was ~~paral~~ paralsis on his
9 left side. She Was really

10 doing a lot for the patience
11 She Introduced myself
12 she asked him How was
13 he feeling. remark was,"
14 XXX, can't you see 'Im in
15 pain?" he telling the nurse
16 he was in so much pain.

Page 2
17 he really didn't won't
18 to answer her. Before
19 she was ready to give
20 him his I.V. Are Anything
21 XXX "you're killing me,
22 you XXX."
23 Oh this going to Be a great
24 Day I said to myself
25 just thinking alone.
26 I have pride in What
27 I Do I am going to get
28 pad no matter what I am
29 still ~~am~~ going to collect
30 my money no matter
31 what happen I do Believe
32 and I no that In ~~my~~ mind
33 My thoughts were similar
34 but deep down.

Page 3
35 What was the approach?
36 A Registry nurse
37 was so descriptive.
38 impossible for me to
39 find a replacement.
40 My second and thirddays
41 she decided she ~~won~~ wouldn't
42 <u>Abuse</u> any longer and
43 ~~Also~~ also left the case
44 felt Abandoned was an
45 understatement; even
46 this doctor In this case
47 she Really liked what she
48 was doing But was getting
49 treated Right Respect.
50 She had chance of getting
51 A another job But Don't
52 she wanted to But ~~I~~ then again
53 She wanted to.

Tanya's summary is the kind of writing that feeds everyone's worries about the consequences of illiteracy and the failure of our schools. It will also suggest to some people that this writer is somehow cognitively and linguistically deficient, that she is incoherent, can't think straight. But if we examine this piece of writing in context, taking into consideration the student's past experiences with schooling, her peculiar notions about reading and writing, the instruction she is currently receiving, her plans and goals for her future—that is, if we assume a coherence, if we assume that a learner's performance at any time has a history and, as Mina Shaughnessy taught us, a logic—we will think about this text and the student who wrote it quite differently.

Part of the seeming incoherence of Tanya's text falls away when we look at the text she was summarizing (see table 1). Tanya marked up the text she was reading, underlining and bracketing sentences and paragraphs that she considered important—paragraphs 7 and 11, for example. When we examine Tanya's summary against her marked-up source text, we see that she lifted some of these

Table 1. Juxtaposing the Case Study and Tanya's Summary

Original text	*Student's summary (lines 23–39)*
"Oh, this is going to be a great day," I said to myself. [paragraph 4]	23 Oh this going to Be a great 24 Day I said to myself 25 just thinking alone.
I have pride in my profession [paragraph 11]	26 I have pride in What 27 I Do I am going to get
But I can give the minimum, too. I can sit here most of the day and still collect my 35 bucks at the end of the shift. [paragraph 11]	28 pad no matter what I am 29 still ~~am~~ going to collect 30 my money no matter 31 what happen I do Believe 32 and I no that In ~~my~~ mind.
My thoughts were similar, but deep down I really wanted to help him. What was the right approach? [paragraph 7]	33 My thoughts were similar 34 but deep down. 35 What was the approach?
. . . the report she sent to the Registry of Nurses was so descriptive that it would be almost impossible to find a replacement. [paragraph 8]	36 A Registry nurse 37 was so descriptive. 38 impossible for me to 39 find a replacement.

sentences and parts of sentences from the original and situated them in her summary, though not in the way we would expect. For example, lines 23 through 39 of her summary are bits and pieces drawn from disparate parts of the original text.

When we examine what Tanya takes from the case study, how she modifies those sentences and phrases, and how she situates them in her summary, we notice two things: she makes slight modifications in the original, changing a word here and there but copying whole chunks verbatim, and she juxtaposes segments of the original without connecting them each to the other. For example, a phrase taken from paragraph 11 in the original is put next to one from paragraph 7, which comes next to one from paragraph 8, with no apparent attention to the features of discourse that allow readers to construct a coherent text.

Tanya had a patchwork approach to writing a summary, and, when we began to talk to her, we learned why. We pointed to some of the sentences she had lifted from the case study and modified slightly before patching them into her summary. For example, she changed the nurse's statement "I have pride in my profession" to "I have pride in what I do." In response to our question as to the purpose of her modifications, she answered, "I have practice from when I try not to copy. When I get a little bit from there, a teacher'll really know what I'm talking about . . . then if some parts from there I change a little bit, they know I'm not really that kind of student that would copy, 'cause another student would copy."

Tanya seems to be operating with two intentions here: to display and convey knowledge ("a teacher'll really know what I'm talking about") and to show she's "not . . . that kind of student that would copy." Tanya wants to be a successful student this time around, so displaying knowledge is for her a powerful and understandable signal of her good academic citizenship. What is intriguing here, though, is the procedural rule she invokes when writing her summary: change a few words so as not to copy. This injunction against plagiarism is probably a holdover from some past instruction. The thing that interests us about this rule is that it is a good reminder what a powerful hold negative injunctions can have on students; it also recalls for us that school has been mainly punitive for Tanya. In our formal interviews with Tanya, in our talks with her after class, in her essays and writings throughout the semester, we heard many variations on this theme: being kicked out of five high schools during her senior year, being hit on the hand with rulers, being chastised in the middle of reading class for not coming to school, feigning sleep for fear of being called on. Here is an example:

TANYA: I was scared a lot.

INTERVIEWER: Just scared of reading out loud or . . . ?

TANYA: 'Cause see, the only reason I was scared was 'cause the teacher, she would look on an attendance list, and she would see who was that person reading. And she would call out that person's name and ask you, "What is your problem?" and look at my attendance and know that I ain't been coming to school. And she would get on me, and that's what I would be scared of. 'Cause she'd call my name out, have me to come up here and just stop everything.   (interview, 6 Oct.)

We heard so many negative memories of schooling and literacy instruction from Tanya and other students that we began to appreciate anew the power of directives like "Don't plagiarize," even when they aren't explained or aren't contextualized or in some other way don't make sense to students.

Another rule that seemed to govern Tanya's construction of the summary had to do with selection. Remember that she had marked up the case study, picking out things that interested her. We learned from our interviews with her that she changed whole sentences around not only because she wanted to avoid plagiarism but because "the parts about the nurse are something about me . . . you see 'I have pride,' you see, I can read that for me." In her construction of the summary, then, she seemed to privilege propositions that related to herself. While some of the details she included in her summary contained its gist, she tended to choose details not because they were important to the original text but because they were important to her; their placement, therefore, had more a personal than a textual relevance.

We saw this again and again in both her reading and her writing. Texts sometimes didn't appear to have a coherent identity apart from Tanya as a reader; the importance of the text tended to be in direct relation to its importance to her. This practice led some of her teachers to think she was a flake, but we should also recall that the practice resembles the kind of reading strategies that teachers may encourage her to use, that actually resemble expert ones: interact with the text, relate it to your own experiences, derive your own meaning from it. In fact, Tanya's reading teacher encouraged all her students to take what she called star notes—notes that would make them star readers. These notes were a dialogue that students were supposed to have with the author of the text.

Another way to understand Tanya's penchant for privileging propositions that related to herself is to read this strategy as an interesting assertion of her own self-worth in relation to a life and a school history that had left her feeling that she wasn't worth much. A theme that rises, phoenixlike, from our many pages of transcripts of tutoring sessions and interviews is Tanya's assertion that she can do it, she can make it, she can learn and succeed.

"I'm going to get a little bit better in my reading and my math. All the rest I think I'm capable of doing."   (9 Sept., first interview statement)

"I can do that, too [write a comparison-contrast essay]. I can do a lot of things." (20 Oct.)

"I know I can do it. I know I can do it. That's what I really need [to improve her writing and math]."   (27 Oct.)

The way Tanya aggressively appropriates the meaning of a text to suit her own interests parallels for us the chorus she repeats over and over again: I can make it, I have pride and confidence in myself, I really am going to be a nurse. Such goals and dreams allow her to identify with the nurse in the case study, and it is likely that they orient, to a disproportionate extent, her construction of that reading and writing task and perhaps other school literacy tasks as well. Tanya had a lot of strikes against her: kicked out of school, on the outs with her mother and an overbearing stepfather, living on her own in a drug-infested apartment complex, pulled by a legion of boyfriends—"the only thing good in my life," she once said. Tanya has got to hold on for dear life to the idea that she can be a nurse, that she is important, that she can succeed.

Tanya's bizarre word salad is, perhaps, not so bizarre after all. Still, one's heart sinks when one places Tanya's statements about her hopes and dreams next to a text that, though now better understood, is still exceptionally flawed mechanically, grammatically, and orthographically. Her errors are the stigma of illiteracy. What is a teacher to do? First, we want to recall that Tanya's essay is a first draft, and our experience with her has shown us that, with instruction to revise and proofread, she would most likely correct some of her punctuation, capitalizing, and spelling errors. Still, a revised version would be littered with many errors, and it would be hard to ignore them. One of the rewards, though, that comes from working with marginal students is that they force you again and again to scrutinize your own reactions, to question your received assumptions about literacy and pedagogy, about cognition, and about the purposes of discourse. After wrestling with our own concerns about the errors in Tanya's written language, about all those markers of illiteracy, it struck us that something profoundly literate is going on here. A fundamental social and psychological reality about discourse, oral or written, is that human beings continually appropriate each other's language to establish group membership, to grow, and to define themselves in new ways. Socially oriented linguists discuss the way this impulse plays itself out in speech, but it can occur as well with written discourse (see Bartholomae; Lanham; Witte).[2] Tanya's appropriation of the nurse's text, with enough words changed to signal that she's not the kind of student who would copy, is related to her desire to redefine her life, to make it, to be a nurse's aide or a licensed vocational nurse. Tanya is trying on the nurse's written language and, with it, the nurse's self.

A powerful pedagogic next move with Tanya would be to temporarily suspend concern about errors and pursue, full tilt, her impulse to don the written language of another. What she seems to need at this point in her reentry into the classroom is a freewheeling pedagogy of imitation, one that encourages her to try on the language of essays like the nurses's case study, essays related to health care that are accessible and tie in with Tanya's hopes for herself. Then, gradually, the teacher could begin calling attention to certain sentence patterns through a focused imitation; could help Tanya make and develop discourse patterns, like the chronological one she's trying to follow in the summary we presented; could show her some simple ways to effect coherent transitions from one bit of language to another; could teach her a few conventions that would enable her to use the texts of others in ways that show she's not copying. The teacher could, in short, help Tanya shape her writing in the way the nurse and other such authors are shaping theirs.

At the same time that we outline a pedagogy to move Tanya toward a conventional discourse, we are aware of what her unconventional performance can teach us. We are struck by her "plagiarism," for example, not only because it is a startling departure from traditional ways of using a source text but because it puts into the foreground what is often an unquestioned practice in the Western essayist tradition. We academic writers internalize rules and strategies for citing source texts, for acknowledging debts to previous scholarship, for separating what we can claim as our own ideas from the intellectual property of others. And we do so, once we have learned the tricks of our trade, almost without thinking, producing essays that seem to mark clearly where other people's ideas end and ours begin. Such clearly documented writing may let us forget or even camouflage how much more it is that we borrow from existing texts, how much we depend on membership in a community for our language, our voices, our very arguments. We forget that we, like Tanya, continually appropriate each other's language to establish group membership, to grow, and to define ourselves in new ways and that such appropriation is a fundamental part of language use, even as the appearance of our texts belies it.

We have given one snapshot of some of the social and cognitive variables surrounding one piece of writing from one of the students we studied in a community college. As we and those working on the project with us continue to examine our data—texts, videotapes of classroom interaction, audiotapes of tutorial sessions, speak-aloud and stimulated-recall sessions—we hope that our research will provide answers to the following questions:

1. What productive and counterproductive strategies, habits, rules, and assumptions tend to characterize the writing and reading skills of underprepared students?
2. How are these strategies represented in the students' minds, and what personal, social, and historical forces may have influenced these current representations?
3. What tends to happen to these strategies, rules, and assumptions during instruction?
4. What mismatches or points of convergence tend to occur between pedagogies or programs and the students' background knowledge, experiences, and goals?
5. What are the social and institutional processes whereby students like Tanya are defined as deficient or remedial or substandard?

We are hoping to bring to bear several layers of information on the problem of underpreparation in reading and writing. By comparing the data we collect in our three sites—the community college, the state college, and the university—and by making sure that our work is many-layered, we hope to construct rich descriptions of the knowledge, assumptions, and behaviors that characterize and influence underprepared students' creation and use of texts. In the process we hope to devise a social and cognitive framework for analyzing the discourse produced by underprepared students, a framework that allows us to go beyond merely describing textual features, to understanding the production of those features. Moving from textual features, whether written or oral, to a description of those knowledge structures that yielded those features and moving from a description of those knowledge structures to an understanding of their origins in a broader context is the tough problem that we want to work on. We hope, finally, to construct a set of vivid examples that may be used in teacher or tutor training, examples that illustrate dysfunctional reading and writing strategies and reveal the social and cognitive factors influencing them. We hope these vignettes will provoke some epiphanies, that they will move us all toward a different and richer representation of literacy instruction for underprepared students—toward a redefinition of *remedial*, away from the deficit orientation it currently has and toward a richer, more informed, and generative conception.[3]

NOTES

[1]This piece of writing is also discussed in Hull, "Literacy, Technology and the Underprepared." In that essay Tanya was identified by the different pseudonym of Ariel, a rather literary name used to capture what seemed to be her essence, a mischievousness and a wonderful lightness of being in the face of difficult circumstances.

[2]Our thanks go to Stephen Witte for helping us shape this discussion.

[3]An extended version of this essay appears in *Written Communication* 16 (Apr. 1989): 139–54.

We would like to thank our colleagues for their assistance at various stages of this project: Kay Losey Fraser, Marisa Garrett, Peter Simon, Susan Thompson-Lowry, Smokey Wilson, and Stephen Witte. Our work has been supported by the Spenser Foundation, the Center for the Study of Writing, and the James S. McDonnell Foundation's Program in Cognitive Studies for Educational Practice.

WORKS CITED

Bartholomae, David. "Inventing the University." *When a Writer Can't Write*. Ed. M. Rose. New York: Guilford, 1985. 134–65.

Hull, Glynda A. "Literacy, Technology and the Underprepared: Notes toward a Framework for Action." *Quarterly of the National Writing Project and the Center for the Study of Writing*, 10 (1988): 1–3, 16–25.

Lanham, Richard A. *Style: An Anti-Textbook*. New Haven: Yale UP, 1974.

Rose, Mike. *Writer's Block: The Cognitive Dimension*. Carbondale: Southern Illinois UP, 1984.

Shaughnessy, Mina. *Errors and Expectations*. New York: Oxford UP, 1977.

Witte, Stephen P. "Some Contexts for Understanding Written Literacy." Right to Literacy Conference. Columbus, Ohio, Sept. 1988.

Cross-Age Tutoring:
The Right to Literacy

J. Elspeth Stuckey and Kenneth Alston

In 1987–88 the Bread Loaf School of English funded a project in South Carolina to improve the literacy conditions of rural students. The project was based on a model called cross-age tutoring that was developed by Shirley Brice Heath to encourage the acquisition of second-language literate behaviors in young Hispanic children (see Hoffman and Heath). The South Carolina project expanded and elaborated the model to involve a broad spectrum of ages, groups, and disciplines.

We offer this essay for more reasons than description. We think that the project works because it is imbedded in theory and politics. The theory concerns the articulation of educational purpose; the politics is the calculated practice of that purpose. The two are really not separable, but we begin with politics.

According to our view, most public education in the United States reproduces the status quo. In so doing, it systematically and successfully restricts the opportunities and aspirations of minorities and the poor. No educator can walk the halls of a public school and not discern a visible class structure. Remediation is a condition of the underclass. Further, standardized testing, teacher education, and exit criteria ensure the failure and the disfranchisement of those who are racially identified and poor. Because literacy in the late twentieth century is the chief instrument of this domination, literacy in the schools is the chief location of struggle.

To instantiate the politics, the project works with rural, poor, and black students. The common term for these students is *at risk*. We assumed from the outset that at-risk students are capable of acquiring abilities, the supposed lack of which identifies them as at risk. As we have come to understand and as others before us have understood, the students at the bottom of the bin are competent human beings who have interests, talents, and the desire to learn. They are simply poor.

The only value of politics is to invent ways to implement change. The cast we would like to give to politics is impatience. We suggest that politics can succeed in the face of daily sadness, wastefulness, and poverty. We believe that the direness of conservative praxis (if there is such a thing) can be replaced by human and economic concerns. The South Carolina project is most useful in this respect because it suggests how a particular approach to literacy yields ends that in school today are ordinarily denied by literacy.

The project intertwines speaking, reading, and writing. Twice a week a set of tutors meets with a set of tutees. The tutors are older than the tutees, but not much; some tutors are only a few years older than their tutees, and some high school students tutor students in elementary school. The tutoring sessions usually last for approximately twenty minutes; some last longer. The older students read and write with the younger students. They concentrate on whole texts, reading entire books or writing complete stories. At the end of each session, the tutors spend ten or fifteen minutes recording field notes in journals. At the end of each week, the tutors write letters to an adviser to describe the activities of the week. The adviser writes letters back to the student tutors with appropriate responses and inquiries. At some sites the participants have access to computers to record notes and to write letters. No matter what technological capability is available, the participants at all sites maintain regular tutorial sessions, keep records, and correspond with advisers.

How South Carolina elaborates the mechanism is a wonderful thing to see. In 1987–88 there were five sites. They spanned the state. One was in the low country, one was in the high country, one was on the North Carolina border, and two were in the midlands. Two of the sites involved junior and senior high school students who tutored elementary school students. One site involved college students tutoring ninth-graders. One involved a college tutor, a college teacher, and elementary school tutees. One involved six fourth-grade tutors and six first-grade tutees.

Site A. The per capita income at site A is under the poverty line. The tutors were sixth- and seventh-graders; the tutees were compensatory first-graders. Compensatory first-graders are very small children. They appear swallowed by the desks they sit at most of the day. They suffer various injuries and often come to school patched up. They have gained entry into the compensatory first grade because they cannot pass skills tests in the first grade. In the compensatory first grade the students must work on those skills to bring them up to standard. Theoretically, the time spent in compensatory first grade is limited, and students are transferred back to the original class. Unfortunately, most of the compensatory first-graders stay in the compensatory first grade. The next year, they enter the standard first grade. During the project, there were three successive compensatory teachers.

The tutors ranged in age from twelve to fifteen. One had lived in more foster homes than her age. One tutor was suspended from the project for allegedly breaking a yardstick over a first-grader. The student was simply repeating an educational tactic practiced on her. Most of the students in the project were black; all were poor.

Site B. The tutees were first-graders, the tutors were fourth-graders. Most of those in both groups were black; all were poor. The black children's ancestors were slaves on the rice-growing plantations in the area before the Civil War.

In the last ten years the area has been bought up by developers and gentrified by retirees and middle managers, whose children and grandchildren have flooded the local school.

Site C. The tutees were sixth-graders, and the tutors were from the ninth through the twelfth grades. Some of the tutors lived in a home for abused and difficult children. This school differed from the others in only one respect: when we were there, the entire school was white. Few blacks live in this industrially desolate part of the state, nor have they ever lived there. The unmistakable revelation is the consistency of economic misery for whites and blacks in poor, rural settings.

Site D. The tutees were three small boys, all black, impoverished brothers and cousins who were despaired of. The youngest was in the first grade for the second time; the next was in the third grade but had failed the first grade; the oldest was in the sixth grade for the second time. The sixth-grader, mid-way through the project, was discovered to be congenitally blind in his right eye. The tutor was a college student, the first black male teacher encountered by any of the children.

Site E. Sophomore-level college students from a historically black college tutored ninth-grade students at a nearby black high school. The average income level of the college families is under $8,000 a year. The average verbal Scholastic Aptitude Test score of the entering freshmen is 282. Of the twelve ninth-grade tutees, six dropped out: one to get a job, one because of pregnancy, one because of home problems, one because of illness, and two after repetitive absences from school.

In all, approximately ninety students were involved in the project.

The background stories of the students are necessary not to belabor the usual pieties of failure and social damnation of poor students but to decry their inimitableness. The mean circumstances the students found at home were endemic in their school lives as well. All these small, medium-sized, or maturing children were systematically informed of their inadequacy and inferiority. They were not the ones with privilege; they were the ones at risk.

Neither the parents nor the teachers of these students were mean, inadequate, or inferior. The teachers and the parents have no personal investment in the damnation of their children. Yet—and we say this with trepidation and conviction—teachers and parents are co-opted by a system that they wish they could change or wish they could beat but are convinced that they cannot. (Of course, we would be dishonest not to admit that some teachers believe in the system and do their best to keep it running.) Good teachers and parents are plentiful; so are rules and regulations to shut them down.

That these students and their teachers were the ones to ratify the cross-age theory is the theory. In this respect there is one other unique aspect of the project.

The project is a literacy project. As such, its usual institutional framework is English—sometimes linguistics, sometimes English education. Consequently the students and the teachers usually come from remedial English classes. The only reason for this association is tradition; the argument against it is the necessity for literacy across the curriculum, the necessity for all teachers to be teachers of reading and writing. To this end, one of the sites set up shop in a science laboratory. This was Site E, the site that involved sophomore college tutors and ninth-grade tutees. The content of the project consisted of the chemistry experiments to be done as part of the tutors' normal course work. Once a week, the tutees traveled to the college to participate in the three-hour lab. Their role began as observers and notetakers. Increasingly, they took part in the experiments until they ultimately began conducting the experiments themselves, using the tutors as references, rather than guides. When the college year ended, the high school students continued to conduct experiments in their own classroom, ultimately becoming tutors to younger tutees from another site.

The literate exchange—the benchmark of the project—evolved around the needs of experimentation. The students had to read and understand complicated laboratory instructions. They had to keep field notes on the progress of the experiment, and they had to write up lab reports at the end. Finally, they corresponded with the adviser, as well as with each other, on the week's experiment, explaining both the science and the scene. This site also incorporated electronic mail during the second semester; the students inputted their correspondence, which was downloaded by the recipients and responded to in a similar fashion. The speed of the correspondence increased remarkably. By the end of the project, several ninth-graders, as well as the sophomore tutors, were accomplished at both chemistry and computers. Clearly, the concept of cross-age tutoring is not restricted to a single discipline.

The question is, what is the concept? To say that the theory of cross-age tutoring is its at-risk population is less to explain than to justify, a justification around whose edges, for better or worse, doubt always hovers. Does grouping older and younger at-risk students in congenial settings of reading and writing simply produce improved literacy? Are we somehow confusing literacy with compassion, counseling, or common sense? The questions would not be so problematic were not the tacit maintenance of such confusion necessary to underpin the current educational system. (Doubt arises most charmingly in situations of oppression.) The concept of the project must be described in two ways: first, as distinct from an ideological, psychological principle and, second, as antithethical to the usual theories of literacy. The first way may imply a critique of the psychopathology of Western education, especially the ubiquitous notion of self-esteem. The second way simply explains how the project understands literacy.

Whereas the project is compassionate and values self-esteem (how artless to have to say so), the notions of compassion or personal attention and self-esteem serve to excuse schools for isolating poor and minority populations of marginally literate students. The project was praised often. The praise usually came in one repeated line: "The students have more self-esteem now." The second most repeated line was "Personal attention is all these students need." The third line began, "The home lives of these students . . . ," presuming no personal attention or self-esteem there either. To be sure, many of these presumptions strike a chord. Yet what was usually taken for a rise in self-esteem was simply the recognition by the students and the teachers of the reality of the students' lives as people, not as blighted parts of the social landscape. The equation of learning with individual attention to self-esteem is wrong; passed off as theory, the equation empties education of content and reduces the stature of some persons and groups. (There is no telling how many middle-class students fail the self-esteem test and receive slight personal attention but somehow avoid remedial reading classes.) The practical results are that schools abnegate the responsibility to change because they claim they cannot fund nurture.

The point is that, as long as an image of smiling faces occupies the vision of educators, the issues of race and class and literacy will remain unaddressed. It is almost malign to observe the educational accomplishments of at-risk students and then to attribute those accomplishments to a rise in self-esteem. It is dishonest to attribute lack of self-esteem to lack of attention or to poor performance on standardized measures of learning. To do so is to miss the import of endeavors like cross-age tutoring. This is more than a bone to pick with school administrators or teachers, for their concern for the quality of the lives of students is genuine. This issue runs to the heart of the remedial mentality and its relegation of illiteracy to the realms of psychic woe. The cross-age project succeeds precisely because it refuses to equate literacy with virtue. The project in no way fools itself into thinking that it, not the institution, sets the conditions for literacy, including the conditions for the project. Many schools politely refuse the offer. Any school can shut down volunteerism at any point. What the project believes about literacy can be said economically.

Literacy is a technology unlike any other. Not a means to an end, literacy is a means to other means. Because the invention of means is the meaning of learning—when conditions are even slightly conducive to fair education—literacy is the most valuable technology. The stronger version of the claim that literacy can promote conducive conditions is tantalizing, but the more likely explanation is that the effects of literacy on programmatic change are the effects of human change. The human condition reveals more about literacy than literacy reveals about the human condition (a conclusion not simple but often not simpatico with the wishes of the literati.) Yet to say so is less to undermine the power of literacy than to translate it, translation itself being a means to other means. This is literacy's unique strength. It explains how the cross-age model of literacy is both portable and local. The model works not because it reveals the symbiotic relation between literacy and class but because it reveals the artificiality of the relation. The concrete, everyday classroom efficacy of the model is that it reveals the difference between students having something to say and their having a place to say it. The first thing the project affords is a place.

At-risk students are rarely asked to do what their more privileged peers routinely do. That is, they are rarely asked to speak, to think, to plan, to collaborate, or to evaluate. A typical cross-age tutoring session asks the tutors to do all those things; literacy is the agency. The tutor meets with the tutees. Together, they decide on a book to read or a composition or story to write, and they sort through the available selections. They sit down together. The tutor begins to read out loud, modulating voice and adjusting the book to the vision of the tutees. When a tutee's attention wanders, the tutor calls it back and asks open-ended questions, a skill learned in training sessions. The tutor may stumble over words but keeps going. The tutor points to pictures to solicit responses, tells stories, listens to stories that the tutees tell. If the task is writing, the tutor and the tutees may discuss their efforts and may read aloud what each has written or what the tutor has transcribed for the tutees. At the end of the session, the tutor records the activity in a notebook and takes time to reflect and recall. After several sessions, the tutor writes a research report, a letter to the adviser to describe the tutoring sessions. In response to the letter, the tutor receives requests for clarification, offers of advice, praise, and references to future activity. The cycle repeats, and growth in observation, analysis, and linguistic maturity manifests as artifacts of literacy. A usual pattern is for the student tutors to progress from hesitant banality to making plans to making requests. A student may write in early field notes and letters, "I am having fun." Soon, the tutor writes: "My tutee needs a magic marker and paper. We are writing a story." Then the tutor asserts: "Send me a computer. I will give you my allowance every week. I can do much more with a computer." With older age groups, the activities merely vary with interest and peer possibilities; the effects and the evidence remain consistent. The revelation of out-loud reading to someone whose interest is interpretation, not correctness, is striking across all ages.

Perhaps for the first time, the tutors encounter occasions essentially of their own making. They learn how to plan ahead and how to understand progress, failure, frustration, and epiphany. The ideas of goals and needs evolve, and the tutors learn, first, to voice their observations and then to trust them. That these things are not solicited in the usual remedial environment hardly needs to be pointed out; that these things are solicited in cross-age tutoring as normal activities cannot be overemphasized. To be sure, the project does not pretend that some students do not have great gaps in their learning or that progress will move at an even pace. Nonetheless, students who can behave as readers and writers, who can be admired for occupying such roles, and who can take risks without fear of penalty are students who can become literate.

In ordinary lives these things sound ordinary. They are characteristic habits of the owners of literacy. They are not characteristic habits of the at-risk. Clearly enough, silenced people have words. Therefore, the one question that remains is the one that literacy cannot answer: What is the value of all this?

What is the value? No school principal, teacher, or superintendent fails to ask that question, and no one has any question about the meaning of value. Does the project improve standardized test scores? If so, proceed. If not, our hands are tied. Are principals, teachers, and superintendents aware of a notion of education apart from tests? Most are aware. It really does not matter. We rarely dealt with teachers, principals, superintendents, state department officials, or even consultants who did not feel that they were on the line concerning test scores. A third-grade teacher describes a typical situation. Every year, standardized-test scores for districts are published in the newspaper. The teachers are not identified. However, some districts have only one class at a particular grade level. Anonymity is hardly preserved for anyone.

Cross-age tutoring is statistically significant. In the first year of the project, the at-risk students improved on a state-mandated standardized test more than any other group in the school. In the second year, the students in the project tested out of remedial reading classes altogether. The college students, in stark contrast to the usual results, took and passed the state-mandated teachers' exam; the students went on to scholarship programs in their fields. The youngest students who had previously failed a grade were passed into the next grade. The data, still being analyzed, are positive.

Statistical significance is not, however, the answer to the question of value. As peremptory as it may sound, if the value of cross-age tutoring is to catch a few students as they fall, cross-age tutoring is worthless, though not callous; it is another epiphenomenon of standardized testing; it simply prolongs the misery of students indelibly incriminated by test scores. The value of the cross-age model is its ability to produce nonstandardizable results, to produce the conditions and the occasions for thought and action to ratify, rather than restrain, student learning. This the project can do. A thick description of any site suffices. A close look at the science project in site E is exemplary.

Chemistry laboratories are not congenial to underprepared students; laboratory manuals are incomprehensible. Sophomores in college are only slightly more equipped to negotiate them than are ninth-grade students. Negotiation is the form that experimentation takes. From some experience the older students tend to know the arcane terminology; they explain it. The younger students tend to gather materials and learn the terminology. When experience is insufficient and comprehension fails, the tutors and the tutees find solutions in the teacher. When groups of students become stymied, the teacher calls everyone's attention to the meaning of a direction in the manual.

Experiments proceed in steps. Each step shuttles between text and laboratory. Again and again, students read a direction; again and again, they measure, heat, pour, observe, calculate, and reach the next step. Reading brings results. Mistakes mean starting over. Knowing the experiment involves keeping notes of the progress made. Experiments succeed, experiments fail, and figuring out why is what matters.

The students explain the experiments in letters to the adviser. The adviser is an English teacher, not a scientist. The adviser is often confused. The lab reports make no sense. The reports have little in common with what happens in the lab. In the lab the students yell at each other, break beakers, leak water on the floor. In the reports, beakers fill themselves, no water spills, experiments resolve. What is going on, this contrast between reality and report? Explain an acid, explain a base. Explain the difference between talk and a report in science.

What is teaching, what is learning? The scientific experiment is an example of the negotiation between the two—an example of the continuum of learning and teaching—which is an example of an authentic practice of literacy as well. The science professor writes the English adviser: "You missed the point in the last write-up. The students were right." The English adviser responds, "Okay, so what am I to do, pretend I understand?" The science professor writes, "Come to the next lab."

The ninth-grade students in the project—the ones who are able to stick with it—learn to learn. They complete an experiment, arrive at an answer. The college sophomores—the ones who are able to stick with it—learn to teach, which is to learn. One kind of evidence is almost humorous. The college tutors complain rancorously of the inattention of their charges. If only the tutees were motivated, if only the tutees listened to the tutors, then all would be well. When the tutees become tutors, the tutors complain rancorously: Tutees don't listen. Tutees don't sit still. What the tutees need is discipline! The usual structures of education emerge. That is when the structures can be examined.

Literacy denied is not the same as literacy availed. Denial changes literacy. Literacy is not difficult to deny. In South Carolina the basic-skills assessment program assesses the need for remediation. The basic-skills test asks that students be able to do several things: decode word meaning, identify main ideas, understand references and inferences, and analyze literature. In the decoding segment the student is tested on sight recognition, phonetic decoding, contextual word meaning, and structural word meaning. Main ideas must be identified as restated, paraphrased, or inferred. Analysis of literature is a matter of information, structural elements, rhetorical devices, and critical analysis. Students who can do these things need no remediation; they are literate. Students who cannot do these things find themselves in classes devoted to their becoming literate. One wonders if inference is a really a problem. Students in the project clearly infer the difference between their usual schooling and the project.

A seventh-grade tutor writes: "Do you have to go to collage to be a teacher? What kind of education do you have to have? If you do have to go to collage how many years do you have to go? . . . I really would like to know." A participant in the project is asked to describe the difference between a teacher and a cross-age tutor and replies, "I guess a good teacher is a cross-age tutor."

During the summer, a young tutee writes for the project newsletter: "My name is Dennis. I gat your letter. thank you I had a good summer I passed to the Second Grade I will be happy wheen school starts." The editor of the newsletter, a tutor in the science project, prefaced the newsletter by saying, "It is through education that we succeed." Plenty of inference here.

The model of cross-age tutoring is an alternative, a different literacy. It sets a course. What is to become of the course?

The underlying purpose of cross-age tutoring is to change education. In the face of the bureaucratic mess of state mandates, teacher powerlessness, and chronic shortfalls in funding, change may not seem possible. Change may seem slow. Small, poor schools sigh to gain small, inexpensive changes, hoping that large changes will come later. They are paralyzed by test scores.

They are wrong. The forms of education today, particularly the batteries of standardized tests, are very much different from the past forms. The miserable treatment of poor and minority students in the United States is perpetuated; it is not a natural disaster. Arbitrary changes in policy can radically reorganize a school's curriculum, routine, and accountability. In South Carolina, policies change with stunning regularity.

Nothing is shown more clearly by the cross-age tutoring project than the eagerness with which students embrace opportunities to learn. Nothing is clearer than the speed with which the students do it. In an hour's time, two small boys can work together to achieve a literacy that one or two or six years of schooling have not been able to produce. In one semester, six middle-school students can jump two grade levels on reading tests, can test out of remedial English altogether. In a thirty-minute training session, five fragile little children can acquire the ability to tutor five fragile little children and, when a sixth fragile tutor joins the group, to show her how to do the same. In a college chemistry lab, ninth-grade physical science students who have had no hands-on contact in a laboratory setting, who have minimal reading skills, who have no familiarity with complicated terminology, and who have little experience with sophisticated computation can learn to successfully conduct and document college-level chemistry experiments. Change is not only fast but profound.

It is the mechanisms of educational change that are slow and that impede the possibilities of literacy. The cross-age model, as much as anything else, undermines mechanistic behavior. It demonstrates the power of students—even very young students and especially poor and at-risk students—to empower themselves and to change education in the process.

In the 1990s the image of a cadre of dustbin students going up against the system is Dickensian with a twist. The industry of labor is now the service of information. Those of us who have the luxury to pun can afford Dickens; those of us who are the pun cannot. The choices we make in literacy education today determine the lives of students. We have several choices. Cross-age tutoring is merely a suggestion of one choice.[1]

NOTE

[1]The cross-age tutoring project in 1988–90 continued to produce remarkable results. Test scores improved, and more students became adept at electronic mail. Sites continued to multiply across the state. A new twist to the program proved particularly successful: a group of students became both tutors and tutees. The teachers named these students double-hitters because these middle-level students were tutored by high school seniors, and then they themselves tutored first-graders. The school superintendent for one of the smallest and most impoverished districts, an unusual superintendent in his concern and willingness to take risks, worked with the project to write a $300,000 three-year proposal to the state for programs for the at-risk students in his district. The project was not funded.

WORK CITED

Hoffman, Diane M., and Shirley Brice Heath. *Inside Learners: Guidebook on Interactive Reading and Writing in Elementary Classrooms.* Stanford: Stanford UP, 1986.

Enacting Critical Literacy

John Clifford

One difficulty with the traditional training of readers and writers has been the avoidance, perhaps repression, of our explicit social and political purposes. Do we want our students to write correctly formed, grammatical, sophisticated essays that reinscribe what society already believes, or do we want them to create alternative ways of being in the world, however imperfectly transcribed, however tentatively formulated? These are different goals. The first preserves a society's dominant values; the second skeptically interrogates them. Not only the conservative education critic William Bennett but many professors endorse this conserving, wagons-in-a-circle tactic as a bulwark against fragmentation. Most current progressive reformers from Henry Giroux to Gerald Graff, however, acknowledge the multiple and competing stories of what our society is and should be; they want education to alter society, not just pass on one particular version of its values, beliefs, and symbolic truths. Without an inquiry into first principles, the tactics of our instruction in literacy have to be deeply flawed, if not mindless.

I can remember in graduate school being impressed by Louise Rosenblatt's wise reminder when I told her I taught high school English. "Oh," she said, "not high school students?" Her point is relevant to the current controversy over the locus of literacy. Should it be primarily a content-oriented skill, connected to competence in understanding, preserving, and producing particular kinds of texts? Or should it be primarily student-oriented, concerned with an alert and critical quality of mind, in an ability to understand how readers create meaning? I suggest that a critical theory of literacy be tied directly to the consciousness of readers and writers, for only in the hearts and minds of wholly literate people can a different society be envisioned. The spirit of a critical literacy hopes for change, for social justice in a more humane democracy. The pulse at the center of a critical literacy is personal, dynamically inward. It is surely grounded in the contingencies of a sociopolitical context, but flawed institutions change only when the people who inhabit them are transformed, when they can see differently. Through critical literacy students and teachers become agents of change, enactors of attitudes and beliefs rooted in democratic values and a celebration of difference.

The historical narratives of our teaching of reading and writing now being written strongly suggest that this transformative goal of internal growth in perspective and self-consciousness has never been widely accepted. True, it has always been there at the margins in the reform movements of the nineteenth and twentieth centuries, in James Hosiac and John Dewey and later in the work of Louise Rosenblatt and Ann Berthoff. But the plan of the dominant ideology has not been to alter and mend but to seamlessly weave students into the fabric of our society through the efforts of conscientious English teachers understandably more concerned with managing crowded classes than with the apparently remote abstractions of cultural hegemony. This plan has been largely successful; schools have rarely been concerned with a critical literacy beyond advanced decoding and formulaic inscription.

Most practicing and would-be English teachers are encouraged to see their tasks unproblematically, without much sense of dissonance and unaware that they can decide the nature of the reading and writing they profess in classrooms. The commonsensical tradition that English teachers unravel canonical texts for students and then require deductive, literary critiques that are faithful to the intentions of those works seems a given. But this unproblematic given is the antithesis of critical literacy. It reifies tradition, it privileges the past, and it prevents scrutiny of the status quo while creating the illusion that we aren't responsible for continuing a tradition, that affirming a static past over an evolving present is not in itself an ethical and political commitment. I believe the ordinary classroom teacher can, even within the awesome constraints of today's educational environment, pursue critical literacy, allowing an interrogating and empowering spirit to inform, enliven, and sustain all reading and writing activities. Let me explain some ways in which this may happen. But first a necessary digression.

An interesting indication of the hierarchical influence of the literacy training I am opposing is the advanced-placement exam our most prepared students take in high school. It was developed during the heyday of the New Critics and represents the extent to which theoretical formalism trickled down to the schools without much thought about its pedagogical implications. The questions on the exam ask for close textual analysis of the work itself, a method some traditional professional critics still use. And because advanced-placement English is seen as the ultimate literate achievement, attention to form and unity has attained high status, implying that, since this is what our best students can achieve, it is the goal toward which all might strive. Unfortunately, the pedagogy that follows from this theory of reading discourages the active involvement of readers, obviates their experiences, and negates the ethical and social dimensions of their lives.

Questions about the ways that poetic form supports theme and about the ways that tensions are resolved are rigorous and often valuable techniques to combat impressionism, but they ignore the reader's felt experiences, emotions, history, and society. T. S. Eliot's belief that poetry was "an escape from emotion" gave rise to a denigration of the reader's active contribution. The affective fallacy necessitates a pedagogy unconcerned with the experience of novice readers.

Reading is better conceived of as an event in time and place, with specific readers bringing to texts their own personalities, cultures, syntactical and semantic habits, different values, assumptions, and expectations. They live, therefore, through different works. These multiple subjectivities come to the fore if instructors allow them, if they are encouraged and nurtured. Yet research suggests that, in the traditional honors English classroom, lecture, recitation, and silent study dominate the activities; only two percent of the time is given over to group work, and much of this work is attention to textual patterns and devices. In such an environment students may grow as explicators but probably not as self-refective readers knowledgeable about the ideological reasons for diverse interpretations. That, in fact, was the ostensible reason for New Criticism's development in the 1930s—to let the work of art speak for itself unmediated through the confounding subjectivities of readers. It was and still is a strategy to calm the turmoil of our public and private histories. But for the majority of students, especially those with little interest in careers in literature, close reading may seem frustrating, alienating, and disempowering.

Although the authority of formalist readings has been suspect for some twenty years, many critics still think close reading is an uncontested given, instead of just one limited and specialized way to approach texts. Fortunately, for students in high school and college there are more promising and accessible ways to read—promising, however, only if your goal is to allow students to use some of the authority that teachers and critics have hoarded away for generations.

I want the average student to feel a sense of power in dealing with texts. Readers develop a sense of strength when they can bring their own experiences, values, and beliefs to bear on texts, when they are not disoriented by adopting the meanings of their more informed instructors. This unnerving sense of distance was particularly acute for thousands of working-class men and women, blacks, homosexuals, and non-Westerners who for generations were trained to read like specific men, albeit under the guise of objectivity and scholarly detachment. Most students are not able to mount the sustained, insider assault on the hegemony of reading that the feminists did. They simply abandon the effort to relate fully to texts, to treat them as artifacts, inert and unavailable—thus diminishing the possibility of being truly literate, truly empowered. That does not have to happen. I offer the following not as a model but as a representative anecdote, one concrete way to enact a critical pedagogy.

In an Introduction to Literature course I recently taught, I began by handing out William Stafford's poignant poem "Traveling through the dark," a haunting narrative of a driver who comes upon a recently killed pregnant deer on a dark, mountainous road, her fawn still alive, waiting to be born. The driver agonizes beside the still warm body of the doe and, with the car engine purring and the wilderness listening, pushes the doe and the unborn fawn into the river below. I asked the class to respond to two simple questions: Why do you think the narrator decided to abandon the fawn? And what would you have done? After I asked a number of students to summarize their responses orally, we discussed the differences between the driver's decision and theirs. Some agreed with the driver, citing practicality and concern for the fawn's life in captivity; others differed and held out for the value of all life, for compassion, for simple fairness. The focus on the driver's decision is only one of many possible ways into the text, and so far this sequence is fairly typical in a response-oriented pedagogy.

But what students think about the ethics of the driver's decision is only as important as their gradual understanding of the reasons why they think that all life is valuable or that unborn animals don't have rights or that an animal's life among humans is worse than death or, in a wider interpretive context, that ethical decisions are either clear absolutes or murky, unsatisfactory trade-offs made in the dark. And so on the first day of class I began calling into question the assumptions underlying these ethical judgments. Why is human life more valuable than that of an unborn animal? Why are you saying that life is sacred? Under all circumstances? Why do we believe these things? Where do these implicit values come from? How come your reading is different from the person beside you or the same as the person next to you?

Quite naturally these responses are at first vague and tentative: we get them from our parents, from school, from our peers, from television, from movies. Again, some leading questions: Would college students in Kenya respond this way? Would hunters in Canada? What if you were a vegetarian, old, poor, rich, born five hundred years ago, with friends, with your parents? Would a different context in the poem's situation change your response? How? Why? And then the point of all this: What do these responses tell you about the origin of your values and thinking? How have these assumptions influenced what you said about life and practicality, about values being absolute or situational? And what do these responses tell you about reading and writing and how one can understand these "simple" tasks? In discussions, students gradually realize that my intention in the last question is to create a link between their characteristic way of seeing the world and their approach to reading and to disabuse them of the notion that there is an obvious, natural way to read. Feminists in today's English departments confront canonical texts by using their values and experiences, struggling against New Criticism, actively reading against the grain. I like my students to take that critical stance, to reread and rewrite the texts they encounter in relation to their own ideologies.

I like to have the responses to my questions written in a journal modeled on Ann Berthoff's double-entry notebook, a procedure that asks students to write their ideas on one side of the page and later to worry over these entries, making comments about them on the other side. Students are being asked à la Kenneth Burke to interpret their interpretations, to know their knowledge. In this way writing parallels reading: both nonlinear processes encourage a metadiscourse that can raise the student's consciousness about how we come to know, how we understand, and how complexly situated and varied the processes of reading and writing are. When real readers share their responses and interpretations and then self-consciously analyze the reasons for those responses, it is difficult to maintain that there is meaning *in* the text.

After the students read from their journals in small groups, the focus of the ensuing discussion is neither on the reader's ideas nor on the text's message but on the transaction that occurs between the reader and the text, on the coming together of two different ideologies. Students adapt quickly to this new method of reading, finding it neither mysterious nor eccentric. On the contrary, its apparent naturalness both creates and reinforces a democratic climate of informed involvement. I say *apparent* because no method of reading is natural: students are taught to read specific texts in specific ways. We all are. We are taught either to look to authorities for a text's meaning or to look inward; we are taught to be passive or active, involved or detached. Therefore, if responses are encouraged, students begin to realize that their interpretations are, in fact, intimately connected to their own world views, to experiences, to gender and race, to the social contingencies we are all enmeshed in.

This self-consciousness needs to be extended to the theory undergirding critical literacy. Students do not need elaborate theoretical explanations, but, as Gerald Graff says in *Professing Literature*, our reasons for reading and writing in particular ways should be made explicit, both to demystify how the teacher is always able to see more and to provide a vantage point from which students can situate themselves knowingly within the theoretical debates raging in the profession. Students can then understand that they can choose an approach that makes sense to them, that may give them some control over their own literate processes. Without at least a rudimentary sense of why teachers say what they do about texts and why they require such specific critical essays, students can never be truly literate. To imitate academic authority figures out of bewilderment or a false sense of achievement is antithetical to a literate consciousness.

Students begin to see that what they say about a fictional character's values, how a plot unravels, how cultures are depicted, how fictional universes are created also says something about their own values, about their place in our culture, about their tolerance for diversity and conflict. These discussions about their responses to literary texts often involve heated defenses of family and subcultural values and are often lively struggles to assert minority beliefs against the larger culture's domination. These discussions are about the connections between culture and identity, about who is allowed to define words, about who has power and who doesn't—in short, a microcosm of the ongoing social struggle to create a sympathetic reality for oneself. In the uncovering of the layers of beliefs, values, and histories that constitute our identities, students begin to see how meanings are created and defended not from some received literary criteria but through alignments of influence, through the negotiated construction of standards based on personal and social values. Wisdom, truth, and insight do not transcend particular contexts, however much Allan Bloom and his Neoplatonic apologists assert otherwise.

Although the soul of this approach is to foreground the experiences and beliefs that students bring to the classroom, it is not an exercise in values clarification. Initially, students put forth mostly received opinions or, at least, ideas not closely examined. However, the dialectical atmosphere enables them to wonder why they are defending this character's values or that poem's obliqueness. Eventually, if there is goodwill and trust, opinions are altered, positions are modified, the point of view of the other has its effect. Nevertheless, if we value multiplicity and the need for conflict, we must accept an inevitable diversity in the ways that students read texts and in their attitudes toward texts. To work toward a consensus only substitutes mystification for false consciousness. A more intellectually and democratically exciting goal than agreement is for each student to feel strongly about a considered response to a text and then to write—vigorously defending that reading while respecting how others see the world—in other words, to be an informed voice for mutiplicity and against artificial consensus.

The question of authority—of who has the right or the credentials to comment on texts, to resay what is in them—has been a source of intense religious and political debate since at least Plato. Many elites do not want ordinary readers to challenge their norms, their meaning. However, if reading is defined transactionally, with the reader's experiences foregrounded as much as the text's specificity, accepting an expert's reading is tantamount to embracing that person's way of seeing the world. Why would we want students to let others read and think for them? One unpleasant but plausible answer is to control and dominate, to repress the effects of the social contingencies on our lives, to deny the skepticism and the transformative will that can be an antidote to the corrosive docility of our time.

Students come under innumerable influences in their college careers. The influences are, in poststructuralist terms, written by many contradictory discourses. Other classes may reinforce or extend my attempts at empowering students to be confident, literate commentators. But that is not typical. As much as Allan Bloom and others denigrate the quality of the popular culture that our students participate in, we are all deeply influenced by its values and by other diverse, contradictory, and conflictual versions of truth, justice, and the American way. My course and all the students' courses are blended into a complex social and cultural mix. I don't want to imply that, since any given instructor's effect is small, the project of critical literacy is quixotic. In fact, I think just the opposite is true. We are all affected by the ideological assumptions that exist in the many discursive environments that envelop us all. If we could live exclusively within just one environment, somehow eliminating the noise from all others, we would probably never change. We would never sense the dissonance, contradiction, or oppositional impulse that goads us to interrogate and problemize the givens of traditional reading and writing instruction. But exposure to a univocal discourse is practically impossible. Except for some hermetic religious communities, we are all subjected to conflictual and antagonistic discourses that leave their traces in us, even if we ultimately reject them.

The possibility of altering one's perspective lies in having to inhabit and deal with the contradictions that inhere in different subject positions. Being challenged in a response-oriented classroom to unravel the ideology of one's reading and then to confront other authentically held positions is to move from being a passive consumer of reading to being a participant, a maker of meaning who understands explicitly the social significance of a critical literacy. That is a subject position I want my students to assume, however transitory and tentative it may be. In a universe of discourse replete with repressive and hegemonic intentions, any potentially liberating discourse must be heard, must struggle for legitimation. The enactment of a critical literacy is, finally, not a question of sanguinity but, in the hope of more democratic vistas, an ethical necessity, a professional imperative.

WORKS CITED

Berthoff, Ann. *Forming-Thinking-Writing: The Composing Imagination.* Portsmouth: Boynton, 1982.

Bloom, Allan. *The Closing of the American Mind.* New York: Simon, 1987.

Graff, Gerald. *Professing Literature: An Institutional History.* Chicago: U of Chicago P, 1987.

Stafford, William. "Traveling through the Dark." *Stories That Could Be True: New and Collected Poems.* New York: Harper, 1960.

Adolescent Vernacular Writing: Literacy Reconsidered

Miriam P. Camitta

Vernacular writing is traditional behavior that proliferates throughout culture, is integral to cultural process, and is organized by conventions and aesthetic judgments that derive from cultural experience and social life. The forms, styles, and uses of vernacular writing are expressions of literacy, although they do not enjoy the same standing as standard or official literacy.

Vernacular writing is most often associated with domestic, community, and local contexts. For this reason it is noncanonical, a category into which Barbara Herrnstein-Smith places "modern texts, especially highly innovative ones, and such culturally exotic works as oral or tribal literature, popular literature, and 'ethnic' literature" (18–9). Vernacular writing may be considered noncanonical because it shares features of modern, oral or tribal, popular, and ethnic literature. The personal, recreational, and creative texts of vernacular writing are innovative—deriving and departing from those sanctioned by canon—as are modern texts. Like traditional oral literature, vernacular writing is both for-mulaic and schematic. Its form and its content are influenced by popular lit-erature and culture. And it draws on traditional themes and community-based, localized forms of expressions, as does ethnic literature.

For Ivan Illich, vernacular culture is nonhierarchical and nonhegemonic and is more closely associated with the local, familiar, and everyday, rather than with the elite or institutional. It is a wholesome counterpoint to the culture of bureaucracy and to the shadow economy that supports it.

However, other commonly held definitions of the vernacular that are powerful in our popular understanding of literacy are interlarded with words that are loaded with negative connotations. Vernacular languages and dialects, which are the languages of family and of community life, are not the languages of power. Rather, vernacular languages are associated with both political and social subordination, an association that may threaten the serious study of vernacular literature. The vernacular is recognized as the source of multiple, plural literacies (Szwed), but its relation to the standard remains far from mutual.

In literacy scholarship, in spite of the work of Ron Scollon and Suzanne B. K. Scollon and of Sylvia Scribner and Michael Cole, which demonstrates that literacy exists in vernacular languages and dialects, vernacular literacies are known, at best, as cultural alternatives to official literacy; at worst, they are believed to be partial, incomplete forms that are subordinate to the real thing, by which is meant essayist prose (Cook-Gumperz and Gumperz; Scollon and Scollon; Scribner and Cole, "Unpacking Literacy").

This conflation of essayist prose with literacy leads to a "serious underestimation of the cognitive skills involved in non-school, non-essay writing, and, reciprocally, to an overestimation of the intellectual skills that the essayist text 'necessarily entails' " (Scribner and Cole, "Unpacking Literacy" 76).

A thoughtful consideration of everyday writing practices and a close reading of vernacular texts reveal that canonical tradition cannot account for literature outside its borders. In anthropological approaches to the study of literacy, ethnographies of literacies provide descriptions of reading and writing in vernacular languages and dialects (Heath; Scribner and Cole, *Psychology of Literacy*). These studies are helpful in that they interrogate a premise that is implicit in much of the literature: that *standard* and *literacy* are the same and, by extension, that literacy is an either-or proposition (see Szwed; Street). In addition, the studies' findings point to the inadequacy of hierarchical and dichotomous constructions of language—folk and formal, oral and literate, unofficial and official—by delineating forms and processes of writing in everyday situations that depart from the conventions of essayist prose and the genres sanctioned by canon.

For example, an ethnographic study of the vernacular writing of adolescents reveals that they often ignore the boundaries and distinctions that have traditionally served to separate literature from other kinds of writing by drawing on a variety of sources, styles, and genres in the construction of vernacular written texts (Camitta). The study further shows adolescents mixing genres and styles to create new genres through a process resembling creolization, experimenting with formats, and drawing freely on literary, popular, and folk conventions and aesthetics. As a result, adolescent writers create texts that are not simply composites of several genres; nor are they bungled versions of a single genre; rather, the texts are innovations, what have been called the subtexts of canon (Michie).

The nonsectarian approach to the writing and literature of adolescents represented in the study can be seen in their practice of creating writing collections and informal anthologies. The collections include poetry (a traditional literary genre), autograph book verse (a traditional folklore genre), letters to friends, original verse, song lyrics, and slogans. The collections of memorabilia hold verses and prayers clipped from newspapers or copied from published anthologies; letters and greeting cards; the verse and song lyrics of friends and acquaintances; programs from funerals, graduations, and proms, often with original verse and prayers; obscene parodies of popular and traditional texts; and self-edited books of verse, letters, and personal thoughts.

Classicism and innovation, creativity and convention, typify the writing practices of adolescents, as a look at their composing techniques and processes shows.

Patchwork and mosaic are two composing techniques that adolescent writers use to create texts that are not represented in the literary canon. Historically, patchwork and mosaic are conventions of a vernacular writing tradition that dates to the Middle Ages, when it may have functioned as a populist reaction against the texts of classical, canonized genres (Bakhtin). In both patchwork and mosaic, the texts are composed by appropriating words and phrases from oral tradition, popular culture, or literary texts. Texts that use the mosaic technique are constructed wholly with materials appropriated from various cultural sources. Texts that use the patchwork technique insert the appropriated materials into the writer's original text.

Mosaic:

Help! I need somebody! Help! Not just anybody! Help! I need somebody now. Lady love never smiles so lend your love to me a while, do with me what you will, break the spell and take your fill. On and on we rode the storm the flame's back and the fire's gone, on this empty bed is a night alone, I realized that long ago. Is anybody out there? Is anybody there? does anybody wonder? Does anybody care?

Patchwork:

Dad's Obstacle Course

Why do you confuse me so?
So many questions unanswered, untold
Should I stay or should I go?
Which way is up?
(I think you went down.)
Where's the door 'gotta get out of here.

In these examples from students' writing collections in 1982, the mosaic technique pieces together borrowed lyrics and phrases. None are original to the writer; yet the finished piece is a creation that can be associated with the writer. The patchwork technique inserts borrowed song lyrics into an original poem. The references to the sources of the borrowed song lyrics in both techniques are implicit, relying on the readers' knowledge of popular musical culture, an example of intertextuality.

Another way of looking at the cultural borrowing that adolescent writers use when they create either patchwork or mosaic texts is to compare both practices with the modern and postmodern practices of assemblage and montage. In the writings of cultural theorists like Jacques Derrida, assemblage and montage are vehicles by which traditional constructions of *author* are dismantled. (For discussions about the disappearance or the death of the author, see Foucault; Barthes.) The ideas of originality and of the author as owner of the text are deconstructed by assemblage and montage as images and texts are recreated, juxtaposed, and recontextualized in the new piece. Patchwork and mosaic as acts of authorship in the vernacular tradition are expressions of cultural process, by which culture is made and remade through the appropriation and reorganization of its materials. In this process the notion of original author is subordinated to the text, which is disseminated over time through multiple authors, in whose hands the texts are embellished, elaborated, and recreated in new contexts.

Another composing technique used by adolescents involves play with traditional generic boundaries by merging two or more genres or by embedding one genre into another. In the first technique a poem is merged with a letter by a process that selects aspects of each and then merges them to create a new form. In the new poem-letter text the adolescent uses poetic diction, rhyme, and meter narratively within the larger format of the letter, adding metaphor and imagery, instead of the reporting mode typically associated with an epistolary form. This composing strategy accomplishes several rhetorical functions: it allows the writer to express feelings and ideas through poetic tropes that are narratively linked, mixing the mimetic and diagenetic functions of language. In the second technique one genre is embedded in another. Poems, raps, and excerpts from popular songs are embedded in letters, in which case the diagenetic and mimetic functions remain separate but are used to complement and amplify each other. Shakespeare uses this technique extensively in his plays, embedding songs, sonnets, monologues, and plays of different categories within the larger format of the play.

In the following poem-letter the writer has merged the letter frame with the diction of poetry.

> Let's go back in time,
> Let's do it all again.
> Give life a second chance because
> everyone needs a break.
> Last year we were young,
> we laughed at love and lovers.
> They were so blind. But we
> Soon began to walk hand
> in hand and we slowly began
> to feel what they felt. Our hearts
> grew, for no reason, we would
> cry. For no reason we felt the feelings
> that for so long we only
> laughed about. Now our hearts
> are broken and a part of
> us has died. We are still young
> but no longer children. Now
> We are the ones being laughed
> at. But we know what they
> don't know. Let's go back and
> start again. Love will fool us
> again.   (Student's notebook, 1984)

Composing or writing has been discussed here as a variety of activities that accomplish cultural process by appropriating cultural materials and by manipulating expressive conventions. In addition, the study sheds light on the processes of vernacular writing, in which performance and a related phenomenon, collaboration, are central to the composing process. Both performance and collaboration occur at several points in a text's career and represent a context and a process for a recursive and open-ended revision. Performance may occur during drafting, as it does in the construction of personal letters. Partially or wholly composed letters are frequently read aloud to an audience with at least one sympathetic listener or are given to a reader, who offers advice about rhetorical strategies often considered crucial to the effect of the letter on its intended receiver. Or performance may occur after drafting, as it often does in rap composition, when written rap texts are performed in a rehearsal setting. The audience often acts as a consultant, offering advice about rhyme, diction, and meter that is later incorporated into the next draft of the rap text. Participants in rap composition recognize that their product will be refined, polished, and professionalized through this kind of collaboration.

The performance of a rap or of a letter is a collaborative venture, engaging audience and author in a critical dialogue. The experience of the individual is brought into focus with that of the group through the interplay between author and audience that reshapes experience for each by means of the text. Thus, a text not only is subject to the conventional rhetorical strategies that reflect the collectivity of cultural expression but is often collectively shaped during its composition.

In this way, aspects of cultural process attributed to folk or vernacular culture—such as performance, appropriation, and collaboration—are enacted in the processes of vernacular writing, in which the text is the vehicle for accomplishing culture. Dialogic performance, appropriation and collaboration, especially through the techniques of assemblage and montage, are central concerns of deconstruction and postmodern theories of culture (see Ulmer). The vernacular text, like the postmodern text, is open and indeterminate, subject to endless change and interpretation precisely because of its position to its author and its audience. The ethnographic study of writing elucidates that position, making explicit the dynamics of the dialogue between individual and collective experiences suggested by critical theory, in which texts are continually open to revision through a drafting process that refines the relation of the text to the individual and to the group.

The study of vernacular writing has implications not only for the study of literacy but also for theories of language and culture and for educational practice. Hierarchical and dichotomous models of language that maintain the exclusivity of the categories of vernacular and official accommodate plural literacies by making their use nonmutual. However, if language is viewed as the individual and collective enterprise of culture, as a dialogic process, communication crosses boundaries, instead of creating them.

This brief examination of adolescent writing practices is offered as another possibility for the study of literacy. It is not enough to assert democratically that vernacular or popular literacies must be validated and respected by academics. Rather, literacy scholarship must be informed by a theory that both accounts for and explains the various uses of language—standard and nonstandard, official and vernacular—a theory that begins with culture as the basis for language use and proceeds with full descriptions and critical analyses of the many texts and practices of literacy. Such an approach subjects the texts of vernacular writing to the same close scrutiny applied to the texts of canon and will result in the same appreciation of their artful and thoughtful construction and use. This approach suggests the logic for looking at vernacular writing as a range of significant and meaningful literate skills and resources that are mistakenly disconnected from the process of literacy education as it is officially conducted. Ultimately, the study findings may reveal some phenomena about writing that are now unrecognized because they are not canonical. These phenomena are related necessarily to culture, and their description may contribute to the emergent refiguration of culture that is the postmodern project.

WORKS CITED

Bakhtin, Mikhail M. *The Dialogic Imagination: Four Essays*. Trans. Caryl Emerson and Michael Holquist. Ed. Michael Holquist. Austin: U of Texas P, 1981.

Barthes, Roland. "The Death of the Author." *Image, Music, Text*. Trans. Stephen Heath. New York: Hill, 1977. 142–47.

Camitta, Miriam P. *Invented Lives: Adolescent Vernacular Writing and the Construction of Experience*. Diss. U of Pennsylvania, 1987.

Cook-Gumperz, Jenny, and John J. Gumperz. "From Oral to Written Culture: The Transition of Literacy." *Writing: The Nature, Development and Teaching of Written Communication*. Vol. 3 of *Variation in Writing: Functional and Linguistic Cultural Differences*. Ed. Marcia F. Whiteman. Baltimore: Erlbaum, 1981. 80–109.

Foucault, Michel. "What Is an Author." *Language, Counter-Memory and Practice: Selected Essays and Interviews*. By Foucault. Trans. D. F. Bouchard. New York: Cornell UP, 1980. 113–38.

Heath, Shirley Brice. *Outline Guide for the Ethnographic Study of Literacy and Oral Language from Schools to Communities*. Working Papers in Language and Education 2. Philadelphia: Graduate School of Education, U of Pennsylvania P, 1978.

Herrnstein-Smith, Barbara. "Contingencies of Values." *Critical Inquiry* 10 (1983): 1–35.

Illich, Ivan. *Shadow Work*. Boston: Boyars, 1981.

Michie, Helena. *The Flesh Made Word: Female Figures and Women's Bodies*. New York: Oxford UP, 1987.

Scollon, Ron, and Suzanne B. K. Scollon. "The Modern Consciousness and Literacy." *Narrative, Literacy and Face in Interethnic Communication*. Norwood: Ablex, 1981. 45–56.

Scribner, Sylvia, and Michael Cole. *The Psychology of Literacy*. Cambridge: Harvard UP, 1981.

————. "Unpacking Literacy." *Writing: Functional and Linguistic Cultural Differences.* Ed. Marcia Farr Whiteman. Hillsdale: Erlbaum, 1981. 19–40.

Street, Brian V. *Literacy in Theory and Practice.* Cambridge: Cambridge UP, 1984.

Szwed, John F. "The Ethnography of Literacy." *Writing: [The Nature and Development] of Written Communication.* Vol. 1 of *Variation in Writing: Functional and Linguistic Cultural Differences.* Ed. Marcia F. Whiteman. Baltimore: Erlbaum, 1981. 13–23.

Ulmer, Gregory L. "The Object of Post-Criticism." *The Anti-Aesthetic: Essays on Postmodern Culture.* Ed. Hal Foster. Port Townsend: Bay, 1983. 83–110.

The World, the Text, and the Reader

Paula M. Salvio

Literacy is often defined in the narrowest terms, emphasizing the decoding of lexicons. Many elementary school students, in an effort to establish prepared-ness, are required to identify sight words and punctuation marks and to recite vowel and consonant sounds according to the rules of phonics. Despite symbols designating the life of the child—brightly colored story rugs; the gentle, constant hum of fish tanks; and the arrangement of family silhouettes above each child's seat—the process of learning to read in the classroom creates a distance between the familiar world of home and the public world of school.

Western literature abounds with myths of the great hero who leaves home to conquer mysterious, foreign lands. Like our own children, these heros are taught to repudiate knowledge of the domestic, the familiar. At an increasingly early age, children are brought to the world of the classroom and taught to honor abstract, rational forms of thought. If we are to explore the context in which children learn to read and write, we must reinterpret the meaning of literacy, seeing it as a process that continually unfolds not in isolation from but in relation to the fluid, lived-in spaces of our lives. To be literate is to be intimate; it is to be familiar not simply with the lexicons of language and literature but also with the meanings embodied in the sounds and the textures that shape the context of the reader's life. These meanings are embodied in the animated movements and gestures that characterize the way the reader walks out the screen door and down the path to the classroom space, where experience and text, the word and the deed, are mediated by the knowledge of the reader's body.

In her book *Bitter Milk* Madeleine R. Grumet writes of the body's exile from the curriculum we create to teach our children to read. "To bring what we know to where we live," writes Grumet, "has not always been the project of curriculum, for schooling, as we have seen, has functioned to repudiate the body, the place where it lives, and the people who care for it" (129). Drawing on Maurice Merleau-Ponty's concept of the body-subject, Grumet develops the term *body-reading*. To be a bodyreader is to place the project of reading into the hands, feet, and belly of the reader. Our bodies possess profound knowledge about the relations in which we engage, the rules governing our behavior in public and private spaces, the texture of October leaves, the din of city nights, the early-morning smell of toast and tea. Bodyreaders bring this knowledge to the reading of texts (Grumet 130). Where do bodyreaders reside? They sing the knowledge embodied in the pulse and the rhythms of our movements. Through their gestures and movements they make physical what is often unexpressed, lodged deep in our bellies. The knowledge of bodyreaders is not always vocal, but it is always gestural.

In this paper I introduce the knowledge embodied by bodyreaders. Although the reading and writing curricula in our schools do not intentionally invite bodyreaders into the classroom space, they often slip in uninvited. By exploring three curriculum forms used to teach reading and writing in the classroom, I locate the moments where bodyreaders intervene to mediate the relations between action and language, world and text. I begin by exploring three curriculum forms most often used to teach children to read: underwriting, the language-experience story, and the memorization of sight words. These forms characterize the formal activities we engage in most often as we teach reading and writing. What do these forms offer us? How do they mediate between the familiar world of the student and the strange world of the text?

In one typical school I visited, the kindergarten students were asked to form circles on their story rugs so that they could begin a work sheet lesson. Elliot's animated monologue about his uncle's new dog was deemed inappropriate by the teacher as she instructed her students to "pay attention" to the directions she was giving on how to underwrite their names, an exercise that consists of students' imitating the spelling of their names underneath what the teacher had written. In a first-grade classroom down the hall, the students opened their reading workbooks to pages of sight words. The sight words were arranged in rows across the page in different colors. Under each sight word was a dotted line. The students were asked to underwrite each sight word, using a different color pencil for each word. In another first-grade classroom the students wrote a language-experience story. Each class member contributed a detail about their school; the rule was that they had to use a sight word. The teacher copied what the students said on the board. After having copied this story from the board, the students were instructed to circle all the sight words they could find.

Where are the bodies in this curriculum? What are they doing? What do they reveal? Let us look for a moment at the act of underwriting or overwriting a phrase or word. What moves is the hand and the eye. When children underwrite, they copy a word or a phrase underneath the teacher's handwriting. While the initial phrase or word may be suggested by the children, the inscription of the message is encoded by the teacher; it is the teacher's handwriting the children must mime if they are to learn to read and write. The assumption is that children have had no experiences with print before entering the world of formal instruction; consequently, knowledge about how to form letters and orient messages, from left to right, must be taught.[1] Take my hand, and I will lead you. The question is, where are we going, to your place or mine? This curriculum takes the child's experiences, intentions, movements, and desires to an empty space, one devoid of situation. This act of mimesis is only one moment on the educative journey. Underwriting and overwriting, language-experience stories, sight words —all give our children words. What they do not give them is language. Language is nurtured by situation, desire, and action. John Dewey maintains that language unfolds in a context; it is a social thing, fused by human interest:

> [I]t hardly needs to be said that language is primarily a social thing, a means by which we give our experiences to others and get theirs again in return. When it is taken away from its natural purpose, it is no wonder that it becomes a complex and difficult problem to teach language. Think of the absurdity of having to teach language as a thing by itself. If there is anything the child will do before he goes to school, it is to talk of the things that interest him. But when there are no vital interests appealed to in the school, when language is used simply for the repetition of lessons, it is not surprising that one of the chief difficulties of school work has come to be instruction in the mother-tongue. Since the language taught is un-natural, not growing out of the real desire to communicate vital impressions and convictions, the freedom of children in its use gradually disappears. . . . *When the language instinct is appealed to in a social way, there is a continual contact with reality. The result is that the child always has something in his mind to talk about, he has something to say, he has a thought to express, and a thought is not a thought unless it is one's own.* (34–35; emphasis added)

Where, in the curricular forms I describe, is language used in a social way? Are there moments when the student is a bodyreader? Elliot literally sings a song about his uncle's new dog; his voice is lyrical, enthusiastic; he addresses his whole class when he says, "His dog thinks I am terrific!" The eyes and the hands of the students do not mime the handwriting of the teacher without interruption; their desire to plan recess kickball teams and to discreetly exchange stickers interrupts the flow of this activity. Their faces nearly touch; they whisper; they gesture, miming, "I'll trade you this one," rather than the inscription of their names. Present in each curriculum are social situations, created by the students, that provoke them to generate language.

Social situations are contexts. The word *context* is associated with the Latin word *contexere*, meaning "to join together, to weave." Contexts and situations are joined together, made coherent by characteristic objects, feelings, beliefs, desires. In *Philosophy in a New Key* Susanne K. Langer makes use of Carl Buhler's description of context. She writes:

> The context is the situation of the speaker in a setting visible to the hearer; at the point where their thinking is to converge, a word is used, to fix the crucial concept. The word is *built* into the speaker's action or situation, in a diacritical capacity, settling a doubt, deciding a response. (121)

Context is lacking in the workbook exercises, yet the workbook exercises unfold in the context of the classroom. Elliot transforms this curriculum, if only for a moment, by supplying it with context; language, his dog, his uncle, his body—all gather onto his story rug so he can bring them to story form in the oral tradition. The theater work I do with elementary and high school students creates shared, immediate experiences that the students can draw on to generate language about their participation in the world as readers and writers. Like Elliot, we all have stories to tell, experiences to share. Allow me to usher you into the world of the classroom where we do our theater work.[2]

The students with whom I worked in an E.S.O.L. (English speakers of other languages) classroom in Rochester, New York, were seriously involved in writing creative stories. Many of the ideas for their stories came from the readings they shared in class, from their everyday experiences at home and at school, and from their childhoods. The writing project did not unfold in isolation from the reading project; rather, the two projects were interrelated. We often began our theater work by sitting around one of the tables and asking someone to discuss a problem that person had been having with a story. After a student read the story aloud, we began discussing the parts of the story that the students enjoyed and the parts that they felt needed more work. This phase of our work is similiar to the editing and revision process developed in the research of Donald Graves: students develop a repertoire of standards for reading one another's work and help one another communicate their ideas to the classroom community. Our work departs from Graves's work at the point of revision. Rather than relying solely on discursive codes and grammatical schemas for our revising and editing, we look to the rehearsal methods of the modern stage. By creating an improvisational exercise that focuses on the problems a student is having with a story, we create a community of speakers and performers who communicate specific concerns and motives through a virtual alphabet of movement—gestures, mime, tableaux, facial expressions, sounds, and intonations. This movement transcends the customary limits of discursive language, making coherent the knowledge and the understanding that students may not be able, at first, to express in spoken language but that, once embodied in movement, can be translated into spoken and written language.

One day, Juan, a sixth-grader, read a story he had been working on about his trip to the zoo. He told us that he was having trouble deciding how to proceed. In the beginning of Juan's story, he was fully engaged with the sights and sounds of the zoo: "One sunny afternoon I was going to the zoo. When I got there it was like a jungle. There were lots of strange sounds and horrible smells. It smell like an outdoor toilet." Juan then proceeded to describe the movement of a snake. He wrote, "The boa constrictor slithered along the log like a slow train." Juan told us that he did not know what else to write; he was stuck. Our project was to provide Juan with an improvisational situation that captured the world of the zoo and gave him the language he needed to continue writing his story.

What is most interesting about the moment when Juan feels that he can no longer find language to write his story is that the simile he ended with, "The boa constrictor slithered along the log like a slow train," was mimed from a storyteller who visited the class a few days earlier. If Juan can appropriate the language of the storyteller to his story so that it fits the world of the zoo that he has experienced and now writes about, he can assume ownership of this simile. This process of appropriation involves both mimesis and transformation. The storyteller—like the teacher, the mother, and the text—gives Juan language that he comes to realize is not his own. To represent his world, he must adapt this language to his own image. Grumet writes that, "for all of us, the process of development has required this mimetic tracing of the other's relation to the world, and then the negotiation, once we have arrived, of a new itinerary that will bring us back to ourselves" ("On Daffodils"). Juan maps out this itinerary by locating the words given to him by another as his point of departure to assume ownership of his story.

We asked Juan to take us back to the beginning of the story and to continue reading until he came to his description of the boa constructor. We wanted to create an experience of watching the boa, to carve a distance between the phrase that Juan mimed and what he experienced at the zoo. We closed our eyes and listened for the sounds this image created. The children answered: "The sound of a train," "The sound of a train on a log," "A shhhhing sound." Some of the children began to move like snakes, curving their bodies and moving from side to side. They began to bring sight and rhythm together. Grumet, who was invited to this classroom to create a theater lab, asked the students if they could see and hear the movements of the snake from afar. They replied that they could not, that they needed to move closer. Through these simple exercises the world of the zoo became one that Juan could move in; the children lived out, with their bodies, the life they wanted to get into their stories. Once the problem had been identified and discussed, we began to score an improvisation.

The action, we imagined, took place at the zoo. Grumet asked each child to be a different animal; we had boas, polar bears bathing with their cubs, an elephant teasing the audience, and lions napping by the pool. To score the polar bears bathing together, we asked two of the children to be a mother bear and her cub. The other children acted as the audience, looking at the polar bears the way we all do at the zoo, crowded at the fence, waiting, watching.

Because the two children who played the polar bear and her cub were a bit shy, not sure about how to act like polar bears, Grumet talked them through the movements, getting down on the floor with them, beginning from a resting position, then moving them onto their big paws, stretching our their limbs, and playfully shaking the water from their heavy coats. The other students imitated the gestures and the sounds of an audience at the zoo—laughing, calling out to their babies not to get too close to the bears, and feeding the bears in spite of the signs not to feed the animals.

The children attended to the dramatic score with two intentions: to carry out their assigned roles and to generate language for Juan's story. Throughout this improvisation, bodyreading is used. The children look beneath the masks we wear to the zoo and play with being the other. This act creates possibilities for a multiperspectival consciousness; students imagined not only what actually happens at the zoo but what is possible at the zoo. As the bears became more comfortable and began to tease the audience, the actors moved as if they were at the zoo (see Stanislavsky 51–67). During the enactment of this improvisational exercise, the possibilities for Juan's written text blur with the possibilities of the improvisation. Through the interplay of knowing and not knowing, the students probed at different angles of the zoo experience—that of the polar bears, that of the audience, that of the snakes. Within this probing lies the willingness to risk all preconceived assumptions about the course that Juan's story could take.

Once the improvisation was complete, the students immediately moved to their tables and wrote a few sentences about what happened to them. Luisa wrote, "I got splashed by the polar bear"; Kaila wrote, "The polar bear made me laugh because he was so clumsy." As the students began to read the sentences they had written, Juan received more and more language to continue his story. Later, Juan returned to his story and incorporated some of the language he and the ensemble had generated into his revised work.

This improvisational exercise creates an immediate, common experience on which participants draw to perform and to discuss their understanding of a specific problem they encountered while writing a creative story. A bodyreader's movements provide concrete imagery that can be translated into both spoken and written language. Dewey observes that the ability to read, to write, and to speak can develop only among those who have a desire to express vital impressions and convictions; it is the experiential, concrete, communal qualities of the theatrical experience that engenders this desire. The theories and the methods of the modern stage offer myriad possibilities for creating curriculum forms that summon the bodyreader to mediate the distance between public knowledge and private knowledge, the familiar world and strange worlds. Literacy is this act of mediation.

NOTES

[1]For a detailed account of the epistemological and pedagogical implications of underwriting, overwriting, and the language-experience story, see Harste et al.

[2]This work took place in Choji Schroeder's E.S.O.L. classroom in Rochester, New York. I thank Ms. Schroeder and her students for the insight they gave me into this work.

WORKS CITED

Dewey, John. *The School and Society.* Carbondale: Southern Illinois UP, 1976.

Grumet, Madeleine R. *Bitter Milk: Women and Teaching.* Amherst: U of Massachusetts P, 1988.

————. "On Daffodils That Come before the Swallow Dares." *Qualities of Inquiry*. Ed. Elliot Eisner and Allen Peshkin. New York: Teachers College, forthcoming.

Harste, Jerome, et al. *Language Stories and Literacy Lessons*. Portsmouth: Heinemann, 1984.

Langer, Susanne K. *Philosophy in a New Key*. New York: Scribner's, 1942.

Stanislavski, Constantin. *An Actor Prepares*. New York: Theatre Arts, 1936.

Collaboration, Resistance, and the Teaching of Writing

Suzanne Clark and Lisa Ede

What model of literacy is implied by current theories of collaborative learning in composition studies? Until recently, it would have been difficult to answer this question. For, as John Trimbur notes in "Collaborative Learning and Teaching Writing," in the 1970s and early 1980s collaborative learning in composition was not "a theoretically unified position but a set of pedagogical principles and practices worked out experimentally" (91). Thom Hawkins and Kenneth Bruffee, early advocates for collaborative learning in writing classes, experienced collaborative learning in the peer-tutoring programs with which they were involved (at Berkeley and Brooklyn College) before they developed theoretical constructs to explain and support these practices. Like many literacy workers, they moved from an awareness that collaborative learning could help them resolve a specific problem—in their case "the arrival of nontraditional students [to universities] through the open-admissions programs of the early seventies" (Trimbur 90)—to the recognition that, in Bruffee's words, "a new conception of the nature of knowledge [as a social construction] provides direction that we lacked earlier as we muddled through, trying to solve practical problems in practical ways" ("Collaborative Learning" 638).

Between 1984 and the present, however, major theoretical formulations and assessments—including Bruffee's two *College English* essays ("Collaborative Learning and the 'Conversation of Mankind' " and "Social Construction, Language, and the Authority of Knowledge"), Karen Burke LeFevre's *Invention as a Social Act*, and Anne Ruggles Gere's *Writing Groups: History, Theory, and Implications*—have appeared. Although Bruffee's, Gere's, and LeFevre's discussions differ in important respects, all broadly support what can be called a social constructionist epistemology. This epistemological position assumes, as Bruffee writes, that

> entities we normally call reality, knowledge, thought, facts, selves, and so on . . .
> [are] community-generated and community-maintained linguistic entities—or, more
> broadly speaking, symbolic entities—that define or "constitute" the communities
> that generate them.   ("Social Construction" 774)

Bruffee's emphasis on communities in the above definition is not accidental. Theorists of collaborative learning, such as Bruffee, as Anne Gere notes, have tended to "emphasize the communal aspects of intellectual life" (75). Terms like *conversation*, *collaboration*, and *community* are hardly value-free, however. In *Keywords*, for example, Raymond Williams observes:

> Community can be the warmly persuasive word to describe an existing set of relationships, or the warmly persuasive word to describe an alternative set of relationships. What is most important, perhaps, is that unlike other terms of social organization (*state, nation, society*, etc.) it seems never to be used unfavorably and never to be given any positive opposing or distinguishing term.   (66)

Similarly, in *The Political Responsibility of the Critic*, Jim Merod comments on the closely related phrase *interpretive community*:

> No term in critical practice is more beguiling than *interpretive community*. The phrase proposes a body of closely affiliated writers joined to maintain group identity and mutual interests, people on the same side of reality who, even in disagreement, face common tasks and privileges.   (107)

Collaborative learning theorists' emphasis on community results, a number of critics believe, is an oversimplified, naive representation of discourse and intertextuality, one that ignores powerful cultural, political, and ideological realities. In "The Idea of Community in the Study of Writing," Joseph Harris argues that theorists have erred in treating community as a monolithic construct, forgetting that "one is always *simultaneously* a part of several discourses, of several communities, is always already committed to a number of conflicting beliefs and practices" (19). Rather than granting an "organic unity to the idea of community" (20), those in composition studies might best, Harris suggests, view community metaphorically as a city, one where not only consensus but conflict is commonplace, where residents recognize the inevitability of "difference, of overlap, of tense plurality, of being at once part of several communities and yet never wholly a member of one" (11).

In "Reality, Consensus, and Reform in the Rhetoric of Composition Teaching," Greg Myers also questions what he sees as the tendency of advocates of collaborative learning to appeal to consensus and to devalue or ignore entirely the reality of conflict. "Bruffee shows that reality can be seen as a social construct," Myers notes, "[but] he does not give us any way to criticize this construct." Such a stance has potentially significant pedagogical consequences. Despite teachers' intentions, collaborative learning practices can enable teachers merely to embody their authority "in the more effective guise of class consensus," which, according to Myers, can have "a power over individual students that a teacher cannot have" (159).

Ironically—to return to the question with which we began this essay—despite collaborative learning advocates' commitment to democratic and liberatory literacy education, theories supporting collaborative learning in composition stud-

ies imply a restricted view of literacy, one that inherently denies the importance
of culture, ideology, and politics in daily life. Collaborative learning theories
implicitly if reluctantly contribute to an autonomous model of literacy, one that
assumes that the classroom can function as a neutral site of learning, a magic
epistemological circle of chalk dust separating students and teachers from the
world at large.

In *Literacy in Theory and Practice* Brian V. Street discusses the limitations of
the autonomous model of literacy as articulated by David R. Olson and others.
This model, Street argues,

> assumes a single direction in which literacy development can be traced, and
> associates it with "progress," "civilization," individual liberty and social mobility.
> It attempts to distinguish literacy from schooling. It isolates literacy as an inde-
> pendent variable and then claims to be able to study its consequences. These
> consequences are classically represented in terms of economic "take off" or in
> terms of cognitive skills.   (2)

In his work Street discusses research in a number of disciplines—including
anthropology, linguistics, and history—that contradicts the major assumptions
of the autonomous model. One of the most pernicious effects of this model of
literacy, according to Street, is its tendency to encourage researchers and teachers "to judge any particular literacy as either 'restricted' or as having the full,
rational qualities of the essay text ideal" (130). The autonomous model also
obscures the ways in which traditional literacy education, as a "form of political
and ideological practice" (110), has provided one of a dominant culture's most
powerful and effective means of insuring hegemonic control.

In view of the limitations of the autonomous model of literacy, it is essential
that advocates of collaborative learning in composition studies reconsider recent
theoretical arguments supporting collaborative-learning practices and develop a
theoretical construct that explicitly recognizes and fully explores the roles of
culture, politics, and ideology in literacy education. It is not enough, in other
words, that collaborative learning developed in response to the cultural, political, and ideological needs of real students and teachers in real colleges and
universities. Theorists who have thus far emphasized epistemological issues must
now explore culture, politics, and ideology in equally critical ways. We would
like to contribute to this process of theoretical grounding and enrichment by
exploring a concept that connects epistemology and progressive education, the
concept of resistance. This concept enters into our discussion of collaborative
learning in two ways: as a mode of opposition to ideology and as a mode of
learning.

All teachers are in a sense familiar with resistance: we have all seen students
who do not just fail to learn but actively resist our efforts to help them collaborate
effectively or develop habits of critical thinking. Why does this happen? Is this
refusal a mark of our complicity with oppressive ideology? A mark of educational

failure? Perhaps the bleakest view of resistance is represented by Louis Althusser, who believes that the dominant state ideology uses schools (ideological state apparatuses) not only to reproduce social conditions but also to construct students as subjects of ideology. Students can oppose this process, but their resistance is futile; resistance itself is complicit in reproducing inequality. Support for this bleak view comes from studies like that of Paul Willis, whose working-class lads, for example, seemed unerringly to opt out of any possible change in status by their opposition to school systems. Under such a model, collaborative learning can only represent, as Myers charges, a means of enabling the teacher to embody "his or her authority in the more effective guise of class consensus" (159). Collaborative learning, thus, is inevitably a poor trick played on students by well-meaning teachers.

A number of radical theorists in education, ethnographers, and scholars in cultural studies have argued that, since literacy is in culture—and thus not homogeneous but multiple, heterogeneous, and contested—the reproduction of ideology through schooling cannot be as seamless as those who cite Althusser imply. The notion of resistance developed by Stanley Aronowitz and Henry A. Giroux helpfully complicates the way we may think about conflict in education. They argue that "the mechanisms of social and cultural reproduction are never complete and always meet with partially realized elements of opposition" (71). That opposition, not absolute but part of the sociology of learning, provides the opportunity for students to act as agents—to rewrite the ideologically, culturally, and politically embedded narratives of their lives. This rewriting is resistance.

Aronowitz and Giroux emphasize that, however futile some kinds of failure might appear to be, even such forms of student resistance are not just mute opposition but a refusal to participate in an educational program that needs to be questioned. Students practicing resistance are not simply refusing to learn; they are resisting not just a culture that is strange to them—the culture of schooling—but an ideology that oppresses them. In resisting, students know something that their teachers, however politically aware, do not and cannot know in quite the same way. Students' resistance to the ideology of schooling can provide a critical wedge that opens up questioning, that unsettles teachers from their own participation in a mode of learning that is hierarchical and domineering.

But how do the refusals of students become validated as resistance? What sanctions or makes struggle meaningful? We think here of the model presented by Judith Fetterley, interpreting texts as a feminist, as a resisting reader. Rhetorically, her unconventional interpretation takes the form of a refusal to be part of the addressed, the audience—a refusal to identify with the misogynist ideology that she reads in the texts of, for example, Ernest Hemingway and F. Scott Fitzgerald. What she does is likely to make any interpretive community uncomfortable. This voice of resistance labels what seems perfectly natural and thus dissents from primary agreements. As the case of Fetterley suggests, the voice of resistance often takes the form of a polarizing opposition, so it may often seem extreme, perverse, a misunderstanding of a much more diverse intention. It is the hope of many (of Paolo Freire, Ira Shor, and a number of feminists) that, by giving voice to this refusal and thus taking the place of the speaker in an active role, a speaker will move unconscious, passive resistance into active, critical thinking. This hope for an articulated and theorized resistance to empower learning is what needs careful exploration.

Do resistance theories give us what Aronowitz and Giroux call for, a "language of possibility" (139)? In "Accommodation, Resistance, and the Politics of Student Writing," Geoffrey Chase, following Giroux's suggestions, argues that we should look at the moments when students *fail* to learn academic discourse as moments of possibility and that we should make those ruptures and breaks the focus of our inquiry. This is an important suggestion. However, Chase's discussion poses several problems for us. Chase seems naive, first of all, about the realities of students' lives. He criticizes the first student he describes, Bill, for viewing "his project as an exercise that had to be completed following a certain time line" (16), and yet Bill's project is, in an important sense, precisely that. Chase's reluctance to credit Bill's interpretation of his experience—"that he wanted to graduate on time and that his senior project would demonstrate to a future employer that he was capable of doing quality work" (16)—may represent a dangerous, if unwilling and unconscious, arrogance.

More important, perhaps, Chase oversimplifies what is at stake in Bill's conviction that "there were certain conventions he needed to follow" (16). Bill has not arrived at either his conviction or his understanding of the conventions of academic writing haphazardly. Chase notes, in fact, that "the outline [Bill] described to me was laid out by the senior workshop coordinator in class" (17). In interpreting Bill's apparent need to adhere to conventions, Chase fails to take Bill's rhetorical situation as student seriously.

As Patricia Bizzell reminds us, students need to learn the conventions of academic discourse, and what Chase sees as disempowered accommodation may by a different interpreter be viewed as empowering experimentation. Furthermore, even progressive teachers can unintentionally turn political positions into forms of domination. The teacher who already knows what the political unconscious will reveal has foreclosed a collaborative practice of understanding. In Geoffrey Chase's article, for instance, the student examples fall with suspicious ease into a hierarchy of three, with the "best" student, Karen, writing about Meridel LeSueur, "a left-wing, feminist labor writer" (18).

How do we recognize productive resistance when we see it? Chase favors the student who identifies with her subject: "Karen chose LeSueur because there was something about her fiction that spoke directly to her" (18). And Karen resists the efforts of academic historians to impose a form on her writing. Chase concludes: "Her failure to follow the guidelines handed to her was, in fact, a tremendous success, because it involved seeing herself in history, in a context, and as an individual who experiences her own sense of agency and power" (19). What Chase wants to encourage is an attitude of resistance, rather than accommodation. However, his notion of resistance is itself reductive and provokes other problems. By encouraging Karen to identify with LeSueur, Chase is also, as Bertolt Brecht has argued, encouraging her to reproduce the construction of the bourgeois subject. Reading Chase, we found ourselves wondering what would have happened if Karen had chosen a less politically correct subject for historical analysis. Would Chase still have seen the choice as a form of resistance? Street's ideological model of literacy cautions researchers and teachers against setting up "polarized absolutist statements which can result in overstatements" (130). The ease with which Chase characterizes Karen's work as a "tremendous success" (19) while determining that Bill "focused on conventions as a way of limiting his engagement with his project" seems questionable.

We have critiqued Chase's essay not because we believe its errors are pernicious but because Chase's approach is similar to that of other radical theorists, such as Ira Shor—theorists whose projects we endorse. We find much of value in Shor's work and in Chase's. But radical theorists err in failing to consider adequately not only their students' rhetorical situation—their situation as students in classrooms—but also their own situation. Such a failure is hardly insignificant, for, as Street argues, "the processes whereby reading and writing are learnt are what construct the meaning of it for particular practitioners" (8).

Focusing on the rhetorical situation of the classroom complicates and enriches our understanding of resistance because it reminds us that teachers must always contend with the authority that their position constructs; students must always deal with their own lack of authority. As Ann Murphy notes in "Transference and Resistance in the Basic Writing Classroom: Problematics and Praxis," the power of government and institution enters the classroom and must be recognized, but the power of culture enters in the classroom process, in the rhetorical situation that both elicits and defines particular identities. Social and political explanations of resistance remain external and do not extend to the interior of the rhetorical situation of learning, which constructs ideology as a function of knowledge. What the teacher knows about ideology does not by itself, in other words, open up possibilities for students to resist. Because of this, literacy programs—at the very moment of trying to encourage literacy—can simply repeat the discourse of domination, rather than provide alternatives.

Linda Brodkey's analysis of the literacy letters exchanged by middle-class teachers and working-class adults in a basic education program shows how a middle-class discourse can alienate the other with no explicit attempt to dominate or exclude: this occurs because "educational discourse [itself] defends its privileged subjects against resistance" (140). Brodkey's essay represents a close reading of the kinds of failures collaboration may encounter by not recognizing differences of class and gender. Brodkey closes with a recommendation: "Resistance inside educational discourse is then a practice in cooperative articulation on the part of students and teachers who actively seek to construct and understand the differences as well as similarities between their respective subject positions" (140).

How does a practice of resistance avoid the traps of educational discourse itself? To answer that question, we must first locate the hidden place of value within educational discourse, challenging its alleged neutrality: the repressed other of knowledge we might call upon to serve as a place for resistance. The devalued term in the discourse of teaching is *ignorance*. The failure to know exists in an apparent opposition to knowledge and so can be deconstructed. If education values knowledge, it also assumes, as the other part of a binary construction, that ignorance is bad. By asking if ignorance itself may be valuable, may be the mark of a learning superior to a knowledge that does not admit its uncertainties, theory can resist the metaphysical processes of educational discourse. Then the final step after the deconstructive reversal needs to be taken—that is, to see that the knowledge-ignorance opposition covers up the struggle of multiple differences that cannot be reduced to either alternative. But what does resistance as ignorance look like?

Resistance as ignorance has to do with the failure, rather than the success, of the subject who is imbricated in knowledge. Can this ignorance provide a mode of resistance to the position of authority, a resistance that allows the teacher to give up dominating the construction of knowledge? In the place of ignorance, may the student finally speak what has resisted and has appeared as silence? Aronowitz and Giroux point out that ignorance provides a possible source of the "language of possibility" (159), a form of knowing. However, they do not examine the psychoanalytic dynamic inside the mechanism of resistance; they recognize the need for a critical psychology but seem to understand ignorance as a mark of repression. That is, even though they admit that "theories of resistance . . . have not given enough attention to the issue of how domination reaches into the structure of personality itself" (103), they do not take seriously enough the particularities of people's lives or the way that ideology appears as natural, unconscious, and profoundly subjective.

The psychoanalytic situation has important resonances with pedagogy. The work of Jacques Lacan has made more explicit the implications of psychoanalysis for the study of discourse, as articles in the two issues of *College English* edited by Robert Con Davis reflect. Like the teacher, the psychoanalyst is what Lacan called the subject-supposed-to-know, an authority. But what does the psychoanalyst know? What can the teacher teach?

As Freud describes the working of language, there is never a straightforward transfer of meaning from one person to another. The unconscious erupts to disconcert and deflect our words and to reveal our ignorance. What psychoanalysts know does not eliminate their ignorance, for they do not know what their patients have repressed. And at the same time, the patients are ignorant of what their words, charged with symptomatic significance, are telling the other. Similarly, however expert we are, we, as teachers, do not ever know what our students will learn from us, and yet that is precisely what our students think we know. The moment of learning is the moment of ignorance, of seeing the gap, the blank—feeling the lack. Our situation is paradoxically hopeful: not only should we not work to impose on our students what we think it means to be literate, but, no matter how hard we try, we cannot entirely do so. Repression does not exercise a totalitarian control over either the political or the personal unconscious. Furthermore, the linear model for the transference of information, like linear models of communication, misleads us by its apparent efficiency. Teaching literacy is not like going bowling, dependent only on the aim of the one who rolls the ball.

Shoshana Felman argues that psychoanalysis provides a model for learning that, unlike the ineffectual linearity of repressive education, would produce the paradoxical condition of knowledge:

> Proceeding not through linear progression, but through breakthroughs, leaps, discontinuities, regressions, and deferred action, the analytic learning process puts indeed in question the traditional pedagogical belief in intellectual perfectability, the progressistic view of learning as a simple one-way road from ignorance to knowledge. (27)

Like education, however, psychoanalysis has at times fallen into the temptation of prescribing the form of the cure, sometimes of prescribing conformity or social adjustment. Like the return of the repressed in neurotic symptoms, the symptoms of social exclusion mark the classroom with reminders of what has been pushed outdoors. The recurring gaps and silences about the cultural context are taken up as the act of silence by students, inscribing themselves as subjects of alienation. The subject has difficulty with the critical moment of saying the words—ungrammatical? not literary? illogical? too emotional? too worried about the price of books or the economy of grading? too filled with unacademic rage?—words that would introduce the other, difference, into the exchange, breaking the silence. And yet the possibility of critical thinking depends on some kind of violation, difference, negation. A mutual speech is the context for a cure, even though the cure is analysis terminable and interminable, a process of spoken resistance that is the process of learning. In other words, resistance to what is already known marks the starting point for collaboration.

Julia Kristeva argues that the task of the analyst is not to resolve the crisis in subjectivity caused by questioning social constructions and past histories but to help patients enter into language:

> Help them, then, to speak and write themselves in unstable, open, undecidable spaces. . . . It is not a matter of filling [their] "crisis"—[their] emptiness—with meaning. . . . But to trigger a discourse where [their] own "emptiness" and [their] own "out-of-placeness" become essential elements, indispensable "characters" if you will, of a *work in progress*. What is at stake is turning the crisis into a *work in progress*. (380)

What is effective collaboration but a work in progress? Doesn't the very act of defining literacy have to be collaborative? Doesn't resistance teach us that the meaning of literacy cannot ever be defined for another?

By now it is clear, we hope, that—in critiquing theories of collaborative learning for their privileging of epistemological issues and their avoidance of culture, politics, and ideology—we are decidedly not rejecting these theories. We want to oppose such oppositional thinking—the kind of thinking that catalyzes wave after wave of educational reforms yet leaves our educational institutions fundamentally unchanged. Instead, we want to challenge theorists like Bruffee and all who engage in collaborative-learning practices to take the liberating power of collaborative learning seriously and to insist that our theories adequately confront and critique the nature of this experience.

In "Collaborative Learning and the 'Conversation of Mankind,' " Bruffee notes that collaborative learning harnesses "the powerful educative force of peer influence that has been—and largely still is—ignored and hence wasted by traditional forms of education" (638). We agree. But we believe that, by uncritically accepting constructs like peer influence, Bruffee and others oversimplify their own experiences. And by conflating the knowledge imposed by education with the ignorance exposed in the struggle of collaboration, social-constructivist theories of knowledge have overlooked the significance of resistance.

Resistance is not simply oppositional. Resistance opens up possibilities for learning for teachers and theorists, as well as for students. Resistance threatens education itself because it crosses the borders between the classroom and the world, but the threat is also the promise. What happens in a writing classroom can make differences that matter in students' lives. If that isn't true, education has nothing to do with literacy. Our own collaboration and investigation of resistance has forcibly reminded us that the mutual interrogation of ideas does not inevitably lead to critical dominance and repression. Instead, resistance can catalyze a fruitful complication and a more rewarding, enabling understanding.

WORKS CITED

Althusser, Louis. "Ideology and Ideological State Apparatuses (Notes towards an Investigation)." *Lenin and Philosophy and Other Essays.* Trans. Ben Brewster. New York: Monthly Review, 1971.

Aronowitz, Stanley, and Henry A. Giroux. *Education under Siege: The Conservative, Liberal, and Radical Debate over Schooling.* South Hadley: Bergin, 1985.

Bizzell, Patricia. "Arguing about Literacy." *College English* 50 (1988): 141–53.

———. "What Happens When Basic Writers Come to College?" *College Composition and Communication* 37 (1986): 294–301.

Brecht, Bertolt. *Brecht on Theater: The Development of an Aesthetic.* Ed. John Willett. New York: Hill, 1964.

Brodkey, Linda. "On the Subjects of Class and Gender in 'The Literacy Letters.' " *College English* 51 (1989): 125–41.

Bruffee, Kenneth. "Collaborative Learning and the 'Conversation of Mankind.' " *College English* 46 (1984): 635–52.

———. "Social Construction, Language, and the Authority of Knowledge: A Bibliographical Essay." *College English* 48 (1986): 773–90.

Chase, Geoffrey. "Accommodation, Resistance, and the Politics of Student Writing." *College Composition and Communication* 39 (1988): 13–22.

Davis, Robert Con, guest ed. "Psychoanalysis and Pedagogy I and II." *College English*, 49 (1987): issues 6 and 7.

Felman, Shoshana. "Psychoanalysis and Education: Teaching Terminable and Interminable." *Yale French Studies* 63 (1982): 21–44.

Fetterley, Judith. *The Resisting Reader: A Feminist Approach to American Fiction.* Bloomington: Indiana UP, 1989.

Freire, Paolo. *Education for Critical Consciousness.* New York: Seabury, 1978.

———. *The Pedagogy of the Oppressed.* New York: Seabury, 1973.

Freud, Sigmund. "Analysis Terminable and Interminable." Vol. 5 of *Collected Papers.* Trans. Joan Riviere. Ed. James Strachey. New York: Basic, 1959. 316–57.

Gere, Anne Ruggles. *Writing Groups: History, Theory, and Implications.* Carbondale: Southern Illinois UP, 1987.

Giroux, Henry A. *Theory and Resistance in Education: A Pedagogy for the Opposition.* South Hadley: Bergin, 1983.

Harris, Joseph. "The Idea of Community in the Study of Writing." *College Composition and Communication* 40 (1989): 11–22.

Hawkins, Thom. *Group Inquiry Techniques for Teaching Writing.* Urbana: NCTE, 1976.

Kristeva, Julia. "Extraterrestrials Suffering for Want of Love." *Tales of Love.* Trans. Leon S. Roudiez. New York: Columbia UP, 1987.

LeFevre, Karen Burke. *Invention as a Social Act.* Carbondale: Southern Illinois UP, 1987.

Merod, Jim. *The Political Responsibility of the Critic.* Ithaca: Cornell UP, 1987.

Murphy, Ann. "Transference and Resistance in the Basic Writing Classroom: Problematics and Praxis." *College Composition and Communication* 40.2 (1989): 175–87.

Myers, Greg. "Reality, Consensus, and Reform in the Rhetoric of Composition Teaching." *College English* 48 (1986): 154–74.

Olson, David R. "From Utterance to Text: The Bias of Language in Speech and Writing." *Harvard Educational Review* 47 (1977): 257–81.

Shor, Ira. "Equality Is Excellence: Transforming Teacher Education and the Learning Process." *Harvard Educational Review* 56 (1986): 406–26.

———, ed. *Freire for the Classroom: A Sourcebook for Liberatory Teaching.* Portsmouth: Boynton, 1987.

Street, Brian V. *Literacy in Theory and Practice.* Cambridge: Cambridge UP, 1984.

Trimbur, John. "Collaborative Learning and Teaching Writing." *Perspectives on Research and Scholarship in Composition.* Ed. Ben W. McClelland and Timothy R. Donovan. New York: MLA, 1985. 87–109.

Williams, Raymond. *Keywords: A Vocabulary of Culture and Society.* New York: Oxford UP, 1976.

Willis, Paul. *Learning to Labor: How Working Class Kids Get Working Class Jobs.* New York: Columbia UP, 1981.

Part Five

TOWARD THE RESPONSIBILITIES OF LITERACY

The Fourth Vision:
Literate Language at Work

Shirley Brice Heath

In the 24 November 1985 issue of the *New York Times* book review section, Harold Brodkey, novelist and short story writer, wrote an essay entitled "Reading, the Most Dangerous Game." To his readers he gave this warning:

> I think reading and writing are the most dangerous human things because they operate on and from that part of the mind in which judgments of reality are made; and because of the authority language has from when we learn to speak and use its power as a family matter, as an immediate matter, and from when we learn to read and see its modern middle-class power as a public matter establishing our rank in the world.   (45)

Brodkey, as a literary writer, wishes, of course, to promote, encourage, and enrich what he calls "the most dangerous human things" of reading and writing. In analyzing how reading and writing are dangerous, he gives us three visions, which precede a fourth of my devising, to which the title of this chapter refers. Brodkey reminds us that reading and writing operate on and intensify "judgments of reality"—the abilities we have to imagine and then to bestow the authority that language can have. He terms reading and writing dangers because they must bring unpredictability, change, reassessment, redefinition. Brodkey tells us:

> novels, plays, essays, fact pieces, poems, through conversion or in the process of argument with them, change you or else—to use an idiom—you haven't listened. If the reader is not at risk, he is not reading. And if the writer is not at risk, he is not writing.   (44)

Reading and writing thus remove us from ordinariness, commonalities, uniformities. They bring about and, most frequently, are our only ways to ensure the creation and the exchange of ideas. Hence, a central danger within reading and writing is the growth and spread of ideas, as well as the power of problem identifying and problem solving that can come through speaking about and acting on their imperatives. The conversion or process of argument that changes us as we read and write leads us to have to place first ourselves in authority and then, immediately after, others with whom we want to extend the argument. As Deborah Brandt points out in this volume, literate knowledge has to become a craft knowledge, because what sustains literateness is not the *what* but the *who*.

Brodkey speaks directly of the authority in the first three visions of literate language—the authority we have when we learn to speak and use its power— as a family matter, immediate matter, and public matter establishing our rank beyond primary associates to our rank in the larger world. To these three visions I add a fourth—its authority and power as a work matter. Within American society, this fourth vision has risen in authority and power in the past decade, while the first three visions have diminished. Perhaps not surprisingly, the literate language of reading and writing at work now draws on the manners and methods through which such language used to work in the first three—family, daily life of schooling, and public matters of leisure and religious life. For some, the literate language of work now provides in some cases models for talk and idea exchange that home, school, and community provided in earlier eras.

Let's look briefly at the first three visions and where they stand today in American life. How do their conditions affect the fourth vision?

Language within the Family

Language as a family matter includes those uses of spoken and written language that scholars and laymen alike have long argued should help establish our identity, our referencing to the world, and our ways of both seeking solitude and putting ourselves forward to the world beyond the family. It is that language through which children are nurtured and play games, explore their immediate physical and social world, and express curiosity, emotion, and basic needs. The average American thinks of young children learning language within a rich, stable network of interactions with parents, siblings, playmates, and family friends.

But rapidly changing patterns of employment and child-care arrangements are not compatible with idealized images of consistent, verbally supportive care givers. All families—mainstream and nonmainstream—are in constant states of change, and the leisure patterns, family mealtime exchanges, and joint adult-child projects of several decades ago face considerable competition in households of single parents and families in which both parents work full-time (Suransky). In 1986 only seven percent of the families in the United States could be described as the traditional ideal or typical family—a two-parent family in which working fathers and homemaking mothers provided sustenance, structure, and support for children (Hodgkinson). Single-parent households, dual-career families, and extended households made up of nonkin and nonconjugally linked temporary residents give little time to extended spoken or written language interactions with children. As a result, America's children receive far less language for learning in families and through family events than in the decades that preceded the 1970s.

America's children are silent and lonely across socioeconomic classes and in cultural and linguistic memberships. Evidence for this silent loneliness comes from a number of sources. In the late 1970s a team of psychologists in Chicago enlisted seventy-five adolescents of middle-class families to take part in a study of their daily lives (Csikszentmihalyi and Larson). Researchers collected data through the experience sample method; for one week the participants carried electronic pagers and responded during one random moment within each two-hour period to a pager beep. The responses consisted of the adolescents' filling out self-report forms to record their activities, feelings, and thoughts at that moment. These high school students continued their normal activities during the week of recording and participated as well in follow-up individual interviews about their daily experiences.

The teenagers indicated that leisure time with their families consisted primarily of noninteractive, unchallenging, passive activities. The warmest memories these adolescents had were of family times together that involved a trip. At home, the parents and the children rarely did things together, so they seemed to have to leave home to be together as a family. The typical happy-memory scenario pictured relatives around a fireplace after a day of active winter sports, eating and joking or singing and playing games together. These memories were of structured times for talk and interactions that served as cornerstones for the adolescents' self-concepts and projections of their own preferred future family habits.

Being alone was the context in which teenagers felt the worst. They confessed that they were unable to fill solitude with any productive activities. For them thinking took the form of worrying. When teenagers could not do anything, they questioned their own existence. For them the unstated rule of living was "to *be* one must *do*. To know that we exist and that we matter in the world, we must act in ways that prove our existence" (Csikszentmihalyi and Larson 197). Talk is a key feature of this doing-being, and talk and athletic activities take up the bulk of time that adolescents spend with their friends. However, these teenagers spent less than five percent of their time exclusively with a parent or parents; among a sample of one thousand self-reports, they reported being alone with their fathers only ten times, and five of those times included watching television. The adolescents spent approximately half an hour a week, less than five minutes a day, interacting exclusively with their fathers and less than fifteen minutes a day with their mothers.

But we must look at patterns in families of other social classes and cultural-linguistic membership to avoid drawing the conclusion that the patterns of life implied by these teenagers' reports occur only in middle-class families driven by perceived economic pressures and aspirations of upward mobility. An ethnography of Trackton, a black working-class community in the Piedmont Carolinas in the 1970s and early 1980s, pictured families and friends spending long hours outdoors or on porches that looked onto the plazalike center of the neighborhood (Heath, *Ways with Words*). Children and young people moved on and off this stage, always likely targets for jests, conversation, and teasing challenges. In the late 1980s, as the children of Trackton moved away to urban centers to establish independent households, the language environment of their children bore little resemblance to that of their own childhood. High-rise public housing projects, often poorly maintained and heavily targeted for criminal activities, provided few public stages on which children could perform for and interact with familiar caring adults. Young mothers tended to stay shut up in their own apartments, passing their days by watching television and waiting and hoping for some bureaucratic miracle that would bring a change in their lives.

For example, detailed notes and tape recordings kept by one former Trackton child, the single parent of three children in the late 1980s, revealed that she spent most of her waking hours as a passive spectator of television and reader of magazines featuring the lives of movie or television stars. During the occasional visits from her girlfriends, they talked nearly eighty percent of the time. In a random selection of twenty hours of tapes made over two years, approximately fourteen percent of the recording sessions included talk between the mother and her children. She asked direct questions about the children's immediate actions, offered comments on those actions, and gave directions or requested certain changes in behavior; these exchanges of talk usually lasted less than one minute. Of those occasions when the talk of mother and child continued for as much as four turns, ninety-two percent took place when someone else— usually a girlfriend or the neighbor girl who served as a baby-sitter—was in the room. In thirteen instances in twenty hours of taping, the mother initiated nondirective talk to one of the children. On nine occasions, she used some written artifact, a newspaper or magazine advertisement, as the basis of her talk to her children (Heath, "Children").

The spatial, occupational, and temporal changes in the lives of Trackton's children who later located in project housing in urban centers dramatically constrain talk and other interactions between adults and children. In Trackton, from infancy to young adulthood, everyone had immediate access to family and neighborhood friends. Living and talking were largely public affairs, involving many speakers of varied ages, goals, and affiliations. In the late 1980s, public housing, new types of threats from drug-related criminal activities, and the absence of extended families or close friends walled young mothers and their children in urban centers into self-protective noninteractive isolation.

Patterns of daily life that cut the young off from supportive talk that recognizes their roles and responses appear in families at all points along the continuum from middle class to the poor of inner-city high-rise housing projects. A mid-1980s study of nearly 500 teenagers from a wide range of classes and regions of the country who left home between the ages of twelve and nineteen reported that approximately sixty percent of the youngsters who left home felt compelled to do so (Lefkowitz). They felt that they had no support for the numerous responsibilities they had taken on in their daily lives: care for younger siblings, jobs outside of school, moderate school achievement against peer pressures to goof off. These young people reported leaving in the hope of finding supportive listeners and occasions for telling their stories and for taking in others' stories.

Language in School

Where were the teachers of these students? Were there not teachers who saw them daily and provided some forms of verbal support? Public promotions of literacy and basic skills in the 1980s and issues of accountability have worked to silence teachers and students in many ways. Across the United States, school districts, individual schools and their teachers, as well as their students, face assessment by standardized tests that ask students to manipulate discrete isolated elements of written texts. Relatively little class time can go into students' and teachers' talking together about any topic. Thus, back-to-basics programs, oral and written fill-in-the-blank exercises, and teacher-dominated classrooms focus primarily on the mechanics of language and remediation at the sentence level. Under most dominant philosophies of pedagogy at the end of the twentieth century, classrooms cannot foster teacher-student relationships that build a sense of expertise and responsibility in students. Numerous studies indicate the brevity and the limited scope of language in classrooms that set the teacher as the question asker and the student as the responder: Applebee tells us that students spend only three percent of their time in secondary English classes writing discourse that extends to a paragraph's length; studies of classroom language use repeatedly illustrate the limited amount of oral participation students have (e.g., Cazden). Guidance counselors have their attention turned almost exclusively to students headed for college; in addition, in many urban schools there is a ratio of one counselor for every 500 students (Lefkowitz).

Textbooks and tests do not, with rare exceptions, ask students to identify problems; instead, they ask students to *solve* problems already identified and stated by others. Requests for direct action research that would require speaking and listening skills (e.g., interviews with local figures and comparisons of radio and television coverage of current events) usually come primarily in extra-credit sections of textbooks or from teachers of advanced placement or honors sections. Numerous studies of classroom language report the scarcity of occasions on which teachers sit back and let the students talk or ask open-ended questions; even teachers who express the goal of wanting to improve their students' oral language skills find it extremely difficult to give up their central position as talkers in the classroom. Perhaps somewhat paradoxically, in the past decade those occasions of the greatest amount of talk by students interacting with each other have come from the introduction of computers. With this event, many teachers felt free to admit that some of their students had more knowledge and expertise than their elders; thus, students and their teacher often worked together as experts and novice.

In earlier eras, in spite of the prevalence of rote memorization and recitation, the blending of different grades and ages in the same classroom offered occasions for cross-age talk on academic topics. Students were asked to prepare speeches on topics that related to the values of civic life; they participated in planning and producing school programs for affairs that drew a large portion of the community to the school. Textbooks and teaching materials, in contrast to later patterns, provided questions that drew from students' experiences, asked for argumentation, counterpropositions, and comparisons of one's own experiences with those of characters presented in the textbooks (deCastell, Luke, and Luke).

Language in the Community

It is within the community—usually in our leisure activities and in community organizations, such as the church—that we first learn to contend with language, in Brodkey's terms, "as a public matter establishing our rank in the world" (45). When we leave our homes to explore play and to find recreation in our communities, we first meet the need to explain ourselves through language, to acknowledge that it is possible that our familial nonverbal and verbal habits will not be understood by those beyond our households. For many young Americans of the late 1980s, the first such venture into organized patterns of leisure came from participation on neighborhood basketball courts and baseball fields. Youngsters learned early to align themselves with a team, a group for affiliation beyond the family. Occasionally, for big games or special events, members of the family came to watch, and there could follow considerable talk about the who, what, why, and how of the game. But, in the main, leisure-time activities brought together only those of the same age group, and cross-age talk with adults, with the exceptions of coaches and community park directors, rarely occurred.

Adult Americans spent an extraordinary amount of their leisure time as either sports spectators or sports participants. They watched experts of professional or collegiate affiliation, and they took up individual pursuits of athletics, often as a form of physical exercise. Neither as spectators nor as participants, however, did adults find many occasions to talk with the young about these events. National team sports, such as football and basketball, focused the attention of the spectators on events planned, administered, and monitored by others. Audience members for these games were strangers who focused their observations on the game. For events such as tennis matches and golf tournaments, the spectators centered their attention on celebrity players and observed strict rules of silence during play.

Exceptions to these spectator sports were local events, such as high school basketball games, Little League baseball, and neighborhood soccer games. These games often brought together fans who were not strangers to each other, and much talk by participants and spectators alike surrounded the planning, execution, and follow-up appraisal of these events. The patterns of interaction parallel those of earlier years, when a weekend baseball game, church supper, or town parade could involve nearly every member of the community in arranging and successfully carrying off the event. For these events and for some of the most commonly played outdoor games (croquet, horseshoes, sack races), some role for participants of all ages was usually assured. In the stories that circulated after such family or community events, everyone could share in the telling, since all had various degrees of experience and points of view from which they had experienced the occasion.

In an earlier era, indoor leisure activities across classes and ethnic groups often centered on building the mind and the wits. Labor outside the home—whether for pioneers, farmers, sailors, or merchants—provided substantial amounts of exercise for their bodies. Spending time at home and in neighborhood activities to sharpen the wits and to expand knowledge about the world held considerable attraction for men and women, old and young. Throughout the first centuries of American history, men and women wrote in their diaries and letters about the ways in which family activities around games, photographs, and books centered on talk that would build the mind and hone the wits. Parlors were made for talking, reading, and playing games that were often word challenges, tests of memory and interpretation, and ways of practicing negotiation (consider the game Monopoly, for example). In addition, a considerable amount of what contemporary psychologists call "reciprocal teaching" (see Brown and Palincsar) went on during these cross-age family events.

At the end of the twentieth century, a large portion of leisure time for the middle class centers on developing the body and not the mind. Participation in these activities is, more often than not, guided in large part through specialized books, magazines, audio tapes and videotapes, and advertising that insists on the "proper" shoes, clothing, and equipment for these activities. Moreover, the majority of these activities are age-graded and gender-segregated. Men run and play golf with male colleagues and not with their children or female associates; similarly, women find female associates to share their activities, and the most affluent hire baby-sitters to care for their children while they work out at the gym or join an aerobics class. Jogging, walking, biking, and playing tennis or racquetball take on a hyperreality—outside actual participation—through the accoutrements and sources of professional knowledge and institutions (clubs, weight rooms) that surround these activities. The former habits of learning by listening to the experiences of close associates have given way to heeding the advice of professional models, advisers, and promoters. Thus, the ready give-and-take of extended occasions for talk that formerly accompanied leisure events in the family and the neighborhood have almost passed from the everyday experiences of middle-class Americans.

At home these changes in preferred leisure activities have come with rearrangements in the organization of both time and space. The living room has replaced the parlor of earlier days, and it is now often the location of the television set and the video recorder. If the living room is not the location of these artifacts, they are in the family room—a paradoxical name since the family as a unit rarely gathers there. In many upper-middle-class families, children and adults have their separate spaces for their preferred leisure activities. Teenagers have a computer and a stereo in their room, while adults may have small television sets or portable compact disc players in several rooms of the house. Games are age-graded and kept in separate locations, so there may be no central site for storing family games.

Throughout American history the church has been a central institution of community life. In the first two centuries of United States history, temples, churches, synagogues, and mosques in towns and cities served not only as religious centers but also as educational, recreational, and social avenues beyond the family. Protestant church activities tended to center on texts—biblical, instructional, and musical; reading, talking about, and listening to written texts took up much of the time spent in religious activities. Implicit in many of these occasions of interpretation was the expectation that reading and talking about written texts would lead to altered actions and reformed views of one's own performances in the public world.

Beginning in the 1920s and with a dramatic increase in the 1970s and 1980s, churches that took a hostile view of diversity in cultures moved to restrict their parishioners' access to various interpretations of the Bible, instructional materials, and music. The separation from the world that came from being born again led to a reliance on ministers as leaders and interpreters; the chosen followed the ministers' words (Marty). Institutions of fundamentalism and neoorthodoxy drew their congregations close to reading—to the written word—but without open interpretation through speaking about the word. Ritualized language in the words of authoritarian leaders and through recommended study sessions made sure that readers knew how and what to speak about the texts. Institutions increasingly prescribed actions for their congregations, discouraged wide reading, and accepted only approved religious materials prepared for their specific groups. The goal seemed to be to fix a boundary on belief and on practice (Goody xvii).

Decidedly anti-intellectual and fearful of examinations of alternative premises of decision making, fundamentalists helped spread throughout the public a resurgence of faith in educational basics to reinforce children's learning of fundamental reading and mathematical skills. Opposed to open-ended interpretations of literature, personal writing, and textbooks that encouraged alternative viewpoints and stressed America's pluralistic culture, fundamentalists came in the 1980s to be highly influential in designing the curricula of language arts and science in public schools (see Moffett).

In short, from family life and our immediate daily life in school to the more public institutional domains of leisure and religion, children in the United States in the late 1980s, in comparison with their counterparts in earlier decades, had fewer opportunities to follow a single topic or line of thought through a sustained conversation with adults. Extended occasions for talk between those of different levels and perspectives of expertise diminished in the home, the church, and the school. In earlier eras it was commonplace for families to insist on the presence of the young for family dinnertime, parlor games, and numerous other occasions attended by family members of different ages. These occasions provided numerous multiply patterned, redundant opportunities for the young to hear debates, stories, and long explanations of ways to accomplish certain feats. The adage "children are to be seen and not heard" attests to long hours of enforced listening skills. In addition, well into the 1950s, radio programs, such as the *Jack Benny Show*, depended for their entertainment value on long, involved verbal arguments, puns, and wordplays.

The philosopher Walter Benjamin has lamented the decline of storytelling that began with the rise of the novel and greatly accelerated with the newspaper. He claims that the grip of the press on the middle class lies primarily in the centering of the press on information: "the information which supplies a handle for what is nearest gets the readiest hearing" (89). Benjamin goes on to remind us that the art of listening has receded as the middle class has come to focus primarily on information that can lay claim to immediate verifiability, to being "understandable in itself" (89). Every reported event from the news media comes wrapped in a simple explanation that does not have to rely on readers' having "intelligence coming from afar", either geographical or historical (89).

In contrast, storytelling and conversation laced through with mininarratives allow listeners to interpret, to give tales amplitude and extensions in time and space. Information that aims to explain itself without losing time does so through explicit tellings of psychological and social connections that stories never release directly. Lived and relived experiences communicated in stories become re-membered experiences, repeated over time and space by a community of lis-teners. Those who listen, truly listen, know they are the remakers of knowledge through the shared experiences of not only the stories heard but also their stories remembered, related, and released on other occasions that remind the listeners of old stories and analogous times, places, or situations.

Language at Work

What of the fourth vision, literate language at work? How does this language relate to the diminished habits of conversation, storytelling, and communicating experiences in the home, in immediate life, and in the public world? Ironically, in the late 1980s, situations in which work took place increasingly provided occasions in which we could create narratives and share our observing, thinking, and listening with those with whom we worked. The example most immediately at hand is that of those teachers who worked then to promote and extend literate behaviors and not just the basic skills of literacy. My discussion of language at work focuses primarily on teachers who have acknowledged the power of ex-panding spoken and written genres in their work and then offers a brief com-parison with other workplaces.

Numerous portions of this volume tell the stories of teachers who call on students to pool, share, and compare their everyday knowledge before they move on to taking in new information. Moreover, many of those whose work is represented in this volume are fringe dwellers, professionals who cling to the edges of institutions in part-time jobs and in programs that claim no place in the regular catalog of institutional activities. Those who teach basic English, study skills, adult basic education, remedial reading, and English as a second language always stand astride the theory and the practice of both politics and pedagogy.

Yet, as the essays in this volume illustrate, these teachers have visions with their students not of literacy skills but of literate behaviors. Within the programs and the philosophies included here, being literate means "having counsel" for oneself and for others through communicable experience (Benjamin 86). Being literate means being able to talk with and listen with others to interpret texts, say what they mean, link them to personal experience and with other texts, argue with them and make predictions from them, develop future scenarios, compare and evaluate related situations, and know that the practice of all these literate abilities is practical. Counsel is practical advice, but it is often "less an answer to a question than a proposal concerning the continuation of a story which is just unfolding" (Benjamin 86). Thus, counsel depends on our ability to let ourselves and our situations speak to identify problems, to hypothesize futures, and to compare experiences.

How paradoxical it is that, within those institutions of home and school on which the United States has historically depended for instilling literate behaviors, we can find few extended occasions for literate behaviors. There are few occasions for learning through social interactions to provide reinforcement and to assure us that our knowledge is appropriate. Without extended opportunities to talk through and about what we know and have experienced, we have little hope of writing extended coherent prose. Repeatedly, research on writing in the world of work beyond school tells us that the vast majority of writing is first draft only—jottings and incomplete messages to ourselves or intimates to record, remind, or prod us (Mikulecky and Winchester). The relatively small percentage of writing that goes beyond the first draft emerges from a considerable amount of thinking and talking, both self-talk and social exchange with others. Subsequent drafts, especially those of institutions, move through talking and responding before final execution. Much of the talk that surrounds such writing is that of "having counsel"—considering at a practical level questions or possible scenarios—about the purposes of this writing or its continuation as part of a larger story (Flower).

Several essays in this volume illustrate how these literate language behaviors at work can reenter those classrooms in which teachers and students see themselves as members of a learning community. For example, the adult basic education and English as a second language teachers featured on the *Teacher to Teacher* videotape series produced at City University of New York demonstrate four major features of literate language at work: (1) The students and the teachers are highly interactive; they compare and evaluate real-world knowledge and information reported in written texts. (2) They look behind the surface information, a characteristic that can spring up readily within those who have developed habits of storytelling. (3) The storytellers tend to begin their stories with the circumstances of their own learning by locating themselves in relation to the experiences of the story. (4) These students and teachers demonstrate repeatedly how a collective of learners sharing responsibility for building and analyzing bodies of experience "move up and down the rungs of their experience as on a ladder" (Benjamin 102).

Other essays reflecting the whole language approaches inspired by the work of Kenneth and Yetta Goodman echo across age levels the interactive nature of learning. Bringing young students into literature studies validates their life experiences and enables them to include the reactions and the realities of others within their own responses. The experience of the self and its communication to steady listeners enable students to let their own life habits become the net with which they sweep in information from beyond their daily spatial and temporal worlds.

Several essays in this volume illustrate ways in which we can engage students in assessment. The predominant pattern in most schools reflects dependency on assessment tools that come from beyond the teacher and the students. Reported in this volume are numerous efforts to involve students in analyzing their own spoken and written products. Students examine papers written at different times for various purposes and with different kinds of support. They create portfolios of the writing they consider best, and they consider what goes into the making of particular pieces of writing for different audiences, purposes, and topic knowledge. These students go far beyond receiving assessment from others; they take in principles and practices of assessment as part of their own daily monitoring system. Students learn to observe, reflect, analyze, and report on their own selections of the evidence they produced through their own writing, reading, speaking, and listening.

Teachers of these students are learners. They need environments in which together they can exhibit healthy skepticism about too narrow a range of ways of assessing their students' growth. Teachers need to feel free to turn their own and their colleagues' attention to ways they can learn about their own teaching. Currently, assessment tools beyond the teacher and students' construction hold both accountable. This situation reinforces the view that knowledge is simply accounted for, that it is a commodity of one-way transmission, and that it is not interactive. Common sense tells us otherwise. Conjoined learning at the task and with others of similar intention or social engagement provides the bulk of lifelong learning. Thus, learners—students and teachers alike—need consistent and intense attention to their own growth in the accumulation of facts and the awareness of ways of knowing (collections of accounts of such teachers include Newkirk and Atwell; Goswami and Stillman; Lightfoot and Martin).

Aside from such evidence that some groups of teachers and students are working together in collective efforts to further their literate behaviors, what encouragement comes from the world of work beyond these classrooms? Increasingly, American businesses look ahead to the dramatic increase in jobs that require independent problem-identifying skills, oral communication abilities, and experience in collaboration. In several ways some corporations are trying to reshape their own institutions and to reorient their approaches to workers. One example comes from the Creative Education Foundation, an independent, not-for-profit foundation in Buffalo, New York, that became in the late 1980s a strong influence on American corporations. Business executives and managers joined musicians, teachers, scientists, and physicians in seminars that led the participants to talk, exchange ideas, and seek ways of making new connections by interacting with others from different experiences. Regional meetings throughout the year enabled workers to stay in touch with creative approaches to their work and to communicating experiences within their work. Fundamental within the approach was the need to intensify common approaches to everyday experience: to observe with new concentration, to imagine situations, to bring unlikely concepts together, and to listen.

Beyond the learning activities of the Creative Education Foundation itself lay recommendations about patience and common sense in expecting institutions to change. For some corporations the return of managers from creativity education was not always immediately well received or even acknowledged. The recommendation of the Creative Education Foundation to those returning to their jobs sounded similar to what teachers give each other after attendance at especially effective workshops and regional and national conventions: put new creative skills to work quietly in one's own area of responsibility and be willing to share with others who notice and ask about changes.

Another creative approach to collaboration and problem identification comes from leadership seminars provided by the United Auto Workers at the Fremont, California, General Motors-Toyota plant. Several hours each week, workers from the plant came together with other workers across sections and levels of the automotive plant to identify problems; to consider ways of collecting evidence that could suggest solutions; and to record, analyze, and compare collectively their observations, talks with other workers, and deliberations in their own problem-identifying and problem-solving setting. These leadership seminars stood in the place of literacy classes that other automotive plants offered. Here a work center put into action the belief that literate behaviors, through commitment and responsibility to group efforts, bring greater returns than individually acquired literacy skills that may be gained in a traditional classroom approach.

Numerous research studies and panels of corporate executives reported in the 1980s the need for workers to organize tasks verbally, communicate directions to colleagues, and generate coherent spoken and written texts for a variety of audiences (Carnegie Forum on Education and the Economy; Mikulecky and

Winchester; Mikulecky and Ehlinger; Scribner; Sticht). Former low-level white-collar jobs are now combining traditional clerical functions with professional activities that formerly belonged to management. What is being predicted for clerical workers, for example, is "more sophisticated reasoning ability [and] a wide understanding of company policy and procedures" without the degree of autonomy that formerly attached to managerial and professional positions (Feldberg and Glenn 96). One of the ironies often overlooked in the discussions about the deskilling of the American work force through computers is the way in which the demands of computers parallel those of humans: computers at work have had to become multifunctional and highly interactive (Bair). Humans must now follow this pattern to improve information accessibility, sharing, and collaborative problem identification and solution. Researchers within and outside industry and technology increasingly reported in the late 1980s that taking full advantage of technology would require closer attention to the social significance of human-machine interactions "embedded in on-going human interactions" (Blomberg 195).

These interactions work, both literally and figuratively, because they provide occasions for socially distributed cognition that brings human minds and machines together to solve increasingly challenging problems. From such collaboration by those in medicine, aviation, space control, ship navigation, and law enforcement, each of us benefits daily. Our initial challenge is to see the communication of experience and the collaborative problem-solving spirit behind these advances as the key components of literate behaviors. A second challenge is to expand the learning strategies and situations described in this volume and to cooperate with those representatives of the education and business sectors who share humanistic goals. Researchers from a variety of sectors began in the late 1980s to acknowledge the power of such concepts as socially distributed cognition (see Wertsch) and ensembled individualism (see Sampson). Other researchers reinforced these theoretical notions with close examinations of what happened in a variety of workplaces (e.g., Odell and Goswami; Blomberg; Forsythe; Helander). Perhaps most important for direct effects on rethinking literate behaviors is the renewed interest in communication in the workplace (e.g., Porter and Roberts).

All these institutional changes and research efforts appear to be coming together to diminish the focus on the autonomous person working in isolation at discrete mechanistic tasks. Within academic psychology and sociology, proponents for ensembled individualism began in the mid 1980s to argue against either the historical or the sociopsychological validity of self-contained individualism. To those who argue that firm boundaries, personal control, and an exclusionary concept of the person are necessary to support the core American cultural values of freedom, responsibility, and achievement, others point out that ensembled individualism is supported by cross-cultural, historical, and intracultural evidence. This work demonstrated the achievements of cooperative groups who engaged in mutually obligatory communal relationships and should lead to the reconsideration of case histories that heretofore seemed to highlight self-contained individual efforts (Clark, Mills, and Powell).

The fourth vision is, then, one of learners talking and considering together. Three conclusions seem to point to past achievements that we must use to challenge both the future organization of institutions and simplistic definitions of literacy:

1.   All of us—children and adults, students and teachers, shop workers and supervisors, clerical workers and managers—learn most successfully with and from each other when we have full access to looking, listening, talking, and taking part in authentic tasks we understand.

2.   We can complement each other in particular areas of expertise if we learn to communicate our experiences; sharing what we know helps bring the group to higher performance than private reflections of individuals do.

3.   Humans must move beyond information and skills to meaning and interpretation for learning to take place and to extend itself. So-called at-risk or slow learners frequently have learned in out-of-school experience a multitude of approaches that allow them to move away from the mere display of learning to the creation of learning. Schools too often demonstrate in their assignments that the meaning is that there is no meaning to be interpreted from self-experiences or comparisons between direct learning and the knowledge found in books. The clear message often seems to be that the meaning lies in the text and not in the active engagement of text and reader together.

Seeing How We See

There is a Socratic parable, well-known in some quarters, about a teacher who gives students two magnifying glasses and invites them to look at the one through the other. When each student has told all that he or she has learned, the sage delivers the lesson in the form of a question: "Of what have you told me—the thing you have seen or the other thing through which you have seen it?"

This same conundrum lurks behind the study of literacy. Is it an object of analysis through which we circumscribe our examinations of it, or is it an experience that will, when we look closely, point out beyond the mere direct image of text and reader or writer to illuminate significant aspects of human existence? Brodkey's reflections on reading and writing, along with some comparative framing of the uses of leisure time in families and an examination of the nature of interactions in the lives of schools and churches, have led us to look beyond these three visions to that of a fourth—literate language at work. In so doing, we find that collective bonds and shared goals in work settings from adult basic education classrooms to clerical offices can facilitate oral collaboration to identify and solve problems creatively. Groups, more easily than individuals, can move beyond simplistic single-cause explanations to multiple causes that are context-dependent. Moreover, facilitating opportunities for workers to observe, record, retell, and compare stories in groups with different levels and kinds of expertise promotes rapid learning.

The major institutions of literate behaviors in American life, the school and the church, have in the past decade increasingly chosen to play it safe by restricting, limiting, and even punishing those who speak too much or too freely and those who act beyond the words of their leaders. These institutions have attempted to eliminate, it seems, the dangers but also the creativity that come from reading in any follow-up through speaking and acting. Those social institutions historically responsible in the American context for the care of the mind and the body of the young have seemed to lose their literate behaviors. It is as though these organizations have chosen to leave aside any responsibility for creating and re-creating information and interpretations. The full meaning of *responsible*—being able to respond in something other than a prescripted formulaic and almost ritualistic manner—is not easily found in schools. Other institutions historically promoting such responsiveness and responsibility, religious organizations and families, have also altered their earlier functions and priorities. The major places of such responsibility are businesses that reorient to involve workers in leadership and some neighborhood-based organizations, such as youth centers, Boy Scouts, junior Sierra Clubs, and Future Farmers of America.

This volume brings together several accounts of the efforts of those who focus on reading, writing, speaking, and listening as the bases of learning. Most of the accounts contained here are, however, alternative or marginal programs and practices within their institutions. The philosophies, actions, and results presented here do not easily simplify into programs, step-by-step methods, or simple pedagogical recommendations. A public that wants to simplify the literacy problem will find extraordinarily complex the theories of learning, human interaction, and understanding of socioeconomic forces and their relation to power that underlie these alternatives. But resistance or misunderstanding from the public must not tempt those who are involved in the theory and the practice of literate behaviors to become reductionists. We must be cautious that the flexible, dynamic, and highly creative approaches to reading, writing, listening, and speaking represented in this volume do not become reinterpreted as simplified ready-made teacher-proof programs. The overwhelming tendency of education today is to simplify, standardize, and make predictable. What society must recognize is that literate behaviors allow us to address complexities, promote creative problem identification and solution, and chart new directions for learning.

We have numerous magnifying glasses by which we look at other magnifying glasses. We have numerous ways of reading and of reading literacy. Our theories and our research become more elaborate, more sophisticated, and often more specialized as we look more microscopically at some elements of reading or of literacy. But perhaps the sage's simple lesson of the conundrum—"Of what have you told me—the thing you have seen or the other thing through which you have seen it?"—is the best lesson. Without acknowledging before and during our look through the magnifying glass its larger context and the value system we have adopted that forces much of the community to look at only the smallness of reading, we cannot know what we have seen.

It is a fourth vision then—one beyond that of the mere labeling and numbering of literacy, beyond that of preserving and transmitting, and even beyond expanding what we must work for. We must decide that we wish to use literate behaviors to create and re-create beyond our current authority and power. It is in our ensembled individualism that we can be free from the limitations of ourselves as individuals and bound into a new condition of creation and re-creation of literateness and humaneness.

WORKS CITED

Applebee, Arthur. *Writing in the Secondary School: English and the Content Areas.* Urbana: NCTE, 1981.

Bair, James H. "User Needs for Office Systems Solutions." Kraut 177–94.

Benjamin, Walter. *Illuminations.* New York: Schocken, 1968.

Blomberg, Jeanette L. "Social Interaction and Office Communication: Effects on User's Evaluation of New Technologies." Kraut 195–210.

Brodkey, Harold. "Reading, the Most Dangerous Game." *New York Times Book Review* 24 Nov. 1985: 1, 44, 45.

———. *Stories in an Almost Classical Mode.* New York: Knopf, 1988.

Brown, Ann, and Annemarie Sullivan Palincsar. "Reciprocal Teaching of Comprehension Strategies: A Natural History of One Program for Enhancing Learning." *Intelligence and Exceptionality: New Directions for Theory, Assessment, and Instructional Practice.* Ed. Jeanne D. Day and John G. Borkowski. Norwood: Ablex, 1987. 81–132.

Carnegie Forum on Education and the Economy. *A Nation Prepared: Teachers for the Twenty-First Century.* Washington: Task Force on Teaching as a Profession, 1986.

Cazden, Courtney. *Classroom Discourse: The Language of Teaching and Learning.* Portsmouth: Heinemann, 1988.

Clark, Margaret S., Judson Mills, and Martha C. Powell. "Keeping Track of Needs in Communal and Exchange Relationships." *Journal of Personality and Social Psychology* 51 (1986): 333–38.

Csikszentmihalyi, Mihaly, and Reed Larson. *Being Adolescent: Conflict and Growth in the Teenage Years.* New York: Basic, 1984.

deCastell, Suzanne, Alan Luke, and Carmen Luke, eds. *Language, Authority, and Criticism: Readings on the School Textbook.* London: Falmer, 1989.

Feldberg, Roslyn L., and Evelyn Nakano Glenn. "Technology and the Transformation of Clerical Work." Kraut 77–97.

Flower, Linda. *The Construction of Purpose in Writing and Reading.* Working Paper 4. Berkeley: Center for the Study of Writing, 1988.

Forsythe, Diana. "Engineering Knowledge: An Anthropological Study of an Artificial Laboratory." Twelfth annual meeting of the Society for Social Studies of Science. Worcester, Mass., 12 Nov. 1987.

Goodlad, John I. *A Place Called School: Prospects for the Future.* New York: McGraw, 1984.

Goodman, Kenneth. *What's Whole in Whole Language?* Portsmouth: Heinemann, 1986.

Goody, Jack. *The Logic of Writing and the Organization of Society.* Cambridge: Cambridge UP, 1986.

Goswami, Dixie, and Peter R. Stillman, eds. *Reclaiming the Classroom: Teachers' Research as an Agency for Change.* Portsmouth: Heinemann, 1987.

Heath, Shirley Brice. "The Children of Trackton's Children: Spoken and Written Language in Social Change." *Cultural Psychology: Essays on Comparative Human Development.* Ed. James W. Stigler, Richard Shweder, and Gilbert S. Herdt. Cambridge: Cambridge UP, 1990. 496–519.

———. *Ways with Words: Language, Life, and Work in Communities and Classrooms.* Cambridge: Cambridge UP, 1983.

Helander, Martin, ed. *Handbook of Human-Computer Interaction.* Amsterdam: North-Holland, 1988.

Hodgkinson, Harold. "What's Ahead for Education." *Principal* (Jan. 1986): 6–11.

Kraut, Robert E., ed. *Technology and the Transformation of White-Collar Work.* Hillsdale: Erlbaum, 1987.

Lefkowitz, Bernard. *Tough Change: Growing Up on Your Own in America.* New York: Free, 1987.

Lightfoot, Martin, and Nancy Martin, eds. *The Word for Teaching Is Learning: Essays for James Britton.* Portsmouth: Heinemann, 1988.

Marty, Martin E. *Religion and Republic: The American Circumstance.* Boston: Beacon, 1987.

Mikulecky, Larry, and Jeanne Ehlinger. "The Influence of Metacognitive Aspects of Literacy on Job Performance of Electronics Technicians." *Journal of Reading Behavior* 18 (1986): 41–62.

Mikulecky, Larry, and David Winchester. "Job Literacy and Job Performance among Nurses at Varying Employment Levels." *Adult Education Quarterly* 34 (1983): 1–15.

Moffett, James. *Storm in the Mountains: A Case Study of Censorship, Conflict, and Consciousness.* Carbondale: Southern Illinois UP, 1988.

Newkirk, Thomas, and Nancie Atwell, eds. *Understanding Writing: Ways of Observing, Learning, and Teaching.* Portsmouth: Heinemann, 1988.

Odell, Lee, and Dixie Goswani, eds. *Writing in Non-Academic Settings.* New York: Guilford, 1985.

Porter, Lyman W., and Karlene H. Roberts. "Communication in Organizations." *Handbook of Industrial and Organizational Psychology.* Ed. Marvin D. Dunnette. Chicago: Rand, 1987. 1553–85.

Sampson, Edward E. "The Debate on Individualism: Indigenous Psychologies of the Individual and Their Role in Personal and Societal Functioning." *American Psychologist* 43 (1988): 15–22.

Scribner, Sylvia. "Studying Working Intelligence." *Everyday Cognition: Its Development in Social Context.* Ed. Barbara Rogoff and Jean Lave. Cambridge: Harvard UP, 1984. 9–40.

Smith, Joel D. "Literacy in the Workplace." Conference Broadening the Definition of Literacy. Center for the Study of Writing. Berkeley, 5 May 1988.

Sticht, Thomas G. *Reading for Working: A Functional Literacy Anthology.* Alexandria: Human Resources Research Assn., 1975.

Suransky, Valerie Polakow. *The Erosion of Childhood.* Chicago: U of Chicago P, 1982.

Wertsch, James V., ed. *Culture, Communication, and Cognition: Vygotskian Perspectives.* Cambridge: Cambridge UP, 1985.